Life Among the Yanomami

Life Among the Yanomami

*The Story of Change
Among the Xilixana on the
Mucajai River in Brazil*

JOHN F. PETERS

CANADIAN CATALOGUING IN PUBLICATION DATA

Peters, John F. (John Fred)
    Life among the Yanomami
Includes bibliographical references and index.
ISBN 1-55111-193-4

1.   Yanomami Indians – Social Conditions. 2. Yanomami Indians. I. Title.

F2520.1.Y3 P47 1998   306'.089'98   C98-930544-9

BROADVIEW PRESS, LTD.

is an independent, international publishing house, incorporated in 1985.

North America
Post Office Box 1243, Peterborough, Ontario, Canada K9J 7H5
3576 California Road, Orchard Park, New York, USA 14127
TEL (705) 743-8990; FAX (705) 743-8353; E-MAIL 75322.44@compuserve.com

United Kingdom and Europe
Turpin Distribution Services, Ltd., Blackhorse Rd., Letchworth, Hertfordshire, SG6
1HN TEL (1462) 672555; FAX (1462) 480947; E-MAIL turpin@rsc.org

Australia
St. Clair Press, Post Office Box 287, Rozelle, NSW 2039
TEL (612) 818-1942; FAX (612) 418-1923

www.broadviewpress.com

Broadview Press gratefully acknowledges the support of the Ontario Arts Council,
and the Ministry of Canadian Heritage. We acknowledge the financial support of
the Government of Canada through the Book Publishing Industry Development
Program for our publishing activities.

This book was designed and readied for the press by
Colin MacKenzie and Zack Taylor, Black Eye Design.

Printed in Canada

10 9 8 7 6 5 4 3 2 1

To Lorraine,

Dean, Rae, Kim, Kelly, and Andrea

Together, we share so many of these Yanomami experiences

and

To the future of the Yanomami

Contents

Part II *Past and Present: The Xilixana Then and Now*

Part III   Social Change

Acknowledgements

It is impossible to recognize all who have contributed in some way to this project. One should rightfully begin with one's parents, siblings, intimate friends, teachers…, persons who contributed to one's values and aspirations. In some way, all these individuals contributed. That list is long.

More specifically, Neill Hawkins, Marawenare, and Mawasha accompanied me by dugout down the Takutu, then the Rio Branco, and finally up the Mucajai rivers in November 1958. Soon thereafter Don Borgman was my companion during my early residence among the Yanomami. In particular, four young Xilixana men became friends, assisting me in the fundamentals of jungle livelihood and serving as informants. Hemalo, Blena, Wakop, and Hopopoha left a deep impression upon me. Three are still living, and the latter two have adopted Portuguese names, João and Paulo, since my permanent residence with them. I value their friendship as well as my ties to many, many other Xilixana.

In more recent years I have received assistance from others: missionaries Carol James, Carole Swain, Steve and Dawn Anderson, Dr. Timothy Faul, Donald Borgman, Milton and Márcia Camargo, and Alex and Daura Junqueira. Their hospitality, reflections, and direct responses in interviews, e-mailings, letters, and facsimiles have been invaluable. Steve Anderson and Kurt Kirsch have provided photographs.

Dorothy Lim and Karen Webber gave unstintingly of their time and skill in typing many drafts of my Yanomami research. Rae Peters has generously contributed her talents in art in the illustrations. Pamela Schaus gave assistance with figures and maps. Kathy Nagel, Lorraine Peters, and Lynn Graham suggested changes to these written documents. Colleagues such as Laird Christie and Tom Headland have been supportive in urging me to write the book. John Early has been a collaborator in the analysis of data as well as in the organization of the book. Jacky Early has graciously given hospitality during consultation with John Early. The technology of computers and software has been an asset.

During the collection of data I have been assisted by the Social Science and Humanities Research Council of Canada as well as grants in money and time from Wilfrid Laurier University. Their policy of support for research is greatly appreciated.

My wife Lorraine and our children Dean, Rae, Kim, Kelly, and Andrea have been supportive in many ways. (Four of our children were born during our family sojourn in Brazil.) Immersed in research I was often not the most communicative person. Lorraine often bore more than her share of parenting responsibilities. In Brazil I was absent from home while on expeditions to some neighboring tribe. In Canada I was also periodically absent, making field trips to the Xilixana. Upon returning home my family was eager to hear of recent developments. They shared my enthusiasm. On one field trip they accompanied me. (On another, Rae, as an adult, wished to accompany me, but the government had restrictions.) Our Yanomami experiences have left their unique impact upon each of us. We will never be the same.

Michael Harrison of Broadview Press had faith that this story of the Yanomami had to be told. Robert Clarke, as editor, did a great service, applying his writing and organizational skills to the pages I had written. I recognize their contributions in this production.

All monies from royalties for this book will be given to health care services of Yanomami and other indigenes who are confronted with medical needs far beyond their financial resources.

Preface

I came to this book by way of a career path that many readers might find rather strange, and circuitous. I first went to the Amazon rainforests of Brazil in 1958 as a young missionary taking part in a project to set up residency at a new mission station on the Mucajai River, in the heart of the Amazon-Orinoco watershed. Our venture took place during the initial period of Yanomami contact with outsiders, and very little was known of them at the time. I would spend most of the next eight years living among the Xilixana community of that area. I would learn the language and customs, share their food and celebrations, hurts and joys, and travel with them to visit other tribes. I would get married (to a Canadian wife) and have children of my own there.

I enjoyed life in the rainforest—I was always to find the time spent with the Yanomami stimulating and enriching—but in 1967 my family and I left our missionary calling and returned to North America, where I pursued my undergraduate degree in anthropology, then Masters and Ph.D. degrees in sociology. My doctoral thesis was an analysis of the change in bride price and bride payment among the Yanomami. My specialty in sociology became family.

Once back in the university community I couldn't shake my passion for the Yanomami. I recognized that every time I spoke about the Yanomami in elementary and secondary schools, university classrooms, and the community at large, the audience was always engaged and eager—although after one lecture a member in the audience made it clear that he had found the talk incredible. He concluded that my account was nothing but one big lie.

In due course I found that the literature on the Yanomami was being augmented. At this time John Early contacted me and stimulated me to do depth population research (Early & Peters 1990, 2000). I returned to Brazil on field trips to collect data a half-dozen times in the 1980s and 1990s. By then the words "Yanomami" and its variants were becoming household terms in anthropology circles. I felt I had something unique to offer, in part because of my initial lengthy residence with the Yanomami and in part because of my familiarity with these people from the time when they first made contact with *naba* (civilized) people.

Over the past decade, several good publications have expanded our understanding of earlier Yanomami writings. These and earlier writings have focused upon warfare, population, spirits, and life in the rainforest. No work has sought to give a complete or holistic ethnographic and historical portrayal of Yanomami people. This book attempts to fill that gap, by telling the story of Yanomami life in the rainforest over the past four tumultuous decades as well as for more than a quarter-century before contact.

Specifically, the book is a history and ethnography of one particular group, the Xilixana. I mean the writing to be a "warts and all" story. It will, I hope, reveal this indigenous people's life through time: their hopes, passions, aspirations, obligations, and tensions; the fluidity, expectations, and alterations that have occurred because of contact with other Yanomami, Brazilians, and missionaries; their culture of reproduction, honor, hostility, hunting, eating, fishing. It shows the role of health care in the well-being of the tribe. It exposes the fragility of their daily lives, of the search for food and safety, and their preoccupation with the mystical world of the spirits, a domain central to their social organization but alien to Westerners.

In writing this account I have chosen to use language in its most directly translated form from the Ninam dialect of the larger Yanomami group to English. Readers, I fear, may find this language somewhat distorted or clumsy, but given the cultural gap between the two societies, I believe that few concepts are really equal. I believe we can obtain a truer picture of the Yanomami by using Ninam words in an attempt to better indicate the indigenous meaning. While, for example, we speak of the termination of a marriage as separation or divorce, the Yanomami say that the spouse threw the partner away, or the husband plucked her out. Similarly, they identify what we know as "diarrhea" as "the liver hurting," not as frequent bowel movements.

I have been profoundly influenced by the enormous changes confronted by the Xilixana and other Yanomami in the past 40 years. They jumped from their isolated rainforest habitat to frequent Western encounters in an amazingly brief period of time. During the time when they began to make contact with Europeans, the Xilixana also began, for the first time, to meet numerous other Yanomami from the surrounding region. In many ways the story of the Brazilian Yanomami parallels the story of North American "Indian" contact with Europeans beginning three centuries earlier, but it is also different. World history has changed, political and economic agents are different, world sentiment has altered, modernity has reached its apex. The Yanomami have been exposed to the good and bad of Western peoples. The odds for their survival as a distinct people with their own culture and identity are meagre. Through this book I want to contribute in some small way to their place in the changing world, as a people of fortitude and dignity.

List of Maps, Vignettes, Figures, and Tables

Maps

Vignettes

Figures

Table

Glossary of Terms

Vocabulary

alawalik	al-a-wa-lik	any substance used in sorcery
bata	ba-ta	mature person, respected one, chief (written *pata* in Ninam)
bèk	book	people
Bola bèk	Bo-la book	Xilixana, people of the rapids (written *Pola pék* in Ninam)
Casa do Índio		government health-care unit for aborigines in the state of Roraima, located just outside the city of Boa Vista
caxiri	ca-shi-ri	intoxicating drink, usually of sweet cassava but also of yams and sugar cane, in which the food is chewed, then spat into a container, then cooked and left to sit for at least 24 hours. Yanomami learned to make it from the Caribs (Portuguese word)
hekula	he-koo-la	spirits that shaman seek to manipulate and control
Kasilapai	Ka-sil-a-pai	Xilixana, long-lipped people
lix	rish	alter spirit of humans

naba	na-ba	a person who wears clothing or has steel tools (written napa in Ninam; the same word also means mother)
nihpolep	nih-bo-leb	spirit of the dead, who eventually go to the third layer of the cosmos
Ninam	ni-nam	dialect spoken by Xilixana, also means Indian
õkla	ok-la (nasalized)	sorcery used to avenge an enemy
pole	bo-le	a black jaguar-like spirit who haunts the kin of someone recently deceased
theli	te-li	people
xapoli	sha-bo-li	shaman, witch doctor
Xiliana	Shi-ri-a-na	distant relatives of the Xilixana, who also speak Ninam
Xilixana	Shi-ri-sha-na	Yanomami people of this study
yãno	ya-no (nasalized)	large circular cone-shaped dwelling
yãimo	yai-moo (nasalized)	ceremonial feast honoring the deceased

Note: In English the Ninam phonetic p is pronounced "b," and x is pronounced "sh," t is pronounced "d" and th is an explosive, forceful "t."

Indigenous Peoples

Aica   Waica living to the southeast and south of the Xilixana,
                some of whom migrated to Mucajai after contact

Bola bèk   people of the rapids, one of the two Xilixana villages
                encountered in 1958

Hewakema   Aica who lived to the south of Mucajai, who were raided
                by the Xilixana in 1967

Kasilapai   a group of the Xilixana with their own distinct village in
                1958. Long-lipped people

Kooxuma   a group of the Xilixana with their own distinct village but
                who joined the Kasilapai

Macu   now extinct. Lived on the Uraricoera River

Macuxi   live in the savannah area in the state of Roraima and have
                had contact with Brazilians for many years

Malaxi theli   reside at the headwaters of the Mucajai river, friends of the
                Xilixana, some of whom migrated to the Xilixana

Palimi theli   reside on the Uraricoera northwest from the Mucajai post;
                friends of the Xilixana, some of whom migrated to the
                Xilixana

Moxatotau   isolated and feared Waica living on the Apiau Mountain to
                the southwest of the Xilixana

Waica   any Yanomami who are not Xilixana or Xiliana; they are
                considered somewhat inferior by the Xilixana

WaiWai   Carib people who live in the rainforest between Guyana
                and Brazil; they were first contacted in the late 1940s and
                were used as guides to contact Yanomami between 1958
                and 1963

Xili theli   a people whom the Kasilapai raided in 1960, stealing three
                women

Xiliana   a Ninam group residing on the Brazil-Venezuelan border;
                friends of the Xilixana around 1900

Xilixana   a Ninam group composed of the Kasilapai, Bola bèk, and Kooxuma peoples

Yekwana   Carib people also known as Makilitari, or Maiyongong, who live on the headwaters of the Uraricoera River; some have married Sanuma Yanomami

Abbreviations

CCPY   Committee for the Creation of a Yanomami Park, renamed Pro-Yanomami Commission

FAB   Força Aérea do Brazil, Brazilian Air Force

FNS   Fundacão Nacionál do Saúde, Brazil's health agency for indigenous people

FUNAI   Fundacão Nacionál do Índio, Brazil's Indian Protection Agency

MAF   Mission Aviation Fellowship, a mission agency providing air travel for Protestant missionary groups, known in Brazil as Asas de Socorro

MEVA   Missão Evangelica da Amazonia, Protestant mission of Brazilian, U.S., and Canadian missionaries in the state of Roraima, some of whose personnel serve at the Mucajai station

NGO   non-governmental organization

UFM   Unevangelized Fields Mission, renamed UFM International

One
Yanomami, Xilixana, and the Anthropological Approach

For over two decades after the mid-1930s the Yanomami living on the Mucajai River in North Brazil—a people who call themselves the Xilixana (Shirishana)—remained a closed and isolated community, with a population not exceeding 140 persons. Then, just over 40 years ago, the walls of seclusion burst open when the Xilixana initiated contact with Brazilian farmers and ranchers. Other peoples in the Yanomami grouping had first made contact with Europeans only slightly earlier in the 1950s—making them one of the last preliterate peoples to both voluntarily and involuntarily make contact with non-aboriginal peoples. For these groups the contact with outsiders loosened the closed portals of Yanomami culture to vistas and encounters even beyond the mystic world-perception of their shaman.

Yanomami contacts with residents downstream became more frequent over the following years, and by 1987 a deluge of mining activity had begun in the area, exposing the local people to a new era: gold on their lands, government intervention, prostitution, a new form of malaria resistant to existing medication, and warfare with the miners. Bonds between Yanomami groups had become more significant, to the extent, unfortunately, of involving three revenge raids.

The Yanomami's Amazon home is one of the world's richest ecosystems and the largest tropical rainforest. Its waters drain 5.87 million square kilometers (2.25 million square miles) of land. The Amazon's many tributaries originate in the countries of Peru, Ecuador, and Colombia, and in central, west, and north Brazil. The river, filled with a variety of fish, including the piranha, discharges four times the amount of water of its closest competitor, the Zaire River in Africa (Bodley 1997: 60). The watershed's rainforest contains such a huge variety of plant and insect species that they have not all been fully documented. Yet destruction of the Brazilian rainforest has been particularly severe, led by a government eager to exploit the area's economic possibilities.

A few pockets of people living in this huge region have still never made contact with Westerners. Brazil as a whole has 185,000 aboriginals, 40,000 of whom are "unacculturated" (Salzano and Callegari-Jacques 1988). Of these, the Yanomami (also known as Yanomama and Yanomamö) number about 22,000, with about 12,000 of them living in Venezuela and 10,000 in Brazil (see Map 1.1). They were not identified until the middle of this century, when James Barker contacted a group in Venezuela in 1950. Most of them live in mountainous terrain, but some make their homes near the banks of navigable waterways and use canoes extensively. As a result some of them have close and frequent contact with neighboring villages (a half day's trek), while others remain quite removed. Hunting and fishing vary according to habitat.

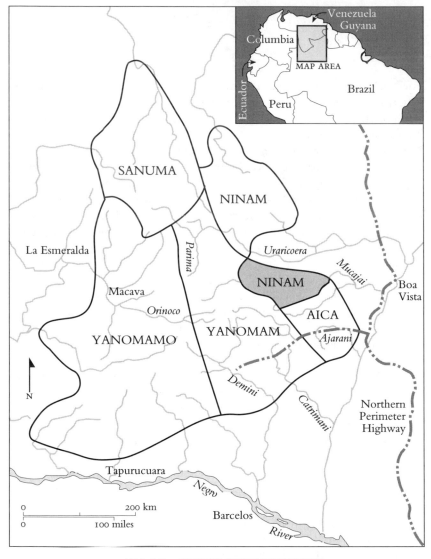

MAP 1.1 – REGIONS OF THE YANOMAMI

Yanomami villages—about 125 in all—vary in size from 16 to 250 inhabitants, with the norm probably between 40 and 70. Villages also vary in age distribution and sex ratio, factors that contribute to fertility as well as to the proportion of those who solely consume food and those who in some way contribute to providing food. Their dispersed and isolated locations have led to a variety of distinct language dialects: at least four (Migliazza 1972) and possibly five. One of the smallest language groups, the Xilixana and Xiliana (Shiriana), located in two different regions with a possible combined population of about 400 in 1958, refer to themselves as Ninam, which is also the name given to their specific dialect (Migliazza 1996). The other groups are the Sanuma, Yanomamö, Yanomam, and Aica. (See Map 1.1.)

The Xilixana first initiated contact with Euro-Westerners in early 1957 on the lower Mucajai River, a tributary of the Amazon, about 2,300 kilometers from the mouth of the Amazon and 160 kilometers from the Venezuela border. Around the same time, and quite independently from the Xilixana, several Xiliana had ventured to a Macuxi post in the central Uraricoera River region (Migliazza 1996). Missionaries in Brazil made contact in three different locations in 1958, and an anthropologist (Napoleon Chagnon) first met the Venezuelan Yanomami in 1963 through Protestant and Roman Catholic missionaries. Throughout the book I use the name Xilixana to refer to all the Yanomami who initially lived in three villages on the mid-Mucajai River at the time of their contact with Brazilians in 1957. Between the roughly 20 months of their initial contact and the missionaries' arrival, one of these villages disbanded after the death of its headman; its members joined one of the other villages. Occasionally I refer to one of the two remaining villages as Kasilapai and the other as Bola bèk. These two villages relocated several times, increased in size, and through the years fissioned into two and four villages respectively.

Yanomami Commonalities and Contrasts

We now have an accumulation of about 30 years of research on the Yanomami done by a variety of writers. This research has included matters of culture, population, health, linguistics, geography and non-Yanomami influences. The variation and similarity of characteristics among the Yanomami will have an impact on their future.

Yanomami life, whether in Venezuela or Brazil, is centered around three primary and three secondary concerns. The first consideration is food. Produce from the field, game and fruit from the forest, and fish from the water are generally sufficient for survival.

The availability of food is unpredictable. Though there is considerable human control for a constant supply of produce from the field, periodically there are droughts in some areas. Fields are developed in the slash and burn fashion, and abandoned after about three years. Manioc and banana are the chief crops. The yield of forest fruit and game varies with the wet and dry season. Fish are more abundant in the dry season, the red howler and tapir more accessible in the wet. Animals and fowl may roam near by, or they may be very distant. Success in stalking and shooting game depends on the skill of the hunter.

The fear of spirits is the second chief concern. Spirits may be seen in the forest, at waterfalls or near the yãno. The Yanomami fear spirits both because they cause illness and death and because they can be manipulated by the enemy. The only revenge is through sorcery or warfare. Yanomami restrict their sphere of travel, and expend much psychic energy on spirit matters. This preoccupation has not declined with the presence of Westerners.

The third Yanomami concern is taboo violation. Because illness may lead to death, Yanomami respect taboos which cause sickness, and are preoccupied in finding a cure to any taboo violation. Shaman play the primary role in the healing process but since contact, many have come to rely on Western medicine. There is a similar concern about taboos relating to hunting, pregnancy, birthing, and rites after an act of murder, in which custom is meticulously observed.

The three secondary matters that absorb the Yanomami psyche and behaviour are less central than food, spirits, and taboos. The first concerns marriage and reproduction. The age, sex, and kin structure of the population, and alliances with other Yanomami villages determine whether a male can readily acquire a partner. In most cases a husband makes payment to his wife's family for at least a 25 year period. Single men and married men whose wives are preoccupied with infants seek coitus with other women. Such action often results in fisticuffs. Marriage patterns of bride service, bride payment, and preference for cross-cousin marriage are common among all Yanomami.

The second concern is warfare, which is initiated for several reasons. It may avenge some form of sorcery, be used to obtain access or maintain participation in a system of steel goods trading (Ferguson 1995), or serve as a means to gain women. Yanomami will post sentinels, build stockades, or temporarily relocate to a neighboring allied village or forest site. A common reason for fisticuffs among the Xilixana is conflict over the reluctance of offering or altering a promise to give a woman in marriage. Other duels arise because of infidelity.

Third, the yãimo feast where an abundance of food and game is consumed in honor of the deceased, is common to all Yanomami. It is an event of heightened social activity, and shows cooperation, generosity, and humor as well as reverence for specific deceased individuals. The artery of much trading and the area where disputes are made public, it is an event that unites the family and community—the muscle of Yanomami social cohesion. Because men consume the hallucinatory drug ebene during its rituals, it is also the place of explosive collective arguments and duels.

Yanomami differ in a number of conspicuous and inconspicuous ways. There are, for example, at least four distinct dialects among the Yanomami. Also, dwellings are different in shape. Many have large donut-shaped *shabonas* (Chagnon 1997) housing up to 250 inhabitants. The Sanuma (Ramos 1995) have smaller rectangular dwellings of between 20 and 40 people. In the early contact period one found a circular dome-shaped yãno among the Ninam, Palimi theli and Malaxi theli, measuring 15 to 23 meters in diameter, which contained all the 30 to 90 inhabitants of the village. The center section of the *shabona* (open) or yãno (enclosed) is important to Yanomami culture, because this is where the yãimo takes place. Yanomami readily and frequently interact with one another, and are aware of the more delicate social exchanges in other households. Privacy is limited. Males and families experience privacy only when they leave the yãno and retreat into the forest.

While tobacco is prepared and consumed in all Yanomami communities, there are differences in its use. Among Xilixana, only men use tobacco, while in other groups women and sometimes children are included. The tobacco wad used by the Xilixana at the time of contact was larger than that of other Yanomami, measuring three by ten centimeters. It is placed across the mouth, or between the teeth and cheek. (Language work is difficult with a tobacco-sucking informant!)

There is also variation in the covering of genitalia. Perception of nakedness differs. Children under age five are naked. The Apiau Aica and others in the Palima mountain region originally wore a string around the lower abdomen as "covering." Men attached the foreskin of their penis in an upright position to a string around their waist. In some groups women used a round roll of cotton measuring two centimeters in diameter around the waist. At the time of contact, Xilixana women wore a small apron of shredded thread which covered their genitalia. Men wore a cotton loin cloth with several independent wraps around the waist. Xilixana never expose their genitalia, and when they first met the naked Apiau Aica in 1959, the former were embarrassed. Xilixana men are even more modest than Westerners, in that their genitalia remain covered even when they are among other males.

While Yanomami differ between those who do and do not have spirit power, the proportion engaged in shamanism varies. At the time of contact, all Xilixana males over age 20 considered themselves shaman. A village with a strong shaman is feared by its enemies. A female shaman was found among the Malaxi theli.

Some villages are prone to much violence, while others, such as the Sanuma (Ramos 1995), have few incidents of warfare and brutality. The threat of warfare restricts the degree to which a village will hunt or the distance people will travel to visit neighbors. Warfare affects the psyche of the entire community: after the Yekwana-Xilixana war of 1935 the latter remained independent, separate from all other Yanomami.

Some Yanomami practice infanticide of females and infants deformed at birth. Some villages never practise the former while others do so on occasion. The Yanomami at Mucajai frequently kill female infants. In the event of twin births, it is common to kill the female or the smaller of the two infants.

Population is a key variable to social organization. Villages with few warriors and hunters are vulnerable to larger groups. Similarly, villages with young women who are not betrothed are likely to bond with villages in which men are seeking female partners. One rarely finds a single female over the age of 20. The frequency of monogamy and forms of polygamy vary. Due to a sex imbalance the Xilixana had several cases of polyandry between 1940 and 1960 (Peters 1982).

Yanomami differ in their consumption of caxiri, a low alcoholic drink made by masticating the cooked manioc root. Caxiri is restricted to the Mucajai and Uraricoera river regions in Brazil, having been imported from the Carib Macuxi to the Xilixana, Palmi theli, and then the Xilixana. Caxiri consumption affects the social organization in numerous ways: some fields are built exclusively for drinking feasts; drinking at social events is more frequent and more focused; there are more arguments, brawls, and feuds; and at times emergency medical aid is required. At the Mucajai post some persons have permanent physical handicaps, and some have permanent liver damage. The Yanomami practice of drinking a masticated liquid from a common pot and a public gourd makes the control of TB an impossibility.

Yanomami vary in their proximity to and dependence on western people. Matters of medicine, trade goods, employment, and education are considerations. There is no better-established Yanomami center than Mavaca in Venezuela. Here Yanomami school children are taught consecutively through a three-month period, many removed from their parents. In the event of illness, Yanomami who live close to Westerners often have access to immediate medical care. If near an airstrip, the seriously ill may be taken out by plane. Yanomami living near a mission or government post may receive some employment, or trade some food or artifacts for trade goods. This recourse to trade goods is pivotal. Ferguson (1995) states that before the turn of the century, Yanomami schemed, deceived, killed, and made alliances so as to keep well situated in a network of access to western goods.

There are two further contrasts in Yanomami culture, which are relevant to the past decade. The social effects of miners in Yanomami villages has varied. While villages along navigable waters have had considerable contact, those in remote mountain regions have had none. Yanomami on the Demini and Mucajai rivers have become politically active in an attempt to counter this exploitation.

The last contrast is not so much cultural as geographical. Some Yanomami live on tributaries which flow into the Orinoco watershed and therefore are Venezuelan. Others reside amid streams and rivers which flow into the Amazon, which makes them Brazilian. This difference is not that significant now, but it will be in the decades that follow. Each country will establish laws which relate directly to medical care, land rights, education, development, and exploitation. Currently, many Yanomami in Venezuela have more association with non-aboriginals, while the Brazilian Yanomami have been critically affected by miners in the past decade. Venezuela established a "national park" and "special biosphere reserve" of 32,000 square miles in 1991. It is assumed this region will be off-limits to mining and other development programs. Despite heavy opposition in Brazil from the Roraima and Amazonia state officials and the military, President Collor de Mello designated 36,000 square miles as Yanomami land in 1991.

On my air flight to the Mucajai mission in 1994 I could see the park boundary, clearly visible because of the long line of felled trees. When I travelled the same area two years later, the trees in the lush terrain had taken over once again, and the boundary mark was no longer visible from the air.

What remains highly visible on the ground, though, is the massive social change experienced by the Yanomami in the past 30 years. The experience is not unique: other cultures in various areas of the globe have experienced change when contacted by modern societies. Knowing the negative effects of the postcontact process, we might anticipate that present governments would ameliorate some of the stress and tension as well as the cultural upheaval. Unfortunately this has not been the case, although the recent history of the Yanomami does indicate some small areas of success in this regard. What is clear is that the Yanomami will not revert back to what we think of as stone-age times, despite the tremendous costs that so-called "modern ways" have brought in terms of health, changes in social structure, and alterations of culture.

The Clash of Cultures

Even without the Yanomami's brave and daring push into the frontiers of Western life in 1957, the two cultures inevitably would have met. The results, though, could have been different: maybe worse, maybe better. Yanomami solidarity, government intervention, unrestrained capitalism, or a tribal acceptance of Christianity as was the case of the WaiWai people to the east, could have critically altered what we now know of the Yanomami. Missionaries came to live among these peoples with the aim of evangelizing them. Brazilian frontiersmen saw that they might benefit from Yanomami canoes, arrows, and cheap labor. Miners sought the natural wealth of rocks and streams in Yanomami land. The government, for reasons of state security, wanted to establish its control over the country's "frontier areas." Later the government felt politically obligated to regulate and address desperate health needs, exploitation, and homicide. Ideologies, whether that of missionary, academic, Brazilian, or international agents, played a part, especially in claims of protection of or salvation for Yanomami cultures, beliefs, and peoples.

At the time of writing there are still a few Yanomami villages in Brazil and Venezuela that have not seen Westerners or Europeans—terms I use interchangeably. At the same time all Yanomami know of the *naba*—the "civilized" people, the ones who make or possess metal goods. Because of their extensive trading network, every Yanomami has now used an axe, knife, or pot from Western society. All of them have heard the buzz of airplanes or helicopters overhead. All have heard stories of *naba* behavior. Like most other peoples around the world, they have an insatiable appetite for Western goods. Fortunately they have had reasonably good access to Western health care through numerous epidemics that could otherwise have annihilated the entire population.

This book, then, addresses the important issues related to Western societies' push through the last frontiers that have separated us from "savages" or, more correctly, preliterate or precapitalist peoples.

The Yanomami: Why Study Them?

All of us tend to be fascinated with other cultures. We are curious about how and why other people think, speak, and live differently from ourselves. We are fascinated with the clothing, food, games, religious beliefs, myths, and relationships in other cultures. These different "ways of living" exist due to tradition, environment, climate, and relationships, whether personal, public, or cross-cultural. They often tell us much about ourselves.

The culture of the Yanomami has proved to be one of those especially fascinating, especially intriguing studies of a way of life that has persisted for centuries but may be on the verge of disappearing forever. The Yanomami lifestyle is intriguing not only because of their survival in the forest under very adverse conditions, but also because their way of life is so different from our own. There may be no other society in which males have such strict and unquestioned control over the lives and behavior of women and children. Among the Yanomami, gender roles are sharply drawn, with no crossing of boundaries. The Yanomami have been identified as the "fierce" people, because of their ritualistic fisticuff duels, raiding for the sake of gaining women, and brutality in warfare. Kinship relationships are variable in intensity, antagonistic, and fragile. Yanomami marriage customs are based upon the logics of economics and reproduction, rather than love or affection. Hallucination by drug is virtually a daily experience for shaman, and a less frequent activity by others in the male population. Everyday behaviors are inextricably linked with an understanding of the supernatural. Their shaman play a key role in the life of the village. To this day no Westerner has completely unravelled the mysteries of the Yanomami supernatural world.

From an academic point of view, our research in understanding the people of another culture should help us understand universal human relationships and societies. Take the problem of war, for instance. Warfare has been an unfortunate and unrelenting fact of life everywhere around the globe. Some countries have suffered more than others from war; some social classes have suffered more than others; and in some states warfare has a persistence that is not just damaging, but lethal. Warfare, because it is a generalized, sanctioned violence, is the most inhumane act of the human species. Its effects are seen as unreasonable by any sane person; and although it has occurred in virtually all societies it has usually been regarded as a deviation from the norm—perhaps something to be avoided if at all possible, perhaps sometimes a necessary evil. Yet for the Yanomami, as a way of life war is not an aberrant condition but a practice that is central to the society's social structure. Research into the causes, effects, and very process of this mode of behavior in the heart of the Amazon is surely of immense academic interest and value.

Another equally important, though less dramatic, facet of this study is family. Family organization is central to an anthropologist's comprehension of any society, particularly precapitalist societies. Family organization takes many forms, and its form alters considerably when preliterate people encounter Western people. As well, amid the reality of limited resources among an ever-increasing global population, the study of demography is also of prime interest to academics, economists, and the politically concerned. The research done among the Xilixana on the Mucajai River in Brazil holds unique lessons in this regard as well.[1]

Using a structure functional perspective, I seek to present the intricacies of family, kinship, and village structures. For the Yanomami these facets of life—and particularly social practices inherent in the provision of field crops, hunting, food preparation, festivities, warfare, marriage, and village leadership—form a delicate and fragile equilibrium. The relationship between these structures has expanded, contracted, and redefined itself with Euro-Western influence and presence.

I also take a critical perspective. The evolution of Yanomami society has not been void of struggle, paternalism, control, subjugation, and injustice. The actors in this vibrant drama of stimulating and sometimes even fatal syncretism are the government and its variant agents, as well as miners, health professionals, merchants, and missionaries. They also include members of the local population itself: shaman, the *bata* (recognized mature Yanomami), mothers, youth, and those who desperately want Western goods of steel, cloth, and plastic, items of low and high technology.

One cannot help, then, but be intrigued with the Yanomami. But there is another, perhaps more important, reason for us to learn about their lives and practices. For half a century now, people around the world have become concerned about the imperialism and colonization experienced by those living in preliterate cultures. The action of dominant powers in both West and East towards aborigines even before the time of Christopher Columbus has not proved to be of overwhelming benefit to those peoples; indeed, the result has often been the opposite. Western societies have been, and still appear to be, ruthless in their efforts to disturb at the very minimum, and in many cases permanently alter, the culture and identity of indigenous peoples. The drive for power and control by the state and capitalists seems to have no limitation. The exploitation of natural resources such as gold, diamonds, other metals, and the forest, in the name of improved national or global economies, seems to contain no constraint. Large land masses are flooded with the construction of dams to facilitate a "better" standard of living for people who know nothing of the lives or the needs of the people being displaced. Aboriginal peoples are not asked for their opinions on relocation schemes, and if they choose to remain

---

1   A second book, co-authored with John Early (1999), takes population dynamics as its primary focus and provides more detail of the Mucajai people's early history, data-gathering analysis, village distinctiveness, and fissions, as well as population specifics.

in their own habitats they find their native resources forever altered. They become victims of Western diseases, and many of them die. Indigenes are forced to adapt to some aberration of Western life. Few are successful in this process.

A very few states have made limited attempts to compensate the gross injustices done to peoples who have a very different approach to life than the entrepreneurship, capitalism, and, often, disregard for the natural environment that has come from abroad. As well, an increasing number of people around the world have intentionally sought out this much neglected story of change. They have listened to the voices of the disenfranchised. Together with the aboriginal peoples, they have raised their complaints against existing government policies both nationally and internationally. They have raised issues of human rights. They now insist upon the pursuit of alternative directions.

Lobbying groups now exist in many countries of the world. Many have organized a membership of professionals, politicians, celebrities, and more general citizens. They use sophisticated means to place pressure on governing bodies to hear the voices of aboriginal peoples. This book, I hope, will play a part in making others more aware of the human rights issues involving one of these peoples, the Yanomami.

Cross-Cultural Research in the Field: Some Basic Considerations

Anyone doing cross-cultural research in the field must be aware of a series of challenges. Some of the hurdles are fixed; others are at the discretion of the researcher.

The first thing a researcher has to do is gain permission for entrance into the field. Governments and specific aboriginal groups are now much more restrictive than they were in the past: they may place restrictions upon the investigator in terms of time, region, and topic, and the whole process may be fraught with delay or political obstruction. In 1994, for instance, I had planned a field trip for April. Brazil was about to host a world conference on the environment in Rio de Janeiro. To make sure there would be no adverse media communication from its rainforest region, Brazil closed off all travel to the Yanomami region for national and foreign visitors, journalists, and researchers.

Next the researcher has to choose a mode of transportation and, usually, a travel companion or partner. In preparing for the trip one has to purchase sufficient food, cooking utensils, and trade good items (to serve as a form of payment). Will travel be done by airplane, automobile, or trekking? Will the field work be compromised by travelling with the local entrepreneur, government agent, or missionary? Once on location, who will be host—someone prestigious or someone quite neutral in community politics? Does one become a guest of the headman, the mayor, the padre, or someone on the fringe of the society? The choice of host might facilitate or hinder the future solicitation of data relating to the social fiber of the society.

Another consideration relates to the matter of health. Western researchers usually find themselves working in a different climate, among a people with a different diet. Researchers can be exposed to infection and any number of diseases foreign to them: malaria, diarrhoea, food poisoning, tuberculosis, hepatitis, and ulcers are common. Flies, mosquitoes, bugs, rodents, roaming mangy canine, and unwashed human hands and faces may be the norm. Bath and toilet facilities are often less sanitary by Western standards, and possibly more public. Heat and humidity can be oppressive. Researchers have to take care to be immunized against disease as well as ensure proper food consumption during the period in the field.

In my experience, I found the Xilixana to be a hospitable people, especially in the sharing of their food. During the time of my family's residency with them, I ate almost anything they gave me. Their hospitality includes the sharing of their drink, which had been masticated in the mouths of the women. In the 1960s I readily accepted this drink. After the mid-1980s, when TB proved positive in almost all of the families in the community, I reluctantly discontinued taking the drink, though it was extremely difficult to reject their kindness. I admit I capitulated in 1995. My Xilixana "brother," friend, and key informant offered me a special invitation to share in a small festive event that honored the death of his son 20 years earlier. At the feast he held a gourd of drink close to my mouth and said "Drink it." I responded with a big smile saying, "No. I am afraid. I am afraid I will become ill." He responded by saying, "It is good. Drink it." I couldn't resist and drank a bit.

I have had malaria several times. I also contracted hepatitis B, which was only identified 32 years after the initial infection had most likely taken place. Similarly, I contracted leishmaniasis in 1962, a disease of the sand fly, and only discovered its presence by a growth within my nose in 1995. Fortunately, I was able to have it radically treated before it disfigured my face.

Those concerns aside, we also have to deal with language-learning. On our initial trip we had to use the monolingual approach to language-learning among the Yanomami. We had no other choice—no one in our party or in the local community was bilingual. That situation is rarely repeated today. Generally researchers encounter someone who is reasonably fluent in two languages, which greatly facilitates language-learning. Language is culturally bound; words have meaning related to the specific culture. Such common words as family, land, and employer can carry a significant difference of meaning from society to society.

Then, too, despite adequate preparation researchers always encounter cultural differences. They face questions about whether to observe local customs in dress, food, and religious ritual. In most cases the laissez-faire attitude of most North Americans is inappropriate, even offensive. Most cultural contrasts are intriguing, but others can be startling and conflictual. Researchers face behavior that not only appears to be irrational but also disrespectful and hurtful to human dignity and even human life. Researchers not uncommonly have to face difficult questions relating to the role of patriarchy, class, or what Westerners perceive as an inordinate degree of religious devotion.

Other prevailing factors relate to ethics. Researchers need to be cautious about selecting informants as well as determining the conditions under which they will ask certain questions. To fully understand the social organization of the community, they sometimes have to ask provocative questions. To what degree does one push a sensitive issue? How does one handle conflict? When (and where) does one talk to the headman, elderly women, pubescent females, children, shaman, or the marginal citizen? Some aboriginals find a tape recorder, or even a note pad and pencil, offensive. Data-gathering often necessitates rapport, and rapport takes time to build. Researchers must be aware of their influence in the community, not only during their time there, but also after their departure. The food they share, the payments they make to informants, their role as entertainer, the associations nurtured, and the comments made: all of these factors invariably make an impact, however slight or large, upon the social organization. Anthropologists in the field are agents of change.

They also face difficulties of participation. To what lengths does one go to participate in events that one believes are destructive to health and human life? Would one participate in clitoridectomy, infanticide, a raid on a neighboring village? And, finally, to whom is one responsible for the data gathered: to the profession or to the local people? In some cases researchers have to choose among various options, each of which might have its own, or perhaps even similar, consequences. In other cases one option seems much more culturally appropriate than another.

Readers of this book will undoubtedly note some critical decision-making that went on in the field from time to time. You are invited to critique these decisions, bearing in mind appropriate ethical, scientific, and humanitarian considerations.

Cross-Cultural Research: The Academic Component

Reading an ethnography of a culture as different as the Yanomami's can force us to examine our own cultures. Perhaps we will no longer see everyday events and common behavior as "natural." In this exposure to the Yanomami, you might ask, as I often did, "How come … (female infanticide is practised, men squat to urinate, or men furiously beat one another on the chest)?" These questions become a matter of more than mere curiosity. We want to know what social function is being served in a particular behavior. Personally, I hope that we work to push this cultural curiosity to the extreme, while always recognizing that though some questions will be answered, others will remain mysteries.

As students of culture we carry unwanted baggage to our research endeavors. Frequently we attach a moral value to behavior. It is not improper to have values; to be human is to have values. Our moral base of judgment comes out of the values of our own culture. When I lived among the Yanomami I was often struck by (a) the low regard for life (dictated by males), and (b) the fact that the destiny of a Yanomami woman was made on the basis of material exchange (again under a male's authority). While a part of me (the "researcher" or "outsider") might see these as the intriguing differences of a foreign culture, another part of me couldn't help but make a judgment on these practices. I believe we must move beyond the idea that as researchers we bring no judgment to bear on such matters. Ethnographic works prod us to research for values that are universal for humankind. I see the dignity of human life and the equality of all humans, regardless of sex or age, as universal human values. It seemed to me that these particular customs violated basic values of human dignity.

Social scientists in particular face this dilemma. Most of those trained before the 1980s were taught that they should be value-free. They were, presumably, professionally socialized to avoid any cultural bias, and most of them came to believe in the pursuit of a value-free stance. Some actually became convinced that this goal was attainable. In the past decade or two, critical theorists, and specifically feminists, have challenged this value-free stance. To be human is to have biases that emerge within our respective cultures and individual experiences. We do well to acknowledge these value positions in any analysis of individual, group, or cultural studies.

At the same time social scientists encounter another predicament. Scientists may behave or speak in a manner consistent with their own practice and cultures, but this manner can potentially thwart or distort scientific pursuits. Will scientists speak out on their positions on polygamous marriage or their repulsion for the fist-beating feuds? What stance will researchers take on the inhumanity of seeing females, both young and mature, treated as chattel by males? When scientists in the field show their biases, they run the risk that much valuable ethnographic material will not be disclosed. When informants see that the scientists disapprove of something, they might then remain silent or distort matters relating to that practice. At the end of the scientific investigations, the picture received, the data gathered, might be both incomplete and inaccurate.

This brings to the surface another ethical dilemma. To what length will social scientists go to glean data? Will a scientist moving among the Yanomami participate in the curare drug sniffing activity associated with shamanism and the ritual respecting the deceased? Will the scientist accompany the Yanomami on a raid, not as a participant but as a companion, in an effort to collect data? Will the scientist make every effort to persuade the Xilixana not to kill an infant, not to revenge a neighboring tribe, not to place a curse upon an enemy, and not to participate in gang rape? On this score, the record of anthropologists among Yanomami has been both liberal and conservative. Anthropologists have chosen to participate in some matters and taken a non-involvement stance in others. A further question lingers: to whom are anthropologists accountable— the profession, their consciences, the local government, or the indigenous peoples?

Most anthropologists among the Yanomami have used tape recorders and cameras. Some have used movie cameras and professional movie-making crews. Is the use of these technologies an intrusion and violation of human rights? In the contact period the Yanomami believed that a person could take taped speech and perform black magic with it. Similarly, they believed that the camera took away the *utup* (spirit) of those photographed. What means will scientists use to coerce informants to disclose the culture under study? Anthropologists have not always been sensitive to the people under study in their scientific efforts to gather data for a dissertation, journal article, or other means of status enhancement. This naivety needs to be scrutinized.

While I don't question that informants be paid, the key issue is usually how much. Based on the standards of Western exchange, almost any amount paid by researchers is cheap. What Western artifacts should enter into the transaction? Does one give any artifact that an informant requests? While I have little dispute about payment in axes and knives, what about clothing, ammunition, cigarettes, tape recorders, or outboard motors? Do outsiders have the right to control items of exchange in a transaction with a mature indigenous adult? What if the item fulfills a status need rather than a survival need? Or what if the outsider has reason to believe the artifact will be used for the destruction of human life?

Any foreigner among the Yanomami, whether miner, traveller, missionary, or anthropologist, is an agent of change. Anthropologists are overt rather than covert about the effect of their presence. The indigenous people see the researchers' lifestyles—with their cooking utensils, flashlights, food, and clothing. They see the foreigners' response to their insistent requests for food or a Western manufactured item. The Western system of justice, equality, heterosexual partnership, and friendship is different, and the anthropologists' stay is brief. Researchers seldom witness the fallout from their presence. They seldom take responsibility for their own effect as agents of change, while they meticulously document the effects of others, such as the army, government, entrepreneur, and missionary, as change agents.

Data-gathering in the field presents its own challenges. Despite academic preparation, the unanticipated happens time and time again. The Xilixana, for instance, have a cultural expectation about being hospitable. The expectation involves considerable visiting and conversing, and the result can be lengthy visits in the researcher's dwelling. The visits can consume a lot of time during which the ethnographer might want to do analysis of collected and disorganized reams of data. Many researchers find it beneficial to leave the research site for pockets of time to do this analysis. Certainly this was my situation, and I believe the ethnography was enriched through this experience. Interacting with other scholars is a great help as well. My collegiality with fellow anthropologist John Early of Florida Atlantic University proved a great asset. A study of this nature brings frustration. ("Will I receive funds to do this field work?" "But this does not make sense.") It also brings joy ("Here is how it fits." "Now I understand.") The entire process engages the researcher with the people and the dynamics of their social relationships. There is satisfaction in connecting pieces to the puzzle of social organization. In retrospect, I sometimes find myself chuckling about field research among the Yanomami. I lived amid a population where, according to my own calculations, at least 40 per cent of the men were "murderers" and 90 per cent potential "murderers," and yet I felt totally safe (at least 99 per cent of the time). Life is filled with such incongruities.

One final theme in this book concerns *change*. This is a theme found in virtually every chapter, though more pronounced in some than in others. The last three chapters in particular focus on the subject of social change among the Yanomami.

The Author's Own Journey

I can fairly evenly divide the first two decades of my life between three geographical locations. I was born on the Canadian prairies in Saskatoon. When I was in my early years of school my family moved to southern British Columbia where my father managed a grocery store and the rest of us tried to augment the family income through small farming: cows, strawberries, and raspberries. In hopes of improving our economic situation, we moved to a community in northern British Columbia, where forestry was the primary industry. My family had considerable contact with First Nations peoples, then referred to as Indians. I loved the outdoors, and after Grade 11 I left school to work as a logger in the lumber industry. Few students in our community graduated from high school when opportunities for good wages were present. A year later I left the north for religious education, and by the age of 20 I had set my heart on working in some missionary capacity among peoples in the tropics. In due course I was in the Amazon, challenged and happy.

My time among the Yanomami began as a missionary with the Unevangelized Fields Mission in November 1958. I arrived in Brazil in what was then the Territory of Roraima (later a state) as a missionary with one year at the University of British Columbia and some training in cross-cultural studies and linguistics, as well as a stint of jungle boot-camp in Guyana.

At that time the aborigines in the area we were looking at had still not been identified as Yanomami. We knew that the people in the Mucajai River area had descended the river shortly before and made contact with frontier Brazilians, who were rather frightened in the encounter; and later we found that some Yanomami had formulated a plot to kill their hosts. We knew that a degree of risk was involved in this quest, both in canoe travel up the river, and in meeting the people. We did not speak their language, and the circumstance was rife for serious misunderstanding.

I set out on the journey up the Mucajai River in a canoe with an American, Neill Hawkins, and two WaiWai from Guyana who served as guides. The meeting with the Yanomami was positive and exciting, and my life among the Yanomami began in earnest. We set up a base for our mission station at a site nearest one of the villages, choosing a place that we thought had sufficient flat terrain for an airstrip. The site proved to be just across the river from their residence. With the help of the local people, we soon constructed a 200-meter airstrip. A few months later a missionary couple established permanent residency in a palm-slat and leaf structure. After I had been a year in South America my Canadian fiancee, Lorraine Neufeld, came to Brazil, and later, on November 20, 1959, we were married in the missionary airplane hangar in Bonfim, a frontier community of possibly 40 Brazilian inhabitants, near the Guyana border. After a temporary placement in another location we took up residency at the Mucajai mission station. We remained permanent residents (with only a few short absences and one year of furlough in 1962) until February 1967, and four of our five children were born during that time.

Initially we concentrated on learning the language, discovering the syntax, and formulating an alphabet. We initiated a literacy program. We made every effort to grasp the supernatural beliefs of the villagers. I accompanied the men on hunting and fishing trips and, with the Xilixana as companions and guides, I and the other missionaries made exploratory trips to other Yanomami tribes to learn their locales, compositions, languages, and populations. On one trip I travelled alone with Yanomami guides. We also made one unsuccessful, more distant trip southeast to the state of Amazonas, to the lands of the Atrowari. It was perhaps fortunate we didn't find the Atrowari, because, as I later learned, had we met them we would likely have been killed.

My wife, a nurse, addressed the many medical needs of the local communities. The "great yellow parrot" from the skies brought us supplies and mail every 15 days or so. Only after several years did we get permission to use a radio transmitter once a day to report the weather to airport personnel in Boa Vista.

Those years set the stage for a future that we did not fully envision, for both the Yanomami and ourselves. Living with the people at this early stage, during the years of their first contact with Westerners, gave us an unusual exposure to their lives as they must have been prior to the time when Western artifacts such as knives, pots, beads, and clothing became commonplace. I heard the accounts of their continued visits to ranchers and peasants on the lower Mucajai. During this period they also made significant liaison with neighboring Yanomami. Some people from these neighboring villages eventually migrated and married into the Mucajai community.

Raising our children among the Yanomami allowed us to more fully enter into their lives. They were intrigued by our relationship with our children, and we became more sensitive to their system of family: roles, authority, child socialization, food preparation, marriage patterns, interaction. We gradually became more comfortable with what at first seemed an absolutely alien way of life. It mattered to the Yanomami that we were there for the long term. We were able to participate in their lives more holistically. We were in no rush to gather data to meet a scheduled field-experience deadline of eight, or twenty-four, months. It was normal for us to get scattered visits of people (usually women and children) during the early part of the day, or for both sexes to come in larger groups during the late afternoon. Initially they were amused at our lifestyle, particularly the food preparation, and they asked us many questions about our families, the headman of our land, and the game in our forests.

During these years we recorded their language, folklore, myths, and culture. It was also our practice to record the date of each birth and each death, information that would later be of extreme value. To keep my mind stimulated I took several courses by distance education, including "Indians of South America" from the University of Oregon. Little did I know that in the coming years the Yanomami would become a focus for my Ph.D. dissertation, a number of journal articles, and several books.

In 1967, when we left the Yanomami in Brazil, I returned to the university classroom to earn my B.A. degree in anthropology. As an older student I struggled with the subject, knowing the practical dimension of jungle life but finding it difficult to grasp the theoretical. I continued in school to gain my M.A. in sociology, which I then taught for a year. I was captivated by the classroom environment, and knew it was my niche, but that meant even more training. After consultation with my wife, I continued through three more years of graduate work to earn my Ph.D. My specialty was family, and therefore it was appropriate to investigate more fully the practice of mate selection among the Yanomami. I returned to do field work as a researcher in 1972, gathering data for my dissertation on family change. Later, back in Canada, with the help of my advisor I also wrote a journal article on polyandry among the Yanomami.

For the Xilixana, in many respects my new role was not that different from the old. I was warmly welcomed back as family and friend, after an absence of five years. I arrived by missionary airplane, not by a private airplane or one owned by the air force or local government. I was a guest of the missionaries. My stay was tentative. The Xilixana were ecstatic that I was returning to visit. Why had I not brought my wife and children? They offered to build me a house so that I would stay permanently. I felt honored.

They could not really understand my shift in role from missionary to researcher. To that time the Yanomami knowledge of foreigners had covered such roles as miner, missionary, police, pilot, and medical practitioner; a "researcher" was something new. They were unfamiliar with academia, libraries, and written history. But in my new role I remained a friend. As researcher I simply asked more questions, to a greater depth, including queries about the Yanomami's past. They couldn't comprehend how I could spend so much time with "book skin." Much later, on my last field trip, in 1996, some of them understood that I was writing a book about them.

I returned to continue my research several times. In 1979, when I returned for the first time since 1972, the first two weeks of the visit were particularly interesting because my wife and now five children accompanied me. The Yanomami were intrigued, and begged us to stay permanently. They designated native names for each of the children, who were then between 10 and 19 years old. On one successive trip I showed them slides of their people taken in the early 1960s. They were aghast to see men in loin cloths and women in aprons. Were they really their parents? Two years later I returned with a loin cloth one of them had woven three decades earlier. They howled uncontrollably in laughter as I walked through the village wearing it.

Missionaries continued their residence at the Mucajai station. Because of the impact of diseases they decided that they could not leave the post even to go off to a short conference or retreat. From the perspective of the Xilixana the missionary role includes, firstly, conversing about the Christian faith and/or doing biblical translation work, as well as health care, selling trade goods, and doing station maintenance. In recent years the Xilixana came to know that the missionaries' activities are circumscribed by the government: no more gun sales, no miners, immunization programs, improvement of the air strip at the request of the air force. In these matters, activity has a Boa Vista (state) or Brazil (national) dimension. Due to the missionaries' long-term stays they interact extensively with local residents about daily tribal concerns: health, food, a good hunt, visiting groups, parties, and brawls.

The most significant role-change for me, in terms of relationships, was that I was no longer seen as the dispenser of western artifacts, the stock in the store. They could not plead for cooking utensils, soap, knifes, fish hooks, or salt from me. I welcomed this relief. As a researcher my activity was not as varied as that of the missionaries; my task was more focused. I was gathering data, which meant asking even more questions on a wider range of topics with greater precision and depth than I had gleaned during my missionary days. At the same time I found that the knowledge of the language and culture, and particularly of population and the spirit realm, was an asset. But now the pursuit of history and culture entailed a sphere of conversations that missionaries were most likely not so concerned with: residence and village composition from 1930 to the time of contact, the cause of all village fissioning since 1930, the genesis of a brawl or spat, warfare with Yanomami and miners. I pursued topics that missionaries avoided: abortion, infanticide, homosexuality, raids. Other topics such as Yanomami genealogy and names required extreme skill in informant work.

But the very fact that missionaries were present facilitated my research in several ways. They made it relatively easy for me to return to the Yanomami on future field trips. They often provided hospitality. They continued keeping accurate records of births and deaths, as well as of epidemics and general health care. They told me about particular events in the field that served as a stimulus to pursue the subject matter further with my informants. Later, when I was back in North America collating and analysing data and found I had fragments of missing material, they were often able to supply the necessary pieces.

My residency with the Yanomami on the Mucajai River just after they had acquired a few steel goods from the Brazilians provided an opportunity to see them at a time of significant structural change. Raising a family among them over an extended period of time gave me insights that a conventional anthropologist is not likely to see and absorb. For the Yanomami, family relationships were central and in some ways unique. Living with the Yanomami as a missionary over a long period of time gave me a lifelong passion for them. I believe the experience freed me to write without some of the constricting boundaries of the anthropologist. The social-scientist role that I took up in my later visits presented another set of biases and goals. That role broadened my knowledge to other societies, both modern and preliterate. I sought a scientific understanding of their structure and organization. I hope that the combination of these two roles has led me to a more enriching and fuller ethnography of these people.

During field work I was occasionally asked, "Why did you come?" Unabashedly, I responded, "I want to learn about your people, including your life before you met Brazilians." I was recognized as one who "looked at paper." A few were annoyed with this focus, not so much because of my objections, but rather because I now did not always simply sit and converse about their immediate interests. A few of them respected my stubborn concentration on an array of paper. At times visitors near my desk responded to a query of a specific detail that had arisen in my research. More frequently they asked whether I had brought Western goods as payment items, and could they see the objects: T-shirts, necklaces, fish hooks. They insisted in seeing all the T-shirts and shirts and began scheming about how to obtain their choice. Once several items were stolen. During more leisurely periods they would inquire about my passport, Canadian money, and the flight on the jet. Increasingly they came to recognize the authority of the writing—they would ask me about the offspring in a particular Xilixana family or for their specific age. On my last visit one Xilixana was sure I would make enormous financial gain from my writing. He made it clear to me that he did not want himself or his people to be exploited. He was greatly relieved when I told him that royalties from the publication of this book would go to providing health care for the Yanomami and other indigenous peoples. I felt honored to be included in the receiving of meat at a yãimo festivity on my 1995 field trip.

Recent Xilixana History: The Basics

In the precontact period, the Xilixana, like other Yanomami, obtained the artifacts they needed from the rainforest around them—using slats of palm to cut, rocks as manioc grater boards, animal teeth as carving instruments, and friction of wood on wood to produce fire. When they did acquire a few steel knives and axes, those items were highly prized. They lived by practising horticulture, with plantains, bananas or manioc the principle crops, by hunting forest animals, and by foraging for nuts, fruits, and honey (Early & Peters 1990: 3-4).

Xilixana history was profoundly altered when several canoe loads of Xilixana men descended the Mucajai River and met Brazilians living below the huge falls. At the time of contact the three Xilixana villages had a population of less than 120. The year 1957, then, became a pivotal time in Xilixana history, separating the precontact period from the contact period.

The lives of these people were profoundly altered again in what I call the contact period (1957-60), when the presence of missionaries and increased contact with Brazilians downstream brought on a whole series of political, economic, tribal, and familial changes. The missionaries, with Xilixana as their

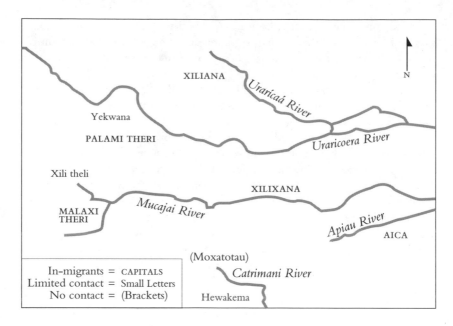

MAP I.2 THE XILIXANA'S YANOMAMI NEIGHBORS

guides, also made contact with the Aica, a Waica people living to the south and southeast, and the Palimi theli to the northwest. Xilixana themselves initiated visits to the Malaxi theli, who live about 100 kilometers upriver at the headwaters of the Mucajai River, and the Xiliana, the other Ninam group living to the north in the Brazil-Venezuelan border area.

What I call the linking period (1961–81) reinforced the irreversible path carved in the contact period. The Xilixana world now included three other non-Xilixana Yanomami communities, each at least four to eight days travel-distance by land and/or canoe. Xilixana men were able to barter to add women to their community, since they now had the advantage of highly prized and coveted steel goods. The marriage bonds with non-Xilixana peoples necessitated retaliatory raids to three very distant Yanomami peoples. They attended other Yanomami festive events, yãimos, and others attended their celebrations in return. (See Map 1.2.)

The missionary presence, once a novelty, became an assumed part of an altered Xilixana social fabric. For most Xilixana, missionaries were welcome because of the trade goods they brought and the medical assistance they offered, and not for the spiritual instruction. While the resident missionaries learned the Yanomami culture, the indigenous population inquired about Western life, fertility, deaths, animals, family bride price, and possessions. The indigenous people were particularly interested in learning about how the Westerners made axes and knives. Unfortunately, the resident Westerners could not adequately respond to these inquiries, because they had never seen the manufacturing process. They took the tools for granted, just like water and air. For a couple of years most Xilixana attended Sunday church meetings. Shamanism decreased or went underground.

A number of the group at the mission post established strong friendships with neighboring peoples. Some Xilixana valued the periodic ties to Brazilians. A few of them received employment for a week or up to two months. The number who had made visits to the district capital, Boa Vista, was increasing. They saw stores with a variety of countless goods. A few attended movie houses. They learned of prostitution, police, prison, alcohol, and the feuds peculiar to "the wild west."

By the end of the linking period all the patriarchs dominant at the time of contact had aged or died, which allowed the youth of the contact period to emerge gradually as leaders. They lived all their adult lives in a milieu of steel tools, medical aid, and significant contact with the surrounding Yanomami villages. The linking period was also a time of increased medical attention. Missionaries made sure that critically ill persons were flown out to the state capital, with others sent out to larger cities to the south. The government participated by spraying houses for malaria and insisting upon blood examination before malaria medicine was dispensed. Eventually they initiated a program of immunization.

In 1982 the Xilixana moved into a fourth critical period, when mortality increased due to increased contact and fatal diseases. This was also around the time when miners moved into the Yanomami lands in search of gold. This awareness period (Early & Peters 2000) takes us to the present. To a few Xilixana, the presence of miners brought hopes for an increase of Western goods. A number of men gained employment, earning larger sums of cash than ever before. In reality miners carried diseases and brought in murder, government intervention, a few trade goods, and an almost global recognition of the exploitation and violation of human rights. The peoples in contact with miners witnessed an abysmal side of humanity: unfulfilled promises, hatred, pornography, prostitution, vulgarity, and store-bought alcohol. Miners and Yanomami met with unnatural death in this confrontation. The period carried with it the potential of Yanomami genocide.

The Xilixana were to learn, too, that as a people they had rights to their land. By the end of the awareness period they had become politicized. As members of the Brazilian nation, they had a right to have their concerns voiced and respected. For the first time the Xilixana were exposed to a broader understanding of the Yanomami people as a whole, which included those in Brazil to the west on the upper Parima River, and to the south and southwest on the Catrimani and Demini rivers. The Xilixana began to talk of the state's obligation to meet their medical needs and to preserve their way of life. The care facilities of Casa do Índio on the periphery of Boa Vista became institutionalized as a site for serious and long-term patients and their caregiving kin companions.

When the Xilixana went to Casa do Índio, in addition to the health care they received they heard stories from other Yanomami as well as from other aboriginals. As the term awareness period is meant to imply, the Xilixana association with other Brazilian peoples, both *naba* and indigenous, will augment in the years to come. This association will mean further adaptation and integration. It will mean a continuous change of the social system.

I do not anticipate this book to be a package that is nicely wrapped and tied. I expect there are unanswered questions, missing pieces of the puzzle, possibly a few startling disturbances. If this is not the case, I will have failed. I cannot claim to fully comprehend the behavior of the Yanomami or the intricacies of their social organization. The tension and collaboration of the powerful and the powerless are always fraught with peril in terms of justice and what is right. That tension exists within any society, but the scenario is particularly tentative when two cultures as vastly different as the Yanomami and Euro-Westerners meet. The Yanomami are on a journey into the wider world that is not likely to end for another century. These fascinating, vibrant people have been and will continue to be at a great disadvantage in this great clash of societies. With contact the gates were opened to an unmapped future to which Yanomami would have some control, but other agents of change would be more powerful, more persuasive.

Part I
The Xilixana Way of Life

Two
Field Entry, Language-Learning, and Cultural Surprises

When my group arrived on the Mucajai River in 1958 we were the first out-siders to make contact, much less establish residency, with the Xilixana, except for their limited contacts during the preceding year with frontier Brazilians on the banks of the lower river. Soon after our arrival we offered a cutlass as a gesture to a man who seemed to be the headman. He accepted the gift. It quickly became clear to us that the Xilixana found our Western ways to be peculiar, mysterious, and often humorous. Over the coming days, months, and years they observed our every move and mood, at times to our great annoy-ance; we, in turn, watched them, learned from them; together we attempted communications.

During our first months with the Xilixana we stretched our creativity to its seeming limit in the attempt to communicate in whatever manner possible. Initially we operated by gesture, and for the first few days in particular we were restricted to grunting and a lot of smiling. We tried our best to seem friendly, and saw that they reciprocated. We pointed again and again to spe-cific objects to learn their words for those things. To denote time, we pointed to the sun, arcing it across the skyline. We indicated the duration of our travel up the Mucajai River by using the fingers of our two hands to point out the number of nights of sleep on the trip. We communicated the strain of portag-ing by bending our backs and groaning to simulate the maneuvering of canoe and cargo on land around rapids and waterfalls. They reciprocated with ges-tures that meant a far distance, paddling a canoe, death, a child, eating.

These strained but simple efforts in a potentially volatile social environment proved largely successful. We made gestures with a hand across the stomach and then towards the mouth, and pointed to a banana, trying to communicate that we were hungry and would appreciate bananas as food. That seemed to work satisfactorily. But their interpretation of our gestures and symbols was sometimes different from what we anticipated. What added to the complexity was our Western mind-sets: scientific, supposedly rational, and a work and achievement orientation to life. Not surprisingly, we thought and acted differently than these people we had just met. Later we learned that particular Xilixana gestures carried a great poignancy. To demonstrate utter disgust, for example, an Xilixana will lock eyes with the speaker, slowly move his head and eyes away, then spit on the ground.

Numerous humorous events occurred in the initial years. When I accompanied the Xilixana on hunts I soon found that my companions appreciated the function of my watch, because using it to tell the time meant that we could locate the sun's position even on a cloudy or rainy day. This was helpful, because a sense of panic could set in if a hunter did not return to the yãno before dusk. One day, though, they asked me to identify the location of the sun without looking up and around for it. I looked down at my watch. It showed 9:00 a.m., and I pointed to the sky in what I thought was the appropriate direction. This drew a great deal of laughter at my expense. It turned out that the sun was in the 11:30 position. My wind-up watch had stopped.

Some of the things I saw I simply passed off as strange, peculiar, and a bit humorous. When someone farted, a few people would laugh, more would say "hmmmm" in disgust, and several others would plug their noses with the index and middle fingers. If a man dropped a knife or small tool, he would pick it up with his foot, while standing erect, the object dexterously clenched between the big and second toes. When someone asked for the direction in which a tapir had been shot, or where a man was making a canoe in the forest, the respondents would move their heads and extend their lips in the direction and possibly add, "*uuha.*" A few habits I found repulsive, such as a tendency to wipe mucous from the nose by hand and then wipe the hand on their hair. I didn't understand how a stick was adequate to clean oneself after a bowel movement, and I was surprised to find that Xilixana men, dressed in loin cloths, squatted rather than stood to urinate.

Like any foreigner I experienced culture shock, and a number of incidents took me by surprise, jolting my own cultural perspective of human life and appropriate interpersonal behavior. One incident, for instance, vividly portrayed a stark value difference. I noticed that one of the two wives of the headman was very pregnant. A few days later I realized that she must have given birth: her abdomen was no longer large. But she was not carrying the infant, which puzzled me. I inquired, but couldn't understand what was said. A day or two later we crossed the river to visit the Xilixana who had constructed temporary shelters on the southern bank of the river so they could continuously view our shelter on the northern bank. They managed to tell me the story graphically. The headman's wife had given birth on the bank of the river, and her husband had shouted, "What is it?" She said, "A girl." He said, "Kill it," and the newborn was thrown into the river.

Another incident revealed another detail of the Yanomami culture, though at the time I didn't recognize its full significance. When we arrived I was single. At least one older man, the local patriarch, saw this as an opportunity. He offered his daughter to me as wife. I estimated her age at about 15 years, and I found out that her betrothed husband, of about age 50, had died because of a cold and resulting health complications after his first trip to the Brazilians downstream. My marriage with her would resolve several problems, as viewed by the local patriarch. For one thing his daughter would have a male to look after her, an absolute necessity in this culture. She could also bear children, and I would have someone to cook for me. In a society with clearly defined gender roles, this female role too was essential. I would also have someone who would faithfully stoke up the fire in the middle of the night when it was cold, and, of course, I would have a sexual partner. The payoff for the patriarch would be my obligation to bride service and bride payment. As long as he lived I would be indebted and obliged to make payment. He would have a lasting source of axes, knives, pots, matches, and whatever else was in the boxes I had in storage.

Luckily, I could resolve this dilemma by telling them that I had already arranged to marry a woman from among my own people. I said I had not taken her as wife because she was still young. Culturally, for them, that meant she had not yet reached puberty. This was the only way I could communicate that, timewise, it was not yet appropriate for us to marry. I still wonder whether they were surprised to see Lorraine arrive as my wife at Mucajai within a year, a woman of 25 and five-foot-seven in height.

MY FIRST ENCOUNTER WITH THE MUCAJAI YANOMAMI

In December 1958, I flew with John Peters into the Mucajai station as John's new bride. John had already lived among the Yanomami for a number of months, and as soon as we emerged from the small airplane I was immediately engulfed by a number of copper-colored people, the women clad in scanty aprons and the men in loin cloths. They chattered away to me and gestured wildly. I smiled, shook my head, and hoped they would realize that I could not understand them. When I did not reply in their language, they began to shout into my ears as if I were deaf, with the hope, it seemed, that I would then understand. I stood there frustrated, wishing I could comprehend what they were saying.

A short, older woman squeezed against me and slipped her hand inside my blouse and felt my breasts. I felt squeamish, but not afraid. She soon withdrew her hand, pointed to her breasts and back to mine, and jabbered something to those around us. She seemed satisfied that I was a woman who had breasts just like the Yanomami women, and I felt that she and the other women had started to accept me, even though, unlike them, I covered my body with clothes.

LORRAINE PETERS

The Challenge of Language

Our first challenge at the Mucajai station was to learn the language. None of the local language had been set down in writing. There was no dictionary or grammar book. We couldn't communicate in Portuguese, the country's national language, because no Xilixana spoke it. The form of language learning had to be monolingual. We had absolutely no simple and useful phrases such as "What is this?" or "What are you doing?" We had as our goal not merely to converse well enough to gain general anthropological data, but also to produce a phonetically accurate alphabet that would eventually lead to writing down the Ninam language. Our language-learning efforts also included deciphering grammar and syntax.

At first we concentrated on using the pointing technique to learn the names of objects. We repeated over and over the collection of sounds that we heard from Xilixana speakers, transcribing them in small notebooks that we always carried with us. I continued this practice for the total of eight years that I lived there. I noted the transcribed utterances and later the same day or the next attempted to make the same utterance with another Xilixana in a different setting, to see whether I got a response of recognition. At times the response was positive, and I was delighted. At other times the attempt yielded a blank stare, and I knew I had made some mistake.

For instance, something as simple as finding the word for "banana" could prove immensely difficult. I would point to the fruit and expect to hear the local word for banana. But that expectation represented my language framework, not the Xilixana's. For the Xilixana there are a number of acceptable responses. My informant could give any one of eight possible words to identify the specific variety of banana. He could use a word relating to its maturity: green, ripe, or overripe. He could respond according to its taste: good, delicious, sweet. He could utter something that indicates ownership. He might make reference to the skin of the banana, or the particular part of it you are pointing to: top, middle, bottom. He might be impressed with the color of the skin of your finger and say "white" or "pale." Or he might never have seen such a clean fingernail in his life, and voice an appropriate adjective. All these utterances are perfectly logical responses for the Xilixana.

My method was to write down an utterance and then try to get the informant to repeat it, though even that request was difficult to express. I soon found that some informants were more helpful than others. The better informants expressed words more clearly and more slowly and appeared to comprehend our efforts to learn words and phrases. Nouns, we found, are relatively easy to elicit. Verbs are somewhat more difficult. Dissecting a sentence into specific words is a challenge. It is especially difficult to get an understanding of the verb tense. Terms and meanings that identify a people's soul and spirit, touching on their sense of what we call religion, were the last and most difficult to comprehend.

I will always remember the time we learned the phrase, "What are you doing?" One day within the first month of our arrival, Neill Hawkins and I were involved in some activity in our small leaf-roofed shelter, which had no walls, and the Yanomami were sitting and standing around, watching and chatting amongst themselves. Neill was reading a magazine that had come to us in an airplane drop. One fellow came to him and uttered some sounds. Neill grunted, hoping the Yanomami would repeat the sounds, which he did. Neill copied down the phrase, *kalewathaha*, and went to a fellow who was squatting near the coals of the fire, carefully holding his arrow shafts over the heat of the fire in an effort to bend them straight. Neill said the same phrase— "*kalewathaha*"—and the native, showing no alarm, responded with another utterance. We went up to others and said the phrase again, and each time it was reciprocated with what seemed a very natural response. Linguistically speaking we knew we had mined a diamond. Many months later we were able to dissect the utterance further and found that *kale* means "what," *wa* means "you," *tha* means "to do," and *ha* is something that makes a word or phrase into a question (putting the emphasis on the last syllable). Having discovered this combination meaning "What are you doing?" we were better able to go on to learn many verbs and understand action activities.

It also became apparent that some communication could not be written. The Xilixana indicates an affirmative "yes" by saying something like "It is" or "I understand" (or "I see"). But also, to signal understanding in conversation a Xilixana will either raise and lower the eyebrows, or quickly breathe in through the mouth. The sound of air entering the mouth is audible. There is no shaking of the head for "yes" or "no." Eventually we heard a "*e e*" for "yes," which we found to be rather strange. Some Yanomami terms are specific to their culture and have no equivalent meaning in the English language. Words found in the Yanomami spirit world are one example. My colleagues and I were surprised to find no expression for "thank you," a phrase so common in European languages. (My personal view and bias are that human interaction and relationship are impaired or shortchanged if lacking some verbal expression of gratitude.)

We could also divide our linguistic work into specific areas of study such as phonemic structure, phonetics, morphology, and syntax structure. Phonetics is the study of sounds and their production. Humans can produce about 300 sounds by means of the mouth, but most languages use only between 40 and 60 sounds. Some use as few as 10, and in a few rare cases as many as 150. In our respective cultures we become accustomed to making a limited variation of speech sounds—our repertoires are not as extensive as they could be. With the use of those human sounds commonly used in our own culture, we often find it difficult to voice the sounds used in speech by people in other cultures. The flap *r* used by the Germans and the people from India is a sound (phoneme) that North Americans find difficult to produce. The click of the Dobe !Kung in Africa (Lee 1984) is another example. Many German and Dutch people find the distinction between the *v* and the *w* difficult. Many speakers of Spanish find the *v* in English hard to pronounce, and therefore substitute the *b* phoneme. (See Appendix.)

Most morphemes—the smallest unit of grammar—are recognized as free morphemes such as cow, dog, and hop. Language-learning has three different categories of transcultural word meanings. Firstly, some words will be identical in meaning to a morpheme in the linguist's native language. In

Yanomami *okolo* means what we know as dog in English, *witihi* means wood, and *tuhu* means jaguar.

Secondly, some words are easily translated, though the meaning is transferred to something that is culturally equivalent. Yãno means more than home: it is house, home, village, and a social complex of numerous families. The yãno structure serves as a town hall, dance floor, hospital, restaurant, and workshop as well as a home. The possible inhabitants that the term refers to range from 20 to 80 people. Yãno is a particular structure (large, round, and made of wood and leaves). Although the word does mean "home," its significance has a very specific cultural meaning. Similarly, the term *ilihi* means earth and land and the trees of that particular region. In the *ilihi* the local population finds game ... and jaguars and snakes ... and can become lost. In like manner, the word *naka* can be broadly translated as "call," but it also has a more significant meaning, in that if you are called, you are expected to respond. You must heed the call, and depending upon the relationship or status of whoever calls, you respond immediately, delay your response, or ignore the call.

Some words in English are not found in Yanomami vocabulary. Ninam has no noun that is the equivalent of "friend," although it has a word for "friendly." There are no words for gratitude, honor, and respect. The language restricts colors to a range of five words: white, blue, black, yellow, and red. The sky and grass are both identified with one Yanomami word. The word used for white can also mean "clean," and the word for red is the same one used for "fire" and "blood."

Because no words existed for foreign items such as airplane, plier, cap, shoe, fish hook, and cow, the Xilixana initially incorporated descriptive terms from their own language. An airplane became "the yellow parrot," plier became "the teeth of crab," cap was "head covering," shoe was "foot covering," and fish hook was "fish tooth." They translated cow as "big, shitty anus" because of the huge amount of excrement the animal produced. They borrowed the words for other terms such as gun and ammunition from Portuguese from the very outset, though they were generally mispronounced. They incorporated more Portuguese terms as their contact with non-Yanomami expanded.

Thirdly, some morphemes in a different language can have meanings that are totally foreign to the linguist's experience. Just learning these terms can richly expand your own cultural experience. Yanomami use something like the Iroquois system of kinship. Their term for mother refers to the mother's progenitors as well as to her sisters. Similarly, the term for father refers to her father's progenitors and brothers. But the terms of parentage do not include the person's mother's brothers or father's sisters. Just as they have many different words for different aspects or types of banana, the Yanomami have no generic word for monkey, but specific terms for each of the five species of monkey.

Their words, we found, could have specific meanings under certain conditions. *Waithili* means "fierce," but it could also mean "brave" and "tough." *Mãlo* means "naked," but significantly could also mean "without its counterpart." *Mãlo* refers to an adult without a spouse, a child without parents, meat without cassava, or a canoe without a paddle. *Hoitaha* refers to the present moment, today, or the very recent past or immediate future. Several words struck me as being particularly effective. The word for really big is *pata-the-pata*. To emphasize the bigness the speaker swells the cheeks and puffs the lips in using the word. The enunciation is a bit garbled, a bit airy, but extremely effective. *Yutuhe* means "long time ago." And if it is a real, real long time ago, the Yanomami extend the second vowel, as in *Yu-tuuuuuuuu-he*.

Syntax structure was one of the greater hurdles in Yanomami language comprehension. How does a learner identify specific words in any given utterance? With the utterance *ya ohi*, it soon became relatively simple to recognize *ya* as "I" and *ohi* as "hungry," and write it down as *ya ohi*. It becomes more complicated to break down *hoitahayaohipalāle*. I know that the phrase is pieced together with *hoitaha* (today), *ya* (I), *ohi* (hungry), and *pa lāle* (am not). Are the last two syllables separate independent morphemes or not? After much study with the use of parallel phrases we determined that they formed a separate word. The Yanomami language has many bound morphemes, even for a single word. In the process of scientifically reducing the language to writing we found it difficult to determine a consistent pattern.

Contrasts in Culture: Startling Differences

As we got to know the Yanomami and developed a rudimentary knowledge of their language, of what they were saying to us and to each other, we began slowly to recognize particular experiences, observations, and objects, though much of it seemed quite peculiar to us. The significance of kinship and kinship terminology was pivotal in understanding the culture. We noted that taboos in the eating of food extended to children, pregnant women, menstruating women, warriors, and hunters. Sexual mores contrasted radically from those of Western societies. Deviance was controlled and punished in ways significantly different from our society's treatment of it.

Most noticeable, perhaps, was the centrality of sorcery and shamanism in the culture. It was incomprehensible to me, for instance, that someone would claim to be the victim of sorcery and resign himself to dying, even refraining from eating food. Before death struck there was always wailing, and in the event of death the wailing lasted for the night, which was perhaps more comprehensible. The Xilixana practised a certain ritual to dispose of the body, then later to burn the bones to ashes, which were used in festivities for many years after the death. Death was a tragedy, except for the very, very old and feeble, yet even after someone's death the Xilixana feared the spirits of the deceased, who haunted the habitat, seeking other relatives.

I was surprised at how openly, and often, the Xilixana referred to matters related to sex and sexuality. Once I saw a small bird dart after another bird, and a 14-year-old girl told me they wanted to copulate. The Xilixana immediately recognized and talked about any large forest animal as being male (usually big) or female. They laughed when they saw dogs copulating. They giggled when they saw a male child act in some sexual manner. Adults teased young naked boys about their penises. When dogs give birth, the Xilixana make clear that they prefer male puppies over females, as they also do in the case of humans. Many fist fights break out over gossip about a male copulating with a woman who is not his wife. There are numerous myths involving sex. There is no greater social crime than to commit incest.

Their greetings are simple and direct. Upon arriving, the Yanomami says, "I have come." To us, the fact that one has "come" seems quite evident. In departing the Yanomami will say, "I'm going." After years of exposure to the Yanomami I now find their terms of greeting just as appropriate as our greetings of "Hello," "Good morning," or "Good-bye."

The system of counting frustrated and infuriated me. Quantity is limited to three words, though the meaning can be modified by gesture. *Mõle* means one, and possibly two. *Yaluku pèk* means something between two and five, while *yalami* means anything more than two. *Yalami* with your hands held together palm against palm with separated fingers means "a fair amount." But if you say *yalami* with your hands placed on the hair of your head, it means "a lot." The highest amount would be indicated by using the term *yalami* together with a phrase meaning "like the trees of the forest." They once told me that there were *yalami* people in a village they had just visited. I didn't know whether the population was 16 or 80. This system obviously would not work in Western society for purchasing a bicycle or six items at the grocery store, but it was perfectly adequate for the Yanomami. Exact numbers were not important.

Direction is more crucial to them, but their sense of it is not distinguished by east, west, north, and south. The terms *ola* and *mana* are sufficient to cover every type of direction. One travels upstream, *ola*, or downstream, *mana*. Thus the bow of a boat is *ola*, its stern *mana*. Similarly the trunk of a tree is *mana*, its top *ola*. As you walk in the forest you travel away from the water (*ola*) or towards the water (*mana*). You walk uphill (*ola*) or downhill (*mana*).

For the Westerner, the Yanomami concept of time is also frustrating and seemingly unintelligible. They frame time in three periods: immediate, recent, and distant. Each of these three time-frames has a degree of latitude. We found that present time has a range of about 24 hours, either past or future. They determine recent time by context and can be referring to a range of two days to about a year, sometimes past and sometimes future. Distant time is a year or more, again in the past or future. They have, then, a wide-ranging sense of the latitude of time. One evening after sundown, for instance, I entered the yãno and found a Xilixana lying in his hammock. He seemed to be absorbed in something, and I asked him what he was doing. He responded by saying that he was hunting, and it was obvious to me that he was not joking. After I learned the language a little better I was able to understand what he meant: at that moment he was fully engaged with or concerned about hunting, absorbed by what he would be doing the first thing in the morning, which would be to go out hunting.

In those early years of language-learning, we had another puzzling experience related to sense of time, only this time of a much more serious nature. A

Xilixana arrived in a panic at our residence and said that someone was dead. At the same time he seemed to be expecting some response from my wife, a nurse. He seemed to be asking for medical assistance and for us to go to where the victim was. We wondered just what we were to do if the person was already dead. We accompanied him at a brisk pace and found that the man was not dead, but rather very, very ill. He was in the state of dying, it seemed, but not yet dead. That experience revealed sharply for us that the English language's tense structure was inappropriate for understanding Yanomami culture.

An understanding of the term *pihi* proved to open a wider window to Yanomami culture. In its simplest form *pihi* means to think, but the *pihi* functions in the chest, not the head. Your *pihi* may be happy, sad, preoccupied, mixed up, angry, bad, or wild. Initially I reasoned that if I thought a lot about my wife or children when I was off on a trip, this was my *pihi* and it was a positive attribute indicating care and love. Later I learned the word really implied a weakness, an obsession for some other person to the point that you can't function properly.

With the introduction of Western goods, the Xilixana translated the names of most objects directly to the Ninam equivalent: a knife was *poak*, axe was *pata poo* (big cutter), matches (and fire and the color red) were *wake*, and salt was *waihok*. Many Western items that were foreign to the Xilixana experience took on indigenous nomenclature. A clock or watch became the equivalent of moon. A hammer with its claws to pull nails was called *kaya nak* after the large rodent capybara, with its beaver-like teeth, which inhabited the banks of rivers and streams. The response of the person who first touched ice from our refrigerator was, "It's hot!" The words uttered from the Xilixana who held the spark plug to my outboard motor as I yanked the cord was, "Electric eel!" I found it most interesting that two words were virtually identical in the Portuguese and Yanomami languages: canoe and clothing. Undoubtedly the Yanomami had borrowed these terms from Europeans centuries ago.

Some objects, such as motors and money, they immediately accepted and adopted with Portuguese words, but with Ninam pronunciation. By the mid-1970s many Western goods had lost their indigenous identifiers and the Xilixana used Portuguese words for them: salt, pot, ball, watch, and book, for example. In the 1980s, when more young Xilixana men and women either had more contact or spent more time with Brazilians, their Portuguese vocabulary expanded. Still, by the mid-1990s only one Xilixana was speaking Portuguese anywhere near fluently. He is a migrant from the Palimi theli, and spent his childhood with a Brazilian family. His ability in Portuguese has given him status, so that Brazilian government officials use him to communicate their intentions. He accompanied Yanomami leader David Kopenawa to several Yanomami "town" or bata meetings in other Yanomami villages as well as to Brazil's capital, Brasilia.

When I was doing field work in the 1990s I thought I was hearing some new indigenous words, but they turned out to be Portuguese words pronounced with Ninam phonemes, and possibly with a syllable missing. I had the same difficulty in my demographic research, when I found individuals who identified themselves with Portuguese rather than indigenous names. For a while I wondered whether these were new people in the population, people I had previously overlooked, but I found out they were people previously identified who had taken on new names.

In the early days, though, along with the many new cultural experiences I was encountering, the Xilixana were equally surprised with our behavior and with aspects of our culture that we displayed. "How could anyone sleep on a flat bed surface?" they wondered. ("Wouldn't you fall off?") "Why would anyone eat greens and eggs?" (Only tapir eat lettuce.) "Give me your partial denture for the tooth I have missing." "Why would husband and wife kiss one another?" someone asked me. "Your wife is always about, working. Does she never have a menstrual period?" another asked. They were delighted once when I expressed some fear and hesitancy about speaking to my father-in-law. They couldn't comprehend why I made no payment to him for my wife.

Data-Gathering: Pursuits of Peril and Pleasure

I quickly recognized that if I were to gain any understanding of the Yanomami culture I would have to learn about their kin structure. I was amazed at the great range of people included in what, in our culture, we would consider the nuclear family. Person x has several mothers, several fathers, and a host of brothers and sisters. This seemed particularly strange until I came to understand that the children of x's mother's sisters were considered siblings, as were the children of x's father's brothers. This meant that your parallel cousins were siblings. Among the Yanomami, the cross-cousin relationship is of great importance, because these members, when heterosexual, are the prime candidates for sexual relations and for marriage. This discovery about cultural family relations opened up a whole sphere of social organization dynamics for me. Yanomami seldom speak to the parents of their cross-cousins, treating the fathers of the cross-cousins with respect and fear. Should they want a cross-cousin as wife they seek permission from the woman's father, and if all goes well they remain indebted to this family for the rest of their lives.

To gain a better understanding of kin relationships, I began formulating genealogies. Initially I went only with the designation of "parent," "child," and "grandchild," noting someone's oldest son and his mother, for instance, but avoiding names because Yanomami are often hesitant to give names (Chagnon 1997: 20; Ramos 1995: 56-59), and in some cases the utterance of a name is followed by great guffaws of laughter; or the names are at times cautiously used in humor and jest. Alcida Rita Ramos' (1995) research among the Sanuma recognizes the significance of names in Yanomami culture. Publicly individuals were originally identified as the brother of x or the daughter of w. They used names somewhat secretly or selectively. At the time of contact Xilixana were a bit guarded, though more public with names than Ramos reports. Some names were publicly acceptable, others were not. The names they did give each other were usually descriptive: blind one, shorty, bearded One, one with heart pain, pain of the liver, hairless forehead, short arms, dark skin. Other names were derived from an experience associated with the person: words of a dance tune, the appearance of their canoe. But these descriptive names could also be derogatory and never used in the person's presence: Ass Hole, for example.[1]

In my research, though, avoiding names became cumbersome in dealing with some 30 or more genealogies. In my more recent research I was tracing up to six generations, and I needed to sharpen my designations. I sought to use names that were not derogatory. Amongst ourselves, after contact, we identified a few individuals as Pretty Girl, Strong One, Happy One, but this was not practical when communicating directly with the Xilixana. As I established a greater degree of rapport, people volunteered specific names. The Xilixana showed no ill feeling at our use of respectable names. They also gave names to the members of my family: for me, Bearded One and, later, White Head; Trumpet Bird for my wife, because of her long legs; and Fierce One, Humming Bird, and White Fish for our children. While recovering from an accident after a tree bashed my lower leg, a month after our arrival, in jest I associated animal names to a half-dozen men. Most of these names are still used: Ilo (red howler monkey), Paxo (spider monkey), Mayop (toucan), Toli (wood tick).

As their visits to the frontier people on the lower Mucajai became more frequent, many of the Xilixana received common Brazilian names such as Pedro, João, José, Carlos, and Maria. By the beginning of the linking period, most of them had Brazilian names, though in the mid-1990s indigenous names were still being used with a number of people over 35 years of age. They no longer observe the taboo on names. Most children now receive a Brazilian name at or soon after birth, in part because the Brazilian medical professionals require a name, preferably Brazilian, in their records. The Xilixana asked the missionaries to name their infants.

In this research of 40 years into population and naming, I find it astounding that a wife now addresses her husband as Carlos, rather than calling "*aahh*" (hey!), that a mother beckons her child as Suzanna rather than "young one." I might add that I could not always identify names as being in the Portuguese language. Names such as Aljir, Edgar, and Cerleia are not pronounced in identifiable Portuguese when used by a Yanomami. Medical records and Brazilian census data show all Mucajai people—over 400 in all—as having the last name of Xilixana.

I found in doing field work on genealogies that the Xilixana had a great hesitation to speak about the deceased. Yet my research required that I find out who had died, when they died, to whom they were related, and the cause of their deaths. These details proved difficult to extract. As a tactic I soon found I had to avoid speaking to relatives of the deceased. In more recent field

---

1   To identify specific Xilixiana persons I use the first two letter of the indigenous names—for example "PE" or "OL".

work my key informants volunteered that they had no hesitation of speaking about those who had died many years earlier. I did, however, encounter another problem. My list of the precontact period population had grown, and I gloated in these discoveries; but I wondered why new persons were surfacing despite my thorough research in earlier years. My exhilaration was short-lived. Further investigation revealed that some individuals had two or three names, and one informant might be knowledgeable of one name but not another. The means I used to check the possibility of multiple entries was to check the cause of death. For example, if I heard that one person had died of a swollen foot and another of being hit by a large fallen branch, I knew I had two persons rather than one. Another way I could check was to identify the married partner. I could also ask for the names of the brothers, sisters, and children of every person who lived and died before the time of contact.

Through a jointly developed trust and my long-term presence, this data was recorded, organized, coded, and thoroughly checked, eventually providing enough data for two books on the population of the Xilixana (Early & Peters 1990, 2000). On one of my field trips, while I was checking abortions, infanticides, and paternity, a female informant hesitated to give details of her fertility history. Her Yanomami companions saw the hesitation and urged her to give the information to me. They told her I had asked for the same information of many others and had written it all down on my paper. Her companions, in other words, helped me to quell her fears. Several times I was checking my data, such as the sequence of births within a third party's family, and the informant said, "I don't know. What does your paper say?" The record on paper held some authority. During my last few field trips I showed literate Yanomami their names in my records, and they showed that they were pleased. My research had become less secretive and less mystical to them. In the end the information about births and deaths has proved to form the base for identifying the ages of almost all the Xilixana listed in medical records and the state's population registration. In my past few visits the Xilixana often checked with me to find out, or affirm, their precise ages.

On my 1996 field trip the headman of one village forbade me to speak to the youth and middle-aged people about those who had recently died. Such a discussion would bring memories of the dead to the surface, he said, and would fill the people with deep sorrow. In indigenous terms, it would make their *pihi* heavy. I had no trouble complying to this request, and after that I only engaged much older people as informants. At that time I was investigating the Xilixana history between 1890 and 1950, a period that predated almost the entire population. A few older people, whom I identified as key informants, remembered incidents involving long-deceased persons from their families or yāno.

Early history, which depends upon memory and oral history, presents another problem. One informant's data may conflict with another's. There may be some biased motivation that slants the telling of a particular event. On a 1995 field trip I was seeking details of specific events in the 1930s, and my two key informants actually competed, each trying to outdo the other, both of them emphatically stating, "This is what really happened." This tension was to my advantage, because the data was augmented with new pieces of information that I would not otherwise have got. Always, in accepting one piece of data over another, I had to consider numerous factors. How reliable was my informant? Was there reason to believe he would give data with a bias? Was he consistent in his reports from one session to the next? Was he reporting on members of his village or on those of another village? Was his data in some way related to his own genealogy? It helped, of course, if I could check the information one person gave me against data from other informants or from events I had witnessed myself.

I also found that some data was the specific domain of men and some of women. Men knew the details of warfare, hunting, and trips to the Brazilians and other Yanomami villages. Women knew the details of abortion, births, infanticide, puberty, female deaths, and the taboos for menstruating and pregnant women. All these factors are central to any ethnographic, genealogical, or demographic study.

The missionaries who had come to the community over the years were helpful in numerous ways. Since their first arrival in 1958 they had kept an accurate account of all births and deaths and had recorded the causes of death. They gave specific dates of epidemics and inoculations, as well as other details of health. They provided the dates of other events and augmented stories for which I had only limited details. They answered numerous detailed questions that surfaced in my writing of this book, by mail and fax. The missionaries assisted in every way possible, including providing me with housing and often food on my later trips.

The Researcher in the Field

I have heard of anthropologists facing the problem of uncooperative informants, but that was never my experience. On occasion I travelled to a specific village, only to find that the informant I was seeking had gone off for several days or was visiting a distant village. Many researchers find that informants, for reasons of their own, don't show up for a scheduled interview or meeting, or that an informant is not as helpful as anticipated.

Making payments and giving gifts to informants and friends as planned can be another problem. Once I asked an informant to select a pair of short pants and a shirt from six items that I had with me. He chose two, then said, "And this one too." He got it. In my field trips in the 1990s women berated me for not bringing my wife's used clothing.

Sometime you encounter situations in which it is impossible to please everyone. For instance, by the 1990s the Xilixana had not had new adzes, the cutting tool for making canoes, for at least two decades. I had sold them curved adzes in 1965, and later on, for years, they begged me to find some more adzes for them. After considerable searching in Canada, I arrived in 1995 with two adzes and got into great difficulty selecting the recipients for this costly and valuable tool. After promising the adzes to two men in different villages, I visited a third village, where as soon as I arrived a man cautiously asked me who would be getting the valued steel tool. That evening and until my departure at mid-morning few people proved willing to converse with me. They were angry that I had not kept an adze for them. They saw my action as a slight, as favoritism.

The challenges a researcher encounters doing field work among aborigines varies. There are few situations in the world today that parallel my own experience in the late 1950s. Most researchers do not witness first hand the insecurity of a previously uncontacted tribe, the sense and reality of isolation, and the restricted means of transportation. Some now have radio contact and the advantage of a GPS (Global Positioning System) instrument (Chagnon 1997: 82) to identify precise geographical location—equipment that did not even exist when we were starting out.

In the field, living conditions are often extremely rough by our own standards, and tasks like food preparation can be more time-consuming. The customs you encounter can be more circumscribed than in our liberal and pluralistic home environments: dresses for women, no shaven heads for men. The conventional social activities of Western life may be completely missing. A researcher may not achieve anything like the planned progress in field work. You are always open to the unanticipated. Your routine can be suddenly interrupted by a family feud, the pursuit of a jaguar, the sudden high fever of the shaman's daughter, or the arrival of guests.

At the Mucajai mission it seemed that we always had a string of visitors who were curious about the foreigner's behavior and property. A second group would arrive upon the departure of the first, because there was antagonism between the two. Interject a whining infant. Interject requests for iodine, Band-aid, needle, knife, salt, paper, pencil. (Do not lose sight of the knife. It may disappear.) You learn much in observation, then further inquiry, of tensions, feuds, customs, and just plain fun. You have moments of sheer delight, in formal and informal settings, when you have uncovered new data and a door has opened to even greater revelation and discovery. Despite the vast differences in culture, you develop strong, lasting friendships.

Three
Village Life and Social Culture: Basic Patterns

For decade after decade the Xilixana followed a certain pattern in their movements from place to place in an area. When they went out on hunting trips they would watch out for areas with good soil and readily accessible water. After about three years, in the dry season, the Xilixana would move to a new area for the purpose of building a new field and eventually a single house, the yãno. Men would cut vines and trees to clear a field. Hunting would be less a problem because game would be more plentiful compared to that of the territory near their older permanent residence. After three to six weeks of activity in this new area, they would return to their permanent yãno, and in another eight weeks burn the partially dried, fallen trees at the new site. They had more work to do in cutting tree branches and throwing them on piles to burn. They did the actual planting near the end of the dry season or in the wet season. They would carry manioc sticks, sugar cane, yams, sweet potatoes, and banana shoots by basket to the new location for planting. Six or seven months later, with evidence of harvest from the new field, the entire village might move and construct a large yãno. In this way they might have two houses in two locations at one time, a fact that produced inaccurate population estimates done in aerial surveys in Yanomami regions by the government and the Fundacão Nacionál do Índio (FUNAI) after contact in the linking period.

This cycle of relocation had other functions as well. After two years the thatched-leaf-roofed yãnos needed repair. In some cases they patched the roof, at other times they put new leaves on the entire structure. More frequently they moved to a new area that had not been as frequently hunted. They also vacated a village site that had become filthy and unhygienic. In other instances they burned the yãno after the death of a family member. Usually they moved into temporary structures before eventually building a new dwelling.

Family activity around the Yãno.

Dwelling with sky-light: new walls of mud are being built.
Note cassava bread drying on the roof.

Village Composition and Decision-Making

At the very minimum the composition of an Xilixana village consists of two families: two fathers, their sons and daughters, and the wives of the adult men. In time this structure matures to include a further generation of married sons or daughters. The ideal village has at least two family patriarchs from whom children may marry one another and thus avoid violating the cultural definitions of incest; in the best of circumstances a village has enough teenage girls to provide marriage partners for all the adult men. That precondition not only

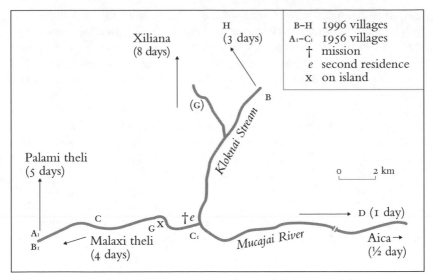

FIGURE 3.1 VILLAGE LOCATIONS 1958 AND 1996

allows young married men to live with their bride's family and provide them with game, but also makes it possible for them to occasionally provide meat to their parents as well. That state of affairs, however, is rarely the case, and men usually have to seek out their wives in another village.

Village members are dependent upon one another: women to jointly uproot manioc from the fields and at times to help one another to care for a small child; men to build fields, a dwelling, and canoes, and hunt for larger game together. This economic exchange is important. There is no one single head who ultimately makes the final decisions. The family patriarch is the final authority within the family. Some older men have more influence in the village because of the number of their offspring, their abilities, political skills, and possibly shamanic powers. These persons are *bata*, or senior, and individually "a canny helmsman of discourse" (Murphy 1989: 182). They have authority as long as they can physically function adequately, but they seldom issue orders; they instead manage affairs by consensus. They demonstrate their power by example rather than by verbal commands. Village members have the final decision as to whether to respond to the leader's wishes or not.

Villages are sometimes located a few hours from one another, which means that a continuing social involvement can fairly readily take place. Relations between villages vary from congenial and hospitable to hatred and fighting. Members from one village may be friendly with another village, while other members may be hostile (Early & Peters 2000).

The village complex of houses has radically changed over the past decades. Until the 1980s each of the Xilixana villages had one yăno, but in a few instances the people had built two yănos five or six meters apart. By the 1980s the Xilixana were finding these arrangements too noisy and crowded. Some were uncomfortable with repeated squabbles between specific adult females in the yãno. Several felt their accumulated artifacts were too exposed to the public. They began to build smaller, rectangular family dwellings adjacent to the yãno. With the exception of one village, this is now the pattern. Each village now has one yãno that is the residence of the headman, and most of their yãimo festivals are held in this structure. As many as six smaller dwellings surround the yãno.

Because of the importance of the provision of health care at the mission and the opportunity to obtain trade goods, as well as friendship with missionaries, the Xilixana may set up their dwelling places at two and possibly three village locations. They might, for instance, build a yãno near the location of their largest field; a second, smaller dwelling might be at the mission station; and a third at a distance of three to four hours walk, at a place where they are building newer fields. (See Figure 3.1.) Eventually they will abandon the older village and field and move to the newer location. In one instance the more distant location remains a second village, with the primary village a 45-minute walk from the mission.

THE DWELLING

The yãno is a circular, covered leaf house, measuring some 15 to 23 meters in diameter and 12 meters in height (Figure 3.2). In the contact period this structure had but one opening, the door. Inside the door was a corridor with palm slats on each side, from the floor to a height of two to three meters. The passage serves to keep the house dark, as well as assuring some protection and privacy for the families living on each side of the corridor. Apart from this passageway, the house construction has no partitions. The lack of light inside the yãno seems to decrease the number of insects inside it. In the linking period the Xilixana constructed smaller rectangular buildings near the yãno.

FIGURE 3.2
THE YÃNO HOUSE

The Xilixana make their lodgings as families at the circumference of the house. They tie their hammocks to the upright posts of the building structure and, where necessary for hammock tying, place other posts about seven centimeters thick into the ground. The outside walls consist of woven leaves. The neighboring Palimi theli and Malaxi theli use palm slats on the walls, which serve as a protection against the enemy's arrows. Palm slat shelves are sporadically attached to the wall, upon which the

FIGURE 3.3
RECTANGULAR HOUSE

respective family members place their personal items, such as cotton spindles and arrow tips. Sometimes inhabitants push a few leaves of the wall aside to permit sunlight to enter. Tasks such as feathering arrows, stringing beads, weaving a loin cloth or hammock, and more recently sewing clothing, require light. The peak of the roof has a bee-hive-shaped structure of three-quarters of a meter across made of finer grass.

Smoke lingers in the yãno, and with a half-dozen fires burning, I always experienced a burning sensation in my eyes. They also need some light in the yãno after the sun has set, so they light four or five dried leaves to provide it at least momentarily, or they throw more wood on the hearth fire. They also retrieve a glazed sappy substance from the forest that lights the hearth area for about ten minutes at a stretch. Since the contact period, flashlights have served this function, when batteries are available. Another common light sometimes used is a small tin container that holds kerosene and yields light from a wick of cloth. This source of light is common in Brazilian peasant homes.

Since contact with other Yanomami and Brazilians, the yãno has been modified, although its basic external appearance remains the same. It is round with the same approximate circumference, and remains completely covered with leaves. While formerly they made the walls of leaves or of palm slats, most now use mud, a technique borrowed from the Brazilians. All yãnos now have one or two vents or windows (skylights) in the roof of about three-quarters of a meter square, allowing sunlight to enter and smoke to escape. This also makes the yãno cooler during the day. At night these "vents" are closed to conserve heat. Yãnos now have two or three entries, with doors made of boards rather than of palm slats. Sometimes they use an old blanket or tarp. When Xilixana vacate the house, the doors are shut tight, and the main door closed with lock and key. In the 1970s most yãnos had three or four protrusions of three-quarters of a meter in depth and two meters in length built extending out of the outside wall. In these "rooms" they stored their valuables, such as cutlasses, a suitcase or box, and clothing. Yãnos now do not have these protrusions.

The yãno is the hub of Yanomami life, and the hearth is the center of family activity. The yãno offers shelter from rain, wind, cold, and protection against gnats and insects. It functions as a lively center of broader social activity and exchange of food. Banana stocks are extended from horizontal poles near the roof. The numerous hearths provide a kaleidoscopic, opaque, television view of Yanomami life—the focal point for food preparation, eating, child care, social interaction, and sleeping. At the perimeter of the hearth men will carve and prepare their bows and arrows, or manufacture rope.

The Yanomami are not a quiet people. Their voices have a wide range of intonation and expression accompanied by hand and body gestures. When they gather around they spend their time telling stories, in the process sometimes building cultural myths. The men vociferously relate stories of hunting escapades or intertribal visits of the past week, year, or decade. They give vent to gripes, or ridicule people, and rumors are created, exaggerated, believed.

The gossip can have long-term consequences for someone's personal identity, or can erupt into physical blows.

Families are located around the circumference of the house. The center of the yãno is used daily as a walkway from the door to the person's specific hearth. It is a place for children to play. In recent years I have seen several ropes hanging from the upper horizontal poles of the yãno to about one meter off the floor, and children play and swing on the ropes. Of even greater importance, the center of the yãno is the place where all the ritual of the yãimo is performed, which includes drinking, dancing, and formal trading. (See Figure 3.4.)

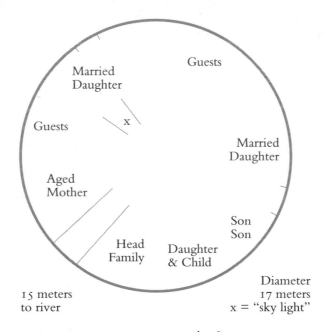

FIGURE 3.4 RESIDENTS IN THE HEADMAN'S YÃNO, VILLAGE E, 1994

Each family has its own hearth, which is the place where all food is cooked and eaten, the social center for all family life. In the dark of the night one will hear the muttering of a husband to his wife in the hammock below to blow up the flame because he is cold. Upon awakening in the morning and urinating just a few meters from the house, a Yanomami returns to crouch near the fire for warmth. When a man seeks shelter after a rain, the hearth provides comfort and warmth. I remain amazed at how long Yanomami can remain in a squat position during conversations with others. From the 1970s on Xilixana began to sit on a piece of wood, or on a crude stool. Some simply sit or lie in a hammock with a friend.

Hammocks are a practical piece of yãno furniture. They serve as chair and bed, as a domain of privacy in the dark. When the Xilixana travel they simply roll it up, place it into a basket, or have it hang from their backs as they trek.

They hang the hammocks of their children in a triangle around the hearth. At night, until her child is about three years of age, a mother will keep him or her in her own hammock and thus is always available to nurse and accommodate the child's needs.

The hearth is also focal as the domain of the mother. She responds, usually unperturbed, to requests for food and drink from young and old. She honors requests for a knife, cotton, spoon, and even cassava bread, often tossing the object onto the dirt floor near the intended recipient.

With the use of Brazilian hammocks in the past two decades, and in one or two cases the use of mosquito netting, hammocks are now not hung above one another, nor are they placed near the fire. They take up more space, and are tightly woven, so that the warmth of the fire does not penetrate the occupant as with locally woven hammocks. The occupant in the Brazilian hammock sleeps in clothes or is covered with a blanket. Possessions are now kept on shelves or in boxes along the wall. I noticed on my 1996 field trip that in one village there was a small building no more than two square meters in size used exclusively for *matohip* (possessions), built primarily to store goods securely for periods when the inhabitants are absent from this village. (See Figure 3.5.)

THE LIFE OF DOGS

Most foreigners view Yanomami dogs as a menace. They are scrawny, lousy, cursed, and kicked. Almost every household has a dog, with the male dogs prized for their hunting ability. In the last decade the Xilixana have recognized that female dogs can hunt as well. Before that, bitches were valued only because their next litter might yield some male pups. Women are responsible for caring for dogs in the yãno. (I saw a woman once in another Yanomami tribe nursing a pup.) Children love to play with pups. The Xilixana will scream and chase a male dog from bitches who are in heat. They prefer their dogs to copulate with large, strong proven hunting dogs.

No Xilixana will kill an aging or ailing hound. If they did, its owner would become ill. Once, after I suggested a hunter kill his dog, which was moaning and in horrendous pain, he refused but urged me to do the task. However, they do feel able to leave dogs in the forest to die. If a hunting dog resists accompanying the hunters, he is shoved out the yãno door with little recourse but to assist on the hunt. To encourage a dog's willingness to hunt, his master will breathe into the canine's mouth several times. To the delight of a dog owner, a missionary sutured a large slab of hide ripped from a dog's back into place. If a good hunting dog dies, his master will remain silent and withdrawn in grief for almost a week.

From whence came dogs? My question was answered simply and abruptly, "My fathers." We know canine are imports from Europe. Undoubtedly the indigenous peoples obtained them from Spaniards or those in contact with Spaniards centuries ago. (See chapter 7 on the mythological source of dogs.)

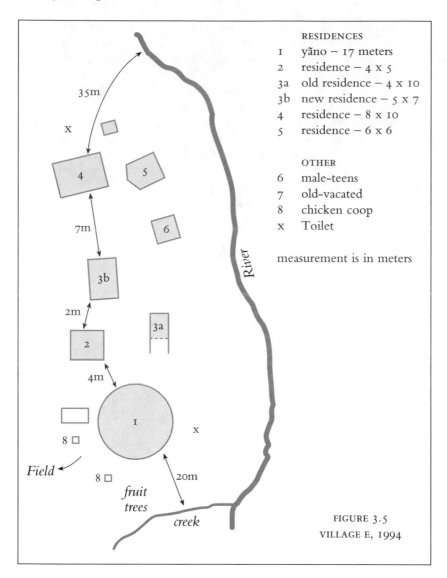

RESIDENCES

1   yãno – 17 meters
2   residence – 4 x 5
3a old residence – 4 x 10
3b new residence – 5 x 7
4   residence – 8 x 10
5   residence – 6 x 6

OTHER

6   male-teens
7   old-vacated
8   chicken coop
x   Toilet

measurement is in meters

FIGURE 3.5
VILLAGE E, 1994

COMMUNITY VISITS

The routine events of life are interspersed with brief or long-term visits from people of neighboring villages. During these events there is a lot of verbal interchange. The people communicate freely and vociferously with their visitors about all aspects of life: food, meat, children, relatives, other Yanomami, Brazilians, missionaries, material possessions, raids, witchcraft, and women. A host family is responsible to see that food is generously given to guests. When ample food is available, the departing visitors will carry some food on their return journey: bananas, sugar cane, roasted meat, and baked cassava. Generosity in sharing food is the mark of a congenial visit and a gracious host.

A large supply of bananas, or an unusual kill of tapir, peccary, or fish is always cause for festivity. Such an event may involve more than one Xilixana village and usually lasts for an entire day and evening. Visiting families simply move their hammocks into the host dwelling, extending the hammocks, which are used for sleeping and sitting, between two of the many posts in the yãno.

Other events punctuate the rhythm of village life. Sometimes a woman or man will explode with deadly venom at another person in the yãno. Occasionally the emotion expands to a fisticuff duel engaging two adults— sometimes all the adults. There are other blips of heightened emotion. When one or several hunters don't return by dusk, the place can go into a frenzy of worry as people talk about whether the missing persons might have been hurt, lost, attacked by a jaguar, or fallen victim to some spirit. The villagers will call out, hoping to hear a response. Several of them might head out on the path, firebrands in hand—or in the past three decades with flashlights—hoping to meet the missing person or persons.

The activities of shaman can also disrupt the atmosphere of the yãno. A shaman may be engaged in sending *hekula* to an enemy, or he may be in a search for some departed spirit that has brought illness to an inhabitant. Family members become preoccupied with recovery by medicine, spirit intervention, or shamanism. If the person's illness is prolonged, or the patient shows little hope of recovery, one or several women will wail. While a patient is ill, the next of kin are not likely to leave the yãno for more than a couple of hours. With death a whole new scene unfolds: remorse, ritual, the destruction of the deceased's possessions, the likely abandonment of the yãno, avenging those who are responsible for the death, and the construction of a new house.

Death, Burial, and Cremation

No event among the Yanomami is as disturbing and traumatic as death. To these people death is more than the nasty result of falling prey to a jaguar or snake, or being a victim of warfare, diarrhea, or an inflamed leg or—in more recent years—malaria or tuberculosis. Death is viewed as the action of spirits: violating a taboo, the haunting of a relative's spirit, or an enemy's black magic. Even after 40 years of missionary presence and the intervention of Western medicine and its explanations for the causes of diseases, the Xilixana still attribute death to the workings of spirits.

When someone is seriously injured, or if recovery appears to be unlikely, women begin to wail—like they wailed over me one month after my arrival, when I was injured after being pinned to the earth by a fallen tree. Upon death, the entire household wails through the night. Amidst the crying, near-relatives spell out the attributes of the deceased. "She made good cassava." "She fashioned my hammock." "She accompanied me to the fields." "He was a good hunter." "He was brave and courageous." After a child's death, several adults will one by one take up and hold the corpse, weep, and express their attachment to the deceased.

Only in a very few cases is there little or no wailing after death. There is one reported case prior to contact where a man was buried alive. In 1959 a living man's burial was aborted by missionaries. He died shortly thereafter. A few years later a man, controlled (possessed) by spirits, was about to be abandoned by his family when missionaries were called to the scene. He lived for another three decades.

The next significant stage is burial, and men on the one hand and women and children on the other are treated differently. The corpses of children and of most women are left in their hammocks, tied to a horizontal pole and carried by designated non-related men into the forest about a kilometer distance from the yãno, at times to an island. The men dig a shallow 700-centimeter hole and place the hammock and corpse into the grave. For the following month the family will weep in mourning. The face of the mother becomes caked with dirt due to her tears and the lack of washing. Parents will trace the areas where young children once walked, and with a knife, dig the earth. The possessions of the deceased are smashed. (In recent years valuable items have been saved from destruction.)

The dead bodies of men, some women, and in a few cases children are carried by men to a hill across the river, less than a kilometer from the yãno, to a place where the Yanomami do not normally traverse or hunt. At the chosen site the men wrap the body in the hammock in leaves and bind the bundle with liana in such a way that jaguar or vultures are likely not to meddle with it. They place the bundle on a stick platform, raised off the earth by at least two meters, and leave the flesh to rot.

After three or four months the same males who initially disposed of the corpse return to the site to perform an ash ritual. Some 200 meters from the site they each don switches of branches and walk directly to the corpse shouting "ho!ho!ho!" to ward off any spirits. They take the wrapped body down from its platform, build a fire, and place the body on the fire. The two men who work the bones have their upper bodies smeared with black to hide themselves from spirits. Everything is burned, and while the coals are still hot, they carefully remove the bones using sticks. They make slits in the upper end of these sticks, using them to grasp the fragile charred bones, which they then place on leaves or a wood slab. They never touch the remains. The men are meticulous in making sure to remove all the bones from the ashes. Their mood is sombre. They may recognize some unusual marking or discoloring of one or several bones, and confirm their suspicion that death was caused by *alawalik* (black magic).

Using mortar and pestle, they ground the bones to a powder, which they place into gourds. They seal the gourd openings with black resin and carry the vessels back to the village. The two men dance into the yãno with the gourds and present them to the ash-keeper, usually the deceased's mother or sister. They place the gourds in a small basket, which is then hung near the hammock by the leaves of the yãno roof. The two men move to the center of the yãno, where hot water is poured over their heads and hands for cleansing. They wash themselves in the water. The people present eat.

CREMATION

O ur task is the cremation of the body of a person who had died about six weeks earlier. Two men, non-relatives of the deceased, commissioned by the sons of the deceased, together with a daughter of one of the men, my brother, and I, all in a dugout canoe, paddle for about five minutes across and down the river. My brother and I consider ourselves fortunate to be able to join in this solemn event.

When we reach the bank and afterwards penetrate the rainforest, the two men soon cut "whips" of about two meters long and slash the air and bushes with loud shouts of "hah!hah!hah!" We are in the area where the bodies of the deceased are frequently hung to allow for the flesh to rot, a first step in the cremation process. The people never hunt in this area, nor do they walk in it. They believe it is haunted, and their shouts and the "whipping" serve to scare the spirits away.

A pile of dry wood measuring one to eight centimeters in width is heaped high in one place, and the body, thickly wrapped in dried leaves, is placed upon the pile. They throw a splash of gas at the base of the pile, light a match, and it all goes up in flames. I stand back from the intense heat. Few words are spoken. There is no jesting. The two men each find two-meter-long straight sticks of wood and make slits in the thin ends. These sticks will be used to extract the charred bones from the hot coals of the fire. Using a cutlass, one carves a small tree to the size of a baseball bat, to be used as a pestle to crush the bones to ash upon a slap of wood.

All the wood is burned. If I look very carefully I detect bones among the coals. The men place a slab of an old canoe that they have brought with them near the perimeter of the dying fire. They reach into the coals with the sticks and gently maneuver the charred bone into the slits, lift, then drop the objects upon the slab. They grimace from the heat. I am impressed with their focus. They are cautious and patient. They continue with their work, remarking to one another, "We don't have the other bone of the ankle," and "Did you get all the fingers?" Once or twice they stop, and after carefully observing what they see as an aberration, an unusual spot or darkness on a bone, make a comment to one another. These might be the markings of an enemy shaman— they could be the cause of death, and necessitate revenge.

After they are satisfied that all bones have been placed upon the slab, they each take turns in the mortar and pestle process of crunching the bone to a very fine powder, which takes considerable time. They carefully place the fine black powder into two gourds about eight centimeters in diameter. They seal the opening at the top with black resin. We put out the fire, and return to the canoe. Back at the yãno, without fanfare the two gourds are left with the family of the deceased. A year or two later, when a yãimo in held in honor of this deceased person, the hosts will honor these two men by giving them select pieces of meat.

JOHN PETERS

The ash is kept anywhere from two to five years, though in one instance—that of a baby—it was kept for 25 years. To the Westerner, this seems a paradox, because at birth they attempted to kill this baby, which had a visible tumor between his eyes. (He lived for 12 years and they carefully treasured his remains for those many years.) A portion of the deceased's ash is used in the yãimo, possibly once a year or less frequently. The emptying of the last ash from the gourd is noteworthy, because this marks the final yãimo, the last formal remembrance of the deceased one.

In several cases I recorded, Xilixana bodies were not burned and ground to ash. The deceased may be an infant or a very elderly person, or perhaps the deceased had no immediate relatives. In a very few cases elderly men have requested that their bodies not be reduced to ash. The stipulation is made because either the *hekula* spirits will return to kill his kin, or he died of some illness such as TB, and it is believed that the use of the ash will have negative consequences. In one case cremation rites were observed but there was no subsequent yãimo.

I asked my informant whether he had thoughts of his father and mother, who had died 35 and 15 years before, respectively. He said, "When someone calls "*paye*" (father) in the yãno I sometimes think of my father. When I am hungry I sometimes think of my mother, who gave me food."

The Yãimo

The yãimo, the apex of all Yanomami activity, weaves together the social, religious, economic, and individual fiber of life. It links the past to the future. It becomes the fulcrum of much social engagement and behavior for months and years after the actual celebration.

The yãimo is a conundrum. It is a strange mix of excitement, dancing, eating, and laughter; and, many times, it is the scene of eruptions of heated duels of fisticuffs, sticks, or knives. Such encounters result in bruises and swellings on the body, black eyes, and serious gashes on the head requiring stitches or special treatment by medical professionals in the district capital, Boa Vista, or in Manaus, where the Rio Negro and Amazon River meet. The social equilibrium of families and the village is often fractured for years.

It is also a time of sadness and deep remorse for the family that is remembering and respecting the death of one of its members. The father or male siblings of the deceased initiate the festive event. Verbally they send invitations to neighboring villages (sometimes only specific families).

The yãimo festivity is never held solely for the residents within one village. There are always guests. Every yãimo is carefully orchestrated in a specific sequence of necessary tasks performed in an orderly fashion. They cut every mature banana stock from their fields and hang them in long rows high in the yãno to speed the ripening process. The Xilixana are known to build, in preparation, a field two years in advance of a yãimo.

All able-bodied men, including visitors who have arrived early, depart for a seven-to-thirteen-day hunt to accumulate as much game as possible. All the meat they bring back is roasted, except the innards or small game, which the hunters consume in the forest or else send back earlier to those preparing for the event at the yãno. If their hunt is not too distant, several men will return to the yãno to replenish their stock of cassava bread. They mark the passing days with knots in a string, though some now follow the weekly days of the calendar. During the men's absence, in the evening the women dance in the yãno to ensure that the men have a successful hunt.

One or two men take the responsibility of tending the fires that roast the meat. Most of the meat is crisp and black. When the father or brother of the one in whose memory they celebrate deems the food to be abundant, he will say, "It is enough. We have enough meat." He and one or two others will trek back to the yãno. Two or three days later the others follow. In recent years, if they are returning by canoe, women will transport fermented drink to the returning large group of men. There is excitement and anticipation in the cooperative toil of this festive preparation. There must be sufficient cassava bread for the men to take on the hunt, to eat upon their return, as well as a larger deposit to distribute to all when families depart at the end of the yãimo.

Two days before the men's return from the hunt, the women dig up the sweet manioc root and carry it back to the house for peeling and cooking. Afterwards they masticate it and pour the soupy substance into two or three small, specially carved, wooden "canoes" in the yãno. They cover the canoe-like container with leaves and leave its contents to ferment for two or three days. More invited guests arrive a day or two before the men return from the hunt. Yãimo invitations are rarely refused. Entire families attend, and some-times all members of the village. If they have to come a long distance, such as eight days' journey between villages, men are more likely to attend than women, and the guests might spend as much as a month with their hosts.

Upon their return from the hunt, the men will camp overnight an hour or two distance from the yãno. Someone informs the "home" group that they will arrive the next day. The entire yãno is cleaned and swept. Hammocks are removed. Fermented drink is ready. The next morning just 300 meters from the yãno the men decorate their hair with white vulture feathers, place large red parrot feathers on their upper arms, and color their bodies with black, red, or purple paint. Visitors, women, and children stand in a large circle as the men enter, each carrying his weapons, displaying his bravado. After a couple of minutes they exit, one by one. They soon return and all the hunters dance. They are dressed in their best clothing. In the last two decades, as clothing became common, men began to wear shorts. More recently women wear brassieres as well as bead aprons, stored for such occasions. The shells and aluminum pieces dangling from the aprons produce a lovely rhythm in the women's dance.[1]

---

1 The strutting, prowess, and staging of the Xilixana men are not as grandiose as the practice of the Venezuelan Yanomami as described by Chagnon (1997: 175).

Serving the drink using gourds, 1995.

The return of the hunters marks the beginning of three days of continuous festivity: drinking, talking, and dancing as well as the rituals of trading and, finally, the ceremony of the deceased. Women extract hundreds of pounds of sweet and bitter manioc root from the fields, and then peel, grate, press, and bake the mass to produce piles of flat cassava cakes. If more cassava is required during the days of festivity, men cross gender roles and assist women in harvesting and processing manioc. Young women between the ages of 15 and 25 serve the drink in gourds of about one liter, dipping the drink from the large wooden canoe-like containers (in recent years aluminum containers) and carrying it to individuals scattered throughout the house. They serve the men first and more frequently. The "waitress" will walk up to someone conversing with others and hold the gourd in front of him without saying a word. After a few seconds he reaches for the gourd and devours its contents, possibly removing his lips from the gourd once. I was struck by the fact that the drinker does not verbally acknowledge receiving the drink, nor does he/she give any recognition to the presence of the server. The "waitress" returns to the source of drink, scoops up another gourd full of drink and serves someone else. (This method of hospitality only increases the possibility of the uncontrolled spread of diseases such as colds, pneumonia, and TB) The drink is served until it is all consumed. Only after several drinks, and the offer of yet another gourd, might a drinker mutter, "But I am full," though this is seen as no good reason to refuse another drink. They might then vomit, either in the yãno, where the mess is not immediately cleaned up from the dirt floor, or a few steps from the entrance, and return for more. The volume of voices escalates. Children and adults play games. In recent years, tapes of either Brazilian music or the dance music of other Yanomami are played. Children, women, and men dance, particularly in the evening. All are in a merry mood except the family with the deceased's ashes. The family of the deceased feels free to give some evidence of contentment only after the completion of the ash ritual.

The yãimo is also a time of liberal sexual license. Though men are more aggressive, women also seek partners. A male may ask another male *wãlima* for permission to have coitus with his sister. In turn the male who grants the request expects that he too will have sexual access to the other man's sister.

The *wayamo wei* (trade talk) is also part of the yãimo ritual. This activity was foreign to the Xilixana until their contact with the Palimi theli, and the Xilixana had to learn the language of this ritual. (Our closest Western analogy is the talk of the auctioneer selling cattle or furniture.) Two men squat facing one another, with arms around each other's neck. They converse in expressive shouts of short staccato words or sentences while swaying from one foot to the other. Most of the people in the yãno hear their dialogue. The exchange covers a range of topics: information about the long journey or hunting trips, warnings not to hit, shoot, or use black magic, or requests for trade goods or a wife. After the encounter the two are exhausted and perspiring. Sometimes there is deception in the conversation. Any trades made are binding, though one member may not reciprocate his item until months later, because it is at his distant village.

Another focal point of the yãimo is the sniffing of the ebene (curare) drug, processed from a sticky dark red substance found underneath the bark of the *yakiana* tree (*virola theidora*). Men warm the bark over a flame and extract the sticky substance, which they then place either on arrow points to shoot monkey or store in small containers to use for the yãimo. They take ebene by placing a pinch of the drug between the forefinger and thumb and inhaling it up the nostrils. Other Yanomami use a half-meter-long bamboo shaft to blow the drug up the nostril (Chagnon 1997: 54). Some women also inhale a small amount of the drug, again a practice of recent years. Shaman use the same drug in their profession. Some Xilixana report that they enter into another world of the spirits when they take the drug. In 1959 and 1985 two men died from an overdose of *yakiana*. According to stories, a similar death occurred sometime before 1930.

Throughout the festivity long-held tensions or recent arguments may explode into duels between specific individuals. Two men will bare their chests and slug one another with their fists, each striking a series of three blows. If their anger is greater, the beaters may clench sharp stones within their fists, and thus deliver more violent blows. One Xilixana now suffers from permanent chest pain because of this means of meting justice.

Near the end of the celebration the deceased's ashes become a focal point. The men are at the height of the effect of the ebene drug. The gourd in the basket is hung from a man's neck, while all the men run vigorously to and fro within the yãno. The women stand on the sidelines, and everyone is wailing profusely. The ash is extracted in part or in its entirety from the gourd and smeared on the backs of both male and female children, including immediate family members. This act prevents the recipient from becoming ill, and helps the child to become strong. Unlike other Yanomami, the Xilixana do not mix the ash in a drink for consumption.

The emptying of the last gourd with the last ash is a particularly significant event. The gourd is smashed and the ash mixed with water, then placed in a hole within the yãno while everyone weeps. They pour banana drink into the hole as food for the deceased. If the deceased had the habit of sucking tobacco, they will also place tobacco into the hole. The deceased will not ever be ceremonially remembered again.

The culmination of the feast comes with the distribution of the abundance of food: bananas, cassava bread, and meat. The father and brothers of the deceased place all the meat from various fires in the house upon leaves in the center of the yãno. In recent years they have used tarpaulin in the place of leaves. Relatives of the deceased will not eat any of this meat. They appropriately cut up the meat, then methodically distribute it. Occasionally they will look about the yãno to make sure all households have received a quantity. The men who buried or hung the corpse, and later did the cremation, are the first recipients of meat. After most of the meat has been distributed, women who helped in the production of cassava bread are the recipients, usually of the legs and arms of monkeys. Finally, adolescent boys pick up any scraps left at the place of the meat cuttings. There is no squabble about any perceived injustice in the meat distribution. The meat is wrapped in leaves and bush rope to be carried home. Most go home content. Some stay to consume the last dregs of drink, become feisty, quarrel and fight, eventually leaving in discontent.

There are exceptions to the shape of this elaborate festive activity. On another occasion several hunters in one household returned with considerable meat. The women in the family made a lot of cassava and some fermented drink. They invited a neighboring village to the feast. There was no dancing, no trade talk, little intoxication, no ebene drug, and no evidence of ash at this event. The visit began at about 9:00 a.m. and terminated by 1:00 p.m. Everyone visited, consumed enough drink to vomit, and went home content with the meat they had received.

Village Fissions, Population, and Distribution

Yanomami villages are always in a state of flux, with the people subject to residential relocation, for a number of reasons. The physical yãno itself has a limited life span. Most do not last more then three years. The leaf roofs rot, as do, eventually, the wood posts. The people move to get away from the unsanitary environment that comes out of living in one place for several years; or they might relocate to be closer to new fields. They abandon and burn a yãno as well as the fields and artifacts of a recently deceased member. They will leave a region that they consider to be tainted with illness. They move to more distant locations to expedite hunting. Sometimes they relocate out of fear of a pending raid. In a few cases the population declines to the point where they cannot function as a political or economic unit, and they join another group.

Several factors contribute to village breakup, or fissioning. Most fissioning occurs under strained conditions, though sometimes it is peaceful and amiable. At Mucajai, hostile fissions were eventually healed. Using Ninam vocabulary, a frequent reason for fission is notha wei, meaning "bad talk," scolding, gossip, or a display of demeaning and derogatory language in a loud voice. In the

Xilixana culture, women are most likely, it seems, to demonstrate this behavior. The topic or story of the *notha wei* may be real or fabricated, concerned with stealth, a woman's inability to produce male children, poor hunting skills, incest, intercourse, or a lack of valor. The talk may be ignored, or it may be countered with more *notha wei* and eventually result in fisticuff duels. When *notha wei* persists, one group might leave the village and seek another place to settle, at least for a period of time, possibly permanently.

Quarrels also often erupt over a betrothal. The members of a potential girl's family may feel they are not receiving sufficient bride price or bride payment from a future husband. In a few cases a verbal promise was made, but the father of the young girl made arrangements with another person. Such incidents are serious and invariably lead to a series of fisticuff encounters, and perhaps a village breakup.

Wãs thethe (meaning noisy, annoying, bothersome) is a second common reason for fissions. The yãno becomes too saturated with noise. It is filled with activity, and particularly the sounds of infants and children who are either crying, calling to one another, or innocently playing in the yãno. Though the parents sometimes reprimand their children, they seldom discipline them. Some individuals, preferring a more serene setting, choose to move out. In such cases the tone of separation is much more subdued.

Other factors relate to village fissioning as well. Population size is directly related to village tension. A large population has a higher degree of *wãs thethe* and probably more *notha wei*. The larger the population the more likely tensions of the past will surface to explosive proportions. Similarly, perceived injustices—for instance, of someone withholding a possible female from marriage—will ferment. The sex ratio and age distribution of village members may similarly create abnormal tensions. At the time of contact there was, roughly, a five to three ratio of males to females, creating stress for monogamous relationships, marriage fidelity, and betrothal arrangements, as well as leading to the pursuit of acquiring women by raiding more distant villages.

Unique events can stimulate a village to fission. A brawl may erupt, resulting in severe physical bruising and bitter hatred. One of the parties may temporarily move to another village, or into the woods, and eventually build a new permanent dwelling. A group of people may be drawn to relocate, as has been the case twice, to a FUNAI post.

A population is affected by four variables: births, deaths, in-migration, and out-migration. Demographics often differentiate a population between those under age 15, those between 15 and 65, and those over 65. The first and last groups are referred to as the dependent population. If this population is unusually high, it often taxes the energies and resources of the population between 15 and 65. Usually, however, a community finds a reasonably balanced sex ratio until age 65. Third World countries generally have a high proportion of their populations under age 15, and industrialized, or Northern, countries tend to have a higher proportion of their population over age 65. Under normal situations, most populations grow.

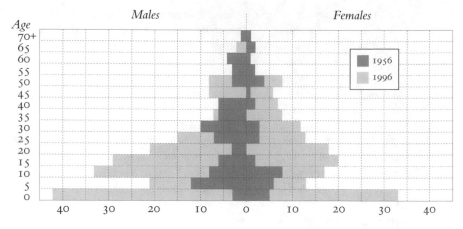

FIGURE 3.6 XILIXANA POPULATION PYRAMID 1956 AND 1996

The populations of small communities such as the specific Xilixana villages or even the larger Mucajai community as a whole fluctuate. Small populations will be affected by warfare and raids. They may show serious decline with diseases and epidemics such as malaria, colds, whooping cough, and TB. One key consideration is the number of women in the population who are in their fertility years. The population balance is influenced by in-migration and out-migration.

The Xilixana population remained very much the same in terms of numbers for the precontact period between 1930 and 1956. During that time there was no migration in or out of the community. There was one epidemic thought to be malaria.

The pyramid (Figure 3.6) visually assists us in recognizing the age distribution and size of the Xilixana population. The population is segmented into five-year age cohorts by sex. One can readily make several observations of the precontact population. First, the 1956 record shows no balance between males and females. There are almost twice as many males as females. Second, several cohorts do not have a single person: ages 20-24 and 35-39 for the females. A closer look shows that females between ages 15 and 44 are proportionately few in number. This is the age when women bear children, the years of fertility. The small number of women in these cohorts will restrict the number of children born into the population. Given the population distribution in 1956, the Xilixana would do well to even replace the existing population. A final observation is that the structure of the pyramid is not "normal." It does not slowly taper to a peak. The child population is small (equal to that of the 25-34 age population).

The 1996 population record indicates that the population has grown in the 40-year period (by 300 per cent). (This stands in sharp contrast to the 1935-56 period when there was virtually no growth.) Among the Yanomami this can be considered two generations of time. The major reason for this growth has been in-migration. The population expanded because Xilixana acquired women in raids carried out in 1960 and 1967. These captives were in their childbearing years and immediately contributed to an increase in the population. The Xilixana men also found Yanomami women in more distant villages, even though they spoke a different dialect than Ninam. Eventually kin joined these migrants.

This pyramid, compared to the first, is fairly normal. The exception is the 30-44 age cohort for the males. The 5-9 age cohort for both the males and the females and the 10-14 age cohort for the females are restricted. The shortage of females in this age cohort is bound to limit growth for another decade. It may have another consequence: men 15-24 years of age in 1996 may have difficulty in finding a marriage partner for a monogamous relationship. It is possible that polygamy, as practised for a generation after 1950, might once again be adopted.

At the beginning of the contact period in 1957 the people of Mucajai were located in three villages, which I have designated as villages A1, B1, and C1 (See Figure 3.1.) Village A1 was the smallest, with 17 residents. The headman, Kooxuma, and two other male members of the village died because of a cold contracted in the initial visit to the Brazilians, and the remaining residents joined nearby Village B1, which had 21 inhabitants. The members of that village have been recognized as the Kasilapai (long-lipped people). Village C1, home of the Bola bék (people of the rapids), lived a day's journey downstream in a single yãno and numbered 81. The missionaries arrived at village C1 in 1958 and established their residency nearby at a place that is still the location of the mission. Some two years later the people of village B1 abandoned their location and built their houses near the mission.

In 1960 a group of 48 people fissioned from village C1 and formed village D. For a year they had a separate yãno almost adjacent to village C1; then they moved to a place almost an hour's walk away. Some three years later two of the three primary families of village D decided to move 10 kilometers downriver. In 1983, after the death of one of the headmen, and an invitation to establish residency at the newly developed FUNAI station further downstream (Comara), these people moved once again. One family with 14 members remained at the original 1960s site, village E, and have stayed in that vicinity, at the mouth of the Kloknai Creek, ever since. By 1998 it seemed that Village E was about to fission due to population pressures and tensions.

By 1984 two of the older patriarchs of village D wanted to live in a more quiet environment, and 18 persons moved downstream about two hours' travel by canoe. That village did not last long. After both headmen died, the village dispersed in 1988, with some members going back to village D and the others to the small Aica village that was located even further upstream.

By 1985 village c numbered over 100 people and they congenially severed, with 65 of them forming village F. The members of village c decided to move further downstream.

Village B1 remained near the mission for only a few years, after which the members built fields and yãnos some 20 to 60 minutes' walk away from the station. Due to internal conflict 38 people in that group fissioned in 1986,

Temporary shelter using tarpaulin from miners camp after the yãno was burned because of a death.

forming village H and building a house adjacent to that of the existing village B. Their next move, two years later, was to an island in the river, and when their headman died in 1989 they abandoned the island. In 1991 they were invited to the new FUNAI base on the mid-Uraricoera River, a distance of some four days' travel over land.[2] By 1996, then, the Xilixana were living in six villages: B, C, D, E, G, and H. By 1998 village G had peacefully fissioned to two additional villages.

---

2   A more detailed explanation of these moves can be found in Early and Peters 2000.

Four
Everyday Life: Food and Child Care, Hunting and Fishing

Yanomami life is not exclusively a continuing pattern of hardship, toil, and struggle. Routine tasks appear to be more the nature of the female role than of the male. At the same time there are ample opportunities and occasions for leisure and pleasure. In the normative events of the day, the early morning through mid-afternoon is taken up with work. The women accompany one another in whatever they do: toiling in the field, carrying water, and working in the yãno. They talk freely with one another during their more individual tasks in the yãno. By mid-afternoon the older men have returned from the fields, and by late afternoon the hunters have returned. The pace of the married women at this time of day increases, with the chopping and gathering of wood and the cooking of game brought in from the forest. As dusk approaches, and for the first hour after twilight, Yanomami of all ages move freely in and out of their hammocks, eating cassava bread, and meat and bananas when those foods are available. They often sit upon some small slab of wood outside the house, conversing and laughing, while smacking their lips on a bone or slurping broth. The Xilixana love to converse and love public drama (Ramos 1995: 44, 49). Two or three of the more industrious men may be carving a paddle, braiding rope, or whittling a knife handle. Children are all about—playing, running, joking, and teasing. Groups of men or families may leave the yãno for several days to construct new fields or carve a canoe.

Children and adolescents play in or near the yãno. At times the play is harmonious, at other times they tease, taunt, and argue, at times flitting back to their mothers for food or to solicit sympathy. They wander to the creek or river bank to bathe and play. At age nine young girls have already begun to assist their mothers in their work.

Inside a dwelling in the nineties.

Daily Village Life

The activities of a family or village do not have any strict daily routine. Activities are governed by daylight and darkness, and by season. The primary concern is food. The harvest of forest fruit varies throughout the year. Fish and game are limited in the rainy months between June and August. Fields are cut in the dry season, and planting takes place when the earth is damp. They are more apt to travel when streams and rivers are not at their peak. Several times a year families leave the yãno and disperse into the jungle for three to twelve days to hunt and forage. Groups of men or families may leave the yãno for several days to construct new fields or carve a canoe. Most Xilixana in the environs of the mission frequent the post at least once a week, to receive health care, purchase or sell some item, or simply to visit the missionaries. On other occasions they visit friends or relatives in another village.

They generally have a cleared area about two or three meters wide around the yãno. In the late afternoon women sit here in the sunlight, spin cotton, and chat. Men tend their arrows, or whittle a handle for their knife or axe. Some may make a paddle or bow. At the edge of this clearing Yanomami urinate in the early morning, or children and dogs defecate. A meter or two beyond the clearing are two or three locations where they throw dirt and garbage from the yãno. Since the mid-1960s, with the encouragement of the missionaries, the Xilixana have constructed pits for toilets, enclosed with two walls of leaves. Most are in disrepair, but they are used. Some Xilixana prefer to walk further into the woods or the edge of the field to defecate.

WOMEN'S WORK DAY

The Western adage of "a woman's work is never done" is highly appropriate for Yanomami women. Women's main work is preparing food for the men and children, as well as themselves, and caring for the children. A woman's work also includes gathering firewood and carrying water from the stream. When she is not doing those tasks she spends her time spinning or weaving cotton. There is always a need for another loin cloth, apron, or hammock.

Women grow cotton in the fields, and pick it. They dry it in the sun or over the fire and afterwards sever it by hand from the black seed. The women loosen or fluff the cotton into a doughnut-size mass that they spiral around a two-foot stick. When a woman is about to begin spinning, she wraps the fluff around her left arm.

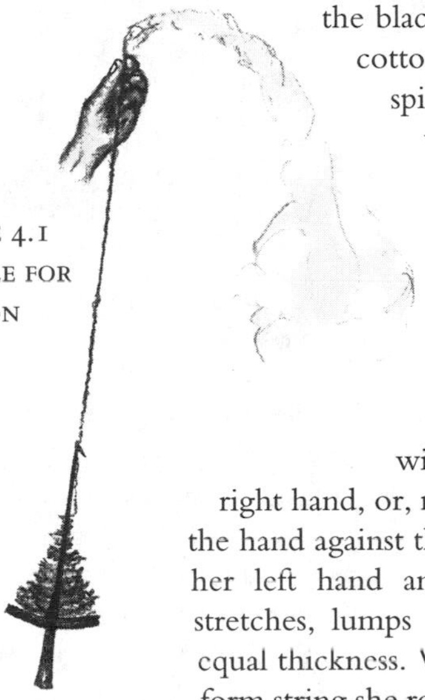

FIGURE 4.1
SPINDLE FOR
COTTON

She attaches one end of the cotton to the hook on the spindle and lengthens the fluff to a string-like appearance. She sets the spindle into a spinning motion, either by twisting the bottom end of the stick with the thumb and middle finger of the right hand, or, more often, by rubbing the spindle with the hand against the thigh. She pulls the cotton fluff with her left hand and with her right hand removes, or stretches, lumps of cotton, forming a cotton string of equal thickness. When she has what appears to be a uniform string she rolls it on to the spindle, hooking the end of the spun string onto the hook on the top of the spindle. She repeats this process over and over again. The women do the spinning at any time when they are not actively engaged in other endeavors.

The spindle used for spinning cotton consists of a sliver of wood 25 centimeters long, the thickness of a match. A piece of gourd eight centimeters in diameter is fixed 10 centimeters from the base with resin. Another short sliver of wood in the form of a hook is attached with tree sap to the top of the spindle, to which a length of cotton required in the spinning process is secured. (See Figure 4.1.)

They traditionally spun the cotton in three thicknesses: (a) thin, to attach feathers to the top of the arrow shaft, (b) moderate, for loin cloths, baby slings, and aprons, and (c) thick, for hammocks. About 90 per cent of all cotton is now spun for hammock purposes. The men often use large balls of cotton for

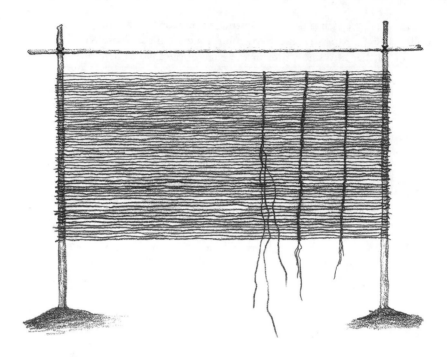

FIGURE 4.2 HAMMOCK WEAVING FRAME

hammocks, measuring up to 20 centimeters in diameter, in trade with other Yanomami. (See Figure 4.2.)

At the time of contact, every male over the age of six wore a loin cloth stained with a reddish-orange die made from the seeds of the bixu plant. (See Figure 4.3.) The loin cloth was held in place by a band made exactly to fit its intended user. Adult men placed five or six wraps one upon the other, making for a waist band that served as a practical place to store a wad of tobacco. After the contact period, men often used it to hold a knife with a blade of about 12 to 20 centimeters long. Lice found this piece of clothing an appropriate place to lodge, and the men would sometimes place the wraps over a flame to remove the lice. By the mid-linking period they no longer wore loin cloths and wraps. In my 1996 field trip, when I showed the Xilixana a man's loin cloth and wrap, as well as a woman's apron, artifacts I had collected in the mid-1960s, the generation under age 30 were absolutely aghast. They asked the older people, "Did you actually wear these?"

All females over the age of six wore cloth aprons (see Figures 4.4, 4.5). Although the aprons were relatively small in size, they were modest in principle, always covering genitalia. Soon after the arrival of missionaries they replaced a cotton "belt" worn around the buttocks with about ten strings of blue beads. Later they wove beads into the entire apron, some with very sophisticated patterns. The symmetry was striking, especially when produced by people who count in terms of one, two, and many. The ends of the aprons

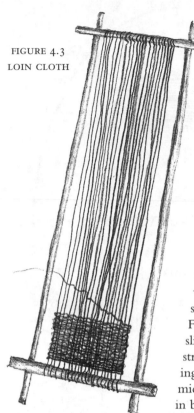

FIGURE 4.3
LOIN CLOTH

were decked with short dangles of seed casing, which made a rhythmic sound when they danced. Later several young women replaced these dangles with small aluminum triangles that produced a more vibrant sound when they danced. With the limited availability of beads in the mid-linking period, and new clothing preferences, they wore aprons less often. However, while dancing, women in the 1990s choose to clothe themselves with beaded aprons and brassieres.

Young girls and mothers use baby slings made of bark or cotton to help carry infants. The slings are worn over the shoulder and go down to the opposite hip, where a child rests his or her buttocks. The sling makes it fairly easy to nurse the child. For travelling, a female places the band or sling around her forehead and the child straddles the upper back, at times even sleeping. A few baby slings were still in use in the mid-1990s. Some women now carry children in bands of used cloth.

Women are also responsible for preparing tobacco for the men. They hang tobacco leaves about one meter above the hearth, each separated by a few centimeters. Just above these leaves hang several beaks, bones from birds or animals, or a leather fragment from a tapir. When the tobacco leaves are dry, wives splash water on them to make them pliable and then slap them on the hearth, now without live embers, before carefully wrapping them. At the time of contact this plug measured ten by two centimeters. Now they are five by one centimeter. Among the Xilixana only men (suck) chew tobacco, while in other Yanomami villages women and even

FIGURE 4.4 APRON

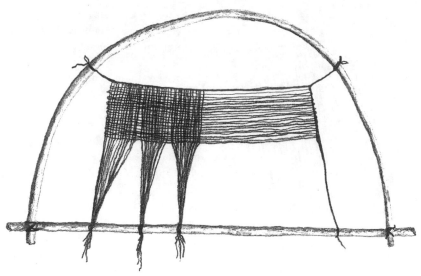

FIGURE 4.5 APRON WEAVING

children use tobacco. A user places the wad across the mouth, or between the teeth and cheek—making language work with a tobacco-sucking informant more than a little difficult.

MAKING CASSAVA

No other task requires more time on the part of women than cassava bread preparation. This food is the staple for Xilixana as well as many other indigenous cultures in the Amazon region. Manioc is, according to Leslie Sponsel (1986: 75), "highly productive: flourishes in poor soils where most other crops fail; [is] storable in the ground up to two years; [is] resistant to drought and pests." Its disadvantage lies in its poor protein content (1.6 per cent) and the amount of labor involved in its processing. The manioc has to be dug out of the ground, carried from the field to the house, peeled, grated, and pressed in a fiber-woven squeezer to extract the prussic acid. After this preparation the women bake the dried mass. They cannot leave the root unattended for more than two days, nor can the cylinder-shaped pressed mass of grated manioc be left for more than three days. Once the grated and squeezed manioc is baked into pancake-shaped coarse bread, the women dry it in the sun to avoid mold.

Mother and daughter returning from the field.

The crude and inefficient grating activity is essential to transform the root to a mass. Until the time of contact, to make the grater stones they built a fire on granite rocks, and after a time the heated rock would sometimes crack and provide a small, rough slab of about 18 by 30 centimeters that they could use to grate the manioc root. Since contact, the Xilixana have purchased WaiWai and Yekwana grater boards measuring 30 (and more) centimeters by 60 centimeters from the mission post. They rasp the root on these grater boards, and the mass falls upon a slab of wood from an old canoe.

They place the results into a cassava squeezer or *tipiti* (Portuguese), an accordion-like cylinder of woven reeds looped through a horizontal pole more than two meters from the ground within the yãno (Figure 4.6). A pole penetrates the lower loop of the squeezer, and the mother or an adolescent daughter sits on the pole providing weight to make the squeezer more taut. The manioc mass contracts so that the poisonous prussic acid and liquid mass drips into a leaf or clay vessel, and since contact, metal container. The drippings from bitter cassava are poisonous, and from time to time a chicken drinks it and dies. (In 1934, the Xilixana say, a hungry man ate the bitter root from a field and died.) The primary function of the squeezing process is to extract the liquid, which contributes minimally to detoxification. Boiling and baking do reduce the cyanide content (Dufour 1995).

After about 30 minutes of this operation, the squeezer is lifted from the hook and pushed together accordion fashion, and in its cylinder form the white mass,

Cassava bread baking using a barrel as stove.

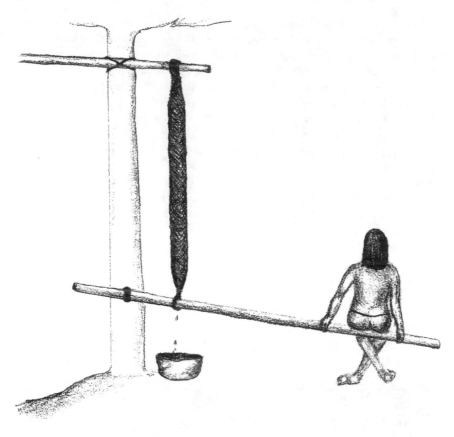

FIGURE 4.6 CASSAVA SQUEEZER

10 centimeters in diameter, is extracted and immediately segmented into pieces of 20 to 30 centimeters in length. (When cassava squeezers are not available, the Yanomami press the mass between their hands, a slow and tedious process.) These pieces are rubbed in the hands forming a coarse flour, which is strained through a sieve that the men make of liana vine. The coarse flour is then spread out upon a griddle to a thickness of one to two centimeters, and pressed down by hand. After it becomes a cohesive mass it is shifted on the griddle and, when adequately roasted, is quickly flipped over to the other side with the use of two hands. After a few minutes it is ready to be eaten.

The cassava bread on their original clay griddles measured 20 centimeters. With the use of metal griddles in the 1960s and 1970s, the bread was twice the diameter. One village now mass-produces this staple on crude barrel-like stoves that yield a "pancake" 60 centimeters in diameter. The Xilixana salvaged barrel-like cassava-making units from miners' camps in the awareness period. Cassava bread can be stored for about four days provided that when not needed it is placed in the sun, usually on the roof of their dwelling, to avoid mold. When taking a lengthy trip they often wrap these chunks in leaves to carry. These cassava cylinders can be stored for about six days. They attract fruit flies and quickly mold. When they keep them inside the yãno women sometimes wrap the cylinders in banana leaves.

Cassava bread is eaten by dipping it into broth, or eating it by itself, or mixing it with water and serving it as a drink. Meat is never consumed without cassava bread. Periodically women also prepare a thicker cassava bread with a gooey center, starting the process by placing the substance that drips from the pressing process out in the sun. The sun evaporates the liquid, and in this process the cyanide escapes, making the substance edible. Then they placed it on a skillet and bake it similarly to ordinary cassava. This type of cassava bread becomes extremely hard if it is not eaten within 24 hours.

The initial stage of processing sweet cassava is much the same as for making bitter cassava. They boil the peeled root and eat it with salt. They also cook and eat sweet cassava much like Northerners prepare and eat potatoes. Since their contact with the Palami theli, women have boiled the peeled sweet cassava root, masticated it, then boiled it some more. After it ferments for at least 24 hours, they use it as an intoxicating beverage. At the time of contact the women made small quantities of the same liquid by masticating the starchy food and leaving it to ferment in a clay pot, with no resulting intoxication because of the small quantity consumed.

Weaving the cassava squeezer requires more skill than perhaps any other item the Xilixana make. In the contact period only five older men had the skill to do this intricate work. At that time I expressed my concern that with the death of these artisans no one would know how to make this necessary tool. In time the fathers of several younger men taught them the art.

The man dries the reeds taken from a three-meter plant in the forest, then weaves them together—starting with the reeds lying on the ground and later moving them onto his lap—into a cylinder shape measuring 250 by 10 centimeters (see Figure 4.6). The tube is flexible and expands in an accordion fashion to at least 20 centimeters when the manioc mass is stuffed into the open end.

OTHER HOUSEHOLD TOOLS

Women made crude, thick, two-to-six liter pots using rolls of clay about one centimeter thick—though the Xilixana quickly came to appreciate the thinner and more symmetrical clay cooking pots made by the Aica. The women also made clay griddles, which were heavy and fragile and thus not practical to carry on trips. They had replaced both items with Western products by the mid-1960s.

They use gourds in several ways. The gourd plant (*Cucurbitaceae*) is found in abundance just outside abandoned yãnos. Although now they have adopted the use of Western plates, they still use gourds as dippers and cups, though supplementing them with others made of metal. They use small half-shells measuring 12 to 15 centimeters as dippers or cups, or as containers for beads and other small items. Larger half-gourds, measuring up to 25 centimeters in diameter, serve as dippers and communal drinking vessels. These items are

Weaving a cassava squeezer.

particularly important in the dispensing of drink at the yãimo. Women use whole gourds with a small loop of rope in the neck to carry water to the yãno from the stream or river, as well as for water storage in the yãno. After a few years of contact the whole gourds were substituted with enamel and later aluminum pots.

The Xilixana make use of several other containers. When they need something to carry wild fruit or meat of considerable weight from the jungle, they frame and weave a back pack from a split palm frond. Often they line the frame with smaller leaves before placing fruit into the pack. Then they tie up the container. The women attach a strip of bark tied in a loop to the pack and place it over their foreheads for carrying purposes.

They use about 20 leaves to make a vessel to carry a smaller volume of weight, or a quantity of honey. They also make a crude basket of liana with a radius of 20 to 25 centimeters, tying it up with bush rope at the neck, and again put it in place with bark around the forehead for the journey back to the yãno. They also use wild banana leaves to wrap up a few small fish. When they arrive at the yãno they simply place the fish with its leaf wrapping on the hearth to broil.

Along with these carrying containers quickly constructed in the forest, the Xilixana also make baskets of split liana that will hold anywhere from a half-liter to 20 liters of goods. A few are woven with one centimeter spaces, but most are more tightly woven. Almost exclusively, it is the women who use these large baskets to transport manioc root from the field or to haul firewood, again carrying the heavy load on their backs by means of a bark strap placed across their foreheads. At times they place an infant on top of the cargo in the basket.

Oval-shaped gourds measuring 30 centimeters in diameter and five centimeters in depth serve to hold smaller goods, such as cotton and spindles.

MEN'S WORK DAY

Men move about the yãno engaged in different activity from that of women. While most men embrace and cuddle small children, they do not concern themselves with food preparation or with making themselves available to help with their offspring. Men are not comfortable with infants—they are afraid, for one thing, of being urinated or defecated upon by a baby. When they carry young infants they do so with their arms slightly extended away from their bodies, reaching under the baby's butt and around its back. Women carry infants placed firmly against their own bodies. If a child cries while a man is tending it, he will quickly pass it to a woman.

A man leaves the house between dawn and eight o'clock to go to the forest or river, to hunt or fish. Older men tend the fields. Men return from a hunt to the yãno anytime between midday and evening, to recline in their hammocks, expecting to be given food by their wives. After some rest they engage themselves in some work in or near the yãno: whittling an arrow point, carving an axe handle or paddle, and, since the 1960s, crafting an artifact to be sold for cash.

Hunting and Fishing

Xilixana men spend more time occupied in hunting and fishing than in any other activity. Indeed, a man's identity is most closely associated with hunting. Men take great delight in making a good kill, in hitting their mark. Their labors of hunting are greatly appreciated by their kin. A wife sometimes withholds sex from her husband if he does not produce game from a hunt. On the other hand, she can be sexually desirous of him if he brings game. Some women respond sexually to a man who is not her husband if he gives her meat. The game they shoot is the primary exchange item used for the continuous payment to a man's wife's parents, and a man's social status is raised by a record of consistently coming back from a hunt with game. A good hunter is prized in the Yanomami community.

In the event that one repeatedly misses his target, the hunter's blood is considered too thick, and must be released. Another hunter will pinch the skin of the arm below and above the elbow, and pierce it with the tail bone of the stingray. More recently they have used the fang of a snake to pierce the skin. The hunter tells the fellow with the stingray tail or snake fang the number of pierces he wishes, as well as the specific locations. Generally several men perform this ritual at one time. They gather any dripping blood in

Return from a monkey hunt.

leaves, then take them outside and place them in the branch of a tree where large black biting ants feed. Though one can wince, you are not to groan in the piercing process. Men show up to 20 such scars on each arm. This practice has not declined since contact.

Boys are socialized at a very early age to aspire to be good hunters. When a boy is age five he plays with a small bow and a reed–like arrow that his father or brother has made for him. Holding his arrow point some 12 centimeters from a beetle, bug, or cockroach in or near the yãno he aims and shoots. By the time he is eight years of age he will own an authentic bow and arrow, a smaller version of his father's. Around the village, at the river bank, in the field, and in the wider open space of the mission post these youth pursue a variety of birds the size of sparrows and robins with great excitement and laughter. After almost every shot they excitedly shout, "Ooohh, I almost got him." Such activity can easily last several hours, and it is all part of honing their skills.

By the age of 14, a boy accompanies his brother or father into the forest to hunt. He knows what arrow point is most suited to specific animals and birds. He has a good sense of direction. He knows the sounds, footprints, and marking of every animal. He has already heard their advice and wisdom as to the tracks of each animal, where they are likely to rest and roam, their scent, and what food they eat. (Once, while we were hiking in the depths of the rainforest, my guide showed me the prints of a tapir, then told me it had passed by recently and was likely a female.) Older boys are already physically strong enough to quickly pursue wild pigs or monkeys. If his arrow comes to rest in a tree, he can climb the tree with ease to retrieve it. In shooting an arrow, he has a good sense of where the arrow will land should he miss his mark. After shooting one arrow, he may rapidly pursue the animal, and return to the location of his first shot arrow some time later. He learns to call the two

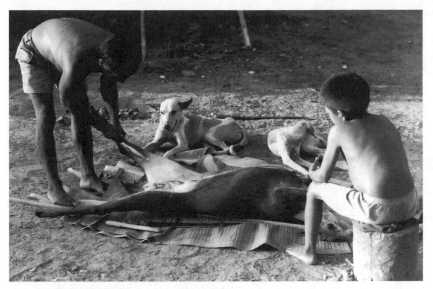

After the hunt. The deer was once taboo meat.

toucan species by placing a leaf in his hands and producing a shrill whistle. With a low hum he calms the trumpeter and curassow birds. Another whistle beckons the tapir, another the furry bearded smaller monkey.

The Xilixana mimic the sound of monkeys and call them. A hunter shouts "*ho!ho!ho!*" along with the others as he pursues a grouping of red howler monkeys. When the monkeys realize they are being pursued, they disperse in the trees. Each hunter vigorously chases one of them. Sometimes, after finding a baby monkey clinging to the neck of its dead mother, they carry the small monkey off to the yãno and raise it as a pet. They never eat anything considered to be a pet, or a domestic animal.

The adolescent boy knows how to smoke the armadillo from its hole in the earth. With time he learns the terrain as well as specific landmarks in the forest. Eventually he will be able to travel throughout the region without accompaniment. Any game shot is particularly valued if it is *ute* (fat).

The macaw fly high and rest on tall trees and are therefore difficult to shoot. These birds betray their location with their loud squawks. Their colorful feathers are valued: the small feathers are used as ornaments for arrows, and the tail feathers adorn a male's upper arms at dances and other festivities. Small birds are sometimes retrieved from the nest and nurtured and reared as pets in the home.

Crafting the tools used for hunting requires a good deal of skill and labor. They carve bows about two meters long from the hardwood redwood tree, hacking, slashing, scraping, and finally sanding the piece to the right shape. The bow is virtually straight, except when drawn for shooting. They loop a course, braided string made from the sisal plant over each end of the bow. After they made contact with other Yanomami, the Xilixana began to manufacture shorter bows made of black palm wood. In the contact period Xilixana hunted carrying a bundle of about eight long arrows, each with their respective points inserted. Later they adopted the use of the quiver from the western Yanomami and began carrying fewer arrows, perhaps three or four—and about 30 centimeters shorter in length. The quiver would contain a variety of points that could be inserted into the arrows when necessary. Arrows have been and continue to be a significant item in trade with other Yanomami. During the contact period they also used a lance made from the black palm tree, to pierce hogs (see Figure 4.7). This artifact has not been crafted since the mid-1960s.

They use five different arrow tips, each suited for specific game (see Figure 4.8). One, with a blunt end instead of a point, with a gnarl of knots, is used by young boys to shoot small birds, knocking the birds out rather than puncturing them. Another is a point with knife nicks that serve as small barbs used in shooting fish and some birds. A third has a distinct bone attachment to make a more pronounced barb. A fourth, a sharp tip of anywhere from 15 to 22 centimeters long, is made from bamboo and used on jaguar, tapir, and humans. It penetrates the skin and leaves a sizable gash that causes blood to flow. Within a decade after contact, the Xilixana were grinding and filing old knife blades to substitute for their bamboo tips. These new tips proved more efficient on their prey: animals or humans. The fifth arrow tip is used for monkeys and has the *yakiana* drug placed upon the wood point. This same "poison" is used in the practice of shamanism, and by celebrants in the yãimo feast.

The construction of the completed arrow requires skill and patience. The arrow shaft, made of cane, is cut from the field, dried in the sun, and heated over the fire to correct any warp in its length. The thinner end of the shaft (which meets the bow string) has a wooden notch inserted and is wrapped with fine cotton thread to keep it fixed in place (see Figure 4.9). Immediately below this insertion two black feathers from the curassow bird are slit in half and attached, again with thread. The thread is also decorated with a few small red, yellow, or blue toucan or parrot feathers. Several purple dabs of dye spot the thread. The other end requires attention as well. The pulp in the middle of the cane reed is pushed further inside, leaving room for the arrow point to be inserted. It is tightly bound with sisal thread, not cotton thread, because sisal is tougher, and the point must be securely inserted—it will bear considerable strain upon impact. After the thread is coated with a water-resistant resin, the arrow is ready for use. From time to time arrow shafts break, but sometimes the Xilixana splice a

FIGURE 4.7
LANCE

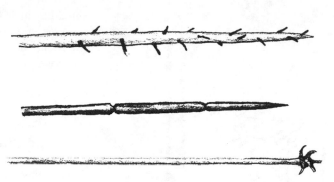

FIGURE 4.8 ARROW POINTS

broken shaft of at least 30 centimeters to another shaft with the use of sisal thread.

The Xilixana consider meat to be superior to any other food; and for them, "meat hunger" (*naiki*) is distinct from any other type of hunger. The Xilixana have a hierarchy of meat preference. The most prized is tapir, followed by bush hog and red howler and black spider monkeys. These animals are almost always hunted by groups of three or more men. After finding the shot prey, the men roll it on its back and check its stomach for fat. The wild pigs vacated the Xilixana hunting region in the late 1980s, though the reason for their departure is unknown.[1]

A second tier of preference consists of other monkeys, alligators, large birds (curassow, guam, trumpeter), the agouti (a rabbit-size rodent), paca (another rodent), and large fish. Following this group are medium-sized fish, electric eel, armadillo, anteater, and medium-sized birds such as parrot and toucan. Small fish and small birds fit the last preference. Although some Yanomami groups to the west eat snake, the Xilixana do not.

Hunters leave the house individually, with a companion, or in groups when they plan to hunt larger game. When they go out together to hunt the larger animals it is usually because someone was out in the forest not long before and had seen, scented, heard, or noted some fresh tracks. They leave the yãno at dawn with dogs, amidst much excitement. Their expectations are high.

FIGURE 4.9 ARROW
NOK AND FEATHERS

---

1   Sponsel (1986: 76) suggests that the peccary, a blackish, wild pig-like mammal [*Tayassu pecari*], is the primary source of protein for Amazonian indigenous people because of the animal's body size and tendency to wander in large herds

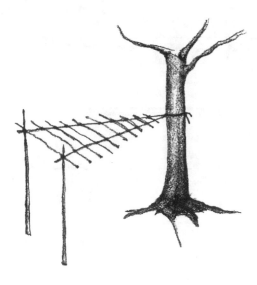

FIGURE 4.10 TEMPORARY SHELTER

Should a single hunter shoot an animal too heavy to carry, he will hang the meat from a tree and have others return for the remaining game. The men might remain in the forest or along the river for several days, living in quickly constructed shelters (see Figure 4.10). The greatest hunting event is in preparation for a yãimo, where a minimum of 15 men hunt.

Several times a year a number of families will jointly leave the yãno and travel for one or two days' journey to hunt or fish. They do not travel as quickly as hunters because they are accompanied by women and children, and more food and domestic goods. The children and women spend their days at camp near a stream, where the people quickly construct temporary shelters. They return to their yãno after from three to fifteen days, generally when their supply of cassava has been depleted. The Xilixana do not spend as much time in the forest, away from their yãno as do other Yanomami in the mountain region. Furthermore, Xilixana consume few insects, while the diet of Yanomami residing in the mountainous region includes a variety of insects.

They observe strict norms for jungle travel. The first several hunters walk in silence and are always alert to the stir of any game. They will quickly deviate from the trail should they track any animal or fowl. The sequence of persons along the path on the trek is kept virtually through the entire day, particularly for the lead person.

Numerous taboos are associated with hunting, and they help illustrate how central hunting is to Yanomami life. For instance, if you have sex before a hunt, you will not be able to hit your target. Shooting after urinating weakens the arm. Often parts of the hide, bones, or beaks of animals or birds are hung over the hearth, which makes the hunter's arm strong. Men do not eat the game they shoot with the bow and arrow—although older men do not observe this taboo rigorously, younger men must. It is a taboo that functions to distribute meat more widely within the yãno. It is acceptable to eat the game you shoot if you were assisted in the hunt by a dog, or if you used a shotgun. It is permissible to eat the fish you catch. If the hunter has someone accompanying him, he will not carry his own game back to the yãno. A menstruating woman may not eat animal or bird meat. In one instance a hunter came home after shooting a tapir, but in the late evening, despite being tired from the hunt, he could be seen at the bank of the river attempting to catch fish for his menstruating wife.

Shaman assist hunters. They indicate where wild pig are roaming. They send the jaguar spirit after the tapir to "eat" it. Then the Xilixana can follow and shoot the tapir. Shaman tell the people where the jaguar roams, warning them not to walk in that area. The hunters lay claim to the hunting area immediately adjacent to their village, making it off-limits to outsiders.

Since contact with Westerners, hunting has been altered considerably. At the time of contact hunters carried lances they used to spear wild pigs. They were plunged into the pigs while still gripped by the hunter. The long-lipped peccary could be fierce, and attack hunters. By the mid-1960s these spears were no longer used. Sometime during the 1960s, a couple of bush hogs wandered in the vicinity of the yãno. All the men were gone, and one of the women went after a pig, piercing and killing it. The men were amused that a woman would actually "hunt."

Every hunter now carries a knife when walking in the forest. If he goes off a long way from the main trail, he will slash half-centimeter-thick saplings with his knife, as markers to help him find the way back. Before knives became common he would have snapped the saplings with his hand, bending them in the direction he was walking. Prior to contact, men would sometimes sever bush rope along the path with their teeth. The use of knives made trails more readily identifiable and more easily walked.

The use of guns means that fewer people are needed for the hunt. Since the mid-1960s almost all villages have had at least one functioning shotgun, although the shot to put into them has been hard to come by. Sometimes the Xilixana could purchase shot from Brazilians downstream. By the mid-1990s Brazilian law was forbidding the sale of shot to a person without a registered gun; and since no Yanomami has a registered gun, ammunition is hard to attain.

The provision of meat has significant social consequences. A husband's and father's primary role is to provide meat for his family. No woman can fill this role. A man may insist on the killing of a newly born female if he feels the infant will add unduly to the burden of his responsibility to provide meat for his kin. He will reward his daughter's suitor's sexual favors with meat. The preferred son-in-law is a good meat provider. Every hunter is noticed for his game as he enters the yãno after a hunt. If he repeatedly returns empty-handed he is insulted by being referred to as *yelawahi* (one who is unable to strike his mark).

Meat is either roasted or boiled. When they have large quantities of meat it is crisply roasted. When meat is butchered the blood is not necessarily washed off before the meat is placed into a clay or metal pot to cook. Smaller game and fish are sometimes wrapped in leaves and broiled on hot coals.

At the time of contact there were two types of fishing: bow and arrow, and using a special liana vine beaten to pulp to create a "poison." To catch fish with bow and arrow they use a scaffolding of about two meters in height constructed at the river's edge. The "fisherman" stands upon the scaffolding and shoots the fish—an extraordinary feat considering the angle of refraction in the water. This method of fishing was discontinued after the introduction of fish hooks. (They did not know of fishing with hook and line until the early 1930s.)

Fishing in 1996, with a line extended across the river.

In the case of using bush vine to stun fish with the drug barbasco, younger men, women, and children chop the specified thick vine in the forest into lengths of 500 centimeters, then beat it to pulp with wooden bats upon a large fallen tree, and finally transport it to the river or stream, throwing it into the water and stomping it with the feet. The liana pulp asphyxiates the fish. When fish surface they are generally grabbed or scooped with a basket. In the dry season, when segments of the river are low, some 12 to 20 people in a group may be engaged in fish poisoning. Smaller groups of five to eight people fish streams. Occasionally, when meat is scarce in the rainy season, a group of five or six composed of an adult male, women, and children will seek to "poison" fish in small creeks. If a shower hits while the vines are in the water, the whole venture becomes futile, much to the disgust of the hungry group. After making contact with other Yanomami the Xilixana acquired plants that they now grow in their fields, and when the leaves of these plants are smashed using mortar and pestle in a hole in the earth, and then placed in the water, they have the same effect upon fish as the liana vine.

The use of fish lines and hooks has revolutionized fishing. They used four different sizes of hooks. Cotton line and, later, in the 1970s, nylon line and hooks have always been available at the mission post. The mission "store" never opens without someone asking for fish hooks. Everyone fishes. Fishing is no longer restricted to men. A middle-aged man or two adolescents might canoe two hours up or downstream and fish for an entire day. Young girls might canoe out to rocks in the middle of the river and fish for a couple of hours. Often one finds women or small children at the river landing throwing a line into the water to catch small fish. One or two Xilixana fish using the *espinau*, a series of large hooks attached to a meter-length of twine knotted to a stronger fish line extending across a part of, or perhaps the entire, river. The line is left in the water for the night, or for several hours. This style of fishing has been learned from Brazilians downstream. A few Xilixana have acquired nets that they throw on the water in a circular form, then slowly pull in to reap the harvest. Several men might fix a net into the water, and examine it for small fish after several hours. Small fish are wrapped in leaves and broiled. Larger fish are generally cut and boiled in water. Occasionally fish are roasted.

The Products of the Land

The forest produces more than meat for the Xilixana. There is a wide array of edible fruits. Jungle food varies by season and desirability. Possibly the most harvested fruit is the purple, marble-sized fruit bacaba (*Oenecarpus bacaba and distichus*), which grows at the top of palm trees.

Bacaba, the size of a marble, is harvested several months of the year. A man climbs the tree to cut off the sheaves of fruit and drops them to the ground. He strips the sheaves of berries and puts them into a basket made of leaves. The tree may yield as much as four gallons of berries. After the berries are brought home, they are cooked in warm water, causing the fruit to soften and making it easy to separate the fruit from the seed. A liquid can be prepared by rubbing the seeds in water between the hands, separating the fruit from the seed. Often the liquid is used as a soup in which cassava bread is dipped. Upon occasion it is used as a drink.

Apart from the bacaba there are three other types of palm fruit. Anaja (*Maximiliana regia*) is light brown in color, a little larger than a golf ball, grows in a cluster of some 40 seeds, and is eaten after being roasted. The palm fruit assi (*Euterpe oleracea*) is purple and oval in shape, and is sweeter and smaller than bacaba. It is eaten after being heated in warm water. Buriji (*Mauritia flexuosa and vinosa*), the third variety of palm fruit, the size of a golf ball, is orange and cooked before being eaten. Only a small layer of fruit covers its large, hard core.

Hajuk, a sweet red berry the size of a pea, is abundant in the jungle during the month of November. The Xilixana break off branches of the tree and carry them home. They eat the berry raw. The wild cashew (*Anacardium occidentale*) is much sweeter than the domesticated cashew fruit and is also eaten raw. This is the only known fruit whose seed (nut) is external to the fruit. While they discarded the nuts in the very early contact period, they soon learned from Brazilians that the nuts can be eaten after being roasted.

They eat brazil nuts (*Bertholletia excelsa*) raw, sometimes after rubbing them on cassava bread, as a spread. On occasion they sell Brazil nuts for cash. There are two types of sweet white pulpy food known as inga, which have black seeds and are found in pods of between 15 to 30 centimeters in length. The white pulp around the seeds is sweet and eaten raw. Occasionally they find cocao (*Theobroma cacao*), eating the white pulp and discarding the seed and shell. Sometimes they also pick and eat avocado (*Persea americana*).

They find honey, known as *yoi*, high up on trees in hives that measure almost two meters in height and half that measurement in width. A Xilixana male climbs the tree and takes up a position well below the hive opening, from which he smokes out the bees by reaching up to the hive opening with a bundle of burning leaves. The bees exit, some lighting on the intruder, much to his annoyance—though luckily these bees have a mild bite. Afterwards, with an axe the man chops at the hive, sending pieces to the ground, with the others below eagerly picking them up and devouring the honey immediately. When the honey is plentiful they wrap it up in leaves, carry it home, and mix it with water to make a drink.

They find another variety of honey known as *oi* inside hollow trees, though not in as large quantity as *yoi*. The Western delicacy of palm sprouts is in abundance in the jungle, but the Xilixana do not eat it.

A number of non-edible products in the forest are critical to Yanomami life. They use trees for building. They use liana in a variety of ways: building, basket weaving, fish poisoning, wrapping. They use leaves extensively. They use wild banana leaves to make roofs on temporary shelters, as well as for wrapping and broiling fish. They use cultivated banana leaves to provide a covering for a temporary shelter in the woods or a blind on the yãno door to restrict insects from entering, to form a protection against dirt when they cut meat on the ground, or to make an umbrella in rain or brilliant sunshine. They use a smaller 30-centimeter dovetail-shaped leaf (*ubim*—Portuguese), which grows on plants about two and a half meters in height in the forest, to roof the yãno and other dwellings. They are picked with a 20-centimeter stem, bundled, and carried to the construction site on their backs, then woven around horizontal liana on the roof or side walls of their dwelling. They use slats from palm trees to make a five-foot vertical wall around the perimeter of the yãno; and they use shorter slats to form shelves. The women tie small scented leaves to their upper arms as ornamentation.

They use sticks from the "fire tree" to make fire. Sometimes they use a whitish transparent sap found at the base of a particular tree as a temporary light in the house at night. They also process a black resin taken from trees to form 4-by-30-centimeter cylinders, which they use on the ends of the arrow shaft to waterproof the thread, as well as to make the arrow points stick into, and stay in, the arrow shafts. The Yanomami also use the resin to plug cracks in canoes. This resin is also a good trade item exchanged between villages. They use long reeds they find in the forest to weave cassava squeezers.

They process the drug ebene from the sap found under the bark of the *yakiana* tree. They use its sticky substance on arrow tips to hunt monkey. Shaman also sniff it on a fairly regular basis. All men also use the drug in the yãimo. The root or more specifically bulb—considered to have magic powers—of another forest plant is placed in the hunter's mouth, then spit in the direction of the curassow and trumpeter birds to slow their movement.

Agriculture

The Yanomami are hunters, gatherers, and slash-and-burn field tillers. The Xilixana tell stories of their forebears at the turn of the century securing a sharp stone to a stick and using it as a kind of an axe to bash trees to make them fall. These tools had not been used in the lifetime of any of the Xilixana I knew, but the rudimentary tree-cutting instruments established a particular pattern of cutting trees from the forests that still exists to this day. They chop about halfway into the stumps of many trees—some 40 to a 100—leaving them erect until they choose a king-pin tree, which they chop completely through to make it fall. In domino fashion, all trees of the forest fall to the ground. At the turn of the century they would tie a strong liana (wood vine, or bush rope) to the top of a tree, and a large group of them would pull it down.

The space in a cleared field may be 50 per cent manioc and 40 per cent bananas. Unlike most Yanomami, the Xilixana eat manioc as their staple food, rather than banana. They grow both the bitter (*manihot utilissma*) and sweet (*manihot aipi*) varieties of manioc, which they plant by pushing young manioc sticks of about 50 centimeters in length from a mature plant into a mound of soft earth. Within eight months the root is ready to harvest, though it may be left in the earth for an additional 12 months. The earth serves as an environment of growth as well as storage.

The Xilixana have at least six different varieties of bananas, plus two varieties of plantain. They eat bananas raw, or squished between the fingers to form a drink. They rarely peel and roast green bananas, a common practice among neighboring Yanomami. In the contact period they cooked banana to form a hot drink. Tobacco is carefully seeded and nurtured in selected areas of enriched soil and potash.

Other edible crops planted in the fields are sweet potato, and purple (*colocasia*) and white (*dioscorea*) bell yams. The white bell yams have been imported from another Yanomami tribe to the west. Yam vines climb a tripod frame built over the young plant. To eat the yams they peel them, then boil. Sometimes they use them to make a thicker broth, almost to the texture of a paste. They also plant and harvest giant purple yams (*aracea*), sometimes weighing as much as 10 kilos. These vegetables are more fibrous. They stopped cultivating this plant in the 1970s, finding other kinds to be more tasty. They plant the sweet potato (*impomoca Batata*) in soft, loamy, moist soil, and boil it with the skin, which they remove at the time of eating.

Several pests play havoc with garden plants and arrow cane. Insects infest sugar cane and arrow cane. Rodents, capybara, and cutia eat sugar cane and sweet cassava.

They plant sugar cane in a similar manner as manioc, sticking short pieces of the tops of the plant into mounds of earth. When the plant is mature they cut the cane, and after ripping off the outer covering (originally using their teeth, but later with the aid of a knife) they suck out the sweet juice. Mothers sometimes suck the juice, spit it into a gourd, and give it to their infants to drink. In the early 1980s the Xilixana adopted the crude sugar cane press from the WaiWai. In recent years women place the juice in their mouth, spit it into a pot, then heat it. After a day or two of fermentation they serve it as a drink.

Peachpalm, (*pupunha Guilielma speciosa*) is a prized, starchy fruit. Its two-centimeter nut is covered with a delicious oil-starchy orange food that they cook, peel, and eat. The fruit grows on a tree whose long trunk is completely covered with spines about 10 centimeters long. It takes several years for the tree to grow to maturity. A lot of skill is needed to harvest the fruit without being pricked. Men mount a scissor-like wood frame and climb the tree to cut the bunches of fruit. They may also climb an adjoining tree, and then

Young manioc plants, the staple food of the Xilixana, in a newly perpared field.

reach to slash the fruit. These domesticated trees are commonly found in abandoned fields to which they return to harvest this valuable fruit. They also grow red and green peppers (*capsicum*) in the field. They pick them, dry them, and sometimes ground them to a powder. This is their only traditional spice. It is used to flavor broth, sprinkle on cooked fish, meat, and occasionally on ripe bananas.

They harvest several other products from the field. They plant cotton seeds and later pick and process the fluff. They have found that the seeds and plants do best when they are placed in the earth in an area where the trees have been burned down. More frequently they plant tobacco in those same areas. Since contact with other Yanomami, they have found that tobacco is a valuable trade item. Gourd plants grow near the environs of the yãno without any effort or care. This is partly because, when the Xilixana craft a gourd, they simply throw out the seeds and pulp as garbage, and these castoffs eventually take root and grow. The bixa shrub produces a pod of seeds that are often used in body decoration. The Xilixana crunch the seeds between the palms of their hands, then mix the result with spital and smear it on their bodies.

Arrow cane is a valued field product and is commonly used in trade. Arrow production in Xilixana fields has diminished since contact, with growth thwarted by burrowing insects. They use the spine-like sisal (*Agave sisalana*), similar in appearance to pineapple, to make rope for bows, canoes, and attaching hammocks to posts or trees. Several plants have been introduced from neighboring Yanomami for black magic purposes. The leaves of another plant are said to cause a woman to become infertile, when spread upon her abdomen.

Today a number of food products have augmented their field crops. The first such fruit was papaya, a good health food harvested on very rapidly growing, pulpy trees found around almost every yãno. They have acquired new strains of bananas and manioc from Brazilians and other Yanomami. Other garden products that have been added to their fields from either the missionaries or Brazilians are pineapple, maize, rice, squash, and watermelon. One community has planted lemon and orange trees in their village, using the seeds of trees found at the mission station. They grow corn and rice intermittently. Some villages have a few grapefruit and mango trees.

The Tools of Life

CANOE AND PADDLE CONSTRUCTION

They make canoes from one of three trees measuring from 50 to 90 centimeters in diameter. After felling a tree, they estimate the required length of the canoe by squatting two, four, or the desired number of men on the log in the approximate sitting distance as in an actual canoe. The resulting length is generally between five and seven and a half meters. After determining the length they begin peeling off the bark.

They use axes, adzes, and long-handled chisels to shape the outside of the log as it lies on the ground. They then turn it over and dig out the inside, with an opening that is about 40 centimeters across. The walls of the canoe remain four to six centimeters in thickness, with the front somewhat thicker in anticipation of its future encounters with rocks in the river. The thickness is not uniform, but only approximated by tapping the axe on the exterior of the canoe. When they have finished the canoe they cut a wide trail through the forest to the bank of the stream or river and lay small trees across the trail, to

Putting the finishing touches on a canoe paddle, 1994.

facilitate the sliding of the canoe. They might place sticks crossway (perpendicular) in the canoe to facilitate the men, women, and children who join to push and pull the canoe to the water's edge, often with grunts and groans and considerable humor.

They gather, and bind, dried palm leaves and place them inside the canoe. They tilt the canoe somewhat to one side, and light the leaves, vigorously fanning the fire with green brushes. The intense heat causes the wood to be pliable for expansion. They firmly place 10 or 14 sticks, 6 centimeters in diameter and 40 to 65 centimeters in length, across the canoe to keep and help expand the walls of the canoe while the heat is applied. They then prop the canoe up on its opposite side, and they repeat the process, with some sticks now placed directly across the opening.

Upon occasion, the fire may burn a hole right through the wood, in which case resin mixed with wood shavings or, more recently, a piece of tin might serve as a patch. If the burned hole is of substantial size, the canoe-makers, in anger, might chop up the canoe, thereby totally destroying the labors of the equivalent of three men for two weeks.

Since contact, the construction of canoes has been somewhat modified. By means of a brace and small bit they may bore several holes in the wood to ensure the correct thickness. The carved canoe is rested on a rack raised off the ground by about 30 centimeters. After the canoe is half-filled with water, they light a fire of wood under the canoe, a method used by the Yekwana and WaiWai. During this heating process they gently insert cross-pieces of wood to expand the width. The Xilixana have borrowed a brace and bit from the missionaries to bore a hole at the front of the canoe, to which they attach a rope to moor the canoe.

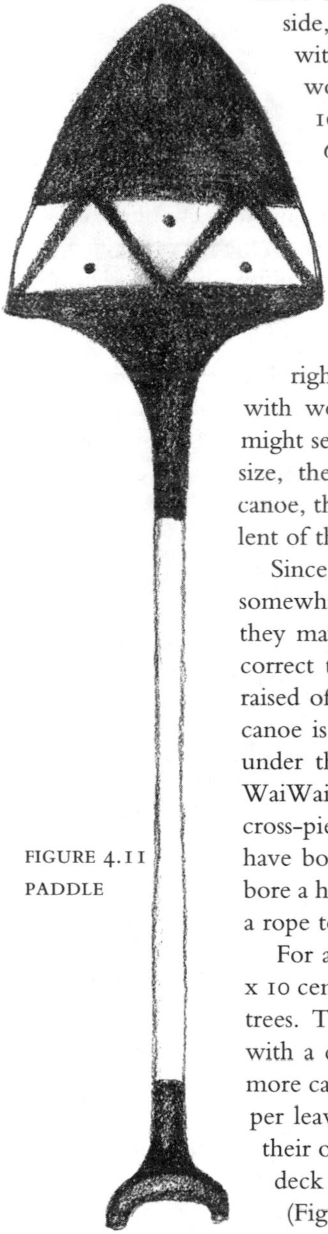

FIGURE 4.11
PADDLE

For a canoe paddle, they cut a crude slab of 150 x 42 x 10 centimeters with an axe from one of three species of trees. They reduce the slab to a more appropriate size with a cutlass, and eventually carry it home to do even more carving with the cutlass, a knife, and finally sandpaper leaves, producing its final form. The Xilixana have their own unique paddle shape, the form of a spade in a deck of cards, with a breadth of up to 40 centimeters (Figure 4.11). The blade is generally no more than 45 centimeters in length. The upper end is widened so they can place their hands perpendicular to the paddle. The shape of the upper handle may be about five percent off from the plane of the base of the paddle. They design the paddle blade with red, purple, or black coloring. Both male and female use the paddles, and sometimes they are used in trade with Brazilians downstream.

FIRE-MAKING

At the time of contact fire sticks had to be only rarely used, because the Xilixana kept fires going continuously in their hearths. They used fire sticks mainly when they made longer trips to hunt or to visit. When families travel short distances into the forest, a woman will carry a stick from the hearth to ignite a fire in the new location. When they need a fire in the field, they will again take out a stick of fire from the house.

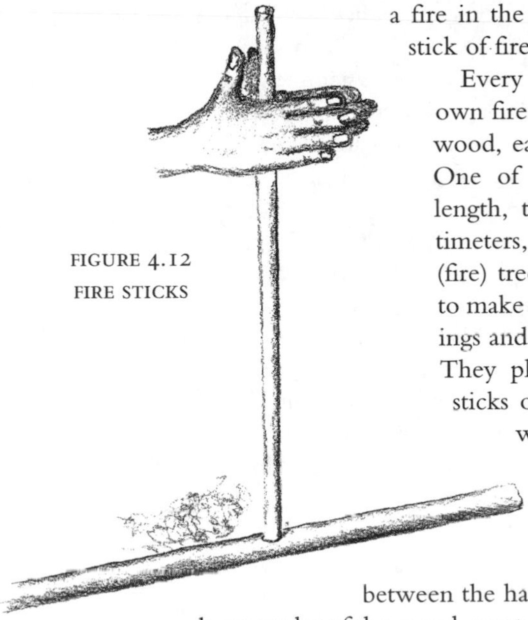

Every male over the age of 20 had his own fire sticks consisting of two pieces of wood, each two centimeters in thickness. One of the sticks is 25 centimeters in length, the other approximately 50 centimeters, and both come from the *wak* (fire) tree (Figure 4.12). When they need to make fire, they make a pile of dry shavings and place it close to some dry leaves. They place the shorter of the two fire sticks on the ground and hold it firmly with the first and second toe. They hold the longer stick vertically with the end placed into a small notch in the horizontal stick. The longer stick is twirled rapidly between the hands, while applying pressure. The hot powder of the wood, created from this friction, is placed near the dry shavings and leaves, and blown upon, producing a flame.

FIGURE 4.12
FIRE STICKS

As a cultivating tool they carved out a dibble stick, a little more than a meter in length, from the black palm tree. The stick, about 130 centimeters long, was somewhat oval, measuring two centimeters in diameter for most of its length, but four centimeters in width at the base, where it had a blunt point. Men over 35 years of age were more likely to use this gardening tool to weed and loosen the earth. Women used it to unearth roots. With the introduction of a metal digging tool, the dibble stick became extinct before 1960.

They used to make another tool by taking the lower long tooth of the agouti and attaching to a 16-centimeter stick using sisal string and resin. That tool also is no longer found in the culture.

All these indigenous items are grown or made in their fields or found in the forest, although, significantly, each item's construction was designated specifically to one gender. Only one item, the cassava squeezer, was seen as a specialized craft, which meant these people had virtually no social status differentiation based upon the production of the tools or items—a condition in marked contrast to our society, where the production of goods, and especially a person's position in the hierarchy related to the production of goods, have a significant bearing on that person's social position.

The production of these tools and items had an important impact upon Xilixana culture. It created gender interdependence. Women spun their cotton thread, which men used to attach feathers and points to arrow shafts. Kin members ate meat shot by the men. Women depended upon men to provide their grater stones (later grater boards) and cassava squeezers. The actual history of the emergence of these field products and manufactured items are unknown. How did they discover if they processed the bitter (poisonous) manioc it could be a food staple? Why is this their food staple rather than plantain and bananas, as with the Yanomami in the mountain region? Who showed them how to weave the cassava squeezer, an item some other Yanomami do not have? Who introduced dogs? Why were female dogs viewed as incapable of hunting? How did they discover that a particular species of liana would "drug" fish? Who introduced them to *yakiana* drug, which proves lethal when overdosed?

MUSICAL INSTRUMENT

The Xilixana have three different flutes they use to make music. The most common one is made from the lower hind leg of a deer. They burn three holes into the bone at three-centimeter intervals, with a semicircle hole as a mouth piece. During the contact period, they often played music with this kind of flute in the early evening. To announce their homecoming, hunters and kinsmen played the bone flute in their canoes when approaching the village. But in the 1990s this mode of making music has become more rare. Instead, occasionally they play tunes on segments of plastic pipes.

They also made bamboo flutes, about 25 centimeters in length and 3 centimeters in diameter, in a similar way, with three holes burned into the bamboo in a row and a semi-circle as the mouth piece. Both types of flutes produce three notes in minor thirds. You might hear young men playing tunes in the evenings while resting in their hammocks.

Occasionally in the contact period they also used a hollow bamboo rod about one meter long and measuring about three centimeters in diameter, with a natural joint in the center. They burned two holes near the joint, and wrapped and tied a leaf around this division. The shrill sound produced by blowing directly into one end increased as the player forced more air into the flute. By the 1980s neither of these two bamboo flutes were still being used. Women never played flutes.

NON–INDIGENOUS MATERIAL CULTURE

At the time of contact the Xilixana had a few very well worn axes, cutlasses, knives, and an adze acquired from earlier encounters with the Macu and Yekwana.

After contact they purchased WaiWai grater boards from the mission post. These were made of small chipped stones embedded with resin in wood. After the mission established a base among the Sanuma and Yekwana in 1963, the mission sold Yekwana grater boards made of small pieces of tin, which the Xilixana preferred over the WaiWai grater boards. More recently they have acquired Yekwana boards from the Palimi theli, and in a few cases obtained them directly from the Yekwana.

For the first three years after contact we saw that the Xilixana had an almost insatiable demand for the very items that had become worn, dull, or possibly broken over the previous 27 years. Having been deprived of knives and axes for so long, with their work on the airstrip and mission station, a number of men purchased these tools in excess of their immediate needs. The headman had six new cutlasses, when two would have been adequate. WaiWai grater boards, matches, enamel pots, scissors, fish hooks and line, needles, and salt were in demand. Other preferred items were soap and mirrors.

Requests for shotguns were persistent, and to some extent the missionaries gave in to these requests. (For other changes in tools, items, clothing, and customs, see chapter 14.)

Five
Family and Social Organization

As in most preliterate societies, family is central to Yanomami life, and so too are marriage and heterosexual relations. Family is the focal point for providing food and shelter, for heterosexual partner selection and satisfying sexual needs, for procreation and childrearing, and social activity. The Xilixana seek social and physical protection from members within their own village, as well as against threats from Yanomami or other peoples in more distant regions, and their social organization addresses these preoccupations. Within the family an individual finds loyalty, support, trust, and cooperation—as well as jealousy, ambivalence, and a certain amount of suspicion (Murphy 1989: 111).

The key to the Yanomami's political and economic structure is kin structure, which, I must emphasize, is not about biology, but rather about social relations and social groups. As anthropologist Robert Murphy (1989: 130, 134) points out, "Kinship terms are maps of the world of relatives, for they outline categories of social statuses rather than biological connections."

Relationship Terminology
and Acceptable Sexual Partners

One of the primary concerns of both anthropology and sociology is social organization. We seek answers to the questions, "What keeps societies together?" and "How is it that we have a persistence of some form of society?" Family has long been regarded as one of the fundamental ingredients for maintaining the cohesiveness of any society, and until recent years this has been a stance supported by anthropologists, especially when they do research related to preliterate peoples. Their focus has been on kinship as the primary means of explaining the complex underpinnings of a people's solidarity and reciprocity (Levi-Strauss 1969; Durkheim 1933); and this focus on kinship has helped in efforts to build an understanding of the dynamics of Yanomami society.

Temporary shelter, 1995.

For the Xilixana, relationship terms are first of all differentiated by family connections. In their terms, family is distinguished by the particular person's immediate family (birth mother and father, birth sister and brother) and his or her parallel-cousins and their parents. Anyone outside those categories, including all cross-cousins and their parents, are not family members. This other category is central to Yanomami life, because it identifies people who are eligible for marriage and sexual relationships.

The Xilixana use family terms familiar to Western culture: father (*paye*), mother (*naba*), brother (*aweye*), sister (*amiye*), but they extend these terms beyond the immediate family to include what we would call uncles, aunts, and cousins—though not all uncles, aunts, and cousins.

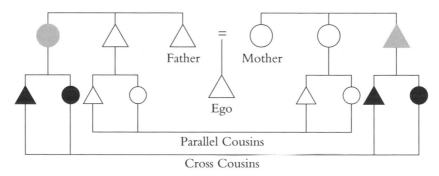

FIGURE 5.1 EGO'S RELATIONSHIP TO TWO GENERATIONS OF KIN   (JOHN EARLY)

The canoe used as a means of transportation.

The Yanomami in general observe what anthropologists call the Iroquois kinship terminological system. In this system, fathers include a person's father's brothers, and mothers include the mother's sisters. Siblings include all the off-spring of these parents. But the person's father's sisters and mother's brothers are not included as "family," nor are any children born to the father's sisters or mother's brothers. In other words, using the term *ego* to designate the point at which we enter a genealogy, in the case of the Xilixana the children of ego's mother's sisters are called brothers, and the children of ego's father's brothers are called sisters. In our society we recognize these persons as parallel-cousins. (Figure 5.1 indicates that all the open figures in the same generation as ego are brothers and sisters.)

The term nuclear family as we know it in Western society does not apply to the Yanomami, who make a distinction between their uterine siblings, and those who are parallel-cousins. In the case of the former, members share the same hearth. The degree of reciprocity is of a deeper quality. The significance of the parallel-cousins and non-biological mothers and fathers is recognized primarily in reciprocity. Members are expected to show generosity, to loan artifacts, and give food when necessary. It is likely that before the age of 35 an adult male will have intercourse with his brother's wife. The Yanomami kinship allows for this option; and children therefore call their father's brothers *paye* whether they have copulated with their mothers or not.

The age range of siblings is broad. A woman is likely to have her first child at age 16 (Early & Peters 1990: 42) and continue to bear children for as many as 25 years. This means that a mother and her older daughters can be raising young children at the same time, although during this time the older mothers will be approaching the ends of their reproductive years, which last, usually, into the early forties. The reproductive period for men stands in sharp contrast, beginning earlier and possibly lasting for a generation longer

(Chagnon 1997: 153). In most cases males have copulated with females before their marriages. In a few cases they have sired children, although they might not have taken on the role of a father. When brides are not available, a male youth might have become a secondary husband and sired children. In other cases, a man might have acquired a second, younger wife when his first wife's reproduction was waning.

In the 1960s, with wives scarce, polyandry was common, and single men over 20 years of age often became secondary husbands to an already married woman. This was often a fraternal polyandrous relationship, with no bride payment or bride service required. The village recognizes the secondary (or even third) husband as the biological father of all subsequent children born. Monogamy is the preferred marriage form, and the secondary husband remains in this relationship only until, if ever, he acquires his own bride. If he remains in the union he becomes the primary husband after the death of the first husband (Peters & Hunt 1975; Peters 1982).

Another peculiarity of the system, from our point of view, is that it does not take into account the role of ego's grandmother and grandfather. Yanomami categories operate within a framework of two generations: a person's own generation and the one preceding or succeeding that person.

While there is much social relevance to family relationships, another level of Yanomami association is also germane to social solidarity. This is the generation whose members, from ego's perspective, are recognized as *wãlima* (known as cross-cousins in the Iroquois system). The Xilixana address these parents as *xowaye* for men and *yapa* for women. The relationship between *wãlima* (cross-cousins) and their parents *xowaye* and *yapa* is one that is generally treated with caution and reserve. The only exception are male *wãlima* who approximate the same age. They sometimes become intimate friends and hunt together, and especially if a male has married his cross-cousin's sister.

The importance of *wãlima* relations rests in its function as the pool of preferred marriage partners. This is a social dynamic that our society defines as incest, but for the Yanomami cross-cousin marriages are the ideal. Women discuss the potential of a marriage almost immediately after a female child is born, and they show a strong preference for potential partners from within the village. This practice is in essence a protection for the village, because it means continued growth rather than the departure of a marriage partner. Still, the preference is not always obtainable because of rules of incest, the small population of the village, and the sex distribution. The ideal arrangement would be a village in which the figureheads are *wãlima* to one another and their wives are unrelated. In this case daughters and sons from one family could marry the sons and daughters of the other family. This was the situation in a village that fissioned from a much larger community in 1962.

The Xilixana showed their concern about finding available cross-cousins for marriage in their conversations with me regarding my own family. When our daughter was three years of age some of them frequently asked us, "Who will she marry?" We would say we didn't know. When we tried to explain that she would eventually choose whomever she wished, the Xilixana found this to be incomprehensible. One day the plane brought mail indicating that my wife's brother and spouse had given birth to a baby boy. The Xilixana were absolutely delighted when they heard this news, because our daughter now had an ideal marriage partner, her cross-cousin.

Village members go beyond what we recognize as parents, aunts, uncles, and cousins. The Yanomami also have terms that designate two generations, one of which, if cross-sexed, is marriageable, the other not (see Figure 5.1). Ego can marry any *wãlima*, the same term used for cross-cousin. The parents of a heterosexual *wãlima* are *xowaye* and *yapa*, again the same terms used for a cross-cousin's parents. Although these classificatory terms tend to be rigidly observed, on occasion they are ignored. Yanomami relationships are prescribed through a group member's parents.

For decades the Xilixana lived in a social cocoon, which they only moved out of in 1957 when they contacted the Brazilians. Since then their contacts with people outside their own group have expanded greatly in a number of different ways—including migration in both directions, and intermarriage— and they have had to find the proper terminology for the "outsiders" they meet and associate with.

When two groups meet, one of the first concerns is to establish correct relationship terms. Considerable thought goes into this process, because social expectations and interpersonal behaviors can depend on the definition. Young men make every effort to "case" the older men, and when they see these older men being accompanied by daughters they will address them as *xowaye* ("father-in-law"), establishing a relationship that legitimates sexual intercourse with the daughter in the first as well as in any subsequent encounters. The naming is connected to the expectations of the social practice, given that every visit includes a feast at which the hosts and visitors consume large amounts of drink and sexual norms become less constraining.

For Westerners, a marked distinction of Yanomami relationships is that marriage or sexual relations are not permitted with every heterosexual outside the "extended family." The practice is that the women considered eligible for marriage come only from every second generation. They consider any violation of this rule to be incest, and they treat these breaches with grave consequences: gossip fights, fisticuff duels. The Yanomami rules of incest are not, then, biologically based. Potential heterosexual partners include a person's cross-cousins, but they use the same term (*wãlima*) only for every second generation in the larger population. Perhaps the rules regarding eligible marriage partners can be better understood as a matter of "privileged unions." Such unions, in which women are regarded as valuables, unfold a wide realm of rights as well as obligations (see Levi-Strauss 1969: 120-32).

Marriages do not have the age constraints commonly found in Western society. In the 1950s and 1960s a husband was generally 8 to 12 years older than his partner, with instances in which a husband was 40 years older. In one or two cases a wife was 20 years older than her husband.

An established pattern of the rights and privileges connects a young man and any of his fathers. I was involved in such a relationship myself. Davi, a man

32 years old, is a son of WA, with whom I established the relationship of brother. Therefore Davi would address me as father, and as a son he could request goods from me. Davi wrote me a note the day I was leaving the village in 1995 to return to North America. He anticipated a subsequent visit. Some ten years earlier I had given him a fiberglass bow, which he had valued highly but later lost in the river. Now, as a son, he asked for another fiberglass bow, and I was under obligation to get him one.

DAVI'S LETTER (TRANSLATION)

> *Father, when you come again*
> *I want a bow*
> *When you come*
> *You bring it*
> *You are my father*
> *That's what I desire.*

As Figure 5.2 indicates, the unit of the nuclear family (A) is focal, particularly during the childbearing years. Though not exclusively so, food, sex, reproduction, and childrearing take place within this unit. The second unit (B) augments some needs of the immediate family. This unit, the extended family, includes a further sphere of brothers and sisters (parallel-cousins) and mothers and fathers. The unit has unique obligations regarding food provision and protection.

A third sphere is the specific family into which ego, as male, marries. There are two categories of (C): one from within the same village, and, failing this, ego from a different village. The preference is from his own village, in which ego has continuous connection with two nuclear units: his family of orientation and his wife's family. Reciprocity between ego and his wife's family strongly cements this unit.

The fourth unit (D) is the other members of the village. From this collective members augment their social relations. A man finds companions to hunt with or harvest field crops with. These other people help one another with house construction; or they loan items to one another. These people celebrate the yãimo together. They exchange news and jokes, and insult one another.

Younger members respect the older generation, and every son-in-law treats his father-in-law and mother-in-law with respect. They strictly observe a practice of mother-in-law avoidance.

One experience in particular gave me a jolt as to the significance of Yanomami kin terms. The Xilixana had asked me about my relationship to two married missionary women, neither of whom were related to me. I had met them and their husbands only two years earlier. I didn't feel comfortable to refer to them as sister, mother, or mother-in-law, all of which are appropriate in Yanomami culture. That left me, given the terminology of the

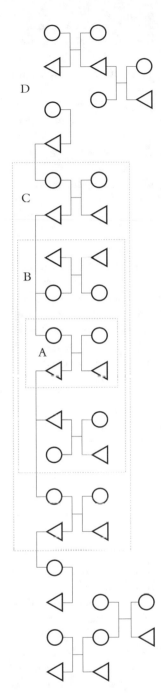

D

C

B

A

FIGURE 5.2 VILLAGE
ORGANIZATION WITH
A FAMILY FOCUS

Xilixana worldview, with only one remaining term, *wãlima*. They smirked at my response, and then it hit me: to them this meant that I was taking these women as female partners, in addition to my wife—that I was not having a monogamous relationship with my wife. From that time on I made a special effort to use correct terms. I addressed my key informant as brother, and I named almost all other relationships based on the kinship terms he used. As an outsider I realized that, to make myself clear, I should use terminology that included father, mother, brother, sister, father-in-law, mother-in-law, and *wãlima*.

Despite the centrality of relationship terminology and its seemingly rigid and fixed pattern, the Yanomami do alter classification when necessary (Saffirio 1985). Most times they do this for the purposes of marriage, in the case of a man seeking a wife. In rare circumstances parents alter or reinterpret terminology to make a marriage arrangement possible for their son. I don't know of any case in which a woman has reclassified a man. In one case a grown man reclassified a *wãlima* as sister, making it easier for him to visit and converse with her. Lee Guemple (1979), in his study of the Inuit, contends that fictive kin brings some flexibility to a rigid structure. In many cases people meet a change in relationship with hostility, seeing it as incest, the worst of all social deviance. The result of this friction is often a fisticuff duel. Napoleon Chagnon (1997: 153) notes that men who are tough and have a high social status are more likely to alter classification.

Other pressures of Yanomami life tend to increase the potential for classification change. The small population of Yanomami contacts is a factor. Each settlement or village might have a population of between 16 and 80 people, and in the marital process of elimination—leaving out children and menopausal women, kin recognized as family, and every second generation of the non-married population—the potential for mate selection can be limited in the extreme. In the 1950s and 1960s some children considered up to five men as their biological fathers. In most cases fathers are fraternal, in which case the plurality of fathers has little bearing upon reclassification. After a girl is four or five years of age the Yanomami might conveniently propose that one of the "fathers" was not involved in the conception, which would allow for a new classification. In the 1960s, when a number of non-Xilixana migrated to the central Mucajai region, the new immigrant women led to an expansion of the population. These immigrants and their offspring were particularly open to reclassification.

The rules of incest are sometimes violated. In the contact period one Xilixana man, BA, married a widow from the Apiau Aica, and after 15 years and the birth of several children with BA (and his brothers), she died. BA returned to her Apiau village of origin and found her earlier-born daughter, who by that time was widowed as well. He "took" the daughter as wife, and she bore him more children. In another case, aging TT took a 15-year-old girl in marriage from the Malaxi theli in 1978, an arrangement he successfully maneuvered because his sons had married women from that village. Though he showed his age, he fathered a couple of children. One of his married sons frequently had intercourse with that same woman and sired a child—though others considered that sexual union inappropriate. The younger man, almost 40 years of age, argued that he had never addressed his father's second wife as "mother," and therefore his sexual behavior could not be seen as incest.

In a few cases reclassification takes place for reasons other than marriage. A married male may dislike the estranged role with a woman considered his wãlima. He has no intention of having intercourse with her. He wishes to converse with her in a congenial social manner, and accepts her as "sister." The Xilixana identify such reclassification as uma pu wei, meaning "as if we are siblings, but not really." The change is made only from wãlima to brother/sister. Such a reclassification does not explode into a community-wide furor as in the case of alleged incest classification, perhaps mostly because it does not involve sex or offspring.

Marriage

The pivotal point for a good deal of Yanomami social interaction involves the partnership of male and female, or mate selection. In the patriarchal Yanomami society the parents determine a young girl's partnership. When females are scarce, as in the decade before and after contact, girls were betrothed as young as age three. In at least one instance, a betrothal was made in advance of birth for a fetus, depending on whether or not it turned out to be female. Upon betrothal the girl becomes identified as the man's woman (or wife), even though cohabitation does not take place until at least a year after her puberty. Sex between the partners before her puberty is taboo, though it is a taboo that has been violated in rare cases.

The betrothal, arranged between the prospective bridegroom and the parents of the girl, has significant economic and political consequences. It initiates the commitment of bride service and bride payment, which are at first intermittent until the girl's puberty, then escalate through to at least the second year of the marriage.

Betrothals can be initiated at one of the three-day feasts, when the young man—sober, drugged, or intoxicated—will make the request of the girl's father or brother. Shortly thereafter he will go out to shoot game, often a large bird, and when he returns with his catch to the village he drops the meat near the hearth of the wife-giving family. The act of accepting the meat and cooking it seals the betrothal, and under normal circumstances initiates a lifelong commitment and association between the young male and the wife-giving family. He commits himself to bride service and bride payment for the rest of his life and identifies himself as an ally to protect the interests and goals of the wife-giving family. In return he will eventually receive a wife, who will offer him sexual relations and bear him children, as well as prepare his food.

At the sign of the girl's first menses the people strictly observe a ritual of female puberty in which she is isolated from all males. About a year and a half later she and her bridegroom begin their cohabiting experience. She bears her first child between her 14th and 17th years. The marriage pattern is matrilocal, with the bridegroom joining the wife's extended household, making himself readily available to his wife's parents or brothers for services of field-making, canoe and house construction, hunting, and, if need be, revenge in warfare on neighboring or more distant villages. If the parents or the bride break a betrothal contract, fisticuff duels are inevitable.

THE FUNCTION OF MARRIAGE

Marriage has far-reaching social functions, along with personal gains. The male acquires a female who will prepare his food and his tobacco, and do much more besides. In the contact period she wove his loin cloth and hammock. But a husband does not view his wife's fulfilment of domestic duties as the primary function. The key task is to bear him children, and not only that but to work at rearing them. In time any daughters she provides will also prepare food for him and look after other needs. Perhaps more importantly, the man also stands to gain when his daughters become of age to be betrothed, after which the son-in-law will provide him with bride payment and bride service. Until the time of betrothal his own sons will help him in making canoes and fields, as well as provide meat.

When a wife reaches menarche, although she is most likely still quite capable of fulfilling household duties the husband will, if at all possible, seek out a younger woman, even if this means providing bride service for a second (or third) time. In some cases men practise polygyny with two fertile women.

Any adult female or male who is not married is considered *mãlo*, meaning incomplete or without a natural counterpart. Single adult women are dependent upon their biological fathers or brothers for game and protection. Single adult males depend upon their mothers or sisters for food preparation. The Xilixana found it difficult to understand why some female missionaries remained unmarried. They felt the fathers of these young women had committed a gross injustice in not arranging a marriage. Marriage, for them, is rarely an act of romance, but rather one of fulfilling specific gender roles. Marriage is a matter of survival.

A woman's motivation to marry is radically different from a man's. Her parents, or perhaps a brother, tell her whom she will marry. Any attempts to thwart their wishes meet up with considerable difficulty. Once she is over the trauma of early cohabitation and the birth of a couple of children, she generally adapts more fully to the demands on her as an adult. Like her mother before her, she bears children for her husband, and rears them. Her status rises with the number of children she bears. She engages herself in the daily task of cassava bread preparation and numerous other domestic tasks. As a wife she is provided with meat. Her husband constructs a field and plants bananas, manioc, and other garden products, which she harvests with other women.

SOURCES OF FEMALE PARTNERS

In mate selection, the Xilixana prefer as cross-cousin marriages from within the same village, followed by sister exchange, the choice of a village female in the proper classificatory relationship, a female from a neighboring Yanomami tribe, or acquisition of a bride through raiding.

If a biological cross-cousin from the same village is not available, they seek a biological cross-cousin in another village. Ego's father's sisters, ego's mother's brothers, or sometimes ego's mature brothers feel considerable social pressure to search out a potential betrothal. If a biological cross-cousin is not available, the aspiring husband seeks a partner from the non-biological *wãlima* relationship. These two patterns of mate selection continue to this day.

A third form of mate selection is based on an exchange of sisters: a man gives his sister in exchange for the sister of his *wãlima*. In such cases the partners tend to be somewhat more similar in age. When I asked a young woman why she had married a particular man, she responded, "Because my brother wanted his sister." In almost all cases the woman has absolutely no choice of a mate. When I asked a widow of 33 years of age with three children whether she would remarry, she replied, "I don't know. It depends upon him," pointing to her brother, five years her junior. In one case a female exchange rather than sister exchange took place: a father of three children gave his wife to a younger man, and in return took the young man's sister. Both male parties gained in the transaction. The younger man got a wife, and the already married man got a partner who had recently gone through puberty. Both families continued to live in the same yãno.

The fourth form of acquiring a wife is through raiding. The frequency of raids varies in Yanomami communities. Chagnon (1997) reports a high frequency among the groups he studied, whereas Alcida Rita Ramos (1995) found few raids among the Sanuma. In the history of the Xilixana, while no raids took place in the isolation and precontact period from 1935 to 1958, since that time they have initiated two attacks to distant villages. In 1960 and 1967 they killed a number of men and grabbed three and six women respectively.

But they seldom make raids for the sole purpose of acquiring women. Generally they have some grievance and a resulting desire to kill males. The by-product is the capture of women. There is no bride service or bride payment for captive women. The Xilixana are geographically so removed from other villages that it is impossible for captured women to flee back to their villages of origin.

If a man who claims her as wife does not jealously guard a captured woman, she falls prey to gang rape in the captor's habitat. She has no male to defend her. If her new husband is not jealous of her, and aggressive in his claim as husband, other men will seek opportunities to have intercourse with her. She is not biologically related to any Xilixana and therefore can be subject to a vast range of sexual partners. Feuds of fisticuffs may evolve. Other women will belittle her for her non-Xilixana behavior or her peculiar accent. Her status improves with time, after she integrates and bears children. Some six years after the Xili theli raid, the Xilixana husbands sent bride-price items such as axes and knives to the remaining family members of the attacked group. In another instance brothers of the captive women migrated to the Xilixana community about 15 years after the raid. The social and political dynamics of inter-Yanomami warfare and the capture of women involving Xilixana are not likely to happen again; what is more likely is the possibility of intermarriage among groups on a more friendly basis.

AGE DIFFERENCES BETWEEN PARTNERS

A husband is invariably older than his wife. The most common scenario at the time of a betrothal is that the male is at least 18 and the female is between 4 and 11 years of age. In one case a husband was 59 years older than his second wife, a captive in a raid. In my experience three other husbands exceeded their spouses by about 40 years. By the end of the mid-linking period the average age difference between partners was 12.9 years. In recent marriages the age difference is 7.9 years, a decline in age difference brought on in part because of the greater number of women available for marriage and because betrothal comes at a later age. In 1995, in 13 percent of all unions the husband was at least 18 years older than his wife, which means there is a generation between the partners.

Age differences tend to be greater when the wife has been taken in a raid. In sister-exchange arrangements the partners are more likely to be closer in age. In rare cases the parents of a young male of age 13 or 14 will make betrothal arrangements with the parents of a *wālima*, which can happen in a village when congenial relations exist between two families. Both parents stand to gain in that their children will remain in the same village.

MARRIAGE FORMS AND PARTNER AVAILABILITY

The Xilixana show a wide latitude in marriage forms, which have altered considerably since the time of contact, due to demographic factors (Peters & Hunt

1975). Female infanticide has played a part in the practice, contributing to a sex imbalance.

Of the 15 marriages recorded at the time of contact, 9 were polyandrous, 5 monogamous, and 1 polygynous. The population had a sex ratio of three men for every two women, and two couples practised a form of group marriage. Those two couples lived next to one another in the yắno; each husband had his own hearth where he lived with one of the two women; and each husband was free to have intercourse with the other's wife.

Almost all heterosexual partnerships start as monogamous ones, but in the contact and early linking periods they began to change to other forms. Invariably co-husbands are fraternal and join the household at the invitation of the married brother. The first husband remains the primary husband, and has his hammock hung above that of his wife's. The previously monogamous male gains in that a second husband contributes additional meat to the household. In sympathy for his brother's single status in not having anyone to fill the wife's role of preparing food, he may acquiesce to his brother joining his hearth and wife. In the contact period as many as four secondary husbands lived in one household. In that particular case the woman living with these five husbands also had brief sexual encounters with other men.

The primary husband is the only one who makes bride service and bride payment. Secondary husbands have their hammocks near by, or reside in the same house as their mothers, in which case the necessity for the younger woman's food preparations are not as essential. Secondary husbands only have intercourse with the woman when the primary husband is not around, and they invariably seek opportunities to form betrothals of their own.

Our research back in time showed a sex imbalance through the 25 years prior to contact. There were few marriages of fidelity, and even in those rare cases other men might also, periodically, have sex with the woman involved. Men more commonly initiate non-marital sexual liaisons, but in some cases women encourage this familiarity as well.

Despite the lower ratio of women at the time of contact, we did see a few cases of polygyny, a form of marriage that has persisted to the present day, though it is not common. A husband in a monogamous relationship might acquire a second wife in a raid or marry another woman for whom he must also make payments and provide service. Some parents want their young daughter to have a partner from within the village and therefore give her to an already married man. Tensions between co-wives are common. The problem is not over the husband's sexual preference, but rather "over real and imagined differences" (Murphy 1989: 84).

Polyandry can occur under several conditions. An older or aging husband might be happy to have a younger man provide meat for his expanding family and thus invite in a partner. In other cases a wife might be amorously involved with another male; rather than see her leave for the younger man, the husband invites him to the couple's hearth.

Xilixana sex imbalance was altered considerably during the linking period (Early & Peters 1990), when they acquired women in two raids and established good relations with three different Yanomami populations, from whom they received women in the fertility years. These immigrant women contributed substantially to the Xilixana population, which eventually brought about a change in their particular marriage form from polygyny to monogamy. By the 1980s among the Xilixana monogamy was the norm, with the exception of three cases of polygyny.

As a married man grows older his power within the yãno increases. In a few cases a husband and father with a number of children will abandon his wife as she approaches menopause, and he will acquire a younger female as wife. The older man's status and history of alliances, as well as his possible generosity, place him in a position of advantage in the marriage market. In the contact period, when wives were particularly scarce, young single men did not challenge this practice. In one instance the head shaman discarded (literally translated, "threw away") his aging wife for a younger woman by giving his son in marriage to a middle-aged woman, who in turn gave him her daughter. Three years later he acquired a third young woman as wife. In at least two instances within the last decade, wives in their late thirties made it clear to their husbands that they would not tolerate living in a household with a second wife.

In 1995 seven men over the age of 20—one of them a man of 52—were not aligned with any partner. Add to this list three men who had been previously married and three widowers who could marry—for a total of thirteen eligible men in the current population. Some 20 per cent of all wives have in-migrated. The total of 74 married women with children includes 18 widows, some of whom could remarry if there were to be a man interested and in the correct classification. Six women were separated with children. Eliminating men and women who are more aged, there was a one to three ratio of available men to women. Almost all of these women would have been married if they had lived in the population 30 to 60 years earlier. In recent decades, then, a radical change in marriage forms and patterns had occurred.

Marriage and partnership relationships as well as extramarital relations have an impact on the rights and obligations of fathers and children. In a 1973 survey of 100 children, 69 recognized more than one male as biological (and social) fathers. Generally the primary husband functions as the one to give the daughter as wife to a male, although brothers have also served this function.

MARRIAGE FIDELITY AND SEXUAL PRACTICE

In this society in which marriage fidelity is rare, men are aggressive in their sexual pursuits, and women seldom forbid men in their sexual advances. In some cases, women encourage the encounter. In other cases they acquiesce in fear. The yãimo particularly is a fertile social climate for greater sexual license, a time when men and women are quite free in their sexual behavior. Arguments and feuds are likely to emerge from many of these sexual diversions. A woman may be rewarded for sexual relations with a gift of meat.

A married couple with an infant of less than one year will abstain from intercourse to ensure that conception does not take place too soon, in an effort to make sure that their baby has adequate nourishment from the mother's breast. When the infant begins to walk, or the eye teeth appear, they again resume having intercourse, initially intermittently. During the period of abstention time with his wife the man is likely to have intercourse with other women, with his wife knowing full well of his behavior. Another contributing factor to this liberal sexual practice is that a husband's brothers are very likely to have sex with his wife. When he discovers this happening a husband may retaliate with fisticuffs, and then again he may do nothing at all. Husbands sometimes punish their wives for infidelity by beating them.

The community knows about, or at least hears rumors about, most of the extramarital sex that happens. In a few cases, though, sexual liaisons are kept secret. In my 1995 field trip I learned of one woman who had kept her relations with a specific man and his siring of her child secret for about 15 years. When a husband perceives that his wife's conception took place with another man, he might insist on an abortion or infanticide. If he acquiesces to the pregnancy, the responsible biological father is culturally accountable for providing meat for the resulting child from time to time, even if he is not husband to the mother or if the woman is not living in the same village. In the event that the child becomes ill, the birth father will spend time visiting his offspring, and if it is a daughter he will have to be consulted about her betrothal. During the child's more mature years he will visit him or her and possibly give counsel.

Since the linking period, men have frequented the brothels in Boa Vista. Some return to the mission post with venereal diseases, and most eventually ask for treatment, in which case the missionaries insist that their wives be treated as well. Wives are miffed at their husbands' behavior, but life goes on.

"MARRIAGE"—TAKING A WIFE

Just a little over a year after puberty the couple will begin to cohabit. Except for captive women, the rule of matrilocality is observed, although it becomes less binding as the years of marriage go by. The rule is binding for Xilixana men who follow the traditional rule of bride service and bride payment for women in non-Xilixana villages. Men spend time in service at the bride-to-be's village, residing there for about two years after marriage and before returning to the Mucajai region. In the succeeding years the family will make periodic visits to hunt and work in the field of their *xowaye*. It is rare that a male permanently relocates in a non-Xilixana village for the purpose of marriage. Most likely the Mucajai people's access to Western trade goods during the first 25 years after contact placed them in a position of prestige.

At the time cohabitation is initiated, there is no fanfare or celebration. The move to cohabitation usually begins when the prospective wife's family arranges a hunting trip into the forest with several other families, including the prospective husband and his family, over a period of 10 to 20 days. While the husband-to-be is hunting, the mother or sister of the betrothed wife will untie his hammock and place it above the hammock of the bride-to-be. When the men return home late one afternoon the prospective bridegroom will make as if to search for his hammock, and eventually find it in its new place above the hammock of his bride-to-be, next to her family's hammocks. Nothing is said. There is no ceremony. The inevitable has happened: the young man and woman are now married.

Coitus may not take place until the second week of marriage, especially for a girl who has not been sexually initiated. The young bride is afraid, and her mother forcefully tells her to submit to her husband's sexual wishes. The transition to the wife role is somewhat ameliorated by the traditional practice of matrilocality, because the young woman is remaining in a familiar social and physical environment.

The woman then provides the service of keeping a fire going through the night, to keep her husband warm. During these initial months they may be seen walking the trail, fishing, or visiting the mission post together. The young wife sometimes accompanies her husband on short fishing trips or visits his family of orientation. In the early years a husband might even assist his new wife by carrying water and wood, especially if the woman is ill or has recently delivered a baby. In the evening and early morning some marriage partners quietly exchange gossip and conversation they have heard from others. During the first two years of marriage the couple may occasionally be seen in the hammock with one another. Apart from this there are few open signs of affection, although since the mid-1980s couples have shown more public evidence of endearment. During this time the male often intensifies his bond with his wife's brothers.

The affectionate bond generally wanes after the birth of a child or two. When intraspouse disputes arise, the husband may beat his wife with his fist or a stick, attacking his wife's face, arms, legs, or back. In one instance a middle-aged Palimi theli husband jabbed his wife in the thigh and legs with his bow, and she eventually died from the wounds. A husband becomes angry and beats his spouse when he feels his wife has treated a child unjustly, when she has not prepared food at the time he wants it, or if he sees his wife as lazy or promiscuous. No brother or sister will come to her defense. But a woman sometimes retaliates by refraining from cooking his food or refusing sexual contact. Only rarely will she pull his hair, scratch him, or beat him with fist or stick. They may exchange harsh words. Either of them might sulk.

Feuds

Most Yanomami feuds arise over women: the resistance of a family to betroth their daughter, a male's clandestine relationship with a married woman, a woman's reluctance to accommodate a man's sexual desire, or perceived incest. The matter of incest is not taken lightly. In a population in which children might have several fathers, sometimes from different patrilineal lines, the question of real fatherhood can become flexible, especially when it involves a mate (Chagnon 1997; Saffirio 1985). At the time of contact, in the Xilixana's small population seven married brothers had sired about half the children under 18 years of age. This meant that biological *wãlima* partners were limited, and the few available women were a prized commodity.

Feuds over sexual partners are very common. Feuds also erupt between brothers, who can be taking part in a legitimate sexual relationship with the same women. In this sense, a brother may be one's worst enemy. In some cases husbands tolerate periodic sexual liaisons of their wives with brothers or other men. But if the husband is jealous and willing to fight for exclusivity, the fisticuffs will emerge. The situation is sometimes fuelled by a wife's compliance with the sexual advances of other men. Towards the end of the contact period one Xilixana, OO, arranged a marriage with PP of the Palimi theli. PP soon became attracted to, and sought the companionship of, OO's younger brother, MM. The brothers came to blows several times, and finally OO was going to end the matter by killing MM with his shotgun. Kin members prevented this from happening. Eventually OO found another wife among the Palimi theli, and the brothers lived together peacefully in the same yãno.

Conception and Birthing

With conception taking place not with a single act of coitus, but many, it follows that several men may be recognized as biological fathers. (This belief is different from the Sanuma Yanomami, who consider only one male to be responsible for conception [Ramos 1995: 225].) As Murphy (1989: 91) appropriately comments about the Mundurucu, the male's semen is the raw material to make the child, and women serve as mere ovens. The centrality of a male's role in reproduction is evident in the language. According to Ramos (1995: 78) the woman does nothing but carry the vessel for the male's seed, known as *mo up* (penis liquid). A male *tha* (makes) a child. A woman *thla* (delivers) a child. In Ramos's Sanuma study, she also found that the people consider the sex of the child to be determined by the male, depending on whether the *mo up* comes from the right or left testicle. The male partner is never considered responsible for infertility. If a Xilixana woman proves not to be fertile—and being fertile is her primary function in life—she is stigmatized—she is the one who is blamed. To make sure this doesn't happen, for instance, during her pregnancy she refrains from eating taboo foods. The Xilixana believe that the fetus is facilitated in the development process by continued coitus.

A number of beliefs relate directly to intercourse and pregnancy. A male is more apt to get ill during his wife's pregnancy. It is not good for a secondary husband to have intercourse with his wife when the primary husband is ill. A man will not eat a double, or joined, Siamese-twin-like banana because his offspring would stick together. However, women will eat a twin banana. If Xilixana are fond of visitors, they wish to have a child from that group. In the hereafter you remain united to your first partner. You become young in the new world.

The Sanuma shaman, with the help of his *hekula*, provides a sling (for a boy) and a belt (for a girl) to wear during sexual intercourse. A male who is restrained from having sex by the woman or her husband may perform sorcery upon the woman so that she will remain infertile. He may put the magical substance on her abdomen, or secretly place it in her drink. In rare cases, should women wish infertility after several births, they request that the magic concoction be placed in their drink. Shaman are said to have the ability to counter a woman's infertility. Sorcery for the purpose of infertility is considered to be a serious infraction, and inevitably results in fisticuffs.

Births take place in the field or forest near the yãno, with only women in attendance. Men are said to become ill if they are present. The pregnant woman squats on a log, and another woman, usually the mother or a sister, holds her from behind. At birth the infant drops onto banana leaves. The baby is quickly picked up and washed with water before being given to the mother. Possibly the water stimulates the infant to use his lungs. The Xilixana were surprised to see Westerners hold infants upside down immediately after birth, and to see them patting the back of the newborn to induce breathing. Some Xilixana women have since adopted this technique.

Before the time of contact they did not tie and cut the cord, but rather severed it by means of a bamboo stick. The slow process of severance caused coagulation of the blood. Since contact they have used scissors and string. They bury the placenta. It has also become customary for the missionary to give a cloth to the mother in which to wrap the infant.

ABORTION AND INFANTICIDE

It is likely that a young woman will become pregnant by age 14 or 15, but in many cases the first fetus is aborted. Ramos (1995: 226) shows that the Sanuma always consider the first-born to be high risk. A similar fear among the Xilixana may partially explain the high frequency of abortions for the first conception. The Xilixana also believe that if girls become pregnant soon after puberty they will harm the development of all their future fetuses; and this fear, too, leads to the abortion of first fetuses. The Xilixana also have abortions when conception takes place too soon after the birth of a child, and thus the living infant would not have sufficient milk; and when the husband attributes the pregnancy to a male other than himself. By the age of 30 almost all women have had at least one abortion.

The abortion methods used are crude. The woman may lean on an object, like the handle of a vertical standing paddle, and work it around her abdomen, applying pressure. With the pregnant woman lying on her back, another woman might stomp with her feet on her abdomen. The pregnant women might refrain from food for about three days, after which the husband, mother, or a sister heats their hands by the fire, searches for the fetus in the pregnant woman's abdomen, and using their knuckles pinches the fetus to death. The expectant mother will be in pain for about a day, with loss of blood. If the attempt is not successful the first day, her family makes a second effort to abort the baby.

There have been suggestions that female infanticide has been more frequently practised among the Xilixana than other Yanomami. There is no clear predictable pattern for infanticide, except as a result of the preference for male children, perceived physically unhealthy infants, and those seen as being sired by unacceptable males. When group members feel that a particular woman has given birth to too many girls, they apply pressure for the mother to kill it. Young mothers of around age 22 or less cannot, or do not, assert themselves when it comes to the life of their newly born children. In general younger women giving birth acquiesce to the commands of the husband, mother, or other women in their yãno.

Infanticide is practised in most cases by a mother, at the birthing site, applying pressure with a stick placed across the throat of the new-born baby. (Ramos reports that among the Sanuma the newly born are sometimes choked with a cord.) As early as 1959 at Mucajai the missionaries discovered an infant had been thrown into the river, and as late as 1995 a baby was ruthlessly tossed into the woods. In that recent case no male had identified himself as the father of the infant, and the brother of the mother was furious that he would have to provide meat for this additional female member in his household. In one or two instances the father has doggedly refused tribal pressure to kill the infant. At the time when his wife is about to deliver and others voice their opinion about killing the infant should she be female, the father may say, "Keep her alive. Let her live to make cassava bread."

In 1962 on a rainy Sunday morning I was told that a child had been born and left in the woods to die. When I asked about the sex of the child, the response was "*pisiali*," meaning "bitch," or female dog. I walked into the forest, found the child, and carried her back to the father, requesting that he look after her. He and the mother did look after the baby then, and she survived.

The Xilixana also practise infanticide when a child, male or female, is born with a defect. In 1965, when a child was born with a growth (meningitis) between his eyes, the new mother's mother attempted to strangle the infant. She was not successful and decided to call the resident missionary nurse. The infant was kept alive and a few months later flown at missionary expense to Rio de Janeiro for an operation. The mother cried when the child was placed on the plane. She had bonded with the child through those first months of his life. Because of that trip away from home, her child was probably the first Yanomami ever to be nursed from a bottle.

In another case, in 1995, the nursing staff in Boa Vista gave a woman malaria medication, not knowing that she was pregnant. The medication can cause damage to a fetus, and the women was later flown to the maternity ward in Boa Vista to have the baby, which was born with two visible grotesque obstructions on his face. The parents abandoned the child, leaving him for the nuns in the Boa Vista maternity ward.

When the Xilixana give birth to twins, they keep alive the male or the stronger of the two infants. They believe that mothers do not have sufficient milk to nurse two infants. In the Brazilian period, under the influence of missionaries, four sets of twins were born and kept alive. In one case the mother nursed and cared for both infants. In the other cases other women took the responsibility to care and rear the child. The decision was not made until after consultation with her husband.

Bride Service and Bride Payment

The indebtedness a man has to his wife's family remains for as long as his wife has living parents or brothers. The husband's greatest and most frequent contribution to his new family will be the game he shoots. Those obligations and expectations have not altered since the contact period, although the type of artifacts given in payment have changed.

Throughout the precontact period native artifacts were the normal items of bride payment: arrows, arrow tips, a paddle. In the contact period, payment included knives, cutlasses, axes, matches, salt, a ball of cotton, and eventually clothing. In the late 1960s the men gave ammunition, and in some cases shotguns, as payment. In the late linking and awareness periods, clothing was a frequent item of payment. Xilixana men do not consider the giving of a valuable item as improper or extravagant.

Payment begins at the time of betrothal, regardless of the age of the female. A mother-in-law to be indicates her consent to the betrothal by picking up game that the young man drops at her hearth. They exchange no words at this point. The husband-to-be will intermittently provide game until the time the girl approaches her puberty, at which point his payment and now service in the form of house, canoe, and field construction will become more frequent. After contact payment came to include metal tools as well as items of clothing. The new wife's brothers may also request bride payment.

Claude Levi-Strauss (1969: 131) addresses the special significance in the exchange that takes place between the groom and the parents of his bride: "Cross-cousin marriage simply express the fact that marriage must always be a giving and a receiving.... One can receive only from him who is obliged to give, and that the giving must be to him who has a right to receive.... The mutual gift between debtors leads to privilege, whereas the mutual gift between creditors leads inevitably to extinction."

With cohabitation the new wife now prepares her husband's meat, with some of it inevitably shared with the woman's family. At times the husband will feel obligated to accompany his father-in-law or brothers-in-law on a hunt, and he will similarly become engaged in other activities carried on by his wife's family: felling and burning trees for a field, house or canoe construction, the gathering of honey or fruit from the forest. The family members will never directly tell him to do a task, but the expectation is evident. His father-in-law may inform his daughter that he needs a paddle or liana from the forest. She in turn will tell her husband. If he does not reasonably fulfill the expectations he will find himself in difficulty. Husbands are obligated to follow the best interests of the family of his in-laws—a fashioning of loyalty that can involve an array of concerns; the husband's obligations are numerous.

In the event of a local feud resulting in fisticuffs, the son-in-law will always join the side of his wife's family. He never evaluates the right or wrong of the contentious issue. Similarly, should his wife's family raid another village, the son-in-law will join forces. Marriage with women from non-Xilixana villages means that some men take on obligations to families in distant villages. Several Xilixana with Malaxi theli and Palimi theli wives have joined those other groups to raid enemy villages far from the locale of the Mucajai mission.

In one case a man asked for and received a gun from his sister's husband after about eight years of marriage. The payment was deemed appropriate because his sister had borne the husband three male offspring. Ramos (1995: 79) elaborates further on in-law responsibilities among the Sanuma. Men are obligated to live in the environs of their wife's family until the parents die, which involves considerable adaptation. According to Ramos, the new husband's move into the sphere of his wife's family is stressful, with some tasks particularly onerous (189). When he leaves his own village for his wife's, considerable adaptation is necessary. Among other things, to be able to hunt effectively he must become familiar with a new forest environment. He is not likely to have his own kin for support in the new yãno setting. Only after the death of both in-laws is the husband relinquished from obligations to them.

A number of men terminate the betrothal within the first years of cohabitation after finding the duties too severe or their betrothed partner uncooperative or resisting sex. In other cases a mother of a bridegroom senses the absence of her son and his game so much that she begs him to return. In such an event the bridegroom can demand the return of any items he has given in payment. Ramos indicates that because of the complexities and weighty obligations in bride payment and bride service, the Sanuma prefer young women who are orphans, or widowed women whose parents have died, because those cases involve no payment responsibility. But among the Xilixana widowed women without parents are the property of living brothers, who have authority over their sisters.

From the time of betrothal and all through the marriage, the husband practises mother-in-law avoidance. Although it is inevitable that they make some limited contact in the yãno and environs, the two will not speak to one another, or make eye contact. If they happen to encounter one another on a trail, the mother-in-law will step aside to allow the man to pass. These strict rules of mother-in-law avoidance have diminished in the linking period.

Marriage Fragility and Termination

Most marriages in the Xilixana society are fragile connections, liable to termination at any time. But certain periods in the life cycle are more susceptible than others to marriage disintegration.

Young woman in the contact period in "native" dress.

The first particularly fragile period is the time between the establishment of a betrothal and the initiation of payment and before cohabitation has begun. If the betrothal has been made while the girl is very young, the male might have lost interest; or her parents may feel the man is not making adequate payment. (Sometimes parents at this stage of their daughter's involvement with a man use the excuse of inadequate payment as an alibi, preferring to give their daughter to someone else.) Even if a betrothal is terminated before the couple cohabit, or before the female reaches puberty, it is viewed as a "divorce," as a union separation, because the couple have in effect been socially recognized as a unit. Each are publicly seen as "his woman" or "her man." The betrothal carries political and economic consequences between the "future" groom and her family. The severity of the act of divorce varies with the age of the female as well as the years the groom has provided service and payment.

A marriage can also terminate around the time when cohabitation begins, or a year or two after the girl's puberty. In this case the young girl is aggressive and refuses her betrothed male partner. Despite enduring continual beatings from her family, who feel an obligation to keep their part of the marriage arrangement, she resists. In a few cases the young postpubescent woman is prepared to bear the beating from her kin because she is amorously attracted to another man.

In the event a groom leaves his village and family of orientation for that of his betroth's village, the groom's family may regret the loss. They feel bereft of his assistance, particularly his hunting. In one case the young bride's family became very attached to the young groom and enjoyed his presence, but the groom's family of origin placed pressure upon him to return. They arranged a partner for him in the yãno of his family of origin, and he returned.

In one case a young girl, BB, was betrothed in early childhood. About the time of her menarche, her middle-aged groom-to-be suddenly died. This man was already a husband to a woman past her menopause. The girl's parents had already promised BB's younger sister to XX, a male of at least 25 years of age from another village. But since XX would have to wait another four years until the younger sister's puberty, he accepted the offer to take BB. After puberty and cohabitation, BB rebelled against this arrangement, saying she was not betrothed to XX but to the man who was deceased. Although her hammock hung below XX's, according to the custom for married couples, she refused to engage in sex, even though her brothers brutally beat her for not complying to her parents' betrothal arrangements.

About this time she and another younger man, DD, became mutually attracted to one another, but for the sake of the marriage agreement with XX, her parents did not endorse that union. Finally, XX became tired of the wrangling with his belligerent partner and returned to his mother's village. At this point the betrothal arrangements became complex. The pubescent girl's family refused to give her to DD, the younger lover. Months later the parents, in a change of heart, consented to give BB to DD. By then, however, DD had seen the young woman involved with several other men and had lost interest. About a year later she eloped with a man from another village—a serious violation in Yanomami culture. The daughter remained estranged from her family for several years.

Tensions can also arise after a couple have lived amicably together for a number of years. The husband may find the expectations and demands of his wife's family overbearing and feel he cannot meet their wishes. In frustration, he leaves. In one instance the groom felt his father-in-law was dictating how he should treat his daughter. The groom told this man to stop his bossiness or else he would have to return all the bride payment. With that the older man ceased intruding into the affairs of the marriage.

Young marriages also terminate if the two members suffer from a lack of satisfaction with one another. Such severance has been common in the Brazilian period, compared to the contact period when women were few in number. Another contributing factor for marriage termination in the awareness period is the later age of betrothal for women, which means that bride service and bride payment have not been made for as lengthy a period of time. The socialization, especially the tradition of a young girl being seen as belonging to a specific male since childhood, is not as concrete. The investment is less. In the 1990s young women also seem to have become more assertive. Young husbands might make travelling escapades to other Yanomami or Brazilian communities, and young wedded women do not approve of the resulting long absences.

The bride's parents sense the responsibility of their daughter's fidelity to the bride-paying husband for as long as three years into the new marriage. Similarly, parents at times invoke their young unmarried sons (until about 20 years of age) not to interfere in a brother's existing betrothal arrangements.

I once witnessed another form of deviance in the marriage pattern. In this case the biological parents of AS (a male of 24) were deceased, but his father's brothers, BB and BA, were classificatory fathers. AS had lived with Brazilians for two years, then returned home. AS was attracted to SI, who lived in a nearby village and had been married for about a year to PE, a gentle and meek young man, not characteristically fierce like others in his age cohort. From time to time AS had coitus with SI, who was subsequently scolded and beaten by her brothers and mother. The affair did not end, and one day in mid-January 1980 AS and SI ran off together, or eloped, a serious offense, viewed by SI's kin as wife-stealing.

The Xilixana thought the couple had fled to the Brazilians downstream. SI's family searched trails and river banks for the missing couple. Both families were angry and made loud threats about retaliatory measures. SI's family said they wanted to bash AS, and they condemned AS's fathers, BB and BA, for not warning or punishing AS for his deviance. Then two days later five men and as many women from SI's household travelled the three kilometers to AS's original household, going there to perform a ritual to redress the deviant behavior. In retaliation for AS's behavior, SI's family went to take BA's 13-year-old daughter XO as wife for one of SI's married brothers. Finding AS and SI there, the five men and women vigorously pulled the deviant young girl by the arms, legs, and head from side to side in the clearing adjacent to the house. After almost two hours of such pulling, the girl's skin was raw and her body limp with pain. One man shouted, "It is enough," and they stopped. BB sharply reprimanded AS, who returned home with the others from his village after the pulling ritual. The anger of AS somewhat abated. Some even laughed over the whole proceedings. Justice had been done.

Some marriages terminate while both partners are in their adult years, and often little drama occurs in those severances. For instance, a widower of about 45 years of age joined a single woman of about 30. He reported that she complained a lot, and the union fizzled after about three months. Another woman reportedly became involved with other men at a dance festivity, so her betrothed partner left. In yet another case one man, LL, appeared to be a happily married husband of three children, at least until he made an exchange of his wife for the unmarried sister of another man. There was no tension, no friction. Both couples continued to live in the same yãno.

Married couples' relationships prove to be explosive from time to time. She may not have his food prepared at the moment he wants it, not comply to his sexual desire, or be promiscuous. He may consider her care of their young children to be inadequate. She may react to his intolerance. Hair-pulling, scratching, and fisticuffs result in bruises, cuts, and swollen eyes. Until the end of the contact period men would beat their wives on the back with firebrands pulled from the hearth. A wife might respond by not cooking her husband's meals or resisting his sexual advances. If she is childless she might flee to her family of orientation. Since she is the property of the husband, her kin will seldom come to her aid in the event of some conflict. Rarely will a member from her family of orientation come to her defense. Verbal communication between the two may cease for several days or weeks. In the precontact period one man performed deathly sorcery upon his wife and another woman who did not comply to his sexual wishes. In the 1960s a Malaxi theli male killed his wife through sorcery. In the 1980s a drunk Palimi theli husband killed his wife with a file. In the 1990s a Xilixana husband living among the Palimi theli missed bashing his wife with a stick but fatally hit his infant son, who was being held by his wife.

As a woman approaches her menopause, her husband may start looking for a second, younger wife. When I arrived on two field trips in the awareness period, I was asked whether I had remarried. The Xilixana thought it strange and humorous that I was still married to the same woman they knew from the contact period 32 years before, and who had long since stopped childbearing. In the event that a man marries a second, younger woman, his first wife will stop cooking for him and move to one of her children's households. After menopause she has no difficulty in relinquishing any rights to the husband, even though he may be living in the same yãno.

Gender Roles and the Status of Women

Within the patriarchal structures of Yanomami life, all of the functions normally considered to be of any importance fall the lot of males, with the obvious exceptions of human reproduction and child care. The Yanomami view semen as the crucial element in reproduction, but they also, somewhat contradictorily, see the failure to conceive as the woman's fault. A woman's activity is always under the authority of a male. He expects her to have water in the house, food ready for his appetite, sex at his will, and contented children.

But people in any society do cross gender lines in one way or another, and such exceptions also occur among the Yanomami. When men hunt overnight they fetch the water, cook meals, and keep the fires going through the night. When a spouse is ill, or even if she has gone to the field for manioc, a man may find himself tending to the needs of the younger children. Once in a while men carry firewood from the forest or field to the house. A single or aged man may tend his own fire in the yãno. In preparation for a yãimo men will collectively dig and carry manioc to the yãno, then assist in grating and squeezing the root to prepare cassava bread. Sometimes a father will carry a child on his back. In recent years, when firewood has to be brought in from further distances, men will assist or even gather, transport, and chop up the wood themselves.

In some instances women participate in conventional male role behavior. Though it is usually the men who fish, in more recent years young women particularly can be seen fishing with hook and line. If a stray armadillo crosses their path on the way to the field, they will pursue and beat the creature to death. On a few occasions a small herd of peccary have roamed near their dwelling during the day and, with the men absent, the women have chased the pigs and killed several with machetes or clubs.

At contact in 1958, only women carried water from the stream, or gathered firewood for the hearth. Men who did this chore were ridiculed. Someone would yell, "You're a woman!" In the 1960s men frequently chopped firewood and carried water for the resident missionaries. At times husband and wife gather wood together for their hearth. During the contact years I once offered a woman the chance to shoot into the air with my shotgun. Reluctantly she did, amidst giggles and laughter from the other women. Women never shoot with the bow and arrow. They are considered "*utmuti*" (ignorant) in this matter. On another occasion, during a month-long trip to several other villages, I left my beard to grow. An hour before returning home I stopped at the river's edge and cut my beard. "Why?" they asked. "For the sake of my wife," I responded. "Do you listen to your wife?" they retorted amidst much laughter.

The intimate contact with resident missionaries and periodic contact with Brazilians have made some gender role change inevitable. They have seen Western men playing what seems to be a less dominant role in relations with women. Among middle-class Westerners husband-wife relations are more complementary, if not always perfectly so. Western husbands do seek to support their wives in at least some of their interests and wishes.

In some cases Xilixana have reversed the gender model exemplified by Westerners. For instance, the missionary women sew, but two Xilixana men are now capable of using the sewing machine. Though missionary men and women both dispense medicine, only Yanomami men have taken the initiative to do so, possibly because the activity is more akin to the role of the male Yanomami shaman. In at least one area Xilixana women have resisted bi-gender norms. They have seen Western women, both in Boa Vista and in the case of missionaries at Mucajai, wearing pants or culottes. In many ways pants would be more practical for Yanomami women, but they have continued to wear skirts and dresses. Undoubtedly the choice of clothing is significant to a woman's identity.

Women are servants to men. Adult women serve their husbands and their children, especially their sons. Girls obey their fathers, mothers, and brothers. If a child defecates, the men will turn their heads and voice their disgust. When a man discovers feces in the dwelling he will tell a woman to clean it up, or in disgust will simply say "shit, shit." Women clean up the feces whether human, fowl, or animal. One of them takes a stick and leaf, scrapes it up, walks to the door, and flings it outside. When an infant being held by a woman defecates, she immediately holds it away from her body and, again, cleans up the mess with stick and leaf. Young children urinate wherever they wish. When a child pees in the yãno the urine is simply absorbed into the dirt floor.

If a baby is colicky and persists in crying in the quiet of the night, somewhere from within the dwelling a man is sure to call out, "Give it food," "Take it to grandmother," or "Give it the breast."

As in Western society, the reproduction activity of women holds little status or reward. With pregnancy a woman's fetus may be aborted, due to pressure from her husband or other women. At birth the female infant may be killed because of her sex, and if kept alive is referred to as a bitch. In childhood she is to replicate what Yanomami women do. She will soon participate in household chores such as baby-sitting, preparing food for the family, and accompanying her mother to the field to harvest and cargo field products to the yãno. All this time males in the same age group are gleefully doing whatever they want to do. As we've seen, a girl or woman has no say over whom she will marry. Her betrothal will be made on the basis of economic and social gain for the males of her family of origin. If she has been taken in a raid, she is likely to be gang-raped. If she is an immigrant with no relatives, she has no one to defend her, no family to flee to. A wife's subservience to her family of orientation continues throughout her adult life if her husband die. Bonds that she forms with other females, even sisters, are tentative (Shapiro 1980: 76). At the same time, men are free to form strong bonds, especially with a brother of his wife.

A wife is beaten by her husband for sexual deviance. She is to blame if she does not bear children and strongly criticized if she bears only females. Her primary life function terminates with the raising of her last infant. Her husband does not find it necessary to provide meat or protect her after she ceases bearing children. At death her body is placed in a shallow grave.

Physically she is weaker than men, which becomes a highly significant trait in a society in which might is right. She is not warrior, hunter, or shaman, all of which are prestigious. She is considered incapable of surviving alone in the forest. She does not comprehend the full scope of the spirit world. She must turn to a male for shamanic assistance. Should a male do some service generally done by women, like carrying water, he is mocked with *Thuwe thai wa pè kii* ("You are a woman.")

THE LIMITED POWER OF WOMEN

Like anywhere in the world, though, despite their subjugated status women do have limited power, the exercise of which is frequently dependent upon structural, religious, economic, and historical factors. It may appear that Xilixana women are chattel, that they must unmitigatedly yield to patriarchal demands and whims, but they do have ways of achieving influence, even though this influence is muffled and restrained compared to that of the men.

For the years just before and soon after her puberty, a girl takes a central position in the fashioning of Yanomami relationships, though she has little power over the direction of those relations. She may resist her parents' intentions of an arranged marriage. She may withhold sex from her husband, and not prepare food for him—though that behavior tends to be greeted with strong blows.

Her primary influence in the village comes because of her reproduction, and especially when she is in her thirties and early forties, by which time her status has become enhanced if she has raised several sons. The rule of matrilocality means that a married daughter remains in her mother's household for a couple of years at least after marriage, during which time the hunting of the daughter's husband augments the family's meat supply. Women also gain village influence through the weapon of their tongues. Their gossip about illicit incest, sexual affairs, cowardice, stealth, or a hunter's poor marksmanship can ignite fisticuff duels between men. Several women in a persistent vocal dispute have caused villages to break up both temporarily and permanently. A woman can influence young pregnant women to abort or practise infanticide.

Six
Socialization and Life Stages

Anthropologists and other social scientists have used "life stages" theory, or the development approach to the study of the family, to explain the socialization processes and growth and learning patterns of people in society. Indeed, the development approach to the study of the family is embedded within family research (Duvall 1971; Aldous 1978). But applying this model to a preliterate people such as the Yanomami—although I will do so at least partially— requires a degree of flexibility. Not surprisingly, the model normally used to explain life patterns in Western societies has its limitations when transported south to explain a life based on survival in the Amazon rainforest.

The patterns of Yanomami life stand in marked contrast to those of Western life. In a Western society the institutionalized schooling system, beginning at about age five and continuing through to age eighteen, tends to be a focal point in the life stages of its members, followed, perhaps, by markers such as marriage, a career orientation, middle age, and the "golden years." The Yanomami life stages do not have the Western markings of a child's years in school, or the legal categories of marriage and divorce. Yanomami life is not centered solely upon a nuclear family. The Yanomami life cycle more closely follows the cycle of nature: prepuberty, fertility, and postfertility.

This distinct life cycle includes a marked gender difference, especially, for a girl, between the age of nine and the time when parenting begins, then again after the woman's menarche. While the life stages of a girl or woman focus to a great degree upon her potential or actual role of childbearing, the life stages of a boy or man center upon his fathering role, whether or not this takes place in a monogamous, serial monogamous, or polygynous relationship.

The particular foci in the various stages through the life cycle of the Yanomami tend to integrate into the cultural concerns revolving around the acquisition of a woman for wife and procreator, food gathering and food preparation, the provision of meat, as well as defensive and offensive attacks upon neighboring Yanomami tribes. Male children are taught to be aggressive and fearless almost from infancy. For most boys hunting skills are acquired early on in life. Female children spend a good deal of their time with their mother and female siblings and soon understand that they are to facilitate and accommodate the whims and wishes of the male members of the community. Their lives become centered primarily on preparing a man's food, fulfilling his sexual needs, and producing offspring. Girls and women carry almost all of the childrearing responsibility.

Taking up this development approach, however loosely, we can discern eight stages in the Yanomami life cycle. (See Figure 6.1.)

STAGE	APPROX. AGE	FAMILY SITUATION		APPROX. AGE
I	0–3	total dependency		0–3
II	4–8	early childhood		4–8
		MALE	FEMALE	
III	9–14	later childhood	later childhood	9–12
IV	15–26	premarriage	puberty and marriage	13–17
V	27–42	first family of production	child bearing and child-rearing	18–44
VI	43–65	second family of procreation	post child-rearing	45–65
VII	66+	appendage	appendage	66+

FIGURE 6.1 STAGES IN THE LIFE CYCLE OF THE YANOMAMI

Stage I: Total Dependency

The first stage, of total dependency, lasts through the third year of life. In the first week after birth a mother exclusively holds and cares for an infant. Although it is socially unacceptable for men to be present at the birth of the child, during the first week of the child's life the baby is considered too frag-

Bathing an infant in the river. Mother has monkey on her head.

ile for the rough, clumsy hands of the father. Besides, he abhors the sight and smell of the infant's excrement. During the first six months a father only rarely fondles and cuddles the child. For the first two years of life an infant is most often with females: mother, sisters, grandmothers, or with her mother's sisters. In moments of anxiety or hunger the mother's breast is always readily available, even if only for a moment or two.

Baby in Yanomami crafted Jolly Jumper

During the first six months the mother will never be found too far away from the child. A child accompanies his/her mother to the field, to the stream when the mother fetches water, on community fish-poisoning trips, or on visits to a nearby village. The mother may be accompanied on these trips by her husband, but she is the one who carries the child, resting him/her on her hip or easing the child's weight in a cloth or bark sling. When the mother carries a cargo on her back, in a woven basket secured by a bark sling over her forehead, she places the child on top of the basket's contents. All the while the husband may walk empty-handed ahead of her along the forest trail.

Infants sleep in hammocks with their mothers for the first two years. When the baby defecates or urinates while in the mother's care or in the hammock, the mother abruptly holds it off to one side to complete this biological function. She cleans the feces and urine from her body or dress, first using a stick and leaf, then with water. She removes any feces on the ground with a stick or leaf. Men never clean up feces—they respond with animated disgust at the offensive smell and sight.

All the other members in the communal house can't help but be aware of the behavior, habits, moods, and general activity of a child—whether the child is teething, has diarrhea, is disobedient, or has temper tantrums. Other household members strongly reprimand the mother of a child that cries incessantly. One night during one of my many sojourns in the communal house, a mother was not able to quell the whines of a child. From time to time one of several men would yell out, "He wants to defecate," "He's got a stomach ache," "He's hungry, give him the breast," or "Give him to his grandmother."

Nursing terminates by the time a child is three, or when the woman gets pregnant again. Both siblings and adults chide children of about four years of age who suckle. Milk is considered infant drink. I, too, was chided because I drank powdered milk. If a mother conceives when she already has a child less than a year old, she will abort the unborn child "for the sake of the living infant."

When the child is about six months old the mother will give him or her other food, perhaps a piece of ripe banana, some papaya, honey, or broth.

Later she feeds the infant meat, after masticating it herself. At about one year of age the child may gnaw on a bone. From six months a father may occasionally begin to hold the child in the hammock, or carry the child in and about the house. It is common to see fathers spending time with one or more of their young children outside the communal house at dusk, when hunting or the day's work is complete. Mothers might then be cooking food or gathering wood to be burned during the cool night. A few mothers sit with their husbands conversing while spinning cotton or stringing beads.

After the infant's first 12 months, when a mother attends to the fire, the meat in the pot, or the grating of cassava, she either plants the infant on the dirt floor, leaves it in the hammock for a nap, or has it attended to by a grandmother or older sister. In more recent years I have seen the Xilixana tie a horizontal stick to vertical posts, 30 centimeters off the ground, using this to help a child stand or otherwise play on its legs. One woman made her young child a playpen, elevated a meter off the ground, by tying closely together a number of horizontal poles of about three centimeters thick. In my field trip of 1995 I saw a baby sitting in a Yanomami-made version of a Jolly Jumper. They had made the seat of cloth, attaching cords extended up to a green but sturdy sapling that provided flexibility and spring as the child of about eight months "bounced" up and down on the dirt floor of the yâno.

After two years of age a mother increasingly leaves a child in the care of others, most likely an older sister, the mother's sister, the grandmother, or even occasionally the father. Should the child ever stumble, be stung by a wasp, be cut or bruised, or fall into the water while in the care of a sibling, the guardian child is strongly reprimanded for carelessness.

The first stage in a Yanomami's life is one of general permissiveness. Children are seldom disciplined, although exceptional moments occur when the mother or caring sibling goes into a fit of rage after being inconvenienced in some way by the young child. The caregiver might hit the child with a stick or brashly shove her or him away.

The Xilixana consider children in this stage as being too young to differentiate between right and wrong. Village members find it amusing when, for instance, a child drags a dead squirrel around the house by the tail, hits a rooster with a stick, pees into the fire, slaps his or her mother, chides the aged, or beats another playmate. On numerous occasions during the contact period irate Xilixana parents have reprimanded the missionaries for disciplining their own children with a spanking. If a child between one and a half to three years of age becomes angry or obstinate, even attacking the mother, whether playfully or not, the mother might respond by laughing at the child's deviance, or she might brutally shove the child to the ground. She might flee in laughter from the child, who clumsily attacks her, stick in hand. A parent who becomes annoyed at a child's behavior will tend to act impulsively, slapping or throwing an object like a piece of dirt at the child.

Revenge, bravery, and the display of physical might are taught early in life, as personality traits considered basic to cultural and physical survival. For instance, in their quarrels with playmates children learn that they must not run in fear to their mothers. A victim of a playmate's cuff is given a stick to retaliate and is prodded to return the blow. In such a case the playmate's parents do not defend the aggressor, but allow him to be beaten, thus teaching the child to bear the physical blows of another individual. I saw one woman pounding her fist firmly upon the chest and back of her eight-month-old grandson. She enjoyed the vigorous, playful "duel." He was being socialized to be tough. The physical responses will serve the male well in his future role as hunter, wife-protector, feud-fighter, and warrior. At least until the middle of the linking period, it was important that villages have sufficient warriors to resist attacks.

Similarly, girls are socialized to react in a retaliatory fashion. Unlike a man in adult life, a woman is not as likely to express requital in physical violence, but rather by making forceful verbal insults against her opponent, both in and out of his/her presence.

In this first stage of total dependency, then, for reasons of physical survival the child absorbs much of the mother's energy and time. The growing child begins to recognize through covert socialization that kin associations are meaningful, and that older kin have an increased degree of prestige and power.

Covertly the female child may realize that she is subservient to any male, particularly her father and brothers. While the female child in her second and third year finds her closest affinity with her mother, sisters, and possibly other females her age, the male child at three not only associates closely with his mother, but also increasingly with his brothers, his father, and other male youngsters. The people around him encourage any possible demonstration of aggressiveness or chauvinism.

Stage II: Early Childhood

The second stage, early childhood, covers the years between four and eight. Socialization for the child's future role within the structure of the society becomes more pronounced in this stage. The distinction between male and female roles becomes increasingly apparent.

A boy of four or five years is given a bow about 50 centimeters long and sliver-thin shafts as arrows, which he uses to shoot cockroaches, insects, and frogs. With vigilance he steps in and around the dwelling and through the fields with his playmates, in pursuit of prey. At age six or seven he is fishing by hook for small fish in a nearby stream or in the Mucajai River. By age eight he is given a larger and stronger set of weapons and is soon shooting chameleons or small birds. By nine he is accompanying his older brother(s) or father on an occasional hunting trip. He learns to differentiate the myriad sounds in the forest and recognizes the markings and habits of small animals: the coati, rabbit, armadillo, turtle, small parrot, grouse, and trumpeter. With dexterity he learns to paddle the canoe with and against the current as well as to adeptly maneuver it through and around the many rapids of the river.

A young boy has considerable freedom in these years. He has little responsibility to his parents or home. When he is not "hunting," he plays with his playmates in the streams, swimming, jumping, laughing—acting the part of a tapir or catfish. Or he may be among the trees near the house, constructing a miniature forest shelter. He will be climbing trees and learning the numerous uses of liana. From time to time he will return to the house to snatch some food or drink, irritate or tease a sister, or younger sibling, then continue with his carefree life outside the house. Occasionally he will quarrel with an older sibling, exchanging a few blows, then sulk or gloat, depending on whether he is victim or victor.

His mother is not likely to ask him to do any task, and his father or brothers will command assistance only on rare occasions. When he is as young as age four his father will encourage him to display an active sense of retaliation and toughness. The boy is encouraged to clench his fists and beat upon the chests of his father and older brothers. This is socialization for the fisticuff duels that are so central to the Yanomami justice system.

The young boy and his peers will accompany family groups trekking into the woods to poison fish or gather wild fruit or honey. In the evening the young male hears an adult man telling accounts of capturing a tapir, peccary, or possibly a jaguar or ocelot. Such accounts serve to underscore his future role as hunter and provider. In the evening young boys will sometimes hear the men around them talking about a raid upon a neighboring village, emphasizing their own bravery in contrast to the fright of the enemy men and women. They might hear other more subdued stories that reveal a man's prowess in some sexual exploit. These accounts of valiant and daring acts serve to reinforce the boy's aim to be courageous, revengeful, and aggressive as a young but maturing Yanomami male.

A young girl's activities are more restricted. She is more confined to the environs of the yãno, and when she does make trips to the field or the stream it is always in the company of older females. At age four and five she accompanies her mother to the stream and plays in the water with other boys and girls, but by six and seven she will bathe only in female company. Compared to the extended, leisurely, and more boisterous play of the boys in the water, her playing and bathing are much more subdued. She will care for a younger sibling while her mother digs out the cultivated manioc root in the field. By age seven and eight a young girl will tend the fire and help cook meat in the pot on the family hearth. She prepares a banana drink, which she serves to her father and brothers.

She learns specific tasks to prepare her for a significant role in the Yanomami society as wife and mother. At an early age she becomes involved in child care, which will become a major activity in her later life. She learns to calm and soothe a crying child, to clean up the feces of a younger sibling or dog, to build a fire, sweep the house, fetch water, and transport a stalk of bananas or a heavy basket of manioc root from the field to the house. Upon occasion she will peel, wash, and grate manioc, or bake the processed mass over the fire. At this stage too she becomes adept at spinning cotton.

Three "dressed up" girls, one with monkey skull.

At the time of contact young girls wore a very small cotton piece to cover their pubic areas. Soon after contact they began to wear small beaded aprons, using beads purchased from the missionaries. The girls learn to wear the apron discreetly because any exposure of the pubis is considered shameful. By the Brazilian period many young girls wore small dresses or panties. In the earlier years boys began to wear loin cloths at about age five, but by around 1975 they had replaced loin cloths with swimming trunks.

Sometimes a boy gets teased about his rigid or stubby penis. By the end of the early childhood stage both boys and girls are aware of sex, having heard youth and adults joke and discuss the subject, or seen a fisticuff duel precipitated by an "illicit" sexual encounter. They have laughed at dogs copulating, and a few youngsters have seen older Yanomami heterosexual pairs having intercourse. Young males have seen, handled, and joked about the genitals of the tapir, peccary, and monkey shot in the forest.

Stage III: Later Childhood

Even though distinct gender socialization is evident in early childhood, it becomes more established in this third life stage. For the male this period ranges between the ages of nine and fourteen; for the female it also begins at about age nine, but ends more abruptly with the onset of puberty at twelve or thirteen.

During this period a boy becomes more competent in his role as hunter. He accompanies father, brothers, or friends on hunting expeditions and eventually shoots larger birds such as the curassow, guan, and trumpeter, and possibly animals such as the monkey and peccary. A boy will spend a night or two away from the permanent dwelling to fish with his peers or older men. Fishing and hunting serve as his consistent uninterrupted preparation for his eventual adult role as provider and protector. A boy increases his skill as marksman and his perseverance and endurance in tracking his prey through the forest. Again he carries minimal responsibility for his own family, and his life is generally carefree. He helps in field clearing, canoe construction, or house-building, for a half-day here and there, interrupted by his own or his peers' whims for more leisurely activity. He wanders in and out of the house looking for a ripe banana, a chunk of meat, or a piece of cassava soaked in broth. His requests for food or attention to female family members are generally curt and insistent.

A female's activity in the later childhood stage, unlike that of the male, is spatially and socially restricted. She remains near her family of orientation and concerns herself with their immediate needs. She becomes proficient at grating manioc. She joins her mother and older women in the field, returning with a heavy load of manioc root and/or stalks of bananas. She helps prepare food for her father and male siblings. She cares for any younger siblings. She accompanies other family members on one-day trips to poison fish in streams, garner jungle fruit, or gather honey. From time to time she finds leisurely moments in the house or when she goes to the river or stream to bathe and fetch water; but she is never alone. When she is bathing and a group of men or boys invade the bathing site, she returns to the house immediately.

Her female role is indelibly marked during this period. She carries heavy baskets laden with produce from the field, even though a boy or man might be walking along behind her empty-handed. She chops and gathers firewood. She plucks the feathers of a bird that has been shot, cooks the meat, and tends the fire. Occasionally she spins and weaves cotton. She will be seen picking the lice from the hair of her classificatory mothers, fathers, sisters, and brothers. She serves the males she is responsible to, irrespective of their ages, whenever it pleases them.

By this time she has established a close bond with her own immediate family and parallel cousins. She is already familiar with kin relationships and responsibilities. She learns that some male members must be treated with distance and reserve, and she does not converse with these men irrespective of age. As the years approach puberty she finds herself possibly becoming subject to the interest of the *wãlima*, who can view her as a target of sexual intercourse. She is warned against incest, and realizes that such an act will receive severe social sanction. Her main defense is to make sure she is never alone. She comes to understand that when she reaches puberty she is to be committed to her husband and compliant to his every wish.

The affinity between the young girl and her betrothed male gradually strengthens, particularly as the girl approaches puberty. Though not common, there have been instances of prepuberty coitus among the Yanomami. The betrothed male, already referred to as husband, will be spending more time with his future wife's family, helping in the field preparation and making bride payment in the form of game. If the girl has a brother near the age of the betrothed, the two men are likely to become somewhat intimate with one another. Should her future husband live in another village, he will come to spend several nights in her family's household. Should she be an orphan or captive she will probably have her hammock permanently hanging adjacent to her promised husband's hammock, even before puberty. In this case she becomes more dependent upon him, because she has no kinsmen for support or protection. The mother of the betrothed young girl will ask her to bring the groom-to-be cooked food from the hearth. This close contact with the betrothed male is normally encouraged by the wife-giving family.

Stage IV: Premarriage; and Puberty and Marriage

For the male the fourth stage, the premarriage years, can vary between four to twelve years in duration. For the female the parallel stage, puberty and marriage, represents an abrupt and traumatic three-year period in her life. For the young woman the stage is initiated by puberty, which, along with the succeeding events of marriage, conception, and possibly abortion or infanticide, plus a likely second pregnancy and childbirth, can all occur in the course of just a few years. In this stage a woman receives what may be the highest degree of social attention in her lifetime. The girl becomes a woman, her parents receive extensive bride payment and bride service, she receives the amorous attention of several suitors, and she cohabits and conceives. The boy, at this stage, is the focus of no such biological or social attention.

MALE: PREMARRIAGE

For a male youth there are no interpersonal ties in socialization or role models comparable to that of the young girl in the fourth stage. Between the age span of 15 to 20 a male youth receives no unusual public recognition and continues to have few social responsibilities. There is no abrupt catapult into this stage, or any great change in status. What happens is that, at a relatively relaxed pace, the earlier socialization is reinforced. In the later childhood stage a boy has already been freed from strong maternal ties. The single male is relatively independent, free of social and familial obligation. Some male characteristics in the early premarriage stage are similar to the Western concept of adolescence. In many ways the boy experiments with and tests his anticipated new role of adulthood. In other ways, the years between 14 and 18 approximate the legendary, but now less common, life of the North American Huckleberry Finn.

The only resemblance to a male puberty rite is a show of stamina by holding the stingers of wasps or of the large black ant upon the chest. But this is a feat practised by males up to 40 years of age, not just youth. The male in the premarriage stage hunts, fishes, travels, and visits at will, often with a friend his own age. The product of his hunting ventures supplements family food. This stage ends for him with marriage, which on rare occasions comes when he is 18, but possibly as late as 29 or 30 years of age. In a very few cases a concerned father negotiates a mate for his son, who might be between 12 and 14 years of age. The fickle fate of demographic variables such as the sex ratio and the reproduction rate of childbearing women determines to some degree how long this premarriage stage lasts. Considerations are: (a) the availability of females in the correct classificatory relationship; (b) the female's age at betrothal; (c) whether he acquired a wife in a recent raid; (d) whether any widow is available; or (e) whether a married couple accepted him as a second husband. In the last case a married woman will show some interest in him, and the primary husband will not strongly resist the amorous bond (Peters & Hunt 1975). In such a polyandrous union the primary husband has the benefit of a younger man to assist in providing meat for his expanding family.

In the event of a young cross-cousin female being available, tribal custom encourages the single male to ask for this girl or woman as his wife sometime during this stage. In a few cases his parents may have already made the arrangement. While the girl is less than 10 years of age, the betrothed man is not likely to spend more than 10 percent of his time in bride service or bride payment. He goes on living his relatively leisurely life, often going hunting, fishing, and travelling, sometimes to other Xilixana or Yanomami villages, or to the Brazilians downstream.

A young man who goes to work for the Brazilians for a few months may acquire shirts and pants, and in a few exceptional cases, a battery-operated record player from his labors there. He might also acquire other items such as a knife, machete, axe, cooking pot(s), and clothing, some of which he will probably give to the wife-giving family as bride payment. This payment becomes essential as his future wife approaches womanhood, in her postpuberty and premarriage months, as well as during the first years of marriage.

This fourth stage is by no means mundane or uneventful for the male. There may be the periods of heightened enthusiasm when all the available man pursue a herd of bush hogs, a group of howler monkeys, or the scent of a tapir. Their emotions may be peaked by a raid on an enemy village. Furthermore, for the single men this is by no means a period of total sexual abstinence. Chagnon (1992: 177) identifies young single men as a social problem in Yanomami society. Most male youth have experienced sexual intercourse by age 18, probably at one of the festive events, when young men copulate with available single or married females. Often a duel of fisticuffs ensues, in which men show their physical duress in a ritual of redressive behavior. Even during non-festive periods, young men may establish clandestine sexual relations with married women, and those amorous pursuits may also lead to a duel of fisticuffs. Young men who have been betrothed must limit these sexual liaisons, lest the wife-giving families retract the promised daughter. At the same time they must be faithful in providing bride service and bride payment.

As a man's betrothed approaches womanhood, he will spend considerable time with the wife-giving family. The promised husband may reside with his prospective wife's family a month or two at a time, assisting in canoe and field-building and following the forest trails looking for game. He (and others) see the girl's developing breasts as evidence that puberty is approaching. He knows that some months after his future wife's puberty he will gain his woman as cook, companion, and conceiver of his children. When his marriage is imminent the young man goes through a settling-down time known as the field-making period. The youth provides evidence that he is taking his marriage responsibility seriously by preparing his own field, in which he will have sufficient food for his household. He clears an area and plants manioc, banana, sugar cane, and yams, and within a year at least some of the products of his toil will be ready to harvest.

This fourth stage has allowed the male to recognize and participate in the dominant Yanomami values of male superiority, self-defense, aggression, and courage. He has matured in physical strength, fighting ability, skill in hunting and fishing, and in canoe-making and field-making.

FEMALE: PUBERTY AND MARRIAGE

Upon the first sign of menarche—usually around the age of 12—the young woman is hustled by her mother to a leaf enclosure measuring about two meters in length and breadth, located within the communal house (Early & Peters 1990). The pubescent girl remains in this small cubicle for almost two months. Before the availability of scissors, a piece of bamboo was employed to cut all the pubescent girl's hair, and on the day that happens she is forbidden to eat anything. Thereafter, her diet is a minimal amount of banana, cassava, small fish, armadillo, turtle, and possibly some wild-fruit drink. She uses sticks to feed and scratch herself. She becomes itchy if she eats sugar cane or yams, gets dizzy if she eats parrot, bush chicken, or bush turkey. If she consumes tapir she becomes tired. If she eats sloth she will move slowly, and sweet potatoes will cause her veins to enlarge. The menstruating young woman leaves the enclosure only for toilet and bathing purposes, always accompanied by another female. The men of the village are warned about her exits. Only her mothers, real and classificatory, and sisters speak to her. No male must see or speak to or about her, lest he be inflicted with *eiana* (bush yaws, or leishmaniasis).

In 1962 I did not respect the "don't see, don't talk" taboo, and when I came down with an ulcer eight months later it came as no surprise to the Xilixana. They offered to cure the illness by taking a knife to cut out the infected area. I gave myself antibiotic injections, and it healed, at least externally.

With the termination of the puberty rite, the young woman assumes normal activity about the house. After her hair has again grown out, her parents generally arrange the hunting trip and other events that lead to cohabitation (see chapter 7). Meanwhile, other potential male suitors may show considerable interest in the girl's postpuberty stage. This is most likely to occur if: (a) the new husband is considerably older than his new mate; (b) the new husband is timid, and therefore not protective or jealous; (c) bride payment was initiated only in recent years; (d) no bride service or bride payment was made; (e) she is attractive and seductive; or (f) the village has several young men in a relationship that makes sex permissible. The problem is exacerbated if this young woman is fickle or favors her suitor while disliking or despising her husband. When a girl has been betrothed, though, the parents and brothers will staunchly reprimand and physically beat her if she does not remain loyal to her husband to be. The wife-giving family has an obligation to give a devoted and compliant wife to the betrothed and bride-paying male.

When women menstruate, they *lo* (sit) on the earth, or lower their hammocks close to the ground so that in lying down their buttocks are on the earth. They observe all activity in the yãno, and may string beads or spin cotton. Since the time of contact they are more likely to be sitting on a small slab of wood during their periods. They refrain from eating any red meat. It is taboo to have intercourse with a woman during her menses. Should a young single woman wish to refrain from sexual intercourse, especially during festivities that bring on greater sexual license, she will *lo*, faking a menstruation. The Xilixana do not understand how Western women can go on functioning without demonstrating this *lo* period.

For the girl a pattern of continuous consistent conditioning is apparent from childhood through to the time she takes up a full adult role. She has been involved with other women, particularly her mother, fulfilling the female role with increasing responsibility. She knows how to prepare food, cut and gather firewood, tend the fire, carry heavy loads upon her back, and attend to children. She has seen, but only partially experienced, her role as one subjected to men. Now she must acquiesce to her husband's wishes of sex and food preparation. Soon she will give birth and rear one, two, and possibly many more children, fulfilling her prime role in the Yanomami society for at least two decades of her life. In essence she experiences no adolescence. The transition into adulthood, including the roles of wife and mother, is abrupt. Some young women fear the first experiences of coitus with their husband. Some feel unprepared in assuming complete and constant infant care responsibilities at age 14 or 16. Young women see their newborn babies killed at birth.

Stage V: Male—First Family of Procreation; Female—Childbearing and Childrearing

For both the male and female, the fifth and sixth stages in the family cycle center primarily upon the family of procreation. These two stages for the female include childbearing, childrearing, and diminishing family involvement. For the male the stages are fathering, initially in the first family of procreation, and possibly in a second family. This fathering stage usually begins at between 22 to 30 years of age.

MALE: FIRST FAMILY OF PROCREATION

In marriage, the climax (though not the end) of many years of bride service and bride payment, a husband now has his own partner and begins his new role-cluster as progenitor, protector, and sustainer of his own family. He becomes fully integrated into his wife's family. He resides in her parent's home and, when necessary, supplements their needs with the produce of his field, as well as with game. They in turn share food with him. At times he is asked to assist in special projects, perhaps making a paddle to replace one his father-in-law had recently broken.

If the men are close in age, an intimate and enduring bond often develops between the husband and the wife's brother—the closest relationship in Yanomami society, even more intimate than the husband-wife relationship. As much as half of all activity during the early years of marriage involves these males in companionship with one another. In the evening they converse with one another in the communal house, further sharing their experiences. As husband, a man is the prime protector and provider of his wife and children. He uses his much-honed skills with bow and arrows to provide a variety of game. His wife cooks the prized meat at the family hearth. He spends at least a third of his time hunting and fishing. He enjoys this activity: it is seldom, if ever, viewed as drudgery by the Yanomami, nor does it carry the negative connotation of work, as do similar necessary daily functions in Western society. Although he doesn't see field-clearing and planting as being as interesting as hunting, as husband and father he takes on those jobs as well. Now he can't work in the field at whim, as he may have done in his premarital years. He knows that being a good provider will please his wife's parents. A married man spends about a quarter of his daylight time in the field, clearing and planting. He spends the rest of his time doing activities that complement the Yanomami lifestyle: making or mending bow and arrows, retrieving arrow cane from an abandoned distant field, gathering jungle fruit with family and friends, carving an axe handle or paddle, braiding rope from the sisal plant, visiting, constructing a canoe, or, every two years or so, repairing, rebuilding, or building a house. Four or five Xilixana men know how to weave the cassava squeezer made from reeds, a craft they acquired from their fathers.

The male role includes all of the skills a boy gets exposed to in his childhood, and which a youth practises in his premarriage years. Now he has become more proficient at them, and carries full responsibility for their execution. As his own sons develop through the life cycle, he introduces these same experiences to them.

The married male, particularly in his later years, increasingly becomes involved in decision-making, which involves not only his extended family but also other members of the tribe. As a mature male he may decide upon relocating, or possibly avenging an enemy camp. From the time his daughter begins walking he and his wife must consider the possibility of acquiring a mate for her. This decision has far-reaching economic and political consequences. Eventually the husband decides upon the betrothal of his own daughter, or daughters.

The mature male is socialized to be fierce (Chagnon 1977). He must stand up for his own and his family's rights. The tendency to revenge is experienced early in a boy's socialization and constantly reinforced in childhood and in later years. Weaklings are despised, cowards are derided, and the timid are scorned. The frequent duels of fisticuffs on the face or chest arise out of alleged or real illicit coitus, thievery, or gossip regarding a man's cowardice, which is considered a serious offense. Emotions can flare up suddenly, and sides are quickly established, primarily on the basis of loyalty to affinal relatives. Verbal utterances are loud, direct, and scathing. The fights erupt quickly and soon die down, but can erupt again months or years later. A male in the late premarriage stage through to the middle of his first family of procreation stage engages himself in these skirmishes.

FEMALE: CHILDBEARING AND CHILDREARING

From about age 18, a few years into marriage, the woman becomes increasingly involved in the role-cluster of cook, childbearer, and childrearer. She spends a portion of every day doing the labor-intensive tasks involved in harvesting and processing the staple food of manioc (see chapter 5). During the first years of marriage and motherhood, the newlywed female is assisted and tutored by her mother. The older woman, still physically strong, assists in the daily routine of duties as well as in child care. She offers her advice in child-training and rearing.

During pregnancy the Xilixana meticulously observe taboos on specific foods. When a woman is pregnant she is not to eat any fish because the spines will prick her baby. She and her husband are forbidden to eat eggs, which will cause the child to become enclosed. After the child's birth, and until it walks, a wife must observe a number of other food taboos: no parrots—the child will become hot and ill; no turtle—heart problems; no spider monkey—child becomes greasy; no smaller monkey—tongue will rot; no *mamoli* (white fish)—child's tongue will be harmed. If the child becomes ill the mother and father will refrain from eating to show respect for their offspring.

A good mother attempts to keep her young from meddling with other children and messing with other people's goods, and to some degree from quarrelling. All of these mild restraints prove difficult in a communal house. Her children are expected not to cry or fuss. In short, they are to be content. She must have enough prepared food available for her husband as well as her children. She is expected to be accessible to her family to meet their needs. Apart from these tasks, a good mother will periodically make a clay pot (in the pre-contact and contact periods), weave a wicker basket or cotton hammock, and sometimes sweep the dirt floor of the house. Interspersed between these activities she will spin cotton, a task seemingly without end. Almost all of a married woman's tasks are done at the house and in the company of other women. She laughs at the humorous happenings of her children, and scolds them for deviant behavior. She has ample opportunity to interact with other women who have similar interests, concerns, and goals, usually in a congenial atmosphere. Her life in this stage is somewhat routine, with business, frequent demands, and endless service.

Stage VI: Male—Second Family of Procreation; Female—Post-childrearing

MALE: SECOND FAMILY OF PROCREATION

By the time a wife approaches 40 years of age, some men have already negotiated a second, younger wife, initiating what is the sixth stage for the male, the second family of procreation. Although not all middle-aged men follow this pattern, it does appear with sufficient frequency, and is ideologically so pervasive, as to warrant the recognition of a separate stage in the family cycle for the male. If a man does not take on a younger partner, he continues to function within what we call the first family of procreation, skipping the cycle of rearing a second family.

The option of taking a second wife is somewhat controlled by factors such as the husband's age at first marriage, his current health, the relationship with his current wife, and the availability of a second mate. Men have been remarried at 63 years of age, sometimes to a female of 13. They might obtain a second wife through a raid, through bride exchange of one of the husband's own daughters with another man's sister or daughter, or through the more usual pattern of bride payment and bride service.

After procuring a younger wife, a husband's interest in his older wife will decrease notably. If his new wife was acquired as a young girl in a raid, she may have been living in his household already for one or two years, with her hammock hung close to, but not below his. If the woman comes from within the tribe and other young single men are also seeking a wife, the marriage might create animosity, but the authority of an older man will dominate. If a man becomes increasingly dysfunctional in hunting and field work, a younger male will inevitably associate with the woman in a clandestine or more open manner. Matrilocality is again observed in any second marriage. In some cases the marriage merely brings about a shift within the large communal house, forming a new nucleus. Usually the marriage revives the husband's interest in hunting, an activity that ordinarily declines for men in their forties. Although men over 50 years of age may not be as agile in tracking animals, they can quite successfully shoot birds or catch slower animals like the armadillo or turtle. An older man spends more time planting and weeding the field.

The husband still has frequent contact with the children of his first marriage. An older woman seldom feels rebuffed, but considers her husband's acquisition of another wife to be quite appropriate. She knows she can no longer bear children. She is relieved of some of her responsibility towards her husband. Younger married women are not as tolerant about a co-spouse relationship. In at least one case, a wife of about 33 years of age and with three young children disapproved of her husband's intention to acquire a second wife. Ultimately the decision is the man's, although it might possibly come at a cost.

FEMALE: POST–CHILDREARING

A woman in the early part of the sixth stage, of post-childrearing, continues the same activities as before except that now she is not pregnant and is no longer nursing an infant, nor does she have the responsibility of caring for a young child. Her time is less regimented by a crying child or the demands of a husband. She continues to meet the needs of her growing children with food and emotional nurturing. She remains a strong socializing agent in the extended family unit. She coaches her newly wed daughters and offers her advice and assistance when they become mothers. At times she may instigate a village feud by gossiping about an alleged act of thievery, sorcery, or illicit sex. Or her incessant disparaging talk of some young person will possibly force the victim and his or her family to vacate the communal house. She participates in the massive food preparation for festive occurrences. If her husband is still around she prepares food for him. She accompanies and assists her married daughters in child care and food preparation. This type of complementarity continues for a number of years. As time goes on she spends less time doing heavy work such as grating cassava and carrying heavy baskets of produce.

As a woman becomes older, her services to her family and the tribe decline. Now younger women are in the role that she once served. She shows her pride in her capable and industrious children, and equally in her grandchildren. She remains attentive to the needs of her prepuberty and postpuberty children. She lives either with her husband or adjacent to the family of a son or daughter. As long as she contributes to basic life functions, she is not abandoned. As long as she is able she accompanies a married daughter to the field or cares for a grandchild in the house. She spins cotton for a hammock for her husband or a son or grandson. In this stage she is a valued and respected person to her children and grandchildren—even at age 35 a man likes to linger near his mother's hearth. As she becomes weaker, she will not be able to travel far from home. Her physical ailments will increase and become more frequent. Her eyesight may not be as focused, so that she becomes less capable of stringing beads or mending clothing. She will tire more easily. She is entering the last stage in her life cycle.

Stage VII: Appendage

Few Yanomami live to the seventh and last stage, that of appendage. The rigors of tropical rainforest life and difficult life conditions take their toll at an earlier stage than in the North, or the culture itself limits possibilities for survival: Chagnon's (1972) Venezuelan study shows that one-third of the male population died in warfare. In more recent years, the elderly, with their weakened resistance, have often become victims of epidemics, such as colds, measles, tuberculosis, or malaria.

The Yanomami dislike any evidence of aging. They pluck their grey hair until they finally become convinced the effort is futile. When my own hair went grey early on, they urged me to pull out the grey strands. One "wise guy" recommended I tint my hair like some other foreigners do. Deteriorating health and feebleness are the prime characteristics of this appendage stage. Aged men are often unable to hunt and clear fields or fish in the streams and river. Even weeding the garden becomes tiring for them after only a brief time. Older women no longer carry produce from the garden or water from the stream. They lose their ability to spin cotton, partly due to failing eyesight and less dexterous fingers. I have seen or heard tell of one or two women who became blind, and who bumped into objects around the house or burned their fingers in the fire. The older women walk short distances about the house, sometimes with the aid of a stick. Children and young boys ridicule the blind and maimed, who tend to be the very last concern of those around them.

The central quality of this group of people is that they have become unable to contribute any resources to Yanomami life. Those who are persistently ill, weak, and elderly impede the normal flow and cycle of village life, and the degree of care they receive is dependent upon the spouse or daughter. If illness strikes and recovery seems unlikely, the family awaits the death. One dysfunctional male was ill for several months, and his tribesmen sought to bury him before he died. They saw no hope for him regaining health. He contributed nothing to the society, so death would now be his only lot. There is little wailing at the death of the old and infirm.

Summary of Stages in the Life Cycle

Family is even more central to Yanomami life than it is in Western society. As with the Western family, the members of a Yanomami family do show variations in the typical life stages proposed here. Death or marital separation might occur during the wife's childbearing or childrearing years. If the young woman dies in later childhood, before puberty, or if she becomes disgruntled with her betrothed in the puberty and marriage stage, this departure from the norm would carry serious and far-reaching social implications. The betrothed male invests considerable time, energy, and trust in the wife-giving family, and the options for another wife in the immediate future are generally not very promising. The grievances that arise in such a situation can linger on for years.

The seven stages differ significantly from those of the Western family in that, for the Yanomami, the family careers for male and female each follow a distinct path in the age sequence after later childhood. The young woman is suddenly hurled into the adult female status of mother, because she is biologically equipped to fulfill that role. The young male lingers for at least a half dozen years in the pre-adult, premarriage stage, seemingly not yet emotionally prepared to be a stable companion and provider for a wife and children. His full adult status comes with fatherhood.

As puberty marked a girl's entry into her prime function, so menopause marks the end of the status a woman once held. She is often substituted for a younger wife. Her husband will spend less time with her. She seeks to complement others, particularly her extended family members.

The retiring years of life are difficult for both Yanomami male and female. If they are unable to fend for themselves in a physical environment which is severe, and in a social environment which is often hostile, they simply await death. The event of death creates considerable consternation if it occurs in any of the earlier stages, but for the weak and feeble in the appendage stage, it is welcomed.

A XILIXANA'S TALE OF PUBERTY, MARRIAGE, AND CHILDBEARING

*W*hen my blood started, they cut my hair with a knife. We lived at the Mulu stream. They hid me behind leaves. I did not talk to men. If I had, they would have got large sores on their skin. I bathed while it was still dark, early in the morning. I ate banana drink. I drank cassava mixed with water. I ate small fish. I did not go into the fields. "The manioc will not yield," they said.

When I was younger my husband-to-be gave pig meat to my mother. He gave meat. At a yãimo he asked for me. I was very, very afraid. I cried. When he took me (as wife) I was afraid. I missed my brother. With my hammock I was placed between them (his older wife and his newer wife). My brother tied the hammock between them. He is the one that gave me. My mother gave me. He was broad. He was a shaman. I did not know anything of intercourse. I was afraid. "Don't cry. Don't be afraid," the older wife beside me said. My fear ceased. Later I became pregnant. There was pain at birthing. Noliwa, Ester, Wahuma, and my mother said, "Take the child." Mahuknini (I call him brother, but he is not my real brother) said, "Pick up the child. We will eat her cassava bread." I was afraid of the newly born's wrinkles. I did not know. My mother carried her at first. Later she nursed. "Let her be one to grate cassava," said Ester. The father said nothing.

She is the one who died, who was eaten in my stomach [died of cancer]. Her ash is now gone. We made a lot of bananas and cassava [during her lifetime]. I think of her a lot.

Ilo [husband] did not get mad at us. Amohik [second wife] and I hit Ilo. His eyes became swollen. We hit with fists. We hit with wood.... After he died I cried a lot. Oliki [younger male] asked my brother for me. "No" I said. "I am God's people." "Laop" [leave it as is—my remaining single]. Men get hungry and demanding.

KONAKXAALIMA XILIXANA

Seven
Myths, Spirits, and Magic

The supernatural and mythical worlds of the Yanomami are fully integrated. There is no dichotomy, no segmentation. The real (visible and tangible) and the spiritual (abstract and ideological) are intricately woven into one colorful fabric. Indeed, often the supernatural appears to be more central than the visible and tangible, and the supernatural seems to determine everyday affairs. For many Westerners it might appear that the tail (the supernatural) wags the dog (the everyday affairs of fertility, health, harvesting, and hunting). The centrality of the supernatural—of myths, spirits, *hekula*, magic substances and their use, and even the sense of a cosmos—explains much of the trappings and realities of Yanomami social organization and life.

Spirits may be manipulated by the enemy, which creates general anxiety for all village inhabitants. The response is generally one of revenge through sorcery or warfare. Because of this fear the Yanomami restrict their sphere of travel and expend much psychic energy on spiritual matters, a preoccupation that did not decline with the presence of Westerners.[1]

Myths

Myths are traditional or legendary stories, usually about some event involving the supernatural. Myths help "explain" the unexplainable, and, as such, the events or personalities in myths are not subject to the scrutiny of fact. The stories are talked about, and believed, just as they are. They give identity to people within a given culture.[2]

---

1   Mark Richie has made a monumental contribution to Yanomami research in presenting the life story of a shaman in *Spirit of the Rainforest* (1996).

2   Johannes Wilbert and Karen Simonean (1990) have collected a large number of Yanomami myths from a variety of sources. The present challenge for scholars is to find the common threads in Yanomami myths and analyze differences among them.

In Yanomami society myths are transferred by oral tradition by men. They are relayed in the yāno for the benefit for whoever wants to listen. These myths are relayed onomatopoetically and in great detail, with frequent use of direct address. In Yanomami stories of creation, humans were created first, and all animals came from humans. In their myths some humans had animal or bird names even before they became transformed into animals or birds. The Xilixana were greatly amused when I told them that the prominent belief in Euro-American society was that humans evolved from animals. They knew we had it all wrong.

THE ORIGIN OF YANOMAMI

These were the only people on the earth. Omano, a male, lived together with his wife and son. (One informant told me Omamo had a brother, a detail consistent with the myth as told by other Yanomami groups.) Through the night it rained and rained and rained. Very early in the morning the young son walked down a trail. He saw the *wasekekekeka* bird (person) and wanted to shoot him. He ran back to the house and told his father, "I saw the one that says *wasekekekeka*."

The father said, "*Uuh*" (showing disgust). "Go back and listen and see what he is doing." The boy went out and soon returned saying, "It is coming this way."

Omano was concerned because he feared *wasekekeka* would attack him and tear off his skin. Immediately he packed his goods to leave. He packed and packed. He took his goods out of the *thaposi* (a hard-fibered, shell-like crescent from a palm tree, sometimes used as a container) and went away with his wife and son, floating way down the river in their canoe. These people undoubtedly were the first *naba*, or civilized people. From out of the *thaposi* there emerged people, male and female. They are our people.

THE ORIGIN OF BATS, ANTEATERS, AND BUSH HOGS

A mature male lived with his wife and mother-in-law. He told his wife to tell her mother to tend the dogs, because he and his wife would be absent from the yāno for a few days. But she followed after them. (There is laughter here, because she should not have accompanied her daughter and son-in-law.) The three went off into the jungle, and walked a long way. At night they hung their hammocks. The male was bent upon doing bad. He copulated with the older woman, committing incest. She became a bat and said, "*se se se se*." He turned into an anteater. His penis was long and dragged along the ground. Eventually some people came along, and the anteater and bat fled into the woods. The bat went saying, "*se se se se*." They were gone. The people sat with the young woman and waited.

There was a shaman with his wife and three children. His wife had walked off into the woods, and she cried because she missed her brother, who had left earlier. Eventually she came upon the encampment of her tribesmen. She saw her people turning into bush pigs, because of their incestuous activity. The women and men grew tails. They took off their beads. They abandoned their hammocks. Their hands became hooves. They became bush hogs. A small bird (person), *talakaom*, appeared and called. The animals responded with "*wa wa wa.*" They spread out into the forest. The little ones became piglets and roamed off into the woods after the older pigs.

The woman returned to her home and family. She cried and told the shaman what had happened. This story reinforces the Yanomami rules of incest.

(The informant's closing comment was, "We don't have any bush hogs anymore." It is uncertain whether the bush hog has recently left the region where Yanomami live because of the presence of miners or because of more natural, ecological reasons. My informant attributed it to the decline of shamanism.)

THE ORIGIN OF DOGS

Our people had no dogs to hunt tapir. They encountered dogs who lived amongst rocks and boulders. They baited the dogs with meat attached to bush rope. The dogs came out from among the rocks to eat the meat, fastened to the bush rope that our forefathers kept pulling. They caught many dogs. Some were black, others red like the deer, and others were striped. They were fierce.

THE DECEASED TERMINATE THEIR EARTHLY VISITS

The deceased used always to visit our living forebears. A recently deceased young woman climbed down the bush rope to see her mother. She said to her, "My skin is dark" (evidence that she had died). The mother did not acknowledge her daughter's deceased state, but simply said, "Yes your skin is dark."

The young woman again sought her mother's acknowledgment of her death, saying to her mother, "Why are your cheeks caked with dirt?" (obviously from her crying in bereavement of her daughter's death). "I was working in the field," the mother said deceptively. The mother was happy to see her daughter. They ate together. The daughter asked for water, because she was thirsty. Her mother had no water.

The young woman recognized the gourd containing her ash in a small hanging basket and asked what it was. "It is a small basket that Molab made," the mother said, again in deception. The parakeet (a person) said, "Get out of here. Go back to your people." He was angry.

Then the mother walked far down the trail to get water for her daughter. Upon returning with the water she saw that her daughter had left. She had gone down another trail and was assembled with others who had deceased. The mother ran down this trail after her daughter. All the deceased ones were climbing up the rope that went into the heavens. The last one up cut the rope. The woman and the parakeet person were left behind with their own people.

(This story is told in a sense of grave disappointment, because if the rope had not been cut they would still be able to visit their deceased relatives.)

THE ORIGIN OF FIRE AND THE ALLIGATOR (WELI)

Years ago our forebears did not eat meat. They could not eat meat because they had no fire. They could only eat bananas and sugar cane.

The Yanomami *Weli* (alligator) had fire, and he kept it to himself. Another Yanomami walked near *Weli* and he saw ashes from burned leaves close to his house. About that time a second Yanomami walked by with a tapir he had shot. The first Yanomami said, "I saw *Weli* and he has fire."

The Yanomami gathered together. There were many. "Let's make merry and go over to *Weli* and see whether we can make him laugh and thereby get fire. They all dressed up with colored feathers. They all went over to *Weli*. They were all extremely joyous, but *Weli* remained straightfaced and never opened his mouth. They did all they could to make him laugh, but he remained sober. One by one they left *Weli*'s house, disappointed that they could not make him laugh.

The last one to leave was *Texo* (hummingbird). "Shall I be the one to make *Weli* laugh?" he said. He made merry, but again *Weli* was not amused. Amidst *Texo*'s glee and excitement, he involuntarily made a dropping (excrement), at which instant *Weli* burst into great laughter. At that point *Texo* dashed into *Weli*'s mouth, snapped up the fire, and flew out, throwing the stick of fire into the air. The person *Koli* (a small bird) caught the fire in flight and passed it on to our forebears, who had circled *Weli*'s house. They took the fire and quickly made a larger fire and cooked their tapir. They also cooked other things like bananas and yams.

Weli was disappointed, and groaned and muttered, "What will I do now that I have no fire? I will go into the water." And he did. He has remained there ever since.

Our forebears took fire and poured it into the *poleihi* tree, this tree, that tree, then another tree. And so they had fire. (At the time of contact the Mucajai people made fire by rubbing together two sticks of this tree.)

PILI UTUP (A PERSON'S REFLECTION IN THE WATER)

This is what we see in the water. *Pili utup* are not fierce. They die when we die. They do not walk on land. One of our forefathers, Mahethexopin, capsized in his canoe and went under water. He brought up bananas from below, for his people. These people have bows and arrows. They fish and shoot game. They have fields of bananas and manioc.

Spirits

The sphere of spirits is perhaps the least understood phenomenon in Yanomami culture, partly because it is involves the non-material—it deals with the abstract and is not readily comprehendible—and partly because it is tremendously pervasive, influencing and penetrating almost all aspects of Yanomami life: their thoughts, dreams, and daily behavior.

Many aspects of the Yanomami spirit world defy the logic of the Western world. These beliefs and practices do not readily fall into categories or some "reasonable" pattern. While it is a source of protection, it is also the basis of tremendous fear. The world of the spirits is also a phenomenon that has undergone significant change since the Xilixana made contact with other Yanomami after 1960.

Life and relationships are fickle. The activity of the supernatural is unpredictable. The Yanomami devote a good deal of time and energy in their efforts to escape the spirits' fickle fingers of fate. The shaman plays a key role in Yanomami safekeeping. No Yanomami has any higher respect than does a shaman. A powerful shaman is known by friend and foe alike. At his death there is much mourning.

Spirits in the Yanomami belief system can be identified as (a) *lĩx*, (b) spirits of the deceased, and (c) *hekula*.

LĨX

Every Yanomami has an alter ego known as *lĩx*. They live in the forest far removed from the actual person. Among the Xilixana a female's *lĩx* is the *hohoama*, a type of river otter that finds its habitation in the water and on the banks of the river. Xilixana men have either the jaguar (*hoo*) or eagle (*pohom*) *lĩx*. A male always acquires the same type of *lĩx*. Other Yanomami who are not Xilixana are reported to have other animal *lĩx*, such as the spider monkey. A person's *lĩx* does not come into being until that person is three or four years of age.

A person's eagle *lĩx* helps the Xilixana hunter to find and kill creatures of the trees and sky, like monkeys and birds. Similarly, the jaguar *lĩx* assists the hunter to get animals that stalk the earth: tapir, pig, deer, and alligator.

The Xilixana attribute many illnesses to the *lĩx* getting lost. They are no longer in association with the person. The *lĩx* must be found, or the individual will die. It is the shaman who searches for the departed *lĩx*. The shaman will work to retrieve the *lĩx* of very aged persons as well. He calls on the squirrel spirit to assist him in this search. The squirrel spirit is a protection or covering for the *lĩx* and can therefore reveal where the *lĩx* might be found. Only a very powerful shaman can find a person's *lĩx*.

If a hunter encounters the physical form of the *lĩx* (eagle or jaguar) in the forest, he will shoot the animal. But when someone shoots the *lĩx*, someone else in another distant Yanomami community will die, though the precise village is not readily identifiable. If the animal is not shot, a member of another community is apt to shoot it later, and a local Xilixana will die. So it is better to shoot the eagle so that someone in another village dies rather than someone in your own. There is also a risk that you might shoot your own *lĩx*, which will cause you to die. If you shoot the *lĩx* of a woman, her child will die. However, if she has no children, there is no negative consequence in shooting her *lĩx*.

When the Xilixana shoot an eagle they observe the strict *inokai* (murder) taboo. The hunter will not take the most direct trail to his *yãno*. He will zigzag through the forest. His hair will be cut and placed in a cut slab in a tree in the forest. He becomes nauseated. His stomach churns with pain. He is itchy and becomes thin. He finds some relief in bathing often. He will swallow the bitter liquid from the quinine tree and vomit. He will not hunt in the area where he shot the eagle for a couple of months. A man observes the same taboo after he kills a person in a raid. He will not touch any food he eats with his fingers, but will use sticks. Similarly he scratches his itchy body with sticks. He will not touch any of his children. He does not eat anything more than a small selection of game for several weeks.

My older informant said he would not shoot an eagle for fear of becoming nauseated and thin and possibly dying. The cost was too great.

Every living person also has a *nihpolep*, spirit which is harmless. It is black and about five centimeters in size. One can see it in a person's eyes. It lives in the chest, and when you die it departs. It roams and is far away. Shaman have the power to kill a person's *nihpolep*.

SPIRITS OF THE DECEASED

The *pole* spirit comes into being after a person dies, and particularly after the corpse is buried or left on a rack for the flesh to rot. There is no *pole* for those who are killed at birth. One does not fear the *pole* of those who die as young children. A male's *pole* is female, and a female's *pole* is male.

Pole roam the forest. They come close to the *yãno* of the deceased to retrieve relatives, including grandchildren. During the day or night they knock at the wooden door, "*tok, tok.*" They say, "*a a a huum*," "*ai ai ai ai*," and, "What are you doing?" People are warned, "Don't go outside. You will be killed." If *pole* appear at night, the Xilixana will be afraid and will not sleep. The *pole* are fierce and have teeth like the jaguar. They are heard but not seen by anyone but the shaman, who sees the *pole* spirit and causes it to move away, leaving the people with less fear. After time and through the powers of the shaman, the *pole* leaves. The *pole* spirits live forever, and after a time cease bothering their deceased.

In recent decades medicine has made the *pole* weak, and they are not as bothersome. The *naba* also have *pole*, but those spirits are not fierce like the Yanomami spirits. *Naba's pole* sing (at least that is what miners have reported to the Yanomami).

During our third year of residence at Mucajai, an elderly woman whose son had recently died appeared at our door about 2:00 a.m. She said she was being disturbed by a *pole*, and asked that I come with my shotgun to shoot or scare it away. I walked down the trail with flashlight and gun, and she followed in fear with her firebrand. I saw nothing and escorted her back to her yãno. I slept the rest of the night, but she remained fearful.

There is another spirit known as *yai* (real). It roams far away, is black and big, and is not feared.

HEKULA

The activity of the *hekula* spirits are central to Yanomami life. *Hekula* are associated with all functions of life: hunting, health, fertility, warfare, death. There are hundreds of *hekula*, generally no bigger than four centimeters. Most *hekula* are animals, and each has a specific task. Only shaman (*xapoli*) can have knowledge of and control over—or are able to manipulate—*hekula*.

In a strict sense, *xapoli* means communication with and control of some *hekula*. In the broadest sense *xapoli* refers to some supernatural or mystical maneuvering. I was recognized as *xapoli* because my use of medicine healed people. A missionary was identified as *xapoli* because by slight of hand he could make a coin disappear, then reappear, a trick Yanomami enjoyed watching.

The function of a *xapoli* is threefold. For hunting purposes he will woo game to the trails where hunters walk. The shaman informs the hunter where game is to be found. Shaman use their power to cast spells upon enemies. And, finally, a capable shaman spends more time in the art of healing than any other activity. In serious cases he will be joined with a host of other *xapoli* in the yãno, each working in sync with the leading shaman. Most shaman have a particular skill with specific *hekula*, and therefore are healers for specific maladies. The most powerful *hekula* are the real jaguar, the real spider monkey, the real howler monkey. They are black and kill. They travel quickly by land, water, and air. The *hekula* that do not kill are tapir, macaw parrot, anteater, deer, and the large squirrel river monster. At the time of contact the armadillo was not a *hekula*, but after contact with other Yanomami it became one.

TABLE 7.1: HEKULA AND THE CURING OF ILLNESS

ILLNESS	HEKULA	ILLNESS	HEKULA
liver	spider monkey	eyes	spider monkey
thorn, sliver	*kokoyoma*	ear	*kokoyoma*
tongue, fever	*kokoyoma*	headache	red howler monkey
heart	tapir, catfish, *tuplasik*	infertility	spider monkey
swollen leg, arm	spider monkey	hit by branch	spider monkey

Alawalik Substances

The use of *alawalik* is not restricted to a shaman, but is available to anyone. In almost all cases it is a work of evil. It is used for revenge and leads to inconvenience, illness, and death. The Yanomami live in constant fear that someone may cast a spell of *alawalik* upon them. Almost all deaths and illnesses are attributed to some form of *alawalik*. The actual substances of *alawalik* are numerous and vary from root, leaf, and bark material to hair or fur.

ÕKLA

The most feared general form of *alawalik* is *õkla*. For revenge or malicious purposes a group of men will travel from four to twelve days to the vicinity of their enemy. Generally before dawn they will stop some 20 to 50 meters from the yãno and perform the ritual: blowing or spitting *alawalik* in the direction of the yãno. They may light a small fire and have the smoke carry the magical powers to the house. The actor designates whom he wishes the substance to strike. Then the *alawalik* party takes flight back to their territory.

The psychosomatic effect of this activity is dramatic. A person or persons will die, being fully convinced that they have been the victims of *õkla* activity. They resign themselves to dying, making no effort to seek healing or recovery. No shaman can cure the curse of *õkla*. However, a shaman will determine whether the malady is due to *õkla* or some other cause. Usually the death is quick. In such cases *õkla* attacks suddenly by breaking the neck, arms, or legs and hitting the body with sticks. This is generally done in the early morning when the Xilixana walk off just a little ways from the yãno to urinate. Other modes of death used by *õkla* are severe headaches, fever, and a severe shaking of the body.

The *õkla*-attacking animals are anteater, cutia, deer, rat, pig, and raccoon. Small children are attacked by black rabbits, *ãle* (a small, sneaky creature), jaguar, piping guan, and the trumpet bird. Animal spirits that do not attack are the red howler monkey, collared peccary, and turtle. The fear of *õkla*, especially regarding the protection of children, has been so pronounced that some villages choose to live on islands, where *õkla* attacks are less likely to occur.

Few people have actually seen *õkla*, though in several incidents people have formed suspicions about its presence, and men have rushed out of the yãno with bow and arrow into the forest in pursuit of *õkla*. Generally any sudden death is attributed to *õkla*: a 53-year-old man in 1961, a 66-year-old man in 1988, a 27-year-old woman in 1989. Just prior to my field work in 1996 a healthy man of 36 died suddenly, with the death also attributed to *õkla*. In 1990, a 43-year-old healthy woman died, supposedly because of *õkla*. In each case the human agent of the death is unknown, allowing rumor to germinate potential reprisals. At times raids are accompanied with *õkla* activity.

OTHER BLACK MAGIC FORMS OF ALAWALIK

The Yanomami use *alawalik* in numerous other ways. A Xilixana may carefully gather the footprint of someone who is not a friend into a leafed container tied with bush rope. He then places an *alawalik* substance into the container, and the person in the far-off village will die.

Some uses of *alawalik* have been taught the Xilixana by neighboring Yanomami after the period of contact. In a process learned from the Malaxi theli, for instance, a hunter shoots a spider monkey, and while the body of the animal is still warm, he quickly pulls hair from the monkey's chest. He wraps it in leaves and burns the hair after returning to his yãno. When convenient he mixes the *alawalik* substance in a drink that a woman is about to swallow— it is usually a woman, often married, who is unwilling to comply to his sexual desires. The woman gets diarrhea from the liquid, becomes ill, and may die.

The curse can be reversed if someone happens to have a similar concoction that came from a spider monkey killed on an earlier occasion. A shaman would assist in this process. Though fatalities from *alawalik* are usually targeted at enemy villages at considerable distance, the technique may sometimes be used in a home village. A young man from the Malaxi theli upriver reported that he had killed his young wife prior to migrating to Mucajai in 1969.

Another such process involves *xapo*, a leaf (root, seed) taken from a domesticated plant and placed in the intoxicating caxiri drink. The person consuming the drink becomes sterile. This is a serious offense in Yanomami culture. Shaman have the power to cure this malady. Similarly, the substance *manakak* is placed into a drink or sprinkled upon small fish before they are eaten. The person, whether male or female (usually the latter) becomes sterile. Men become unable to ejaculate. There is no cure, even by a shaman. The Xilixana identify a woman, now 50 years of age, as a victim of *manakak*. She bore one child who was killed at birth, and never conceived again.

Another *alawalik* substance is known as *katanaik*, extracted from the inner core of a tree. Blood appears on a woman's vagina. Shaman cannot cure this illness. The *kumi* substance is made from the sap of a particular thick bush vine. *Kumi* is placed upon a woman's breast and makes her irresistible to the sexual desires of a male. Husbands generally become angry when this is done to their wives. While the Xilixana used *katanaik* and *kumi* before contact, *oxwak* was introduced by the Palimi theli and is used by women.

Almost all acts of *alawalik* stimulate a passionate urge for retribution. Fear, suspicion, and hatred mount, even when the facts of the case are unknown. The Yanomami mind is fertile with hunches and guesses about the perpetrator and the cause of the act. Sometimes a person fabricates a "story" for self-interest and self-gain. A milieu of distrust is evident. Usually there are fisticuff duels, not once, but in repetition at any succeeding meetings between the two peoples. Sometimes there is murder. In recent times human life has been placed in greater danger in such situations because of the Yanomami's access to guns (Ferguson 1995).

ALAWALIK USED IN HUNTING

To facilitate the hunting of tapir the hunter spreads some of the *alawalik* substance upon his forehead and the sides of his face as he is about to leave on the hunt. When he locates tapir tracks he blows *alawalik* on the hoof prints. The substance magically follows the tracks to the tapir. The hunter whistles to the tapir and it will respond, then reverse itself and come towards the hunter, who in turn shoots the large animal.

To shoot the curassow the hunter takes the specific *alawalik* substance and places it within the arrow notch, as well as in the slot where the point enters the arrow shaft. He goes off on the hunt, and when he sees a curassow he bites off a bit of the *alawalik* and spits in the direction of the bird. This exercise is said to slow the pace of the bird, giving better opportunity to shoot the fowl.

Dreams are a significant part in Yanomami life. Some are pleasant, especially if they bring to mind good experiences with deceased relatives. Other dreams are frightening and unpleasant. For example, a warring party will reverse their tracks, even after a journey of four or five days, if one of them dreams that the enemy has become knowledgeable of the raiding group's pursuits.

The Yanomami Cosmos

The Xilixana report four layers or levels of land or spheres. They do not show much concern for the extreme bottom and top layers, but are well-versed in the two central layers. These spheres are not applicable to all created humans on the earth, but only to Yanomami.

The Yanomami reside on layer two, where they hunt, build yãnos and fields, process cassava bread, copulate, bear children, practise witchcraft, seek Western goods, and die. In any discussion of the sphere above them their concern is upon the availability of field produce, game of the forest, relationships, and shaman power—elements not all that removed from their present earthly existence. The bottom layer, Muhuputu, is inhabited by shaman only. There are no fish or game present. The fields are particularly abundant with banana, cassava, and yams. There are areas of spiked pointed bamboo. Originally the Xilixana came from this sphere.

The uppermost level, Masilim, has both people and shaman. There is ample game, especially curassow and tapir. There is no sickness. There are no õkla.

Thoughts of the third sphere are relevant to the Xilixana in terms of the hereafter. It is the abode of the deceased and is known as *pole* land. Years ago, as the myths indicate, the two groups had frequent communications. The deceased shot game in the forest of earth and took it to their abode, because their game was without taste. Now the game is not tasteless. The fields and forest produce sufficient food and fruit, ample game and fish. There is a lot of water. When it rains on earth, a herd of tapir are playing in the water, and splashes fall upon the earth. Upon death one is met by *Kosikwa* in *pole* land, and he tells you where to hang your hammock. People who are married are reunited with their spouses. They continue to make children. In this level one is youthful and lives forever. One does have fear on earth when *Paxpaxkom* comes down from *pole* land to earth. Women tell him to "Go away. We are healthy."

Taboos

The Xilixana, as we have seen, have strict taboos associated with men responsible for homicide, whether through magic (eagle) or raid. Hunters do not eat any game they shoot. In the event they consistently miss their mark, a bloodletting ritual is said to improve this dilemma. Apprentice shaman must observe sexual abstinence as well as food taboos. There are strict rites related to the treatment of a corpse, cremation, and festivities that respect the deceased.

Women experience numerous taboos as well. During a woman's first menstrual period she is placed in isolation and restricted in food consumption. Similar rules of permissible edible food apply during all future menstrual periods. Taboos apply for the period of her pregnancy, as well as for the first year after the child is born. The father of the child also observes taboos during the child's infancy. No males are permitted at the site of the birthing. They would become ill. Strict rules apply to those with whom one may not have sexual relations.

Any violations of taboo rules have serious consequences. Most relate to some form of illness. In many cases the rationale for sickness is established after one becomes ill, that is, post facto. The plethora of Yanomami taboos places tremendous restrictions as well as psychological stress upon individuals. You blame yourself, others blame you. Furthermore, there is little recourse as regards being freed from these food and social restrictions.

Some 40 years of mission work and exposure to the Western ideology of reason and rationality have not altered these behaviors. Traditional beliefs are evident in the 1990s, in that the Xilixana continue to attribute almost all deaths to spirit powers. In conversation with foreigners, the Xilixana will identify some deaths as being caused by TB, malaria, or colds, but among themselves they recognize the act of *alawalik* or sorcery. They continue to be cautious about going to get medical care at the Casa do Índio, where they will come into contact with other Yanomami and indigenous peoples who, they believe, may well perform *alawalik* on them.

Part II
Past and Present:
The Xilixana Then and Now

Eight
The Precontact Period: A Time of Isolation

Much about the precontact period still remains unknown to Western researchers; and the further we move back in time from 1957, the more we lose pieces of the puzzle of Xilixana history.

While I gathered some general segmented data from as far back as the 1930s during my residence with the Yanomami in the early 1960s, my serious efforts to reconstruct their history began only in the early 1990s, when just a few Xilixana born before 1930 remained alive. But from my association with the Xilixana in the late 1950s I had come to know some of the generation born at the turn of the century. In the 1990s their children and grandchildren were now relating stories told them by their parents. I found their reports intriguing, because the youth in the contact period were so far removed in lifestyle and extra-Yanomami contact from the Xilixana who had preceded them.

I found out that by the mid-1950s they felt the need to replenish their depleted, dull, and worn steel goods. To some extent this finding corresponded with other research into Yanomami history. For instance, in his book *Yanomami Warfare* (1995), Brian Ferguson established the extent to which steel goods have played a focal role among Yanomami over the past century. In the case of the Mucajai community, in their quest for steel goods a number of Xilixana men walked for at least five days to the southeast, though they were disappointed in their futile efforts. In 1957 they mustered their energy to canoe down the Mucajai River, convinced that they would meet the knife-makers. This time the adult men were accompanied by two women and a number of younger men. Xilixana history was about to be significantly altered.

On the lower part of the river they eventually met up with frontier Brazilians, subsistence farmers and ranchers, and initiated a contact that would have short-range and long-range consequences, some of them predictable, others not. The Yanomami were ecstatic to receive a few used axes and knives and some clothing at this historic meeting. A year later they returned. Years later I discovered that several men on this third venture were dissatisfied with the few axes and knives given them by the Brazilians and plotted to kill their hosts. Apparently they were persuaded to exercise patience by younger tribesmen.

On each trip they left numerous arrows for the local people to use. On the last visit the Xilixana left their canoes and returned home, walking through the forest where there was no trail. Later on, when I sought more precise information of this trip, I was told that they thought the Brazilians wanted the canoes, and they believed that on a subsequent trip they would be paid with Western goods. They arrived home with numerous skin sores on their legs. A few months later missionaries ascended the river by canoe and established residence among this Yanomami group, being welcomed because they brought with them treasured Western goods.

Learning Xilixana History

One of my greatest difficulties in setting down details of the Xilixana's history was to give specific dates to events in the precontact period. I was told about isolated incidents from the past, but it was as if they floated in some ethereal time; they were hard to pin down. Much later, in the 1990s, the vague stories I had been told over time began to solidify into specific, marked events, and I probed to find their sequence.

Among others, I heard stories about a violent encounter with the Macuxi, or Macu, who lived further down the Uraricoera River. The Macuxi killed a Xilixana, which led to a revenge killing of a Macuxi on the part of the Xilixana. I heard stories about other raids and killings, of events that happened under sometimes mysterious circumstances. I learned that some time in the distant past (probably between 1875 and 1910) women had been acquired by both raid and payment from at least three different non-Xilixana villages. I heard about what appeared to be a significant event in the people's history: a raid and war with the Yekwana, which happened over a range of eight to sixteen months. Because of that Yekwana attack, the Xilixana had fled the Uraricoera watershed and come to the Mucajai region. The Xilixana often mentioned three other key events in their memory; they had found a cache of steel tools and a bolt of red cloth at the confluence of the Kloknai stream and Mucajai River; some years after that, many Xilixana had died in an epidemic; and, finally, they successfully contacted Brazilians and acquired some steel tools.

As a researcher I needed, as much as possible, to fix dates to the events that they had told me about—a difficult task given a people who do not identify the cycle of years, and whose numerical system is restricted to three amorphous terms: one, a few, and many. A key moment came when, after about two years of study, my colleague, John Early, found a Brazilian geography journal that reported a Brazilian Boundary Commission survey of October 1943 to February 1944. The journal entry provided a specific time-marker between the war with the Yekwana and the Xilixana contact with Brazilians downstream. This knowledge helped us date events such as births and deaths before and after the finding of these tools and red cloth. We also knew about a missionary air drop in January 1957, a date that allowed us to work back to the time when the Xilixana made their first contact with Brazilians. These were the only two precise dates we had.

John Early used the birth data between 1958 and 1987 to compute the average time between births for each childbearing woman (Early & Peters 1990: 42–47). From our data collected from 1958 to 1987 we also knew some women's exact birth dates, dates of puberty, and dates of first children. With these two time formulas we extrapolated births in the population back to about 1900. We also worked at getting dates for births and deaths before and after each of the time markers in the precontact time—the war with the Yekwana, and the Boundary Commission's cache (de Alguier 1944, Reis 1944). This step proved fruitful. We also asked informants about the sequence of births within each family. The task was made easier than it might otherwise have been because the Xilixana always identify sibling order through how they address one another: the Yanomami use two terms that distinctly identify the first and last-born children. Still, the task is complicated because when you ask a mother with five or more children to list them in sequence, she is likely to name at least one of her children twice.

The next point of my investigation was to place the entire population in a birth-order sequence, identifying who was born when. We checked and rechecked these reports over a five-year period. To this data I added the time when and the place where several women had their puberty, a marked event for Xilixana. They identified their field and yãno locations, first as on the headwaters of either the Uraricoera or Mucajai rivers, then on either the north

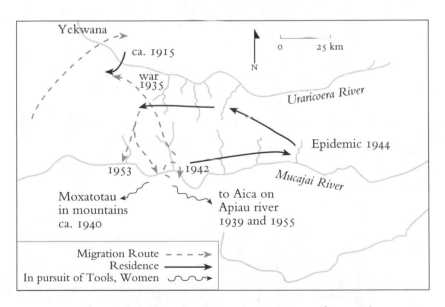

MAP 8.1 RESIDENTIAL REGIONS OF THE XILIXANA, 1875–1956

or south side of the Mucajai. Constructing a map, I followed the sequence of residences at locations on these streams. I made one further check. I located the births and deaths of Xilixana on many of these streams.

Using this data and computation, we designated 1931 as the year of the encounter with the Macu, 1935 as the year of the engagement with the Yekwana, and 1946 as the year of the epidemic. The epidemic was a key, we found out, because shortly after it, and because of it, they relocated once again, this time moving north from the Mucajai River to the Uraricoera watershed. In 1953 they returned to the general area where they had resided after fleeing the Yekwana about 1935 (see Map 8.1).

THE ENCOUNTER WITH THE MACU

The Macu lived some distance upstream from the Xilixana. In about 1930 a Macu family was paddling their canoe upstream, presumably after acquiring steel goods from Brazilians downriver. The Macu were blowing their cow horn, and the Ninam heard it and responded with a "Let's kill them" intent. They lured the Macu family of parents and three sons to the shore and asked for knives, promising them cotton from their yãno. The adult male and his two adolescent sons accompanied the Xilixana to the village, and en route the Xilixana said, "Look up to the ripe palm fruit." The father then looked up. They grabbed his hair, pulled his head back, breaking his back, then beat him to death with sticks and paddles. They did the same to his two sons.

One Xilixana, OL, stayed by the bank with the woman and the youngest child, because he wanted to take her as wife. After the killing incident the men returned to the canoe and asked the other Macu to come, because the father had called for them. After walking a short distance they broke the back of the young boy. The Xilixana covered any traces of the killings and left the bodies in the woods. Later they told me, "We don't bury other people." They used the Macu canoe for a while and later, to hide their actions, buried it in the water with rocks. The Yekwana report that they passed by this area by canoe shortly after and saw a number of vultures hovering. They were suspicious that some type of warfare must have transpired.

From these killings the Xilixana obtained four cutlasses, three small knives, and an axe, though it seems apparent that the Xilixana would have received some steel goods in trade if they had not resorted to the brutality. After all, the Macu responded readily to their invitation to come to the shore. The killing involved a certain deception as well as brutality. The males were all killed, even the youngest of the boys. The reasoning behind this taking of life is that captive men, though potential hunters and workers, have the potential to escape and avenge killings. Women are not likely to escape to distant home villages. The Macu woman was pregnant at the time of being captured, and when her child, a male, was born, he was kept alive. He proved to be an invaluable informant for my precontact data. This first son born among the Xilixana to this captive Macu claims his father is a Macu. After the birth of the second son to the Macu woman, the great war with the Yekwana took place.

From the point of view of the Xilixana, the primary concern in the killing was the acquisition of steel goods, and the gaining of a woman was secondary, which supports Ferguson's theory. The Macu themselves were apparently careful about foreigners intruding in their territory. One of them reported an incident in her younger years where her people killed a *naba* (ones who possessed steel goods). She also reported that in her youth she had visited the town of Boa Vista, presumably when her people had traded for steel tools. As a people the Macu are now extinct.[1]

Shortly after this incident the Xilixana moved from the north side of the river to the south side. The Macu woman lived in a quasi-group marriage relationship, the only known case among the Xilixana. She and another woman partnered two brothers, their individual hearths always being side by side as they moved from one yãno to another. Each woman identified one of the brothers as primary husband. The children of both women readily addressed each of the men as "father." After rearing several children, this Macu woman died in 1972; her two sons and two daughters were still living in the mid-1990s.

THE ENCOUNTER WITH THE YEKWANA

The Xilixana were living near the bank of the Uraricoera River in the early 1930s. It was reported that someone (a Yekwana) had attacked a Xilixana in his hammock and killed him. A man returning from retrieving honey in the rainforest saw the stranger in flight. One older informant gave the incident of a Yekwana killing two Xilixana while they were poisoning fish in a small creek. At another time a man was dragging sheaves of palm and their purple fruit, bacaba, back to his yãno. He was ambushed and killed, his eyes gouged out. The Xilixana did not know who the enemy might be. The Macu woman informed them that it could have been the Yekwana who lived further upstream. They were determined to take revenge.

The Xilixana lived in a very large yãno and celebrated in anticipation of the raid. They set up images of humans made of leaves, and shot at them. There was much excitement in the air. They made three bark canoes and travelled upriver for at least two days' journey. These water crafts were sluggish and moved slowly. From the bank of the river they saw a small dwelling in the distance, and observed it for a time. Later three women from this settlement embarked in a canoe. The women saw one of the foreign bark canoes (the other two were hidden) and paddled near the bank to investigate. The men greeted them with, "Come, Come." In fear one woman jumped into the water and clung to the canoe. The older woman was much bolder because she was *bata* (mature). The women headed upstream and the men in the cumbersome bark canoe slowly pursued them at an ever-increasing distance.

---

1 Note that the Xilixana informants' accounts of this raid do not correspond with the report given by Chagnon et al. (1970).

The men arrived on the island of the Yekwana dwelling. While meandering through the Yekwana field, a hungry Xilixana pulled a manioc root from the earth and ate it. Not knowing it was bitter manioc, he later became ill and died. Shortly thereafter the Yekwana men of the village, who had been off making a canoe, returned. According to custom, the Xilixana asked, "Are you friendly?" The hosts were hospitable and gave them drink. The Yekwana men, tired from their day's work, rested in the hammocks. OL walked over to his brother and said, "Look after the girl you want. Let's kill." To another he said, "Let's kill," and to another, "Guard the woman you want." They then killed "many" men in the house, and out by the canoes one young man was able to flee, eventually carrying the message of the killings to other Yekwana. (Another report says that the incident later became known when other Yekwana who were travelling the river stopped in to visit, and to their horror saw the bodies.)

The Xilixana took the four women, including one young male child belonging to the older woman, and returned to their village. One of the captive women had been visiting this small group of Yekwana from her home in Venezuela on the Paragua River, which flows north into the Orinoco River basin. Some time later one of the men who claimed one of the captive women killed the Yekwana male child in his field. They acquired axes and knives on this raid. They fully anticipated a revenge attack. It did not occur for some months.

One rainy morning the inevitable surprise attack occurred. While the people of only one Xilixana village had made the attack against the Yekwana, all three villages became embroiled in this revenge assault. Although the Xilixana resisted ferociously, they were victims of the gun-toting Yekwana. The Xilixana fired with bows and arrows from their yãno. Fortunately for the Xilixana, that morning a group was out hunting and another group had vacated the yãno to poison fish. With the sound of gun shots they returned, encircling the trails where the Yekwana would take flight after the attack. They waited in the dark, and they eventually heard one lone Yekwana, passing by and carrying a stolen bunch of bananas, coughing. The Xilixana were delighted with this prospective victim. They jumped upon him in ambush. He finally died in a sitting position with a spear pushed through him vertically, beginning at the shoulder blade, then through the liver and anus and into the ground. They also killed other Yekwana. The Xilixana placed the heads of the Yekwana on sticks along the four paths that led from the Xilixana village in the direction of the Yekwana.

Both sides suffered severe losses. At least seven Xilixana were killed, in addition to one of the three Yekwana women taken captive earlier. Two Xilixana women carried gunshot imbedded in their flesh until their deaths in the 1980s.

On my 1995 field trip the only remaining Yekwana fugitive, whose real home was on the Paragua River in Venezuela, told me that she was not present at the site of the shooting. She said she would have fled with the Yekwana warriors had she been around. Among the Xilixana victims was Elema, the great shaman and husband to six women.

Immediately after this raid the entire population relocated at some distance, two groups moving to the watershed of the Mucajai and the other to the east, some distance inland from the Uraricoera River. Many months later some Xilixana returned to the earlier location and saw human feces throughout the house, including on artifacts used in processing cassava. They assumed the intruders were Yekwana.

It would appear that Ferguson's model of killing for the sake of gaining steel goods best fits this warfare. In the story of the encounters with the Macu and Yekwana it is clear that the Xilixana sought valued steel goods, and, indeed, they acquired axes, knives, dogs, four adzes, and one grater board. The revenge and the taking of captive women were secondary to the initial blood-shed for the sake of acquiring steel tools. Still, the Xilixana considered both these peoples to be *naba*. Unlike the Xilixana, both groups were adept at making good canoes. (Periodically they made trips far downriver to Boa Vista to replenish their supply of steel tools.) The Yekwana had guns. Despite the disadvantage in weaponry the Xilixana went to great risk to acquire steel goods.

There is a further puzzle to our research on war, especially as it pertains to the Xilixana. After the Yekwana encounters the Xilixana remained isolated from any indigenous and "civilized" peoples for over 20 years, or one whole generation. It seems that the trauma of the Yekwana war had a long-term effect—so much so that they did not attempt to raid the Xiliana, whose general whereabouts they knew.

At least one other interesting episode took place between the Yekwana and Xilixana in the postcontact period at Mucajai. The same missionary agency that functions at Mucajai opened a station in 1962 among the Yekwana and Sanuma (Yanomami) in the extreme northern tip of the Brazilian territory bordering Venezuela. On one flight from Boa Vista to this distant post the airplane stopped at Mucajai and by coincidence had a Yekwana man on board. I encouraged the Yekwana captive woman of almost 30 years' residence at Mucajai to converse with this Yekwana passenger, and, although with great fear, she did comply with my request. In 1991 some Xilixana met Yekwana at the Casa do Índio in Boa Vista, and the atmosphere was more amiable. In 1993, at the invitation of the Yekwana this same captive woman, now an elderly widow, travelled with her adult children and João, a Xilixana headman and son of a deceased Yekwana captive woman, to visit the Yekwana on the Uraricoera, at a site upstream from the location of the earlier warfare. On this visit they appreciated the prized grater boards and large baskets given them by the Yekwana. There was some discussion of a Yekwana taking a Xilixana woman as wife, but the arrangement never transpired.

The Early History

At the turn of the twentieth century the Xilixana lived similarly to the other Yanomami of Brazil and Venezuela. They hunted and, by using slash-and-burn methods, grew crops of manioc, banana, sugar cane, and yams. They feared their enemies—they feared their raids and witchcraft—and in turn they raided and practised sorcery on their enemies. During those early times steel goods were scarce.

At the turn of the century and for the subsequent two decades the Xilixana were located in the environs of the mid-Uraricoera River. The Xiliana located themselves in the region of the watersheds of the Amazon and Orinoco rivers, where they live to this day.

Several Xiliana villages are located on the Erico River, which flows south into the Uraricoera River. It appears that for more than a generation the Xilixana had frequent contact with these Xiliana. The Xiliana-Xilixana ties are significant in that they are the only Yanomami groups to speak the same Ninam dialect. Like known links between other Yanomami villages, the Xilixana and Xiliana relations were friendly and congenial, and they joined in the yãimo together. Several Xiliana migrated to the Xilixana in the Uraricoera region, and when a noted Xilixana shaman copulated with a Xiliana during a yãimo, the woman conceived and bore a child in her village. (As a grown man and shaman this adult Xiliana connected with the Xilixana in 1961 at the Mucajai station.) However, as is also common among Yanomami, the friendships formed were fragile and affairs and raids and warfare could just as easily transpire: the stealing of women and killing of men. Such tensions led to a separation between these two groups, probably around 1910.[2]

The Xilixana were aware that other indigenous peoples traversed the river, but habitual conflict, including bloody wars between the Xiliana and Xilixana, and the broad expanse of the river for people without canoes, proved to be a barrier to frequent contact after about 1915. They did, however, make contact with other Yanomami who did not speak their dialect. These Yanomami were identified as Waica and were probably people of the central Yanomami district, belonging to groups known as the Wehewe, Thomula, Sithethem, Matalam, and Wakobosibi. Relationships were, again, mixed—friendly and antagonistic, with festivals as well as raids and warfare. The Xilixana acquired wives from the Wehewe and Ahusi bèk (or Wapalum theli). At some point one Xilixana shaman, Elema, was said to be engaged in warfare with the Xiliana, killing many. The Xilixana fled from the Xiliana, moving from the north to the south side of the Uraricoera River.

At some point a group of Xilixana had been fishing downstream from their dwelling, and strangers came, made a raid, and stole a Xilixana woman. Soon thereafter the Xilixana took revenge by killing a male and female. The Xilixana suspect the enemy were the Macuxi from the lower Uraricoera

---

2 Early and Peters (2000) presents the Xilixana and Ninam history prior to 1990. Xilixana informants report that they come from the Surucucu region, and after conflict and warfare among their own people, fled northeast to the Uraricoera watershed. They state that Yekwana contact was first made about 1935. The study of Chagnon et al. (1970) shows the gene flow of the Carib Yekwana and Ninam to have meshed since both Sanuma and Yekwana lived in close proximity. However, the Sanuma and Ninam, while both Yanomami, are different people.

River. They reported seeing large hoofprints, which they later came to believe were made by cattle.

They also report two immense forest fires. The first, which seems to have occurred around the turn of the century, is said to have produced heavy smoke. The second fire occurred, they say, after a young man was bitten by a snake. The father of the deceased, a shaman, called his *hekula* to smite the earth with fire to burn the snake, and the Xilixana eventually put out this fire with the aid of water.

The earliest record of non-indigenous people travelling the Uraricoera River was in 1787 and involved the Portuguese Boundary Commission. In 1838 and 1839 Robert Schomburgk made an expedition up this river, into Venezuela and down the Rio Negro, a large affluent of the Amazon River. The party reported meeting "kirishana" (Xilixana) at the mouth of the Uraracaá River, which flows south from the Venezuela border into the Uraricoera River. In 1911-12 Kock-Grünberg also went up the Uraricoera and reported meeting Xilixana (his spelling was "Shiriana") at the mouth of the Motomoto River. He found them to be "dirty" (Rice 1928). Kock-Grünberg met two groups of Xiliana, describing them as being "very warlike people who succeeded in dominating several weaker tribes" (Steward 1963: 861). In 1924-25 Hamilton Rice followed a route similar to Schomburgk's, meeting Xiliana on the Uraracaá River. According to Rice they used stone graters to process manioc; and they used peccary teeth as a rasp, much like the ones I witnessed in 1958 among the Xilixana on the Mucajai River. Rice reported meeting two different groups of Xiliana with markedly different behaviors. One group strongly resisted any picture-taking. Rice reported that the Xiliana may have pushed the "Maku" (as he spelled "Macu") further upriver. He also encountered a village of some 50 people near the headwaters of the Parima (or Uraricoera) River. These people, he said, drank fermented banana drink and were dirty, repulsive, and repellent (Rice 1928: 216). He believed this village was a Waika area, and considered its inhabitants to be more warlike than the Xilixana.

Throughout the 1920s and 1930s the Xilixana lived on the streams that flowed north into the Uraricoera River, between about 3° and 3° 20' north latitude. (See Map 8.1 for Xilixana locations between 1875 and 1956.) They had no canoes, but were well aware that people further downstream had steel goods. In some of their more lengthy easterly hunting escapades they encountered tracks of an animal even larger than a tapir. Only after the acquisition of two Macu women captives (ca. 1931) did they learn that these animals were cattle. By the 1920s the Xilixana were all living in one general area, but in three separate yãnos with frequent communication between one another. By 1934 the three Xilixana villages numbered about 12, 35, and 56, for a total of 103 (Early & Peters 2000).

The smaller village was identified as the Kooxuma, named after one of its headmen. Its people had their origin in the migration of a couple of Xiliana men to the Xilixana group, most likely shortly after the turn of the century. The second group was known as Kasilapai—a word meaning "long lips" and stemming from the large wad of tobacco, measuring up to eight centimeters in length, that the men inserted into their mouths and lower lips. All men in all three groups sucked tobacco in this manner. Since the time of contact the Kasilapai have not appreciated this nomenclature and prefer to be called Amnas bèk or Oliak bèk, non-derogatory terms associated with specific regions of residence. The last person specifically identified as a Kasilapai, a woman, died at about age 60 soon after contact. The third and largest group was the Alam pèk and Buxenawah bèk, named after the regions they lived in, but they acquired the name Bola bèk, meaning people of the rapids, shortly after 1936 when they moved to the Mucajai River region and began using canoes. At the time of contact the three groups together called themselves "Xidjan," which we recognize as an abbreviation of Xilixana.

The Xiliana and Other Encounters

With time the Xilixana had criss-crossed a very large forest area. Old and abandoned habitats would be revisited, first to get arrows from the field and, later, to harvest the valued peach palm fruit from the planted sliver-spiked palm tree. Therefore, between 1930 to the present, the Xilixana had traversed and become very familiar with all of the region between the Uraricoera and Mucajai rivers, as well as possibly 15 kilometers south of the Mucajai River, covering a strip of about 100 kilometers east to west. To our knowledge no other peoples have inhabited this area over the past century.[3]

In the period before the crafty capture of a Macu woman (1931) we know that each of the Xilixana and Xiliana regions had several villages or yãnos, with some contact between them, though the frequency is unknown. They also had contact with Waica Yanomami. We have records of some ten villages of the Xiliana, Xilixana, and Waica peoples. Several village groups are relevant to Xilixana history: Gilinai, Mokak, Wakoposipii, Thomula, Sithethem, Matalam, Waiyahanakuma, Minaii, Helewas, Koliak, Ahûxi, and Wehewe. Only the Gilinai survive as a group today. The Wehewe lived further down the Uraricoera, and spoke a different language. There were alliances as well as raids and warfare in this network of Xiliana-Xilixana-Waica villages.

At the time of contact the Xilixana had several men and women in their ancestry who were acquired in the late 19th or early 20th centuries from the Waica and Xiliana. Some women migrated under congenial conditions through bride price and bride service. Others were victims of raids and warfare. These women contributed to the fertility of the Xilixana population. At least two Xiliana men migrated to live with Xilixana women, one of whom died just before the contact period.

---

3   Restricting their territory by some state law to their residence over the past 10 or even 30 years would be inappropriate, unrealistic, and unjust. The Yanomami Park, passed by law in 1991, restricts Xilixana land to the watershed of the Mucajai, for about 65 kilometers along the river, and an area about 65 kilometers north and south. The mission post is at the approximate center of this area.

Periodically the Xiliana and Xilixana met for the yãimo festivity. To this day Yanomami travel great distances for this event of feasting, trading, gossip, and sexual license. Sometime after the turn of the century a Xilixana fathered a male child with a Xiliana, a woman who was still alive in the 1960s. Similarly, a Xiliana male fathered a male child among the Xilixana sometime in the very early 1920s. This child died as an adult after the missionaries established themselves on the Mucajai River. After the late 1920s there was no contact between these two Ninam-speaking groups until missionaries arrived in each of these two regions in the late 1950s. These historical connections of sexual bonding remained dormant for about four decades and eventually led to a few exuberant and tension-laden reciprocated visits between the two groups in the early 1960s.

One of Elema's wives and his nine sons and two daughters were still living in 1958. They and their offspring formed the greater proportion of the Xilixana population at that time. Following the strict rules of incest, it was difficult for them and many of their sons to find marriage partners in the three decades following the Yekwana war. Incest rules and the practice of selective female infanticide produced a serious sexual imbalance, which resulted in the practice of polyandry (Peters and Hunt 1975; Peters 1982). The relocation marked the beginning of more than two decades of isolation for the Xilixana.

In the period of isolation the Xilixana made several unsuccessful attempts to either raid for women or find a source of steel goods. About 1940 the Xilixana trekked southwest overland to the Aica, who resided on a distinct mountain, a mountain they could see from a long distance away. A large entourage of men from all three villages travelled the long (55 kilometers by air) journey through a terrain with no previously established trails, southwest to the Moxatotau in what was unquestionably a raid to acquire wives. They did see the Moxatotau people, exchanged arrows, but no one was killed. They returned to their homes, exhausted and extremely hungry. The Xilixana continue to live in fear of the Moxatotau. Even much later, in 1961, because of this fear they moved from the south to the north bank of the river, telling the missionaries present that they might be attacked.

The Xilixana were not engaged in warfare, alliances, immigration of women, and trading of any kind with other Yanomami, other indigenous people, or Brazilians for over a two-decade period. After the Yekwana war the Kasilapai and Bola bèk villages fled the Uraricoera watershed region for the Kloknai creek, which flows into the Mucajai River. Some years later they moved out of this region. The Bola bèk again returned to this region in 1953, near the location where the Kloknai stream meets the river. Five years later the missionaries established a station at this site.

After the Yekwana war the Kooxuma village remained on the Uraricoera watershed. They were reported as not being afraid of the Yekwana. However they continued to associate from time to time with the other two villages, especially the Kasilapai. After being geographically distant for several years, the Kooxuma moved much closer to the Kasilapai village. From that time, and until they contacted Brazilians on the lower Mucajai River, the distance between these two groups varied: at times close to one another and at other times up to five days of walk away.

During this period the relationship between the villages fluctuated frequently between friendliness and hostility, but never reached the point of raids and warfare. From time to time they visited one another. They celebrated the yãimo festival together, during which the men would sniff the drug ebene. They also had the usual fisticuff and chest-hitting duels. They made attempts to negotiate young women for marriage. When expectations for a woman were thwarted, hostility and animosity would surface, often continuing for years. Many harsh words, rumors, and condemning stories were exchanged. Because of this geographical separation and animosity, the groups remain distinct as the Kasilapai (including the Kooxuma) and the Bola bèk. There is much drama as well as social meaning in these formal, festive visits. This is all part of normative Yanomami life. The three groups never killed or seriously maimed one another.

For a very brief period of time before the 1940s the Bola bèk and Kasilapai crossed the river to live on the south side of the Mucajai. For the first time they built their own canoes to hunt and travel. From this location they made more distant trips to the Moxatotau and later to the Aica on the Apiau River, a large tributary of the Mucajai.

While the Bola bèk were living a little upstream from the mouth of the Kloknai stream, an event took place that proved a surprise and joy to the Xilixana. One day in late 1942 or early 1943 TI walked to the mouth of the stream and, to his great surprise, saw several knives and axes lying on the ground, and a bolt of red cloth extended from a nearby tree. (A Xilixana pointed out the exact tree to me in 1996.) With great glee he returned to tell his kinsmen, who together returned for the big find. This was timely, because their tools from the Macu and Yekwana killings a decade earlier had become worn, dull, and broken. The Kasilapai and Kooxuma were visiting at the time, and the gifts were shared. The long bolt of cloth was torn up into pieces to make loin coverings, which were proudly worn by the men. The goods, we eventually found out, had been left by the Brazilian Boundary Commission in late 1942.

Shortly after the red cloth incident the Xilixana moved eastward, again to streams that flowed into the north bank of the Mucajai River. One young man died from a snake bite. Shortly after that a large number of people, especially the elderly, became extremely weak and ill for no known reason. They report no external evidence of skin sores, diarrhea, or vomiting. About a half-dozen Xilixana died. Their symptoms strongly suggest they had contracted malaria. Around the same time some other strange things happened. They saw an airplane flying over their lands. One woman was reportedly grabbed in her field by a clothed man and was only released with the assistance of another woman who happened to be nearby at the time. By the 1990s this story had become embellished to unbelievable proportions. For one thing, the aircraft had become a helicopter, although the incident predated the invention of the helicopter by several years—an example of how oral tradition can stray from fact.

Further away, on the bank of the Mucajai River, the Xilixana saw a shelter that had been inhabited by these foreigners. They did not encounter anyone except the man in the field. They found tin cans in the area, and the Xilixana used some of them to cut meat for a brief period of time.

The people were annoyed by these incidents and believed that they were related. As a result of the many deaths, the three villages of just over one hundred people burned their houses and fled northwest to streams that emptied into the Uraricoera River. About this time, they say, a young Kasilapai male was killed by a jaguar. For the next decade they remained in the forest, in the watershed between the two main rivers. The Kooxuma and Kasilapai lived relatively close to one another, while the Bola bèk remained somewhat separate. For the ensuing years they reunited for visits and for the yãimo and kept abreast of one another's experiences.

About 1953 the Bola bèk village moved back to the Kroknai stream region and constructed a field and house near the bank of the Mucajai River. This specific area later became an airstrip and permanent mission station. About the same time the Kasilapai and Kooxuma villages also left the Uraricoera watershed and moved south to the Peiwa stream, which empties into the Mucajai about 16 kilometers upstream from the Bola bèk village. The two groups were now separated by a day's walk. They again built canoes to use to travel to places where they could hunt tapir and to maneuver on the river and larger streams. They did not yet use the canoe for fishing, because they had no fish hooks, lines, or nets. They fished by building a raised platform two meters in height on the edge of the river and shooting fish with bow and arrow.

The animosity between the peoples of the two locations was evident in at least one recorded incident. The Bola bèk went upriver and smashed one of the canoes belonging to the Kasilapai. Recognizing the scarcity of canoe-making hardware, this was a serious provocation. The latter group retaliated with the same treatment to a Bola bèk canoe.

Quest for Tools

By the mid- to late 1950s their metal tools had again become crude, few, and worn. A younger generation of men had emerged since the warfare with the Yekwana. It had been about 23 years since the acquisition of tools from the Yekwana and 13 years since the Boundary Commission cache. The young men recognized the efficiency of using newer axes and knives for field and canoe construction. Where could they once again acquire these tools? In 1956 a group of seven Kasilapai and Kooxuma men crossed the river and headed southeast to the Apiau River. They met some Apiau Yanomami women, who told them to leave before their men arrived—their husbands would shoot to kill. The women said that steel goods were obtainable further down the Apiau River. Carrying on, the travellers saw an encampment of Brazilian lumber cutters or rubber workers, but met no one, though they saw evidence that Brazilians had recently been in the region. One man dared to steal a wash basin, for which the others chastised him. They returned by foot to their territory on the Mucajai, disappointed in their futile attempt to get steel tools. The man with the basin died shortly after returning, and his death became attributed to Brazilian sorcery brought on because he had stolen the basin.

In 1956, encouraged by the discovery of the Brazilian presence on the Apiau River, a larger contingency of men from all three villages left shortly after the first group's return. Their spirits were dampened when they returned without seeing Yanomami or the "people who make knives." Within five or six days after their return, an airplane buzzed their field and dropped fish hooks. (This was the aerial survey done by the Protestant missionaries in January 1957.) Their hopes for metal goods were once more renewed. The Yekwana captive women, now fully integrated into Yanomami life, urged the Xilixana to travel by canoe downstream to contact the "metal-makers." That same year a number of Kasilapai and Kooxuma descended the Mucajai, portaging around the massive waterfalls known as "the Wall," which marked a boundary past which few Brazilians had ever paddled. After passing the Wall, the Xilixana were shocked to see evidence of the large fresh-water porpoise (Phocoena), which snorted and shot water above the surface of the water. They met some Brazilians, and the encounter was successful: they received four small knives, five long knives, an axe, and some clothing. After that they paddled back upstream. In their home territory they encountered the Bola bèk, who were angry for not being informed about the expedition.

Kooxuma caught a cold and died. The remaining people of his village, including Kooxuma's widow and children, abandoned the house and joined the Kasilapai. Shortly thereafter men from each of the villages and two middle-aged women made the trip down to meet the Brazilians. The next season another large group, this time including a number of younger men, went downriver. As on previous trips the Xilixana and Brazilians showed caution and apprehension, especially because they had no common language. On this third trip several middle-aged men felt the Brazilians were stingy in not giving more tools, and they fashioned a plot to kill the Brazilians. The plot was subverted by the younger men among them, who insisted that the frontier farmers wished them to return to work and thus earn some more trade goods. They left their canoes with the Brazilians and walked back through the jungle, arriving home with many sores on their legs. Some said they walked to avoid the hot sun on the open river. Others said the Brazilians wanted the canoes. Upon returning, a mature adult Bola bèk male died from contracting the cold.

Just before contact the Kooxuma village numbered 17 inhabitants. When the leader and two other males died of pneumonia shortly after their first trip downstream the small village, now with 14 people, abandoned their yãno and joined the village of the Kasilapai. They lived up the river from the Bola bèk village, on the Peiwei stream. The Bola bèk village is the location where the missionaries would begin their residence in November 1958.

Nine
Postcontact History: Enter the Missionaries

The expedition of the Protestant missionaries into Yanomami territory was by no means a haphazard event. The very nature of mission work in the forest region necessitated a support staff.

The Brazilian government did not know precisely which tribes or how many indigenous peoples inhabited the frontier region. Generally the state authorities feared the aboriginals of the rainforest, or saw them as savage, and therefore tended to ignore and avoid them.

The initial players in the saga of the contact with the Mucajai River Yanomami were Neill Hawkins and myself. Neill, an American, married with four children, was a veteran missionary, fluent in Portuguese, knowledgeable of Brazilian custom, and familiar with preliterate South American peoples. He and his wife had first arrived in Brazil in 1944, and he spent the academic year of 1951 in studies at the University of São Paulo.

In 1955 Neill gained written permission from the Brazilian Indian Protection Service (SPI) "to travel among Indians with the purpose of studying their location and eventually of installing services of social and religious assistance" (Hawkins 1955). This included the region of the Yanomami. Through the literature of the Unevangelized Fields Mission (UFM, now UFM International) in North America, Neill requested that 20 young people join in the challenge of Indian work in north Brazil. Sustaining mission work in these isolated regions depended upon aviation. A North American air service organization for missionaries, Missionary Aviation Fellowship (later incorporated in Brazil as Asas de Socorro—"Wings of Aid"), was invited to assist.

In January 1957 the UFM, in cooperation with the Mission Aviation Fellowship (MAF), made a two-day aerial survey of the entire Yanomami region in the Brazilian territory of Roraima. The Brazilian government had granted permission for the survey as well as for the mission's future presence among interior, previously uncontacted indigenous peoples in Roraima territory. The UFM had already established a mission in neighboring Guyana, among the rainforest WaiWai and savannah Macuxi, giving evidence of the organization's long-term commitment to indigenous peoples.

The aerial survey showed a variety of Indian houses in the region. Ten months later two missionaries and two WaiWai guides opened the first mission station among the Aicas on the Uraricoera River. In October of the following year a second aerial survey was made in the Mucajai and Apiau rivers and contact was made with the Xilixana on the Mucajai on November 20, 1958.

Missionary Contact with the Xilixana

The first missionaries targeted for work among Yanomami arrived in 1957, setting up a base on the savannah in Bonfim, Brazil, close to the border with Guyana, where they worked at Portuguese-language learning and acculturation to life in Brazil. They did jungle training among the WaiWai in Guyana. Three Americans—a couple and a single woman as their linguist—moved on in March 1958 to establish the first jungle station on the Uraricoera, near a Palimi theli village. One of the first things they did was build an airstrip about 240 meters long. Several years later these Palimi theli and missionaries relocated.

I arrived a year after the first missionaries—young, single (at least temporarily), adventurous, and idealistic. Based on my three weeks of training among the WaiWai I believed that the jungle and I were a good fit. In mid-1958 we heard reports that aboriginals had appeared earlier on the lower Mucajai River. To get more information about this group, Neill Hawkins made a special trip to Boa Vista, to visit the Brazilian family involved in the contact on the lower Mucajai River. He found out that these Brazilian frontier people had been frightened by the Xilixana visitors, and particularly by the quantity and length of their bows and arrows. The bows, he heard, towered above the heads of the warriors. The Xilixana were also, apparently, apprehensive about the contact. Only men had ventured downstream on the first trip in 1956. On a second trip two women and a number of younger men accompanied the adult men.

In early autumn 1958, after Hawkins' return from his trip to the Brazilian family who had met the distant rainforest inhabitants, he and I embarked on the aerial survey of the Apiau and Mucajai rivers, trying to determine just where we should launch an expedition. The answer soon became obvious. We dropped gifts—metal knives, fish hooks, beads, and a few scissors—attracting people at the village sites we saw (Early & Peters 1990: 7-8). When we circled one of the two small villages on the Apiau, we saw a man with a drawn arrow pointing at our aircraft. We circled a second time, not quite as low, and the warrior was still there, still threatening to shoot. His response suggested a certain hostility to the approach of strangers—which we later learned might have been because of previous unfriendly contacts with Brazilian rubber cutters. From there we flew northwest to the Mucajai River and sighted a large cone-shaped habitat. We dropped gifts both in the field and into the river, and canoeists enthusiastically retrieved the gifts dropped in the river. I was amazed at how capably they manipulated their canoes. We were impressed by a man who emerged from the big house, extending a stalk of bananas above his head, obviously meant as a gift. We interpreted this act as goodwill, circled the village several more times, and returned to our base in the east.

After returning to the base, we quickly finalized plans for the expedition and embarked, in November 1958, with two WaiWai as guides and companions. The route leading to our destination meant travelling for a day's duration down the sandy banked and sometimes shallow Tacutú River, which bordered Brazil and Guyana. Due to our lack of experience, we broke about 60 percent of our supply of springs used for the function of the motor's propeller, in shallow sandy water. We continued into the larger Rio Branco River until Boa Vista, where we stocked up on gasoline and other supplies. We canoed further down the wide river until we reached the mouth of the Mucajai River, where our upstream journey began, at a much slower rate. We passed a few ranches, a number of canoes, a covered river boat that was being used to sell goods to the river dwellers, and several farmers' fields of rice, bananas, and manioc. After a couple of days we were seeing fewer farms. We stopped at the home of the Brazilian people Neill had visited just two months earlier in Boa Vista. Two young Brazilian men agreed to accompany and assist us on the journey upstream. One had met the forest men on their earlier visits, and we hoped this link might help us make a friendly contact with the people upstream.

The first large challenge we encountered on our seven-day journey, about a day's travel beyond the last dwellings of the Brazilians, was the huge series of falls known as the "Paredão," or "Wall." Even though the early group of indigenous travellers had cut a wide path with cross-layed trees through the forest to skid their canoes, our group of six found the task of moving through this area to be formidable, to say the least. Our canoe and equipment were heavy and awkward nuisances. For a time I found myself feeling quite overcome by the difficulties of this travel into the unknown, particularly in negotiating the portage of "the Wall," and I began to think that we should terminate the expedition. Fortunately, I kept these thoughts to myself and didn't mention my reservations to my senior colleague.

After ascending "the Wall" the two Brazilian men decided to return downriver, in part because they were apprehensive about meeting the people upriver. That left us to battle the swift water currents and the uncertainty of the unknown without their capable assistance. We continued upriver in our dugout canoe, powered by a trustworthy two and a half HP Scott outboard engine. The motor proved adequate for the normal flow of the river, but lacked power to push through any rapids. We had to get out into the water and tug and pull the canoe through one set of rapids after another. At least we didn't go hungry: we were amply provided with fish and birds from the water and forest. Our guides were proficient hunters, fishers, river travellers, and companions.

The WaiWai showed symptoms of having colds, so we camped by the river for two days. We did not want to bring this sickness to the tribe. The WaiWai guides had already pointed out signs of human habitation, so we knew we were nearing our destination. I was both excited and apprehensive about the imminent meeting. Would the people we were going to find prove to be friendly, or "killers" as the Brazilians downstream feared? About this time I got a bout of diarrhoea, and once, while chest deep in water pushing the canoe, I had to yield to the body's natural forces.

We soon encountered a section of the river that separated out into five channels, broken up by islands. We decided to select what appeared to be the least treacherous. Our only consolation was the knowledge that just beyond the islands we would find the site of the natives we had seen in the aerial survey just a month earlier. We confirmed our expectations by spotting a small shelter on rocks in the center of the river, a landmark from the survey. We also saw two small but well-used landings on the north and south banks of the river, places where the local inhabitants docked as they went to and from their fields and houses. But as yet we has seen no people. Our sense of anxiety and apprehension escalated.

We shouted out from the canoe in the center of the river, but got no response. Were people hiding in the green of the thick forest foliage? Would there be an ambush? I felt some fear when I heard the leaves shuffle on the distant shore (or was that my imagination?), and I was certain some native was simply taking a better aim along the shaft of his arrow before he would release his fingers from the taut, and very large, drawn bow. We called out some more, and held out a machete as a sign of a gift. We decided not to walk along the well-trodden path that we knew led to their yãno. Instead we crossed the river, tied the canoe to a tree, and cautiously walked along a trail to a field. We didn't meet anyone or see any trace of recent human activity. We returned to the canoe and discussed our options. We decided we might find greater safety by camping on an island about 300 meters downstream.

The next day we went into the center of the river and called out again from the canoe. Later we walked once more to the field on the north side of the river, then went into the forest a short way to see about finding a suitable place for an airstrip. It was extremely difficult, while completely surrounded by trees, to envision a 300-plus-meter flat surface with appropriate approaches. We had a small, hand, topographical level-device that gave us a better idea of how land would slope after a straight meter-wide swath had been cleared in the forest.

The following day our hosts appeared at about 3:30 in the afternoon. We found out later they had returned to their more permanent yãno from a yãimo event at a new field and yãno to the south. They were ecstatic in their greeting and we were happy, and relieved, to find the warm reception. We gave a cutlass to a man who seemed to be the headman and promised other trade goods. We showed them a model airplane, and they quickly identified it as being just like the one that had dropped gifts a few weeks earlier. We tried to communicate our desire to set up residence and to clear a large path in the jungle that would allow an airplane to land. If they would help us, we would give them axes and knives. These people, we found, called themselves "Xilixana."

Our hosts were more intrigued with the WaiWai men than with us. They admired the strings of beads each of the WaiWai wore around his ankles and wrists. The WaiWai permitted the Xilixana to wrap the beads on their bodies. After a while, several people left—later on the WaiWai discovered that a few of the men had carried off some of their beads. There was a lot of chatter by the remaining group, which was, of course, incomprehensible to us.

A few days later we discovered a fact that would have implications for all our future relations with these peoples. The people we met came from two distinct villages. The Xilixana who lived in the immediate area called themselves Bola bèk, the people of the rapids. The others were Kasilapai, and they lived a day's journey upstream. We found that there were kin ties between the two groups.

The next morning all the men seemed enthusiastic about beginning the work program. Men from both villages participated, although the Bola bèk were much more active. They often scorned the Kasilapai. Work on the airstrip proceeded well, though one incident proved to be sobering, almost fatal. On December 1 many of the Xilixana had gone into the woods to hunt. Neill and I took a chain-saw to an island to cut some of the taller trees to clear the approach to the airstrip. One tall tree with a broad trunk started to fall in an unexpected direction, and I couldn't get out of the way—one of its primary branches, just at the point where it met the tree trunk, pinned my right lower leg to the ground. Neill got me out from under the tree, then went for some men to help carry me out. In the end I was restricted to my hammock for several days, and work on the airstrip was curtailed for a while. Neill told me a few months later that he had given serious thought to abandoning the entire project and returning downriver. Although I recovered, the injury turned out to be slightly more serious than I thought. Several years later, during a medical checkup in Canada, I was advised that my fibula had been either broken or seriously fractured.

During the days of my convalescence many Xilixana, particularly the young men between 15 and 25 years of age, visited me on the island where we had set up camp. I used the opportunity to expand my vocabulary, especially the names of the animals and birds of the forest. Time passed, and about two weeks later the airplane returned and dropped food, medicine, and more trade goods. We used the trade goods to buy local fruit and cassava bread. We introduced cotton line and fish hooks to the Xilixana.

The Xilixana enjoyed watching our elementary culinary endeavors, especially our mix of batter for pancakes with cooking oil dropped on the skillet. They wondered why we used paper and pen so frequently. They showed no hesitation when we offered to place salve on their wounds. They swallowed pills. They accepted our recommendation for penicillin injections in a very practical manner. Neill had a boil on his back, and in almost ritual fashion, making sure the Xilixana would take notice, I gave Neill a daily injection, pointing regularly to the diminishing infection. After that example the Xilixana had no hesitancy about taking penicillin injections for medicinal purposes.

During my recovery from the tree accident the two WaiWai, Neill, and I, accompanied by several Xilixana, hiked for over three hours to their new dwelling—the one in which they were having a yãimo when we arrived. A new field surrounded the large-leafed yãno. This walk provided a good test for the capability of my pained right lower leg.

The presence of the WaiWai proved helpful for our emerging relationships. Once in a while during the early weeks of our stay the WaiWai accompanied the Bola bèk young men on short hunting trips. The WaiWai used shotguns to hunt, and they found an abundance of piping guan (bush chicken) in the immediate area. Their culture was similar in so many ways, and despite the language barrier they communicated well.

After the airstrip clearing reached about 50 meters, the Xilixana asked us to call the plane. Quite understandably, they had no way of recognizing the immensity of the task involved in making the area suitable for a landing. Felling the trees, bucking, rolling the logs off the strip, burning the brush, and digging out all roots within 10 centimeters of the surface of the earth without the aid of tractor, mule, or wheelbarrow: these jobs proved a monumental feat.

We had no radio contact, but had scheduled an air drop for about a month after the time we left the base. When that day came, the sky was clear, and we became excited as we heard the hum of the plane in the distance. Before our departure, we had arranged for the pilot to ask specific questions by means of a loudspeaker attached to the strut of the aircraft: Are you well? Are the people friendly? Should we drop the food? Do you want all the medicine? All the axes? The knives? Do we continue with our prearranged plans of another flight and air drop on January 1?

We used a ground sheet to answer, showing yellow for "yes" and blue for "no," and the plane dropped our supplies and mail in several passes. (One box of axes landed in the trees. The Xilixana recovered them, but only told us about their find a few years later.) The pilot circled the area and slowly dropped a bag by wire to us—a manoeuvre we had practised on the savannah before our departure. We placed our mail into the bag and the pilot then reeled the wire back into the airplane as he took off to return to what then seemed to us a remote civilization.[1] That day of contact with "one of our own" was extremely significant to us, even though the colleagues and the lifeline were 300 meters above us in the sky.

By mid-January 1959 we had completed 200 meters of airstrip and the airplane was able to land, again with much excitement on the part of both the local people and ourselves. To their amazement a human being stepped out from the bowels of the "yellow parrot" Piper Cub. We exchanged information with the pilot and his assistant about the events of the past two months.

---

1   For me this mailing was remarkable. I sent a letter to my future parents-in-law indicating my desire to marry their daughter Lorraine. Possibly this is the only such "bucket drop mail service" ever used in match making!

We paced the cleared area and discussed the condition and potential of the airstrip. It soon became evident that the airstrip site we had chosen would only be of temporary value. The strip could not be extended on either end. There was a huge hill at one end, and a deep drop on the other.

Some 12 days later we had the strip in a condition good enough for another colleague, Don Borgman, to fly in and for Neill to return to the Guyana-Brazil border base to resume his leadership responsibilities. We soon began construction on another site, starting at the eastern end of the existing airstrip and moving about 20 degrees to the left, thus avoiding the hill. The Bola bèk consented to our request to cut through a segment of their field, and in return we paid them with goods.

It was evident that the local people were grateful for our presence, which for them meant new and continual access to metal goods and beads. Along with medical work, trading, and house construction, we launched a serious campaign to learn the language and reduce it to writing. We made every effort to not only speak Yanomami, but also to understand the culture, folkways, myths, and mores.

Don and I wanted to understand something more about the habitat of the Kasilapai, who lived somewhere upstream. We informed the Bola bèk of our intention, but were told it was a great distance, and the journey would be extremely difficult. The Bola bèk were guarded about their association with us and wanted to be the sole recipients of all trade goods. Undaunted, we proceeded and found the Kasilapai after travelling about seven hours by canoe, beyond some rather difficult waterfalls. The Kasilapai were not strangers to us, because all the men had been working on the airstrip, although they were not able to work as frequently because their food source was more distant than that of the Bola bèk. We spent the night in their yãno and returned downstream the next day.

Land Expedition to the Aica

In the hopes of possibly establishing another station, Claude Levitt, a senior missionary, and two WaiWai, Yakuta and Wahne, joined Don and me for an overland expedition to the Apiau River. We needed three Xilixana carriers, but brothers and brothers-in-law wanted to assist the "official" carriers, and we ended up with 12 people in our group—quite a troop, more than we had bargained for. We set out following the same forest trail used by the Xilixana in 1956, when they had gone off searching for steel goods.

Game was scarce for the first couple of days. Our companions did shoot and kill a jaguar, though the Xilixana do not eat the meat of that animal. Concerned about the lack of meat, I ate some jaguar and urged the others to eat as well. Some did. And to this date, in an emergency, the Xilixana will eat jaguar. (This could, perhaps, be called a case of cultural borrowing, or at the least a modification of cultural practice. Whether such a change is constructive or not, or whether that even matters, is an issue to be considered.)

We made this trip in the drought season, and so we crossed many bone-dry creeks. In desperation we dug deeply down into one creek bed, found some water, and filtered it, cup by cup, through a cloth. At the sight of any game such as monkey or birds we would either stop or have a group of men leave us to hunt. Even though we carried some 20 liters of water, it ran out, and we again grew desperate. Six men were already travelling somewhat behind, at a slower pace, and we had gone astray from the faint trail that had been used several years earlier. Furthermore, we did not know how far we were from our destination. We needed water. At about 4:00 one afternoon we stopped, sat on the forest floor, and contemplated our next move. We needed supernatural assistance, it seemed. We knew we could not face another night without water.

Then one of the WaiWai noticed that his hand was on a knife-cut sprig protruding from the earth. We perceived this as providential. Obviously someone had walked here before. Claude decided to take compass in hand and head with three men in a southeasterly direction, slashing only a slight trail and moving as quickly as possible. Off they went, and within 20 minutes we heard the call of "Water!"—a welcoming word, indeed. We shouted *maup* (water) to the more tardy carriers behind us and went off to follow the trail to the water. What we found was the Apiau River, now with large pockets of water, none of which were flowing. I plunged in immediately, delighted at the coolness and taste of the water surrounding me. Don did the same, but suddenly blitzed to the shore—he had been swiped by an electric eel.

We set up camp near the water, and our carriers killed several alligators for meat before nightfall. The next day they shot an electric eel with bow and arrow. There was also evidence that non-aborigines had been in the region at one time, because we saw trees that had been tapped for rubber and found a chain and a dish.

According to the pre-expedition arrangements, our airplane was supposed to arrive around that time, but unfortunately we had not yet found the Apiau Indians or any type of clearing that could be used for a supply drop. We decided that an area with stunted growth would have to substitute, though the area probably became flooded during times of high water. We built a fire large enough so, with any luck, the smoke would be visible to the pilot. He arrived on schedule and, using his loudspeaker, asked the expected questions and a missionary assisting him began to drop supplies as well as mail through a door on the passenger's side removed prior to the flight. We welcomed the food— though the missionary assisting the pilot became sick from the circular flight pattern and found it difficult to throw out all the supplies we needed.

We had asked the pilot to search out for us the distance and compass direction of the nearest village. When the Piper Cub returned from that excursion, the pilot started lowering a cloth bucket on a wire to receive our outgoing mail. Claude, the only one of the Westerners who was married, was particularly anxious to send letters to his wife and children. But each of two attempts to get the bag down to us had to be aborted due to the wind. The pilot told us he would make one final attempt and, thankfully, that time all went well.

The bucket touched a small tree some four meters high, and Claude quickly scaled up with our mail packet in hand, dropping it into the bag. He told me to signal the pilot letting him know he could go up now, which I did. The aircraft climbed—but without the mail bucket. The wire had snagged on the tree and snapped off, leaving Claude literally holding the bag. Today, with this event long gone and far removed, I find these happenings amusing, but at the time they were a dismal disappointment.

On the first night of the trip Claude had awoken to find that ants had eaten all the threads of his treasured bead belt. We encountered wood ticks in undesirable locations: in my navel and between my colleagues' toes and on the scrotum. They pinch fiercely when being removed. We were fairly generous with iodine when anyone had a scratch or cut. One afternoon on our return journey, while we were moving along at a good pace, one of the carriers requested medicine for a scratch. The iodine was not readily available, so my colleague used ink from his ballpoint pen to daub the surface. We moved on, everyone quite content.

The visits to the villages were not as fruitful as we had anticipated. In one village, with three triangular-shaped small shelters in this village, each measuring about one and a half meters in diameter, we found only a widow with her small children. She was speaking a dialect we could not understand. We went on to a second village that had a few more people who, we found, had periodic contact with Brazilians. They reported enemies living at the headwaters of the river. We found out the two small villages had populations of only 12 and 24 people. Because this area was readily accessible by water most of the year, Brazilian rubber cutters had been traversing the region for years.

As a result of this visit, one of the Xilixana carriers journeyed to the first village several months later and had the widow and her two children migrate to the Mucajai, so he could take her as wife. He shared the woman with his two brothers. This migration established a lasting bond between her people and this Xilixana family. In 1971 the Apiau woman died, and soon after the widower again trekked to the Apiau and took his deceased wife's daughter, a widow, as wife, and had her also migrate to the Mucajai area.

Also soon after that 1959 visit, a large group of Aica and Hewakema visited the Mucajai. An entire family of four in-migrated, and friendships were established. The Aica clay pots were superior to the Xilixana's—the vessels were more fragile, symmetrical, and lighter. The Xilixana-Aica bond meant an alliance that made the enemies of the Aica the enemies of the Xilixana. In 1967 this would prompt a raid to other Aica living beyond the Apiau headwaters to the Catrimani region.

About 1961 I went up the Mucajai River with Bola bèk guides and visited the Malaxi theli, a group of about 70 people. This trip was followed by amiable visits and exchanges between the Bola bèk and Malaxi theli. As early as 1962 the Xilixana acquired the first of several wives from the Malaxi theli. Again, the alliance between families was binding, and at the request of the Malaxi theli the Xilixana followed in a raid against a village to the south, which resulted in at least two deaths. Even in the 1990s, the Malaxi theli are sometimes a source of wives for the Bola bèk. In the late 1980s and early 1990s, the Bola bèk joined the Malaxi theli in several skirmishes between the miners and Yanomami. Both suffered fatal casualties.

The Further History of the Mission Organization

The Unevangelized Fields Mission (UFM) also worked among the Macuxi on the savannah lands north and east of Boa Vista. After a few years a Brazilian served as president. After establishing firm roots in Roraima, director Neill Hawkins had a vision to engage and integrate Brazilians into the mission. He made numerous trips to south Brazil, and encouraged churches to realize evangelism opportunities among indigenous peoples of their own country. He knew Brazilian men and women were equally able to do language work and Bible teaching. He knew that the permanence of mission work in this frontier region was dependent upon nationals. Young people responded. The first jungle training camp for prospective Brazilian workers was held at Mucajai in 1966. The following year the first workers from the south began their work in Roraima. This was a new phenomenon for Protestant Brazilians, because mission work in Brazil was almost always sponsored by a specific denomination and seldom included indigenous peoples who were monolingual. The UFM International mission board is interdenominational, which meant that financial support and the governing body of the mission activity were separate from the established and organized church.

Brazilians were immediately integrated as equal members in the mission society. All meetings were conducted in Portuguese. In 1969 it changed its name to Missão Evangélica da Amazonia (MEVA). Neill Hawkins remained its leader until his death (of hepatitis B) in 1983. The group elected its first Brazilian president about 1988. By the 1990s MEVA included Brazilian and North American missionaries, active among the Wapishana, Macuxi, and WaiWai along with the Yanomami in the state of Roraima. Several also work among Brazilians in the general Boa Vista area. They are an interdenominational evangelical group, who do not receive funding from one specific denomination. Individuals, families, or specific churches make a commitment to consistently send a certain sum of money for their support on a monthly or bimonthly basis. In turn these missionaries send bimonthly or quarterly letters to their "constituency," reporting on their work. About every four years missionaries return to their home and supporting constituency to report, recuperate, visit relatives, and in some cases to acquire more education. A few missionaries ask for extended stays in their homeland to meet more long-term specific needs; further education that will facilitate them in Brazil, health, children's schooling, or the care of an elderly parent.

This work in the jungle could not be sustained or maintained without the airplane. An agency committed to helping Protestant missions, Asas de Socorro, thoroughly trains pilots and mechanics to fly airplanes in the most adverse conditions. Their record of safe flying is one of the best in the world. While pilots and their families are supported in the same way as missionaries, these moneys are only sufficient to cover living and general expense costs. Missionaries who fly with Asas de Socorro pay for their air travel. Because of this cost missionaries are cautious about the weight they transport into the jungle, and carefully plan the frequency of flights. Missionaries from the south of Brazil find it more difficult to raise funds than most North American missionaries. MEVA is a textbook case of a foreign mission society becoming nationally staffed and sustained.

Missionary Relations

In the history of this mission in the state of Roraima there have been periods of good relations with varying government departments. In 1961 the Brazilian Air Force (FAB) affirmed missionary presence on two Yanomami stations and asked that the missions assist the Air Force to open two others. (One proved to be in Venezuela and had to be abandoned two years later.) In 1962 the mission purchased ground to air radio transmitters for use in the jungle, even though the transmitters would become the actual possession of the Air Force. In the same year the WaiWai and missionaries opened an air field with the Brazilian Air Force south of the Guyana WaiWai mission post in Brazil. The next year the WaiWai helped FAB open two other airstrips. In 1964 FAB and the missionaries opened a Yanomami station on the upper Uraricoera River. Hawkins described the Brazilian Air Force's attempt to open an airstrip in 1963 together with the WaiWai:

> On the expedition's first day at Kanashen, the Major saw Churuma [a WaiWai] come out of the clinic with two dental forceps in his hand and told him, in Portuguese, to put them away before he broke something. Churuma did not understand the Portuguese, but motioning to another WaiWai to come in and sit down, washed his hands, extracted a tooth, and then wrote up the treatment he had given. Even more amazing to the Major and his men was their realization that in the absence of any missionary at Kanashen the keys to most of the houses had been entrusted to two or three of the leading WaiWai men. (Hawkins, Feb. 12, 1963)

At the same time government relations with this mission organization were far from congenial. Attacks against the mission had been numerous. Their philanthropic activity has often been met with suspicion. There were numerous times when missionary work was forcefully attacked by government or other agents in south Brazil. Despite written permission, the MAF plane was apprehended in the spring of 1959, leaving two jungle stations without radio contact. After nine weeks a Brazilian-registered MAF plane came to the rescue.

The apprehended plane was released by an Aeronautics official after being detained for 15 months.

Leading newspapers in 1958 in south Brazil reported that the Americans posed as missionaries but were actually exploiting the territory's mineral wealth. The local governor requested the missionaries be removed. After an investigation by the SPI and the Frontier Commission of the Brazilian army, both groups supported the presence of the missionaries. The following year bishops and other clergy and the media again sought to expel the missionaries. The large daily newspaper of Rio de Janeiro, *Correio da Manha* (Sept. 17, 1959), reported a secret session of the Congressional Committee at which Protestant missionaries were said to be extracting cassiterite sand (a radioactive substance) and diamonds. In the name of nationalism, they pushed for the missionaries' expulsion. Soon thereafter a member of the Chamber of Deputies strongly defended the "Catholic and Protestant missions." This member urged that an investigating team be sent to Roraima. After two years of uncertainty an order was given to terminate all Indian work. Two days later FAB, who set upon establishing themselves firmly in the frontier region, requested the mission "help deal with completely primitive Indians they would encounter during the operation" (Hawkins 1996, July 6). (In this venture a helicopter was forced down in the jungle and a missionary and a Yanomami played an important role in the rescue operation.) After three years, and the transference of several government figures, the degree of tension subsided considerably. However, despite the mission organization's Brazilian leadership and a majority of Brazilians as members, the government once again questioned its presence among the Yanomami between 1987 and 1995.

The history of the mission has been a struggle to hold public legitimacy and acceptance. There have been numerous efforts to oust the missionary presence in the Yanomami region. The Fundacão Nacionál do Índio (FUNAI) had MEVA missionaries evacuated from the Mucajai station for two and one half years beginning in 1987. Since about 1990 the Brazilian government has not permitted new North American missionaries to serve in Yanomami territory. To clarify misunderstandings and political controversy the MEVA president has sent letters and made numerous phone calls and trips to south Brazil. The president once appeared on national television. Some agents, mostly bureaucrats, are still making efforts to oust the MEVA missionaries, while their local hands-on staff voice their support of the missionaries. The Yanomami at Mucajai will not tolerate their expulsion. To many they have become friends and have provided valuable health care to all.

Ten
The Missionary Presence: Translation, Literacy, and Social Effects

With the missionaries present, the Xilixana continued with their normal life of hunting, of making bows and arrows, canoes, of tree-clearing and field planting, pottery-making, food preparation, and childrearing. But there was now one significant difference in their mode of life: Westerners now lived permanently amongst them. They now had easier access to the prized items of axes, cutlasses, knives of various sizes, fish hooks and line, scissors, enamel pots (later aluminium), salt, matches, and valuable colored beads. The new goods facilitated daily Yanomami life enormously. Soon clothing, soap, guns, and ammunition were added to the material culture. The missionary presence also had an important social function in the formation of status positions. The items the Xilixana gained were now significant in bride payment (Peters 1973). Other Yanomami, whom they would soon meet, would envy their Western goods and their access to them.

A series of missionaries have lived at the Mucajai station. The initial plan was for two couples, one from Canada and the other from America, to operate the station. My wife was trained as a nurse. The residence of the two couples at Mucajai lasted just a few years, because an illness required the American couple to leave in 1963. A single American woman, trained as a linguist, came in to assist at that time. After my wife and I and our four small children returned to Canada in 1967, two single women, one a linguist and the other a school teacher, took residence at Mucajai. A couple of years later the senior missionary, the linguist, left, in part due to the overwhelming responsibilities of the station. An American couple replaced her, and later another missionary-linguist came as well. The American wife had training in jungle tropical health care, and her husband knew basic dentistry. After more than a decade of service at the Mucajai station, that couple was relocated to another Yanomami station.

In 1980 the first Brazilian missionary family, with two young children, settled at Mucajai. They were soon speaking the language fluently and involving themselves fully in all aspects of station activities. They earned the respect of all the local Yanomami. After eight years the mission asked the Brazilian couple to serve in Boa Vista, the husband as president and the wife as treasurer. Because he enjoyed jungle life immensely, he found the decision difficult, but ultimately consented. Eventually they were replaced at Mucajai by another Brazilian couple. For medical reasons that couple had to leave the isolated rainforest habitat in 1994. In 1996 the pedagogical teacher returned to care for her ailing, aging mother in New York state, which meant that the station was now being maintained by the senior missionary-linguist of 28 years of experience, a daunting task, plus others who assisted her for short periods of time. In later 1997 the pedagogist returned to the mission.

BRINGING UP OUR CHILDREN AMONG THE YANOMAMI

Our first-born son, Dean, was born with blond hair. "He was born old!" the Yanomami said when they saw him at three months old. When the black-haired Yanomami find a white hair on their heads, they pluck it out, because they do not want to be labelled as old. We explained that in our tribe, blond hair does not necessarily mean that one is old. Many people with white skin also have white hair.

When Dean was eight months old, I became pregnant again. The Yanomami were horrified that I was pregnant so soon while I was still nursing our son. They said our son might die, because I would not have enough milk for him with the new baby growing inside me. They seemed reassured when they saw that we also fed Dean milk from a bottle. They watched carefully as Dean sucked the nipple on the bottle and the milk diminished.

LORRAINE PETERS

The activity of the resident missionaries varied. In the initial stages there was language learning and linguistic work (see chapter 2). Once the language had been analyzed in terms of phonemes, we formed an alphabet. Linguists on other Yanomami stations were always consulted in this process. The missionaries learned more of the culture, including myths and legends. With the help of carefully selected informants, Yanomami stories were recorded. Missionaries also recorded, and later put in print, talk of other episodes such as hunts and visits (especially to Boa Vista, with its first impressions). After a while a few Bible stories were translated into the local language: creation, flood, stories of Jesus' life. With time the missionaries were able to begin translating parts of the New Testament.

As time went on, Bible translation became a priority. There were many challenges in Bible translation because some English concepts or meanings were not found in Yanomami. The linguists struggled with concepts that had their origin in the Greek language within a Hebrew culture 2,000 years earlier. Should "God" be translated as "Omamo," the chief creator in Yanomami legends? Or should we use a new term, such as the Portuguese "*Deus*"? What are the indigenous terms for trustworthy, honesty, caring, generous, and miracle? There is no word for gratitude or the much-used English-language words "thank you." There is no word for "love." Both concepts were considered extremely important to the missionaries in relaying something about the love of God. When an equivalent term was non-existent, the linguist or translator used a phrase that in some way approximated the meaning. "Thank you" can culturally best be translated as "It is good." The missionaries tried the word *pexima*, because a husband would *pexima* his wife, but then found that the same term was used in relation to a knife or food. So we decided *pexima* was inappropriate, because one hardly loves these objects. The term *pihibo* seemed more appropriate, denoting thought towards a family member or another person. To this day the translators still struggle with concepts common among Western peoples but foreign to the Yanomami.

The director of the mission went to considerable length to gather, assimilate, and disperse anthropological information on the Yanomami. His elaborate categories include the ash of the deceased, shamanism, black magic, the yãimo, and kin relationships. Missionaries sent him data from the field, and he worked with it, probing the missionaries on central themes and collating the information.

Daily Life and Mission Tasks

With the coming of the missionaries came another social change in terms of the leisure or sit-down activities of the Xilixana. Women, with their young children, would spend several hours a day at our kitchen, observing our behavior and goods. Along with tribal gossip while they spun their cotton or weaved aprons, they would be entertained by tales of the foreigners' lifestyle and behavior. Men would visit the missionaries' homes in the late afternoon after returning from a hunt or work in the fields. Rarely was our residence void of visitors. While we inquired about the Yanomami culture, the Yanomami would inquire about the Westerner's knife and clothing production, airplanes, families, animals, political organization, and warfare. In the process the Yanomami became exposed to a much larger range of lifestyle, behavior and thought, and so did we.

The missionaries, then, involve themselves in a multitude of tasks, some of which are not so obvious given their calling. They serve as hosts and entertainers on a daily basis. In Yanomami culture, any restraint in hospitality is instantly seen as being uncaring, stingy, distrustful, or unfriendly. In general, missionaries seek to be conversant, helpful, and interested in Yanomami affairs and concerns. The Xilixana arrive in the missionaries' visiting room and often demand attention: an exchange of news, an aspirin or iodine, a drink of water, a plea for fish hooks, matches, salt, or a needle. Some arrive with yams, bananas, papaya, and, on a few rare occasions, meat to sell. Mothers often arrived in the afternoon with their young children, bored with the environs of their own household. While the children fuss and quarrel (at times to the annoyance of the missionaries) the adult women spin cotton and converse. In the 1990s the missionaries provided a chalk board, pictorial magazines, or a 16-piece puzzle for the children's amusement.

Because missionaries are the only Westerners in the forest region, it fell to them to entertain any non-Yanomami who happened by. Most of the visitors were government personnel who came for anywhere from one to several days: to investigate missionary or Yanomami life, to immunize the local population, run a clinic on tooth care, or spray the house for malaria control, for instance. Government officials, such as those of the justice department, police, or Air Force, might arrive suddenly and unexpectedly for an investigation. For decades the Brazilian print and television media had communicated rumors about missionaries' illegal presence in the rainforest, or of people disguising themselves as missionaries when they were really in the gold business. Sometimes travelling miners would stop by. Sometimes there is unexpected business to take care of. Once, for instance, in the early 1960s farmers on the Catrimani road south of Boa Vista were feeling harassed by Aica who suddenly appeared from their habitat to the west. The government asked for a missionary from Mucajai to go and calm the tension and encourage the Aica to return home. So, in this case, at my own expense, I travelled to this locale with two informants and tried to ease the friction. The missionaries could also be confronted with unanticipated and more sobering events, such as the murder of three miners in the environs of the mission post in 1991.

For the future planning of the mission, it was important to know the language spoken, the population, and whether or not the people in distant surrounding villages were friendly. Each trip to other areas carried its risks. In those years we had no permission to use radio contact. We knew that at least one tribe had been hostile to visitors, having recently killed some Brazilians. In another case, when we went into an Aica village, a local man quickly picked up his bow and arrow to shoot. Our Xilixana guide was carrying a shotgun, and I asked him to drop it to the ground.

Several of the young single Xilixana men accompanied me during the contact period on surveys and visits to more distant Yanomami: Apiau Aica, Ajarani Aica, Catrimani Aica, and Malaxi theli. At times another missionary also accompanied me. In 1961 four single young Xilixana men accompanied me by plane to the area of the Palimi theli, where we worked to build a new airstrip for the missionaries and the Brazilian Air Force. These trips expanded the Xilixana horizons beyond their own community of 120 people and the isolation of the previous 25 years. Soon the Xilixana were visiting the Malaxi theli, Palimi theli, Aica, and Xiliana. The Xiliana contact was of particular relevance because they had developed ties with them in the early part of the century and had kin in that tribe, and their spoken language was identical.

UNEXPECTED VISITORS

In October 1963 for a short time I was the only missionary living on the Mucajai mission station. John was away on an expedition with one of his colleagues and several Yanomami guides, in search of an illusive tribe named the Atrowari, who were known to be fierce. I wondered if John would come back alive. A young Brazilian woman, non-Yanomami, was helping me look after our three children, of two months, eighteen months, and almost three years old. As a nurse, I was inundated with treating sick Yanomami who lived near us and people from a neighboring tribe who had come to visit.

One morning a plane landed on the airstrip without warning. Three official-looking Brazilian men walked up the pathway to our house. I invited them in, with one child on my hip, and served them some coffee and cake I happened to have on hand. We exchanged pleasantries and then the men asked if I would take them to see the village and show them what we were doing in the community. Without further ado, I took our two older children with me, and along with a number of the resident Yanomami, I guided the men to the Yanomami houses, where they were warmly received. I also showed them the little store where we sold trade goods, the shelter where we taught literacy classes in Yanomami and Portuguese, and the porch of our home, where I dispensed medicines and cared for the sick.

After two hours or so the men thanked me for my hospitality and flew away. Much later I learned that those men had been sent to evict us, because they had been told that we were really miners, posing as missionaries. Presumably they were looking for evidence to confirm that story.

LORRAINE PETERS

Maintaining the Mission Station

Since the beginning, in addition to literacy work and health care, station maintenance—constructing and looking after the airstrip, buildings, grounds, machines, and trading goods—has taken up huge amounts of the missionaries' time and energies.

At first we focused our efforts on the construction of the airstrip, which eventually included working on proper drainage for the strip and, later, cutting its grass on a regular basis as well as cutting the trees that grew on the airstrip approaches. We also applied ourselves to building and maintaining houses at the mission station. Any building we did there took considerable organization and time. We had to get bolts and nails sent in from Boa Vista. The support posts had to be long, straight, and rot-resistant. Following the example of the Xilixana, we carried in a good supply of leaves, palm slats (for floor and walls), and bush rope from the forest. Within a year it was evident that we needed to have a clinic and a building to house trade items brought in for the local people. Several years later we constructed a small building for a newly purchased generator, which supplied energy for lights from dusk to about 9:30 p.m. A gas engine ran the station's washing machine. Both these machines periodically broke down, as did our small kerosene refrigerators, essential equipment (for Westerners) to preserve food in the tropics. The few ice cubes the refrigerator produces provide a soothing cool drink. In the early 1970s, the mission replaced its leaf roofs with aluminum ones. The downside of this more enduring roof is the noise when pelleted by rain drops. It is impossible to hold a conversation in the home during a heavy rain. In the 1980s, the small refrigerators were replaced with larger units, eventually operated by means of bottled gas, as were the kitchen stoves. In 1994 two missionary construction workers flew in to build a new medical clinic—a building superior to any other structure at Mucajai, with lumber used for floors, walls, and doors—and no palm slats.

CLOSE CALL

The table I used for studying had an open shelf underneath the table top, a place where I kept my language analysis papers. One afternoon I reached for one of the papers and thought I smelled a strange odor. I bent my head to look into where the papers were and to my horror saw a small coral-colored snake curled up in one corner. I jumped up, ran out of the house, and shouted, "There's a snake!" My husband John and several Yanomami came running. When the Yanomami saw the snake they shook their heads, waved their hands, and jabbered excitedly. They told us that the snake was highly poisonous. If it had bitten me, I would have surely died. When the snake slithered out from under the table, one of the men killed it, while I stood by, trembling.

LORRAINE PETERS

Just looking after the equipment we had in the station took considerable time and attention. For instance, we soon replaced the small two and a half HP outboard motor we used to ascend the river in 1958 with a five HP motor. But once, when all of the missionaries were away from the station in 1963, a Xilixana took the motor to travel the river. Later we were told the motor fell off the boat and sunk, though the young man never once discussed this matter with the missionary, nor was he ever reprimanded. We replaced the motor, and by 1970 the station had a larger 10 HP motor. But always the missionaries had to make time to order parts, make repairs, and sometimes send an appliance, motor, and, after the mid-1980s, computers to Boa Vista (or the United States) for repair. Replacing broken parts could take months.

In the 1980s the station installed solar panels to supply daytime energy for computers used in literacy and translation work, as well as for light in the evening. A diesel generator was taken out in the 1988 evacuation and never returned. A solar panel beside each of the three houses now supplies energy for batteries, providing adequate light in the evening. A 500-watt gas-run portable engine provides power for construction work on the station when needed.

In the late 1980s the local people, paid by the missionaries, dug a well to be used by all the local community, including the Xilixana visitors and anyone who remained at the station for long-term medical care. With the mercury-contaminated water, the well was a huge asset. In 1992 a new solar panel was set in place to supply the necessary energy for pumping the water. By the 1990s the Brazilian missionaries had installed indoor toilets, while the two single Americans at the mission were satisfied to keep using their outhouses. Every home has its continuous battle with flies, ants, moths, gnats, cockroaches, and bats. The evening light in particular attracts a wide variety of moths and bugs. After the missionaries' return in 1990, after the forced evacuation, they did some downsizing. They decided to have local women wash their clothes by hand, rather than use motor-driven washing machines, as they did earlier. They decided to keep goods for sale in the "store" to a minimum, both in quantity and variety.

The missionaries have gone to considerable effort to introduce domestic animals—chickens, sheep, pigs, and other livestock—and the growing of peanuts. They complied to the immediate requests of the Xilixana and from time to time had chickens and dogs (later a kitten or two) brought in by plane. In 1962 a Brazilian rancher supplied two Brahma cattle: a bull and heifer, transported by air on separate flights. Even with a Brazilian cattleman on the station for several weeks, the Brahma cattle could not be tamed. They broke through all the fences we tried to put up and wandered into the fields, as well as into the jungle. During the dry season they bravely swam across the river, though they voluntarily returned a few days later. A couple of years both missionaries and Xilixana experienced mixed emotions when the cattle were shot by bow and arrow, like beasts of the forest, and cooked for meat. About that same time the missionaries also brought in two sheep and two pigs. The sheep proved to be a bother. We had no fenced-in areas to place them in, but tied them with bush rope to small plants, and several times they hopelessly twisted the rope. The pigs died of worms and a lack of veterinary care.

During our attempts to raise these domestic animals, a cultural conflict was always apparent between Xilixana and Westerner. The missionaries meant to raise the animals to fatten and eat them. The Xilixana saw any domestic animals as pets, and believed that you did not raise pets to maturity, then kill them for food. In the early years the Xilixana never ate eggs, which were taboo. Later they began to eat both chickens and eggs. The missionaries went to great efforts to grow lettuce, and received rather disgusted looks from the local people. Only tapir, they would say, eat green grass.

During the 1960s we had little concern for security. When we were in the area the only thing we kept locked was our large box of trade goods. If the community was in reasonably good health at the time, the missionaries would lock up their houses and go off to attend a conference or enjoy a retreat of up to three weeks absence from the station. Despite the locked doors the Xilixana could readily enter the houses through any number of open spaces. By the 1970s missionaries were using fine screens on the windows, meant more to discourage annoying small insects from entering than to block out the Xilixana. At the same time, the missionaries did find it necessary to keep most of their possessions, such as clothing and cutlery, in locked barrels. Since the early 1980s, missionary personnel have adopted the policy of not leaving the station all at once, to make sure someone is available for health needs as well as to safeguard their possessions.

Correspondence with the government, the mission organization, and support constituency also takes up the missionaries' time. The government is repeatedly asking for population statistics and the medical history of each Xilixana. Missionaries write reports of their activity for people in their constituencies in Brazil and in North America, people who financially support (and pray for) their work. The mission counsel corresponds and meets in Boa Vista for several days at least twice a year. They place orders for trade items or needed station items on special requisition forms. In the Brazilian period they were able to make requests for specific items by radio before each airplane flight, generally once e.very three weeks.

Literacy Teaching

After health, perhaps the most distinctive contribution of the Mucajai missionaries came in the field of literacy, and, indeed, the development of literacy among the Xilixana is an interesting story. They saw proof that paper "speaks" from the information we communicated to them after reading mail on "airplane day." About two years after our arrival I was on a work project to provide adequate drainage on the airstrip. I told a Xilixana to carry a note to my wife, requesting a hoe. He took the note to my wife, without telling her the purpose of his errand. To his surprise she walked directly to the tool shed and produced the hoe, which he in turn delivered to me.

Within three years of contact the missionaries had initiated a program of literacy, giving children and young adults the opportunity to learn to read and write. At first literacy classes were held in the shade under one of the missionaries houses, first with boys and young men between the ages of 14 and 22. Soon after that the missionaries began holding classes for women. In these literacy classes the Xilixana questioned why the missionary should be so finicky, insisting that the dot of the "i" be placed above rather than below the letter, and why the "a" had a tail on the right rather than the left side. They were intrigued that words such as "knife" and "arrow" could be communicated on paper. These literacy classes also taught the Portuguese language, appropriate greetings, arithmetic, Brazilian currency, and days and months of the year. The missionaries recorded local stories and made them available for reading by the Xilixana. The first school house, with a leaf roof and no walls, was built in 1968. Later one of the villages located upstream from the mission built its own school house, in which a missionary came to teach on occasion. In about 1977 a school house similar to that used among Brazilians in the savannah regions was built at the mission post. The mud-walled interior was bedecked with the letters of the alphabet and numbers as well as pictures. On three occasions the missionary linguist ran workshops of two to three weeks duration for six of the more advanced readers at a retreat center. She trained them to be literacy teachers in their own villages. In 1995 one of these men built a school house in his village so he could instruct children and adolescents himself.

The missionaries went to extensive lengths to endorse literacy. They asked several Xilixana who visited Boa Vista to write down their stories about visiting a school, store, church, or abattoir, and they later published these accounts as a primer, complete with appropriate drawings. When a hunter told of his trek into the forest, they published that too as a primer with drawings. All missionary personnel were engaged in some way in the literacy program. The visiting room in the missionary houses was bedecked with pictures and Ninam phrases.

No other agents who have worked among the Yanomami in Roraima have even approximated the literacy work of the missionaries. While certain agencies have attempted smaller endeavors, those efforts are exclusively in the Portuguese language, rather than in the local tongues. Teaching Portuguese via the medium of Yanomami is always much more effective and provides a greater advantage for the people involved. The missionaries from North America have been cautious about teaching English to the Xilixana, trying to avoid it. There have, for instance, been occasions when the Xilixana reversed roles with me and asked for English words, perhaps "child," "father" and "airplane." They laughed at their attempts to pronounce phonemes that are foreign and difficult. I have heard two or three Xilixana on occasion use two English phrases. One fellow uttered the term, "Honey," because he heard me use the word in addressing my wife. To my ears the word sounded weird coming from a Xilixana. In more recent years another phrase took me by surprise: a young guest departing for his house said to me, "See ya later." He had heard an American guest at Mucajai frequently using the phrase.

The Yanomami found it difficult to make a commitment to have school for a two-week or even one-week period, let alone to sit still for a one-hour period of time. Adult men are busy hunting and making fields and find it difficult to make time to teach. The Xilixana have not yet organized themselves like the Carib Yekwana and WaiWai, who designate individuals for the full-time responsibility of learning. By the mid-linking period, some Xilixana were writing notes to others of their village who were off visiting other Yanomami or being medically treated in Boa Vista. By the 1990s about 10 men were able to read reasonably well. The primary task of one of the current missionaries is to teach literacy.

The Impact of Christian Teaching

The missionaries had two goals to accomplish in their biblical work. They wished to relay the Christian message of God's love in creation, redemption, and preservation. They sought to do this by teaching the Bible, hoping that eventually an indigenous church would be established. To do this, missionaries put a great deal of effort into translating the New Testament into Yanomami, which has always been a focused task for one of the missionaries at Mucajai. This person carried on a close collaboration with other translators working among the Yanomami at other locations.

Throughout the first six years after contact, it appeared as though the Xilixana were responding positively to the new ideology of the missionaries. They were friendly, helped in the construction of the station (for which they were paid), assisted in language work, and readily requested medicine for any and all ailments. Even shaman brought their children to the missionaries for treatment. The religious services on Sunday were well-attended. Four adults were baptised in the Mucajai River, a sign of their commitment to the new life under Jesus' standard. Three years later several more Xilixana were baptized.

The missionaries interpreted conversion to be behavior that exemplified a Christ-likeness, and in practical terms this standard had significant cultural implications. It meant that a Xilixana no longer solicited the attention of a shaman to respond to personal or family members' health problems. It meant a belief in God as superior and sufficient. It meant avoiding or at least restraining oneself in fisticuff duels and harsh gossip that could lead to violence. It meant "honesty," a concept seemingly foreign to the Yanomami. For men Christianity meant fidelity to their wife or wives. All of these qualities were rare in the makeup of Yanomami culture.

It also meant church attendance and individual prayer. Prayer was not a foreign concept to the Yanomami. They interacted with spirits, and with Christian prayer they were interacting with a new spirit, God. Those who were baptized had exemplified this standard of life for about a year. Anyone showing interest in being one of "God's people" was encouraged to attend meetings where stories and instruction from the Bible were given. The missionaries often consulted the baptized ones for advice regarding appropriate practices in Yanomami living. For the first several years, Sunday meetings were held in the space under one of the missionaries' houses, because their dwellings were elevated off the ground by two meters. Around 1964 the whole community joined in the building of a yãno-shaped church. The structure was used for about two years, then fell into disrepair. Roughly 10 years later the missionaries had a second church building erected, with volunteer labor. After its deterioration, they held Sunday meetings in an abandoned missionary house. At times they held a second session of biblical instruction after the church service, for people who had expressed faith in Jesus Christ. From time to time they had prayer sessions in the evenings. Whenever possible missionaries individually encouraged those who showed interest in Christian teaching—whether in village visits, travels, or hunting. In the 1980s, when the villages were located some distance from the mission station, missionaries trekked and canoed to several houses on Sunday to conduct services. On four different occasions between 1961 and 1985 the missionaries baptized a total of 24 adults by immersion off the banks of the Mucajai River.

But several basic Christian beliefs were incompatible with the Xilixana life. One such belief was that human life should be respected whether it be fetus, infant, female, the infirm, or the aged. Missionaries tried to exemplify this principle by discouraging abortion and female infanticide, and although they saved some babies from death, their long-term work of dissuading the Xilixana from these practices was largely unsuccessful. There is no evidence that the frequency of abortions declined due to the persuasion of missionaries.

The missionaries made every effort to heal the sick even if this required long-term medication and care. They resented the patriarchal subjugation of women. The missionaries supported the ideal of family loyalty as well as the Xilixana practice of bride payment and bride service. They showed gentleness to the elderly, who were ridiculed by children and youth and sometimes ignored by adults.

They advocated monogamy, though they did not condemn those already in polygamous relations. They taught marriage fidelity, a practice rarely seen in the community. They advocated sexual exclusivity for partners, rather than the sexual license practised by male and female, the married and unmarried alike. They encouraged married couples to be loving and caring. They wanted to see the Xilixana build a consistent, loving relationship between parent and child, rather than more impulsive behavior ranging from anger and disgust to gross permissiveness. These principles tended to fall on deaf ears.

Christian teaching proved to be radically different from the Xilixana practice of violence and justice. The Xilixana considered the missionary's Jesus to be something of a wimp because he never brandished a cutlass or swung a club. True Xilixana maturity was seen in being *waithili* (fierce). The missionaries challenged the Xilixana to stop warfare and the fisticuff duels. They spoke directly and specifically against the raid to the Xili theli. They successfully persuaded the men not to avenge the Xiliana for two deaths in 1963. They urged them to terminate their overindulgence in the alcoholic manioc drink. In this matter too their efforts proved futile.

The missionaries recognized that the Xilixana had a complex system of spirits that penetrated virtually all aspects of their lives. The Xilixana sought to control spirits for their own good, which meant ordering spirits to harm and even kill an undesirable Yanomami. They feared such a spell from other Yanomami. There was no Xilixana spirit that was eternally good. Missionaries did not doubt the presence and power of spirits, and they could not help but acknowledge the power of a variety of spirits, most of which were evil. But they wanted to introduce the Xilixana to a just, caring, benevolent, and loving spirit. A few Xilixana did convert to the Christian teachings. Many more journeyed the "Jesus path" or "Jesus way" for a year or more, then fluctuated between the life pattern of Christianity and their traditional spirit beliefs.

It was evident that traditional beliefs in *hekula*, *ōkla*, and *pole* had a powerful control upon their behavior and worldview. These spirit beliefs remained central to the Xilixana, but were modified minimally to account for their post-contact experiences.

The Xilixana, it must be said, are masters at deception. They do not see any merit in being truthful. Indeed, they appear to gain personal gratification, and find humor, in hoodwinking another person. Missionaries taught honesty and considered "truthfulness" a prized value. The Xilixana have always stolen from one another. But with Western artifacts that could not be crafted locally, and given the scarcity of these items at times, stealing increased during the missionary presence.

In the mid-1960s the very powerful, respected, and feared polygamous shaman of the tribe converted. It had begun earlier on, when the missionary asked him one day whether he would not want the strong spirit of Jesus in his chest. The shaman said "yes," and the missionary responded that the Jesus spirit would not enter if his other spirits continued their abode in his chest—that Jesus would enter only if his chest was void of other competing spirits (see Dowdy 1995 for similarities among WaiWai shaman). For the shaman this was an extremely difficult choice to make, because he believed that if he ever asked the spirits to vacate his chest, he would die.

A few months later the shaman was in the forest, about four hours' distance from the village, with his two wives and children. They were with others who had gone off for a couple of weeks to hunt in a less trafficked area. A messenger arrived at the mission one day and reported to the missionary that the shaman's young son was ill. The missionary answered by saying that the shaman father was undoubtedly attempting by means of his own craft to cure his son. The messenger said the shaman was not performing his craft, but rather praying for his son. About three days later the family returned, and at sunset the missionary entered the shaman's yãno. Amidst the conversation he asked whether they might pray together that evening. The shaman's response was that he had already prayed. The missionary was astounded that this man had changed his life habits in the forest, far removed from the mission station environment.

Another time the local missionary was urged to come and visit the Kasilapai yãno one morning at sunrise, because a man there had gone into an uncontrollable fit. The yãno, recently constructed, was only about 400 meters away and within minutes the missionary and his wife, as nurse, entered the dark abode, finding that the man's family had tied him up in his hammock. The man had beaten his wife and, it seemed, no person was safe near him. The entire village had packed and was about to move upriver, leaving the sick man alone to die.

The missionary, deciding that the darkness might be part of the reason for the man's wild behavior, asked the family to carry him in his hammock out of doors into the sunlight. They did this, but it brought on no change. When the missionary offered him some food, the man grit his teeth, refusing to take any of it. He rudely brushed the missionary aside, which was an unusual action. When the man was offered medicine by spoon, his teeth remained tightly clenched.

The missionary thought about how, according to the New Testament, Jesus had encountered a similar situation 2,000 years earlier, and how through power from the Great Spirit, a significant change had come upon a demonically controlled person (Luke 8: 27-39). The missionary asked everyone to be quiet, then prayed. In the Ninam language, he asked that the all-powerful Spirit of God release the controlling and enslaving spirits of its victim. He spoke briefly, clearly, and firmly. At the end of the prayer the victim gave a tremendous sigh, and was relieved and released. It appeared that spirit had met spirit, and that the Good spirit had brought liberation to this man.

After this event the victim's kin changed their plans and did not move upstream. Two decades later, when the missionary reminded the man of this incident, although the Kasilapai readily recalled the incident of the forces of release, he could not remember the control of negative forces.

Without question any foreigner in a preliterate society stimulates some change. It may be intentional or unintentional. It may be material or ideological. All societies, including our own, have practices that are not civil, not humane. In this patriarchal environment missionaries have chosen, for instance, to challenge acts of female subordination, or, in the case of female infanticide, female death. Perhaps it does not matter that such acts are done by missionaries, but that they show respect for human life.

In one case, for instance, a woman had already given birth to two females, leading to strong cultural pressure to kill any other females that she might deliver. In the case of another child who was saved, it was only the father's stubborn insistence that kept the girl alive. The father was one of "God's people," and he insisted that his next child, irrespective of sex, was not going to be killed. In 1972 his wife once again gave birth, to a boy, and he was absolutely ecstatic.

We know of one concrete case where missions thwarted intertribal killings, and there may have been others. Several Yanomami have said, "If I imitated my fathers, I would kill," or "If I would not carry God's talk, I would kill."

The Missionary Presence: Mixed Results

By the mid- to late 1960s, the people's general interest in church attendance and matters relating to Christianity had declined. By the end of the 1960s the Xilixana were less concerned about attending Sunday services. It became evident to the missionaries that total tribal conversion, reported by a few missionaries who worked with indigenous peoples in other parts of the world (Dowdy 1964; Richardson 1974), was not taking place at Mucajai. Although the rapport of missionaries with the local villagers remained good, there was a further decline of Xilixana interest in Christianity in the 1990s.

Missionaries had hoped that an increasing number of individuals, especially men in this patriarchal society, would convert, and that their families and possibly their villages as a whole would follow suit. A few individuals did become Christian in the sense that they no longer engaged themselves in shamanism, fighting, or slander, and did participate in discourse with God through prayer. Frequently their marriage partners did not show the same type of commitment as they did, or their maturing sons and daughters were not sympathetic to Christian beliefs. None of the Xiliana believers became fully literate, ambitious in the study of the Bible, and in turn a leader and teacher among the people. These missionary goals have not been realized.

Other factors played an important part in social dynamics, both politically and economically, and in missionary activity. Some two years after missionary contact the Kasilapai moved to the environs of the mission post, increasing the local population by almost 40 per cent. In the mid-1960s one village moved a considerable distance from the mission, and their contact with missionaries declined. A little later a second village fissioned and moved a half-hour away from the station. As it happened, in the early 1960s missionaries had recommended that the Xilixana fission and spread out from the station, because of the limited local game supply, and because insults between women and families were frequent and intense in large populated yãnos. Despite these moves, the mission post continued to be a center for the Xilixana, especially in health care and the trading of items now considered essential.

Contacts further abroad also had their impact. Three of the villages had acquired wives and other persons from three non-Xilixana villages and, as a result, special bonds of alliances and reciprocated social expectations were formed with these more distant peoples. This had an effect on shamanism, which by the 1970s had revived itself as a stronger, more open, and central force once again. Perhaps no one cultural change has been as significant as the frequent and excessive drinking patterns imported from the Palimi theli. Although Palimi theli originally migrated to one of the Xilixana villages, they influenced all villages in terms of alcoholic consumption, an influence that led to an increase in brawls, as well as more frequent festivities that included greater sexual permissiveness.

For their part, the missionaries recognize qualities of the Yanomami culture that may be considered superior to Western culture. The Yanomami have strong family bonds and are in many ways a generous and hospitable people. They are fun-loving and enjoy celebrations. Yanomami life lends itself to the cycle of seasons and days. It is nature-oriented. Time does not have the rigidity and work-discipline found in Western life. Missionaries have formed close personal bonds with a large number of Xilixana.

The missionaries recognize that for the Yanomami issues of life and death are closely tied to the supernatural sphere of spirits. The missionaries believe that the yãimo feast, the central social festivity, has at its roots a fundamental loyalty to the deceased. The Xilixana are understandably reluctant to terminate these rituals for the deceased. The missionaries continue to believe that the fear of these spirits is a form of enslavement, or at the very least a loyalty or sub-servience to a power other than God. Some of them also believe these attitudes are a form of ancestral worship, and therefore contrary to true Christian expression.

The Yanomami tradition of the yãimo is so central and so entrenched, that no one refrains from participating in it. To the Yanomami it means belonging to the community, which carries responsibilities of reciprocating, giving, and receiving. These exchanges include a range of activities that are intertwined with obligations and expectations that have a spiritual base and relevance. Any violation of these norms leads to strong Yanomami condemnation. At the very core of these beliefs is a person's participation in ritual pertaining to the deceased, especially when a particular person's own deceased relatives are the focus of the yãimo. Christianity directly addresses the concerns of the soul in relation to the entire realm of spirits, but no Xilixana have boldly stood up against group pressure to align themselves separately from the yãimo.

This means, from some missionaries' point of view, that no full and unequivocal commitment to Christianity has been made among the Xilixana. In this sense they view their work as still incomplete, as successful only in a small part. Certainly, they would like to see the same results that took place among the WaiWai in the 1950s and which have been, for the most part, maintained to the present (Dowdy 1995). Missionaries have intentionally had the Xilixana meet the WaiWai on a few occasions, in hopes that the some beneficial exchange on these grounds might occur.

The missionaries who have been among the Xilixana have certainly tried to figure out why the Christian teaching has not had a greater impact. Would a more aggressive and authoritarian direction, particularly during the first decade, have yielded greater results? They think not. They recognize that Yanomami culture is strongly community-structured, making it extremely difficult for one individual to live a Christian life. The young convert needs support from other Yanomami. Missionaries have refused to construct a Christian institution and center at the mission post, in contrast to the Roman Catholic program at Mavaca in Venezuela (Chagnon 1997: 228). They believe that the yãimo is central to Yanomami culture, and rather than pushing to have them stopped they have suggested alternatives to the excessive drinking and brawling at those events.

Missionaries themselves learned the Yanomami way of life, spending years in isolation in the forest, when other humanitarians and good-willed persons did not and could not commit themselves to such a project. They have learned the language and reduced it to writing. They have worked to understand the Yanomami culture and have committed themselves to helping them, albeit from a Christian perspective. The Xilixana see the missionaries as trustworthy, stable, and caring. They recognize that missionary men do not sexually molest Xilixana women. Many think of the missionary as a friend.

The character of mission work has changed since the early arrival of the missionaries. Whereas in the first decade their approach was evangelical, the missionaries are now more inclined to see their very presence as a witness of God's care and love. Missionaries are much more engaged in government affairs and in medicine, both of which consume much of their time. Despite the myriad of change, missionaries remained faithfully present to the Xilixana. They interacted with all, freely providing medical aid and basic trade goods for their livelihood as well as a minimum of employment. They encouraged the production of more sophisticated artifacts for sale among tourists in cities, as a further means of supplying income. They have continued to encourage, teach, and train those who respond to a Christian message of hope and charity.

Eleven
"Warfare," Raids, and Revenge

Anyone who is even minimally acquainted with the Yanomami is familiar with the central role of war in this culture. Violence seems always just a breath away in all Yanomami relations, whether husband and daughter, husband and wife, and brother to brother, or between villages or host and guest. Before contact a husband described locally as "bad" killed his wife. At the time of contact husbands would take firebrands and beat the backs of their wives. Soon thereafter an Aica in-migrant youth shot another Aica visitor. A Xilixana almost killed his brother after the brother stole his wife.

Fights and bashing with severe wounds were common during the drunken festivities of the past two decades at Mucajai. A young man accidentally killed his mother with a file in a Palami theli yãimo. Another man killed his wife. In the 1960s a Malaxi theli, according to his confession, killed his wife by sorcery, then moved to Mucajai to acquire a second wife.

The Roots of "Warfare"

The frequency and method of Yanomami warfare have captured the interest of both the general anthropology reader and researcher. Though there is killing in Yanomami fighting it is not the same as Western warfare. Yanomami do not take possession of the victims' land. They do not politically control the besieged. (For further discussion see Chagnon 1997: 185, 189-91; Good 1991: 1) Chagnon has in the past referred to these people as "fierce," although in the fifth edition of his popular ethnography (1997: xii) he dropped the term because of a misinterpretation that comes with the translation.

The protein hypothesis (Ross 1971; Chagnon and Hames 1979; Harris 1984) suggests that violence arises because of limited resources of game. In the patriarchal Yanomami society, the term *naiki* (meat hunger) reinforces the cultural significance of the meat-providing role of men—they provide food in exchange for the sexual and domestic role of women. With population growth, as a village size expands the community tends to deplete the game in the immediate area, and meat becomes scarce. The competition over women increases, leading to brawls, fights, and warfare. Eventually groups fission, and after several years the cycle repeats itself. This perspective glorifies the valor and might of the male, and leaves women in a subordinate and subjected status. Lizot (1991: 68–70) and Chagnon (1988: 986) underscore the place of reciprocity in Yanomami culture. A village is raided, and a strong spirit of revenge sets in. The Yanomami fully anticipate and fear revenge from a village from which women are stolen, or in which someone has been killed. Retribution may also come in the form of sorcery. The old "eye for an eye" and "tooth for a tooth" sense of justice falls short of Yanomami practice, in which revenge may be meted out in a two to one or even five to one ratio. Even seemingly friendly villages may raid or perform sorcery against one another. No Yanomami village lives in peace or considers itself secure from raids or sorcery. Rumor, hunch, gossip, and earlier disputes add to the emotional ferment. Yanomami warfare is brutal and often repetitious. Some villages vacate their yãno and fields so as to be further removed from any retaliatory action.

Brian Ferguson (1995: 353–54) does not find this argument convincing. He makes a distinction between revenge and retaliation. He finds that the Yanomami retaliate as "close agnate groups of the victim rather than the group as a whole." He sees revenge as being a "highly malleable motivating factor" and acknowledges that revenge may be contrived.

Chagnon (1997: 185, 189–91; Good 1991) states that warfare includes the acquisition of women. Chagnon also speaks of reproduction success. My research shows that women are the primary victims of tension. They are stolen, raped, and often belittled when they are taken to a new environment. Women serve the very men who murdered their people. They give birth to children with the men who killed their husbands and sons, and who act as though nothing adverse ever happened. But Ferguson states that the acquisition of women in wars is not in itself adequate evidence that women are the fundamental reason for war. Because women are a component of war does not mean they are the principal cause of the battle.

Ferguson's thorough treatment of warfare (1995) finds the explanations of Yanomami warfare as based upon protein, revenge, women, or reproduction to be inadequate. From the wealth of Yanomami data gleaned, particularly from the central Yanomami region in Venezuela, he finds that these people are not "naturally" violent. I find this stance difficult to substantiate, given the frequent fisticuff duels between men and the hair-pulling and bashing that goes on between women. At the time of contact Xilixana had small stones hung from their hammocks, which they appropriately clenched with the third and fourth fingers in their fists when a fight became vicious. After contact they replaced the stones with flashlight batteries, and not long after that they started to melt down lead pellets to a form that would fit their clenched fists even more effectively. By the 1980s fights included the use of any club or stick available, and sometimes engaged parent against child.

Ferguson's position is one of infrastructural determinism, based upon specific historical situations. The central issue here is one of the availability of steel goods. He contends that the introduction of steel goods is a central variable in village alliances and warfare. He holds this stance not only for the more recent concentrated Yanomami contact period after the 1960s, but also for the turn of the century, when the Yanomami received steel goods through links with indigenous peoples from other tribes. The Yanomami wanted steel goods, and they killed both Yanomami and others to acquire this treasure. According to Ferguson, reasons for warfare go beyond the boundaries of thought that simply link owners and those seeking steel goods. Villages that had few steel goods but a significant connecting link with the source of trade goods made certain these channels were not blocked by neighboring villages.

Although Ferguson places the accessibility of steel goods as central to Yanomami warfare, he also recognizes that other factors can influence the reasons, intensity, and frequency of war. He recognizes that the possession of firearms after the 1950s grossly distorted the already delicate balance between villages. In the fullest sense, firearms were deadly, and the victims were disproportionately those who attempted to retaliate with bow and arrow.

The history in the precontact period shows the Xilixana to be an aggressive and intimidating people. We know that from at least the early 1920s on they initiated all the known acts of violence involving other groups, except for the ambush of the man they found harvesting palm fruit. It is also evident that they lived in fear of attacks, or of being victims of sorcery. More than a generation of time is not enough to rid them of the fear of possible enemy retaliation. In 1962 a Yekwana woman, captive among the Xilixana, was afraid to speak to her own people. In 1961 the Xilixana husband of another Yekwana captive died suddenly. The Xilixana contend that this was an act of sorcery by the Yekwana, 26 years after the war between the two groups.

The Xilixana quest for steel tools was unrelenting, except for a possible 10-year period after the tools were left by the Brazilian Boundary Commission in 1945. It appears that they remained isolated from other Yanomami after this episode. They did not initiate any attacks, nor did others raid. Finally, in 1956 they moved out of this long period of isolation from other indigenous peoples and naba by walking to the Apiau for the express purpose of steel tools. The record appears to support Ferguson's (1955) thesis of the Yanomami's compelling motivation to gain access to Western tools.

Intervillage Killings

THE XILI THELI RAID

The first intervillage killing in which the Xilixana were involved was with the Xili theli. In 1959 four miners paddled to the Malaxi theli, and after several months two of them descended the Mucajai River to return to Boa Vista. On the way these miners visited the Kasilapai village, about 20 kilometers upstream from the Mucajai mission station, and told the Kasilapai that the Malaxi theli would appreciate a visit from them. Most of the Kasilapai men eagerly responded and soon paddled the five-day journey. Undoubtedly the Malaxi theli received several steel tools as a result of this visit, and a number of them accompanied the Kasilapai back to their village. After a visit of several days the hosts made a quick trip upriver once more to escort the Malaxi theli back to their village.

About the time of the Kasilapai's return to their own village, in January 1960, the community was hit with an epidemic of colds, which led to pneumonia. In a brief period of time five people died. We believe they had contracted colds from the Malaxi theli, who had been infected by the miners. This influenza did not affect the other village, the Bola bèk, who lived at the mission post.

The Kasilapai believed the influenza was the result of Malaxi theli sorcery, so nine of their men headed up the Mucajai River, bent upon revenge. When confronted, the Malaxi theli shifted the blame upon the Xili theli, who lived almost three days' travel overland in the mountains to the southwest. The Malaxi theli accompanied the nine Kasilapai men, arriving at their destination about midday. In all the local community numbered about eight or nine men, and many women and children. Several Xili theli men who had been out hunting returned to the village in mid-afternoon. This village had no previous contact with the Xilixana and spoke a distinct different Yanomami dialect. The Xili theli, showing suspicion about the visitors, did not give the "guests" any food. One of my informants said there would have been no bloodshed if they had been friendly. This same informant walked with a Xili theli into his field and asked whether they had performed sorcery. The host showing the field kept repeating, "I do not understand you."

Two Kasilapai asserted their determination to kill. One asked the group to gather together to have a "service" in the manner of the missionaries. The locals did not respond. Then the Kasilapai killed: they stabbed two of the Xili theli, using bamboo arrow tips held in their hands, and killed another with a machete. The also killed a fourth. A fifth man who was stabbed fled, and so too did a sixth "sickly" man. The Kasilapai took three women, and the Malaxi theli took "many," though all the women captured by the Malaxi theli eventually escaped back to their home village. The women captured by the Kasilapai did not have the option of escaping: canoe travel was a frightening experience for them.

About 10 years later the Kasilapai sent a number of gifts as bride payment to the Xili theli, and about 16 years after the warfare a Kasilapai man, too young to be involved in the original killing, was working with Brazilians just south of the Xili theli. The brother to one of the captive Xili theli asked the Kasilapai to have the husband of his captive Xili theli sister come and revenge the Palahudi, enemies of the Xili theli. He never did become involved, but obviously the animosity between the Xilixana and Xili theli groups had dissipated—a point that reinforces the significance of marriage contracts for community solidarity and of social responsibilities even in warfare.

The Xili theli war indicates too the central place of sorcery in intratribal relations. Deceit and deception are also central to these histories. The Malaxi theli shifted the blame upon the Xili theli, which the Xilixana saw as credible. The Kasilapai sought to deceive their targets by calling for "prayer." The Kasilapai clearly did not resort to violence, and killings, with the Xili theli (or potentially the Malaxi theli) for the sake of acquiring steel goods, although perhaps an argument could be made that the Malaxi theli wanted to remain friendly with the Kasilapai in order to keep their newfound resources for steel goods. Still, such an argument does not take into account the Kasilapai's pursuit upstream to avenge those who were responsible for deaths brought on, they believed, through sorcery.

XILIXANA AND XILIANA CONFLICT

Another incident shortly after the Xili theli event is notable because, though bloodshed seemed likely, it did not occur. In 1963 two young Xilixana from the Kasilapai village made the long 10-day trip north by foot to the Xiliana. They never returned, and a second group of Kasilapai went to investigate. The Xiliana informed them that the first visitors had left sick with colds and had probably died in the forest. Another rumor suggested that other, unknown Yanomami had met the young men on the trail and killed them.

But on this visit, while walking through the forest, a young Xiliana boy inadvertently blurted out, "This is where we put them, here at the bottom of this stream." After hearing this the Kasilapai hurriedly returned to their territory, furious about the deaths. The leader of the village approached the missionaries cautiously and told them that he was going to return to the Xiliana for revenge, but since he was now a Christian he would only kill one rather than two people. His revenge party never did go to the Xiliana, and the Xilixana never did find out precisely how the two young men died.

After the death of the two Kasilapai, several Xiliana visited the Kasilapai who now lived at the mission station. There was a point during this visit that the local people were scheming to revenge with murder. The plan was averted when two younger men said, "We will not kill. Let them die of their own sickness." It is possible that missionary teaching played a part, influencing the Kasilapai not to avenge the deaths.

The death of the two Kasilapai young men and the revenge that almost happened are independent of the desire for steel goods. These encounters between the Xilixana and Xiliana in the early 1960s show how quickly mistrust and doubt erupt among the Yanomami, even amidst apparent amiable relations. It also shows that Yanomami sentiment often teeters on an emotional fulcrum: to kill or not to kill. Certainly, the relationship between the two groups in the 1990s would not have been as congenial if warfare had occurred in those earlier years.

THE LOST HUNTER

In July 1967 four hunters crossed the Mucajai and headed south to hunt tapir. In the afternoon, with the help of a dog, they encountered and pursued a tapir. The day was wearing on and the men decided to give up the chase, but one of them, HE, persisted, and later did not return. His relatives initiated a number of searches and found nothing. Two rumors emerged. HE had lost his way, became hungry, and died. From someone in a distant village they heard that HE had encountered four Aica, who, upon meeting, said, "Don't shoot, we are friendly." HE reportedly shot and killed two or three men, and then was shot with a bamboo-tipped arrow while fleeing, and died. At this point the informant said, "If only there had been another person with HE, he would not have shot."

The Xilixana made several unsuccessful trips to find his body. Eventually his sister and two companions found the dog's bones and, later, HE's bones in a thicket near a creek. His bag of shot was nearby, but not his gun. Some distance beyond they saw a temporary Moxatotau shelter.

To avenge his death the Xilixana planned a raid against the alleged perpetrators, the Moxatotau. They encountered another temporary shelter that had been used for hunting purposes, but never met the Moxatotau. They returned hungry. (On this trip they retrieved a stone axe head, which I purchased from them on my 1996 field trip.)

Even today these mountain people to the southwest, the Moxatotau, according to Xilixana informants, remain isolated by choice. The Fundacão Nacionál do Índio built an airstrip a short distance to the south and left steel goods as gifts, although the Moxatotau have apparently smashed most of these offerings. On one occasion, when a plane landed at the FUNAI airstrip, the Moxatotau surrounded the plane with their bows and arrows. In fear the pilot never disembarked and left the airstrip. I heard two reports of Moxatotau clashes with miners. In one incident three miners were killed; in the other one miner and one Moxatotau were killed. There are reports that these people had a fight with the Malaxi theli to the west and made contact with the Catrimani Waica to the south in or before the 1960s.

THE HEWAKEMA RAID

The bloodiest raid since the time of the earlier Yekwana warfare took place in 1968 against the Hewakema of the Ajarani region. Earlier, in 1960, 35 Aica from the Apiau and the more distant Hewakema from the headwaters of the Arajani River had visited Mucajai. Both peoples speak a Yanomami dialect almost incomprehensible to the other group. Thereafter the Xilixana only kept aware of Hewakema activity through what they heard from the Aica.

Three factors attributed to the Xilixana raid. XU's wife died suddenly, and her death was attributed to the sorcery of a Hewakema man. The informant, an Aica, said the Xilixana were a timid people, which enraged the Xilixana. Earlier a Xilixana married an Aica, and her brother, living in the Apiau River region, died. His people sought revenge against the Hewakema.

The revenge party of 11 consisted of men from four Xilixana villages. There was no distinct relationship pattern among the warriors. Several were related or friends of the offended. But other more youthful men seemed to have joined for the adventure, or were caught up in the frenzy of revenge.

After four days by trail they arrived at the village of friends on the mid-Apiau River. An Aica from this village was their guide for the remaining journey. They travelled to the headwaters of the river, then trekked up between two mountains, followed a small creek, and came to a flat terrain and large river, the Ajarani. Because the waters were high, one Xilixana had to swim across the river with bush rope clenched in his teeth, secure the rope, and eventually they constructed a bridge and walked across. They had another four hours of walk to the village. They ran out of food, but eventually came to their destination. Initially the Hewakema thought the visitors had evil intentions, but the guests deceived them, saying they were friendly.

The Hewakema served them meat and bananas and otherwise treated the visitors well. On the second day one of the host men ran to a neighboring village some six hours' distance to invite the people there to come. One morning four days later three Xilixana persuaded three Hewakema to go hunting with them. In the forest the Xilixana killed the three hunters: one with slashes of a machete across the chest and neck; another while he was about to shoot a bush chicken, when his Xilixana partner said, "Let me shoot it" and, taking the gun, shot him. They shot the third while he was gathering worms for fishing at the water's edge.

One of the Xilixana in the village heard the shots and thought, "Aha, they shot one of them … yes, there's the second one dead." The men returned from the forest when the sun was high and hid near the house. One of the older Xilixana realized they were back and fanned up a feverish mood for a mass killing. One Xilixana was diligently sharpening his machete on a stone, very agitated that these people had killed his Aica brother-in-law in an earlier raid. He stood up and asked if anyone wanted his machete, then furiously slashed one of the host men. Another saw the stumbling man and also slashed him, causing his death. The Xilixana shot another man with a bamboo-tipped arrow. Two of the local men stood near by in shock, holding their daughters. Two Xilixana axed one of them to death. One of the Hewakema fled by foot until he tripped on a vine and was killed with an axe. Another was shot at with a gun, was missed, and smashed to death with a stone by two Xilixana. A total of seven men were killed.

The Xilixana fled with women, several small girls, and a boy. Eventually they came to the bush rope bridge, crossed it, and slashed it. It was raining hard. They stopped for the night, placing the women with their hammocks in the middle of the camp, so they could not easily escape. One older Xilixana asked his recently married son whether he would not take one of them for a wife. He said, "No." However, his hammock was very close to the young woman's, so he took charge of her, and by default acquired a second wife.

During the night one woman quietly slipped out with her child. In her exit she rustled some leaves, arousing everyone in the camp, and some of the Xilixana pursued her with a flashlight. She plunged into the water and hid behind a fallen tree in the water. A Xilixana shot near her head to scare her, and the men returned to their camp. All the while they had to make sure the other women did not flee.

They encountered many swollen waters on their return, often walking up to their arm pits in water along the trail. Eventually they arrived at the Aica village on the Apiau River, extremely hungry. From here they sent two men on ahead to the Mucajai to bring food. At the Apiau they encountered several Brazilians, who asked whether they had a good party, and they deceptively answered, "Yes." The Brazilians requested that one particular strong young Xilixana stay to help saw lumber, but his father disapproved, which made the Brazilians angry. The Xilixana arrived back at their village with three captive adult women and three girls. Many years later immediate relatives of the captive women immigrated into the Mucajai population, with no apparent animosity remaining.

Although four of the men involved and one captive woman lived near the mission station, the story of this raid remained undisclosed until early 1973, when I was doing field research of kin and changing marriage patterns for my doctoral dissertation. A partial reason for the restricted disclosure is that most of the raiding party with their captive women lived more distantly downstream. But the main reason is that the local residents knew that the missionaries would disapprove of the killing. The place of the battle was far to the south, and involved a people with whom the Xilixana had little contact. I had established a rapport with one of the men in the raid, but before he gave me any details, he made me promise unconditionally that I would not inform the police in Boa Vista. He knew something of the Brazilian justice system, that acts of homicide were punished with imprisonment, a practice abhorrent to the Yanomami.

Again, in theory the Ajarani incident does not fit the model of violence and warfare relating to the acquisition of steel goods. Both groups had their independent and adequate resources for steel goods. They lived in a social sphere apart from one another, except for the Aica on the Apiau, who had associations with both groups. The argument related to protein is also not sustainable in this case. Both villages had good territories to hunt in, which did not overlap. The case is strongly supportive of the revenge or, specifically, retribution theory. The Xilixana believed that if they did not take revenge in the form of a mass murder, more Xilixana would die through sorcery. The capturing of women simply augmented their original impulse to avenge. The case also indicates, again, the centrality of the custom of giving food to strangers by a host village, and the fear and the suspicion of deception. An obvious tension between, on the one hand, being kind and considerate, and, on the other, being cautious and suspicious. The people have an ambivalence on being hospitable and being *waithili* (fierce). The cultural trait that is clearly evident is the brutality. The incident shows a lack of regard or respect for a person from another group as a human being. Someone who is not in your own group is a threat, is your enemy.

THE RAID WITH THE MALAXI THELI

In 1973 several Malaxi theli died, and one of them was the father to a woman married and living with the Xilixana. Their deaths were attributed to four Maututu theli, who with shaven heads (to avoid illness) and black painted bodies, came near the Malaxi theli yãno. They built a small fire and with the smoke, using *alawalik*, performed sorcery.

The Xilixana son-in-law and two other Xilixana joined the Malaxi theli on the raid (one of the Xilixana had a 22-calibre gun). En route several Anokwa theli joined them, and after three more days of travel they came upon the Maututu theli, who were living in small shelters in the forest. The revenging party shot an adult man, two women, and a boy whom they found gathering purple palm fruit in the forest. The Maututu theli shot and killed one Anokwa theli.

To demonstrate to the Maututu theli their hostile contempt, a Xilixana took the adult body and hacked it into a number of pieces. He hid the pieces in a variety of places. He took the head and placed it into a deep hole at the base of a tree, where they were sure no one would find it. Later, it was discovered. Apparently the leg and arm of the deceased were found. Because they had made clear that they were taking the act of sorcery very seriously, the Xilixana felt confident the Maututu would not seek further revenge. This raid was obviously based solely upon revenge for sorcery.

THE RAID WITH THE PALIMI THELI

One of the Xilixana villages had been allied through marriages with the Palimi theli since 1966. In 1978 seven Xilixana men accompanied the Palimi theli on a raid against the Palahuti. They journeyed for two days until they reached the Maitha group, who joined the entourage for another trip of five days west to the enemy village. As the raiders approached the Palahuti yãno they were shocked to hear a shaman chanting, predicting the enemy's arrival. The Xilixana men wanted to circle the yãno from a close distance, then attack, but the others preferred to remain at a distance. In all they killed three men and wounded another in the early morning, using bamboo-tipped arrow heads.

They could not take good aim because of the density of the bush. The Palahuti fled to another yãno not too distant. One of the Maitha was shot: MÃ, a man who had visited Mucajai years earlier.

THE MASSACRE BY THE XILIANA

At least one other major bloodbath has occurred, although the Xilixana were not involved in it. The incident is significant because it shows the extent of brutality in a case in which one of the warring parties involved has the advantage of firearms. I discovered the encounter during my 1996 trip, and to my knowledge this incident has not yet been reported to either the Brazilian authorities or to the missionaries.

One day while he was building a canoe a Xiliana suddenly died, allegedly because of Palahuti sorcery. His sons were extremely agitated over this incident and rallied other Xiliana for a raid to the distant Palahuti. En route they picked up reinforcements from the Palimi theli, and then the Maitha. Arriving at the Palahuti, they used their guns and shot every person in the village: men, women, and children. There was a second house, possibly an hour's walk beyond the first village. The Xiliana shot two men with firearms in that village, while the Palahuti attempted to retaliate with arrows.

The Motivations for Violence and Warfare

The history of the Xilixana since the time of contact gives no evidence that the acquisition of steel goods was the primary purpose of warfare. They had enough steel tools, and actually traded them with other Yanomami. The abundance of trade goods enhanced their position among other Yanomami.

In the postcontact period, the Xilixana warfare is best understood in terms of the association of the physical and spirit worlds. The Xili theli and Ajarani Maututu theli and Palahuti raids were made to avenge sorcery. The Moxatotau raid was to avenge a death. The Xilixana consider sorcery to be ever present, and children, women, men, and shaman alike fear it. To this day they attribute "natural" death to sorcery. While the Casa do Índio near Boa Vista eventually became an accepted place for healing, they believe the place carries an additional risk, as the meeting place of numerous Yanomami. The Xilixana sense that they are the victims of sorcery even when a death is specified by the medical professionals as cancer, TB, or pneumonia. Any such illness or death must be avenged. Such acts of reciprocity do not readily lead to a state of trust and peace and tranquillity. Suspicion is always present.

Less clear is the priority of acquiring women in raids. In the early 1940s the Xilixana went to the mountain Aica for the express purpose of finding women. Once there, they did not appear to pursue their goal with much vigor. Possibly they found the actual number of the enemy too large to confront. In the Xili theli and Hewakema encounters they stole women, but this bonus only came after they had accomplished their furious avenge motive. Again, revenge appears to be the foremost motivating force.

Two other underlying cultural factors contribute to warfare among most Yanomami. The male is socialized to show himself as tough, brave, and fearless. They are quick to fill the air with verbal denunciations upon anyone they dislike. A man readily raises his fists to hit an opponent on the face or chest. Men see any act that is less than brave as soft and spineless.

The Yanomami practise the art of bluffing. One phrase they repeatedly use is, "You are lying." When they talk together they often ask one another, "Are you lying?" Even if the response is "no," they believe their companion might still be bluffing. After someone makes a statement the listener often asks, "*Unt yai?*" ("really?"). A confirmation that this is *yai* (truth) is still no assurance of truth. Another phrase used less, but portraying the same meaning, is, "His words are not straight." In the Xilixana communities rumors spread rapidly. Arguments and hostility often emerge from incidents or accusations that are untrue or distorted. The Yanomami are quick to show how righteous they are—though this is a trait that is not common only to these people.

Clashes with Miners

At least six times blood has also been shed between the Xilixana and the "civilized," though such incidents are notable for involving one type of Western people only, namely those involved in mining. The events have always happened in Yanomami territory, and in each case the Xilixana believed that an injustice of some kind had occurred. The Xilixana responded to the outsiders in a merciless manner, just as they would with their own Yanomami enemies. Given their customs, the Xilixana would have expected some intervention by Brazilian authorities as retribution for the homicide.

The first miners to penetrate the Mucajai region came in 1959. Four men in a canoe paddled up the river, passing the Mucajai mission station and travelling on to the area of the Malaxi theli. After several months two of this team of four returned downstream to Boa Vista. The other two remained with the Malaxi theli for a much longer period of time, sired children, and eventually went overland to the headwaters of the Catrimani River.

Beginning in 1985 hundreds of miners went up the Mucajai River to pan for gold. They established camps in a number of locations and gouged the river banks from their floats. They used mercury, which contaminated the Yanomami's source of drinking water in the river. At times they asked for food in exchange for Western goods. Sometimes they asked for the labor of Yanomami men, and at times they used Xilixana women as prostitutes.

The first confrontation between Xilixana and miners took place in 1987 in Malaxi theli territory, where a group of Malaxi theli were bent on ambushing the miners' camp and stealing their guns. Some Xilixana happened to be visiting the Malaxi theli at the time, and OX, a Malaxi theli who had migrated to the Xilixana some 17 years earlier, was unsuccessful in persuading his kin not to make the raid. Seven Xilixana joined their forces, including OX. They ambushed the camp. In the exchange of gunfire and bamboo-tipped arrows, at least six miners and four Yanomami were killed, one of them a Xilixana.

The second encounter happened in Xilixana territory during the time the missionaries were ousted and replaced by FUNAI personnel at the mission station (1987-90). The story was leaked to me on my 1995 field trip, when I was walking for four hours north by trail to a more distant Xilixana village. We had walked about an hour when my guides casually announced, "This is where they killed them." The five relatively young killers were from the village of the one Xilixana killed by the miners some months earlier in Malaxi theli territory. They had come across the miners hunched over, eating. Methodically the leading Xilixana said to his companions, "You take that one, and you the other, and I'll get the remaining one." They shot them with bamboo-tipped arrows and left their bodies to the vultures. A short time later a miner's plane landed to check the whereabouts of the missing men. The Xilixana feigned any knowledge of the incident. To this day the miners, apparently, can only surmise what happened.

A third incident happened in the immediate vicinity of the mission station, about 1990, when four miners were walking the miners' path on the south bank of the Mucajai River. They were ill-equipped: no guns, little food. They carried a cutlass. In hunger they stole some sweet cassava root from a Xilixana field planted by a woman who had recently died. A Xilixana saw them doing this and followed them from a distance, locating their evening's lodging. Four of his companions joined him for the kill, using bamboo-tipped and steel-tipped arrows. They killed two miners, and a third hid behind the rocks in the river very near the mission. He was shot in the back but extracted the arrow from his own flesh, then crossed to the mainland, and soon thereafter died. The fourth miner fled upriver and eventually reached his destination "without a stitch of clothing" (as my informant reported with a big smile). The earlier killing of one of the Xilixana and three Malaxi theli undoubtedly stimulated this zeal to kill. The bodies were left in the woods for the vultures. Months later the missionaries took photos of the site of the bones and sent them to authorities in Boa Vista.

Yet another incident took place in Malaxi theli territory in 1992. Like several other Xilixana young men, IA was employed by miners. When the federal police became serious about flushing out miners from Yanomami territory, they hired IA to accompany them on helicopter flights. This experience undoubtedly fuelled his antagonism against miners. His mother was a Malaxi theli and therefore he had relatives and associations with others of that group who had either been bereaved or killed by miners. IA, now aged 24, and his younger brother were walking in Malaxi theli territory when IA was suddenly shot by a miner. The younger brother, age 22, went after the miner and shot him, then took care of his brother's corpse. He returned to the Malaxi theli yãno and rallied assistance to attack the miners. They found three miners working the creek. The sound of the diesel engine used to pump water prevented the miners from hearing the approach of the Malaxi theli, who shot all three with arrows. The warriors went to the encampment nearby and killed a fourth person who was preparing food. A fifth lay in a hammock, drunk, and the Xilixana shot him with one of the miner's guns. A man and woman fled. An airplane came to pick up the bodies of the dead men. One of the Xilixana killers was asked by the Brazilians to help carry the bodies to the plane but refused.

In late 1992 or early 1993 a fifth clash took place about 14 kilometers upriver from the Mucajai mission. A canoe of Xilixana men, women, and children travelling upstream met three miners. They stopped to chat. One miner was about to place a shell in his gun and the Xilixana asked him not to do it. The miner complied, but in anger about the death of IA, they shot one miner with a gun and two with metal-tipped arrows.

In 1997 there was another killing. A miner was returning to Boa Vista from the headwaters of the Mucajai River. He stopped in the area of the mission. Several men from Village E, undoubtedly still carrying grudges from miners' encounters among their kin in the Malaxi theli region, killed him.

Without any coaxing my informant told me of several other encounters of his wife's people, the Malaxi theli, with miners. What they reveal most graphically is the devastation of the presence of miners in Yanomami territory—as well as the deeply embedded Yanomami cultural trait regarding revenge. In one encounter, a Malaxi theli shot a miner dead at the headwaters of the stream where they live. In another, a neighboring people shot two miners and a third fled for his life. One miner shot another miner dead. The federal police shot a total of five miners dead, several of whom were very close to the airstrip. The Malaxi theli lay in ambush and shot a miner who was crossing a bridge over a tributary of the Mucajai River. He was carrying his four-year-old son, who toppled into the water and drowned.

The informant reported that as a number of miners were sitting at the airstrip, the Malaxi theli threw *alawalik* (black magic) at them. (They would not shoot arrows at their enemy on the airstrip.) Many of these men became ill, and a number died. The Brazilians thought it was malaria, but according to the Yanomami it was sorcery. Another miner was shot by three men who had surrounded him on the trail, and I also heard of another incident of a miner shot on the trail. Once a miner asked two Malaxi theli to guide him along the path in the forest. At a certain point they stopped and the Yanomami climbed a palm tree to harvest the purple palm fruit. The miner looked up to watch the climber and his Malaxi theli companion shot him dead.

Xilixana suspicion of and antagonism and hatred towards miners carry the same ferociousness and brutality as warfare against other Yanomami, although the social, economic, and political considerations are somewhat different. While miners often have guns, the Yanomami know the forest and are quick and quiet in their manoeuvers through the rainforest. Miners are singularly focused upon gold, and Xilixana have learned its value as a means of accumulating Western goods: clothing, ghetto blasters, outboard motors.

With the deluge of miners came the Military Police. When the Yanomami learned that miners were in their territory illegally, their animosity against the miners increased. While some miners hired Yanomami and bought food from them, they also copulated with their women. The two groups became suspicious of each other.

The conflict between Yanomami and the miners is evident on many levels. Miners stay only temporarily amongst the Yanomami, but while they are there they pollute the waters and exacerbate the malaria epidemic and other health problems. They are not equipped to physically care for any indigenous people they meet or employ. They do not learn their culture or language. The natives of the rainforest stand in the way of their unrelenting pursuit for gold.

The Cultural Norms of Violence

Among themselves, then, the Yanomami live in fear of encroachment or a raid of other Yanomami. The use of sorcery exacerbates their fear as well as their power to inflict illness and death upon others whom they distrust. Friends of one encounter quickly become enemies, simply on hearsay. A Yanomami is not surprised to find that another person's tale, told with great drama and passion as being truth, soon becomes exposed as a gigantic lie. When one has been "had," whether verbally, in trade, illness, or death (sorcery), there is hardly any other recourse but to retaliate with violence. In this sense Chagnon's use of "fierce people" is appropriate. It appears that deception is common, in the myths of their forebears as well as in their daily life. They apparently feel no embarrassment in lying, no moral wrong. In Yanomami culture, truth appears not to be a moral consideration. They live in a world of deceit, mistrust, and hoax. The Yanomami respond quickly to rumor without seeking to hear, or explore, any mitigating facts.

The cultural norm to be tough, gruff, and rough (or fierce) serves to explode a keg of dynamite. There is no room for compromise, no desk diplomacy. Might is right, and, a Xilixana would say, I am right. In any scrimmage it is never an eye for an eye, tooth for a tooth, but rather eyes for an eye and teeth for a tooth. There is no final killing, no termination of a series of murderous events. A killing incident of one generation may well be revenged in the next. A person is never secure. Retaliation or retribution can take place at any time from quite unexpected sources. Trickery in a revenge in death is commonplace. Humans are killed almost as easily as monkeys in the forest. There is no shame, no guilt, and little conscience in the killing, although there will be a fear that the murder might be avenged by raid or sorcery in the future.

Part III
Social Change

Twelve
Adaptation in a Precapitalist Society: Agents of Change

In a modern heterogeneous and pluralistic Western society, it is not difficult to envisage a wide spectrum of potential change. These same principles of change are operative in a precapitalist society as well. In the precontact period, Xilixana village and family structures were both fragile and strong. The social structure was rarely harmonious or even covertly peaceful. Though their social system maintained recognized boundaries and proved to be enduring, it was nevertheless explosive. The elements of history, geography, environment, and population, and to a lesser degree personalities and leadership, all had the usual impact on social structures. The dynamics of this living and vibrant social organism were also contingent upon latent characteristics that would long remain dormant and then suddenly give manifestation in an almost surprising manner.

In this ever-emerging and changing milieu the structure adapts, and the adaptation made is a selection amongst several options. Adaptations then establish a potential for further change while at the same time closing or limiting the possibility of alternatives. In other words, the ever-evolving structure of any society incorporates both change and a degree of constraint or resistance to change—an evolving development and growth and at the same time a permanence, a stability.

People in collectives or groups act in ways that determine their future, but they act out of their perceptions of themselves as well as their perception of others. These perceptions may be close to or possibly quite distant from a given reality. Furthermore, some actors or members in a social system are better positioned for change than others. Their status in society gives them the potential to influence the direction of society more than others. These key persons have the potential to facilitate change or preserve existing values and behavior. In many societies, the young seek change more quickly than older people. The elderly have more vested interest in the existing structure.

Throughout the precontact period, status positions among the Yanomami were firmly established. The most effective shaman and the older and healthy men, particularly those with large families, had the most power. Women had influence in some matters. Children and the maimed had relatively little power or status. At contact the Mucajai population had a five to two ratio of men to women, in part due to the practice of selective female infanticide. The women worked at preparing food, carrying water, and caring for children. When women were taken in marriage, the bridegroom was obligated to her parents for lifelong bride service and bride payment.

Over the 40 years since contact the Xilixana of Brazil have been confronted with three main, active external agents of change: missionaries, Brazilians and their institutions, and other indigenous peoples. These change agents have goals that are both similar to one another and different, and both the goals and the means used to achieve those goals can change over time. The needs of a changing Xilixana society can themselves modify the varying methods used by these agents to bring about change.

The government operates to some extent on the basis of pressure groups: local, national, and international. People in the state of Roraima want employment, and entrepreneurs want business. Mining brings gold, and gold means big business for the people in Boa Vista and elsewhere. Similar interests exist on the national level, but they expand to include national security (which leads to airstrips in the frontier region, for instance) and development (roads through the rainforest). A countervoice also exists, from citizens within southern Brazil and from around the world, that insists on preserving the culture and the lives of the people in the forests of Brazil. The Committee for the Creation of a Yanomami Park is an example. For almost 20 years a collective international voice from anthropologists and others defending the interests of the Yanomami has also been raised.

Institutions like the Air Force, Indian Affairs and Health Services, various protection agencies, along with miners, other Yanomami, and the missionaries all played a part in transforming the rainforest way of living in both big and small ways. The BR-120 Northern Perimeter Highway—the "Perimetral Norte"—has cut like a swath through the southern segment of Yanomami land. With the highway employees and settlers moving in and causing great ruptures in their environment, several villages in the Catrimani river region, southeast of the Xilixana, lost half their populations, and a third village lost 30 per cent of its population (Saffirio and Hames 1983: 11). Some 13 villages were reduced to eight small family groups.

For the most part the agents of change want to see the Xilixana continue to live in their natural habitat and continue their traditional ways. For the outsiders this might mean the preservation of the bow and arrow for hunting. It means that the animals of the forest, the fish of the streams, should continue to be available to support the Yanomami way of living. Minor changes—metal tips on arrows, fish hooks—and major—health care and airstrips—are part of the "rewards" of closer connections to the outside world.

The Brazilian Influence

As a state, Brazil acts as an agent of change in many ways. While the state's presence has been pronounced during the last two decades, its authority was evident from before the time of contact. It was the government, after all, that gave permission in the mid-1950s for UFM missionaries to move in and meet the previously uncontacted Yanomami in the western region of the Roraima territory, which later became a state.

THE BRAZILIAN AIR FORCE

Shortly after the missionaries had established two mission posts, the Brazilian Air Force (FAB) and the National Security Department became keenly interested in the Roraima territory and endorsed the presence of the missionaries. From FAB's point of view the missionaries were a useful ally. It was in FAB's interests to see airstrips established in the frontier regions, as part of the country's efforts to shore up its national security and defend border regions from intrusion. And the Air Force saw the missionaries as an aid to the establishment of amiable relations with indigenous peoples. The missionaries' abilities with the language and their friendship with Yanomami were great assets.

From the missionaries' point of view, FAB's interest in the region came at a strategic time, because they had recently become subject to numerous false accusations that missionary activity was a disguise to cover over mining exploration. FAB intercepted efforts to expel the Protestant group.

Against the missionaries' recommendation, FAB adopted bold tactics that sometimes went awry. In one case the Air Force landed on bumpy grass terrain without any exploratory ground troop to initiate their presence in the area. (Months later they realized they were in Venezuelan territory and abandoned the airstrip.) On that same trip a helicopter accompanying the forces ran out of fuel and was forced to crash-land in the forest. A search team consisting of a missionary, a Waica guide, and FAB personnel went out to find the helicopter. On a second venture a FAB helicopter hovered over a Surucucu village while the missionary and a Waica guide jumped to the ground from the chopper. The resident Yanomami were asked to immediately help them clear a runway on a grassy plateau some two hours' walk away. (This same strip was in heavy use for mining gold and cassiterite after 1985.)

For a brief period of time FAB became extremely interested in the site of the Xilixana mission post. The existing 420-meter airstrip was too short for FAB's purposes, and its personnel surveyed the area and decided to reconstruct the strip almost at right angles to the existing strip. FAB asked the missionaries to mobilize the Xilixana to cut trees for the approach to the strip, as well as trees on the site of the proposed strip. This work was carried out, but FAB never returned to complete the task. FAB's interest in the project waned, probably because the Mucajai station was more than 100 kilometers from the Venezuelan boundary and thus not considered of great strategic importance. For their part, the missionaries at the station were relieved that their outpost would not be inundated by a flow of FAB traffic and personnel.

AGENCIES TARGETED TO PROTECT THE YANOMAMI

The mandate of the Indian Protection Service, founded in 1910, was to protect the Indians. The national office gave permission in 1955 for the Protestant mission organization, Unevangelized Fields Mission, to establish mission posts among the Yanomami in the Territory of Roraima. (About the same time another group, Baptist Mid Missions, also received permission to open a station among the Xiliana northwest of Boa Vista.)

In the early 1960s the president of the Indian Protection Service paid a visit to the Mucajai mission post. I was asked to congregate the Xilixana, and I proceeded to translate his speech: "I am your friend, I care about you, I will work on your behalf. Let me know your problems." The Xilixana found it difficult to make sense of his mission. How could a stranger, unknown to them, who did not know their language, work on their behalf, represent them? And what is this higher body, the Brazilian government?

The Indian Protection Service was reorganized in 1968 to form the Fundacão Nacionál do Índio (FUNAI), the formal institution with the most power over the Brazilian Yanomami. FUNAI's task is to address the needs of the Yanomami, provide health care, sell goods to them, and make sure unauthorized people are not in the area. Given the size of Brazil, the limited resources available, the multitude of different indigenous tribes and languages, and the isolation of some of these tribes and the different degrees of exposure to non-indigenous peoples, the organization's job is of monumental proportions. In 1972 FUNAI had 140 posts in Brazil, 10 reserves, and four parks (Brooks, Fuerst, Hemming, and Huxley 1973). In 1971 it reportedly had 66 attendant nurses and 10 specialized nurses on the posts, with 10 doctors and 10 nurses available. FUNAI claimed to be running 144 schools with 15,000 students (some intermittently). It also had a staff of four anthropologists.[1] In 1992 FUNAI had 4,500 employees (Rabben 1993).

From its base in Boa Vista FUNAI became involved with other aboriginal peoples, such as the Macuxi. In 1969 the agency established a presence with the Xiliana, where it sporadically placed personnel. By the mid-1970s it had established the small Casa do Índio base in Boa Vista, where all Roraima's indigenous peoples—Yanomami, Macuxi, Yekwana, WaiWai, and Ingarico—could come for proper, if minimal, health care. With time the agency founded other posts, and its presence expanded with the penetration of the miners after 1985.

In 1983 FUNAI built an airstrip on the north bank of the Mucajai River, 22 kilometers east of the Mucajai mission. The Xilixana who in 1964 lived on the bank of the river about 14 kilometers downstream from the mission helped in the building of the airstrip, and when one of their leaders died in 1983 they

---

1 A critique of FUNAI's work was made in 1972 by the British Aborigines Protection Society (Brooks et al. 1973).

abandoned their yãno and moved to the FUNAI airstrip. They now call themselves the Comara people after the name of the post. By 1995 they considered themselves distinct from the Mucajai mission communities.

In the state of Roraima there are now at least six FUNAI posts with airstrips in Yanomami territory. Each post has permanent personnel. When the posts are on rivers the staff provides canoes for the Yanomami to travel from one village to another. Occasionally FUNAI personnel from Comara visit the villages upstream in the Mucajai mission region: to transport Indians, call on the services of a shaman to treat a Comara inhabitant, or make sure outsiders have not illegally moved into Yanomami lands. Their primary function at Comara is to treat the sick. The Xilixana at Comara are often transported by air or canoe and road, a trip of two days, to the Casa do Índio in Boa Vista. After the demarcation of the Yanomami Park in 1991 FUNAI persuaded the small Aica village of Flexal just above the large waterfalls, downstream on the Mucajai, to move upstream just inside the park boundary. This places the Aica relatively close to the Comara Xilixana.

In the early 1990s FUNAI opened an additional post, an abandoned miners' encampment with an airstrip, on the Uraricoera River, northwest from the Mucajai mission. Village H from the Mucajai area, with about 40 inhabitants, accepted the invitation to migrate there in 1991 and 1992.[2] Despite the vigorous journey necessary, three to five days' long, visits between this community and village B at Mucajai are frequent. In 1993 village B relocated a distance of four hours' walk north of the Mucajai mission station. About 1994 FUNAI personnel from their post on the Uraricoera trekked to village B north of the Mucajai post. FUNAI proposed building an airstrip at this site, but the headman said he did not want their personnel in his village because he feared they would sexually molest the women.

In mid-1987 it was reported that a Catholic missionary working among Brazilia Yanomami had acted inappropriately, and FUNAI expelled him from Yanomami territory. Apparently, though, the missionary said he would leave only if the other missionaries were also expelled. As a result, in August, after almost 30 years of continuous presence at Mucajai, the Protestant mission personnel composed of two Brazilians and two Americans had to evacuate the post with a mere 72 hours notice.

This surprising turn of affairs occurred during the height of the miners' activities. FUNAI, and in a few instances miners and Xilixana, moved in to inhabit the missionary houses. The buildings fell into disrepair, and some goods were stolen. Weeds and saplings invaded the compound. More dramatically, during the period of the evacuation two miners were killed by the Xilixana in the woods near the station. After a time the Xilixana began to complain about the lack of medical care. In 1990 FUNAI personnel in Brasilia, in response to the local protests, phoned the Missão Evangélica da Amazonia (MEVA) office in Boa Vista, asking why they had left the Mucajai station two and one half years earlier. They insisted that the missionaries return immediately, which they did,

---

2   For the location of Xilixana villages, see Figure 3.1.

though once they got there they were surprised to find that the FUNAI personnel stationed at Mucajai had not been given a redirecting order—it came that
very day. Within a month FUNAI personnel had vacated the Mucajai mission
post. The whole process of FUNAI's evacuation of missionary personnel and the
eventual request to reoccupy was a scenario of major bungling.

FUNAI has been plagued with the problem of insufficient resources for the
monumental task set before it (Maybury-Lewis 1989 2-5; Brooks et al. 1973).
It has lacked the authority to combat other political interests such as
entrepreneurs (miners), government development agencies, the National
Security Council, and Roraima state interests. In March 1989, Action for
Citizenship, a group from southern Brazil established to defend rights
inherent to Brazilian citizenship, targeted the Yanomami in the state of
Roraima. In June members visited the Malaxi theli post of Paapiu and found
no FUNAI staff present. The Yanomami, who lived only 50 meters from the
airstrip, where numerous airplanes and helicopters roared to land and take off,
were in desperate need of medicine. FUNAI offered them no protection against
the assault of hordes of miners and entrepreneurs. The post had no medical
assistant. The miners had brought in diseases—malaria and an eye infection
known as pneumococcus—that were affecting 90 percent of the local population. The Malaxi theli had been introduced to pornographic movies and now
had pin-ups hung in their yãno ("Roraima, Brazil: A Death Warning," Cultural
Survival Quarterly 1989, 59).[3]

At least until very recently, FUNAI staff had no health training and tended to
dispense too much or unnecessary doses of medicine. They have not addressed
issues of preventative health ("The Threatened Yanomami," 1989:13(1): 45,
46). FUNAI workers have impregnated Xilixana women. They make no attempt
to learn Ninam or the Yanomami culture. The Yanomami would be better
served if FUNAI personnel made a commitment to stay at their posts for longer
periods of time. Their concern should be with the long-term protection of the
identity and culture of the Xilixana. FUNAI personnel have the opportunity to
deal with concerns that might improve Yanomami life, such as better means of
agriculture, control of insects that attack food-producing plants, improved
arrow tips, and the provision of adzes to facilitate canoe construction. They
might be able to aid the indigenous peoples to develop artifact production for
trade.

Another organization, the Commission for the Creation of the Yanomami
Park (CCPY), was founded in 1977 to defend the land rights and health of the
Yanomami. It is a Brazilian and international collective organization, and many
of its members are anthropologists who attempt to work in the interests of the
Yanomami, mainly in advocating the creation of exclusive land for the
Yanomami. Supported at least in part by international funding, its personnel are
located at several FUNAI posts among the Yanomami, even though officially
they have not been given permission to be there. CCPY escalated its efforts with
the penetration of miners and others into Yanomami territory in the mid-

---

3 The film Contact [1990] portrays the dilemma of the Malaxi theli at Paapiu.

1980s. But its members' endeavors were viewed as conflicting with government policies and approaches, and therefore they were prohibited from entering Yanomami lands for a period in 1987 ("The Threatened Yanomami," *Cultural Survival Quarterly* 1989: 13-1: 45).

The Commission sought to establish a park covering 8 million hectares in the Brazilian states of Amazonas as well as Roraima. By 1989 the Brazilian government had reduced the proposal to a little less than one million square miles, or by 70 per cent, with the Yanomami territory divided into 19 discontinuous land areas. This official approach would jeopardize their historical occupation of a wide-ranging area and threaten their social reproduction ("Brazilian Government Reduces Yanomami Territory by 70 percent," *Cultural Survival Quarterly* 1989: 13-1, 47). The government plan would permit some special areas for gold prospecting, which meant an invasion of Yanomami territory. Since the park is now officially recognized, CCPY identifies itself as Comissão Pro-Yanomami.

Towards the end of the 1980s the Xilixana were being drawn into state politics. The Brazilian Military Police hired one young Xilixana man to help in efforts to move miners out of Yanomami lands. The Xilixana became aware of the tension between some government officials and miners and recognized that the Yanomami peoples had a right to "ownership" of their lands. In 1994 the

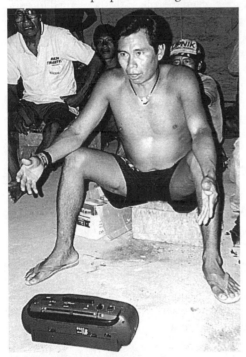

joint bodies of FNS and CCPY hired the only Portuguese-speaking Yanomami from the Mucajai region to assist them in educating Yanomami of their rights. This man, PER, frequented several meetings with Yanomami leader David Kopenawa,[4] and accompanied the leader from village G to the capital, Brasilia, in 1995. With CCPY's financial assistance PER has organized and conducted political meetings in all the Mucajai villages as well as several on the Uraricoera River. These endeavors helped create a Yanomami consciousness, representing a radical shift from the parochial village mentality common among the Yanomami until the mid-1980s. For instance, PER specifically asked

The message of Bata meetings is being recorded.

---

4   David Kopenawa, a Yanomami, summarizes the predicament of his people in *Cultural Survival Quarterly*, 13:4, 1989.

Bata talk in the mid-nineties. Headman takes notes.

me whether I was being paid for writing this book. In the event that I was making money, he said his people felt entitled to some of the profit. They accepted my plan to have money earned from the sale of the book used to assist in the cost of medical care for their people.

In 1996 the CCPY transported a number of Xilixana, including women, to a conference held among the Macuxi, who are claiming the ranch lands of some farmers who have been in the area for generations. A showdown over this issue seemed imminent, with Xilixana warriors prepared to stand with the Macuxi in the demands being placed before the government. Meetings of this nature unite the Xilixana with other indigenous people of the state who feel their rights are not being addressed.

OTHER BRAZILIANS

From the beginning of the contact period, the Xilixana made trips downriver for the experience as well as for trading purposes. They exchanged canoes and arrows for a few used axes, knives, or pieces of clothing. They might stay several days and join these frontier people in hunting, fishing, felling trees, and field work. Compared to the resident missionaries, these frontier Brazilians lived a lifestyle that was not totally alien to the Xilixana. The Brazilians hunted, fished, and practised a similar slash and burn agriculture of garden crops. Most walked or canoed to travel from place to place. Frontier Brazilian life was centered on survival and, for some, a sense of freedom from the constraints of "civilization."

There were new things to see and learn. By 1962 a few young men accepted requests to help farmers build fields or help out ranchers who had large fields of rice, manioc, and banana. A few accompanied their employers to the city, where their horizons were expanded even more: stores with uncountable items for sale, massive houses built of brick (which the Xilixana referred to as "stone"), pavement ("sheets of rock"), vehicles that travelled at great speeds at night, from which they fled in fear. They learned that "police people" who looked "fierce" acted against those who were disorderly. They eventually learned that the police punished acts of violence, both great and small.

A few years later a Xilixana was imprisoned for unruly behavior. He hated the confines of the prison, and especially the smelly toilet in his cell. His mother at the Mucajai station pleaded with me to beseech the authorities to release him.

Some Xilixana have established casual friendships with Brazilians. They see artifacts that the Westerners commonly use. The Xilixana got garden seeds or plants from the Brazilians' fields. The most significant plants imported are rice and maize, obtained in the 1980s. The Yanomami now construct the walls of their houses out of mud rather than leaves. Farmers, merchants, and friends have given Xilixana cigarettes and alcohol, joked about sex, and invited men and women to have intercourse with them. The Xilixana learned to pole rather than paddle their canoes in places where the water was shallow yet swift. They learned new methods of fishing: to use a net or numerous hooks left in a section of the water for the night or for several hours. They recognized the superiority of the gun over bow and arrow.

They also saw drinking and the effects of alcohol more potent than their own. By the late 1980s some Xilixana were taking a bottle of liquor back to their yãno. They witnessed brawls and stabbings. They saw prostitution, a practice notably different from their own sexual license during feasts. When they accompanied missionaries to Boa Vista for language study or medical help, they witnessed urban living. A few also frequented assemblies of Christians who met to sing and worship God.

These experiences on the lower Mucajai and in Boa Vista exposed them, particularly in the 1960s, to the people of the larger surrounding part of Brazil. In time they learned that the Brazilians had a responsibility to provide health care, and that their political destiny rested with people in the capital of Brazilia.

MINERS

The forest breeds suspicion, distrust, and, when non-indigenous people enter the scene, often greed.

The first contact the Xilixana had with miners was in 1959—the time when a canoe of four stopped briefly at the mission station before going upriver to the Malaxi theli. This brief visit left a memory. One of the miners gave medicine to a young pubescent girl who complained of stomach pain. She later died, and the Xilixana blamed the miner. That was also the visit that led to the Xilixana making contact with the Malaxi theli.

Later, when two of the four miners stopped again at the mission station on their way back down the river, they became convinced that the missionaries at Mucajai were really miners. They believed the missionaries were mining gold at several locations in the forest and transporting the mineral out by plane.

About the time of their arrival at the mission from upstream, the missionaries had recently returned from contacting the Aica on the Apiau River. The miners heard that the missionaries had left some of their cargo in the forest near the Apiau River, to speed their return journey. The miners had several Xilixana accompany them in search of this cargo, fully believing they would find evidence of gold mining. The Xilixana told me about their pursuit of this goal, "*João maliãxi hum*" ("Go on to John's metal goods"). They must have been disappointed when they found only an axe, gun, and several one-liter empty cans.

No record exists of other miners entering the region until 1985, when they came in canoes and eventually small barges pushed by 40 HP engines, bringing in machinery, guns, and prostitutes. Some of them stopped at the Xilixana villages to visit and purchase food, and some Xilixana women showed little restraint in having sex with the miners. Several Xilixana men told the miners that they should get their female partners in Boa Vista, not at the yãno. A few miners panned for gold in the creeks in the general area of the Xilixana. Others went further upstream to the headwaters of the Mucajai. The Xilixana assisted in the mining ventures, initially in helping to move cargo, and later they learned how to pan for gold themselves. In 1987 it was reported that there were 80,000 miners in Roraima. (Other reports have estimated the numbers at 140,000.)

At times the Xilixana shared their food with the miners, and in return some miners promised a wealth of goods for Xilixana cooperation. For years the Xilixana had ambivalent feelings towards the miners. The Xilixana's hopes for a Western lifestyle and possessions were quickly kindled, but never fully realized.

In the late 1980s the Xilixana became aware that the government was showing interest in Yanomami territory, and that officially miners were not permitted to go into these lands. But the miners continued to enter through devious routes, and law enforcement agencies with helicopters would "invade" mining camps. The miners would flee to the forest. Later, the Xilixana would root through the miners' abandoned camps, finding pans, tarpaulins, plastic barrels, clothing, maybe a pistol. These goods became scattered in and around the Xilixana residences, including a large, heavy-duty diesel engine once used in gouging soil from the riverbank in search of gold.

Beginning about 1987, when the Xilixana learned to do their own mining, they took their precious finds to the gold dealers in Boa Vista and received money, which they then used to buy clothing and other goods. They had no sense of the actual value of the currency. A village E man bought an outboard motor and gasoline and generously transported Xilixana along the river. More gold provided more gasoline. The engine eventually became dysfunctional, and not knowing how to fix it, and without money to repair it, he sold the outboard downriver. The same man told me in 1987 that he planned to install a television in his house—a statement suggesting a gap in reality when it comes to knowledge of certain technologies.

For a three-year period airplanes droned daily over the Mucajai station, flying between Boa Vista and the airstrips of Paapiu and Surucucu. At least two miners' planes crashed in the rainforest in the area of the mission. When one of those planes was not located, the Xilixana participated in the search to find it. In the other case they were asked to carry the engine to the mission station. They were left feeling that they were inadequately paid for their services.

The miners' approach to life in the rainforest is purely capitalistic. They know there is gold to be found in Yanomami land, and they want to mine it, regardless of the social cost to the Yanomami. The contact with miners exposed the Xilixana to the most brutal, vulgar, uncaring characteristics and behavior of Western people. It showed them the corrupt means used to achieve selfish material gain. Miners also transmitted diseases that brought havoc to many villages.

No organization or agency consistently or regularly monitors the method of mining, the health of the miners, the wage paid to Yanomami workers, or the miners' treatment of the Yanomami. The mining activity has also evolved: first there were small groups of independent miners, and later larger companies that penetrated the entire region. The companies had sophisticated gear and used mercury in their operations, contaminating the river for drinking purposes. The Xilixana along the river now have to transport water from nearby streams.

Other Yanomami

Contacts with other Yanomami—in-migrations, marriages, friendships and alliances, yãimo festivities—have altered Xilixana life significantly. Continued contacts with the Apiau Aica, Malaxi theli, Palimi theli, and Xiliana have brought new influences into their lives. The exchanges with the Malaxi theli, for instance, have not just brought in the all-important factor, for the men, of new wives (and resulting children), but the Xilixana also acquired field products such as more tasty bananas, a new variety of potato, a plant whose leaves are used to poison fish, and a shrub used in black magic.

The contact with the Xiliana has been particularly notable, given that the two groups speak the same Ninam language. About 1970, for instance, a Xiliana widower and his daughter fled the Xiliana community and joined the more distant Mucajai Xilixana village D downstream. In 1991 and 1993 a young man and his sister respectively married partners at Mucajai, after an initial contact had been made at the Casa do Índio in Boa Vista. Other recent contacts may have considerable impact in a decade or two. Through mutual health treatment in Boa Vista at the Casa do Índio, a Yekwana captive in the war of 1935 and her family were invited to visit the relatively recently constructed Yekwana village on the mid-Uraricoera River. She came in 1993, and the Xilixana received grater boards in exchange for cotton. There was talk of a second visit, and of a possible cross-cultural marriage.

In 1992 a young Xilixana woman and younger Macuxi man were romantically drawn to one another in Boa Vista. He followed her to her parents at Mucajai, who were uncertain as to whether the couple would remain among the Xilixana. They remained together and eventually had a child. He is the first known non-Yanomami to marry and integrate into a Brazilian Yanomami community, and he is adapting fairly well to the language and culture, although it is said that his hunting ability could be improved.

After a tumultuous relationship with several men, a young Xiliana from the Comara group, village D, married an Aica. Through this group's association with Brazilians she eventually left the Aica and married a Macuxi, migrating to his home in a Brazilian village near the frontier of the rainforest. She is barren and has frequent contact with her relatives. This could prove to be a gateway for more significant Xilixana-Brazilian interaction.

To anyone who has lived in the Mucajai community for an extended period of time, the effect of other Yanomami upon the Xilixana social organization is apparent in numerous ways. The population has expanded considerably due to migration. The intertribal bonds have obligated the Xilixana to engage in the social activities of other Yanomami in the form of bride service, yãimos, and even raids. Their social world has exploded to a network far beyond that of the two Xilixana villages numbering about 120 in 1956. In addition to acquiring new varieties of plants for their fields they have obtained indigenous and Western artifacts. Perhaps most importantly, the contacts with other Yanomami have reinforced some indigenous beliefs and practices, and notably rituals related to female puberty and the deceased, and various taboos.

The increase of alcoholism is another, less positive but dramatic change. They now consume enormous quantities of "home brew" and engage much more frequently in community drinking events. Before contact the Xilixana had made their alcoholic drink in clay vessels, and they usually consumed it without anyone becoming intoxicated. The practice of preparing large quantities of intoxicating drink was first borrowed from the Palimi theli. For a month in 1961, four young Xilixana men accompanied me to the Palimi theli village to construct a new airstrip for the Brazilian Air Force. The Palimi theli had adopted the drink from the Xiliana, who in turn had adopted this form of drink from the Carib Macuxi. There is no reason to believe that this heavy alcoholic consumption and related violent behavior is due to cultural disorientation or depression of the recent decades.

When they adopted small canoe-shaped wooden vessels, influenced by the Palimi theli, men tended to become heavily inebriated. By the late 1980s they had gained access to large aluminum pots and 15 to 20-gallon plastic containers obtained from miners, or abandoned mining settlements, and Boa Vista retailers, and the large wooden vessels became extinct. The cassava drink could be boiled and stored more efficiently. Women and grown adolescents now become drunk along with the men. In recent years the process of making the drink has become more efficient, with the fermenting process expedited by boiling the liquid after a small quantity is masticated.

Hospitable hosts always have an abundance of the drink ready for any event, and custom dictates that all the prepared drink must be consumed before the visitors leave. Participants are urged to drink more, even if they are full and need to vomit to consume more. This caxiri drink has become the number one Xilixana health and social problem. Frequently the drinking sessions erupt into blows and beatings requiring immediate and special health care. A side effect is that the produce of large fields is consumed in the drinking bouts, leaving food scarce at a later date. Missionaries have discussed this dilemma with the *bata* Xilixana, but indigenous leadership and the will to terminate this social problem have not emerged.

Missionaries

In the remote and isolated community of the Xilixana, the missionaries have been present during difficult times of epidemics and diseases, which had their toll on human life, but would have been much worse if they had not been there. When FUNAI expelled the missionaries at the end of the 1980s, the Xilixana pleaded with government authorities to have them return. The missionaries have coordinated a whole series of immunization and dental treatment programs. They have helped the Xiliana to acquire goods they needed or wanted. During times of drought they provided "make-work" projects so that the Xilixana would be able to purchase manioc grit and rice.

The missionaries, as we've seen, have also had an impact—though somewhat checkered—in the introduction of Christian ideology. For outsiders they have provided an otherwise missing expertise in language analysis and contributions to academic workshops and journal writing. For the Xilixana they have made strides in literacy. The Xilixana have seen the significance of literacy, and have been given the opportunity to learn to read and write, both in the Ninam language and Portuguese. Learning to read in their mother tongue reinforces their identity as Yanomami, and learning Portuguese provides help in their long-term survival in the larger country. The missionaries did not coerce children to attend classes, and they did not offer board to children. Missionaries have used the visiting quarters in their homes to encourage literacy, geography, and biology. Missionaries believe in Yanomami serving as teachers, and have taught more advanced students in this role, training them at workshops in another location.

As agents of change, people like missionaries find themselves placed in a precarious position, having the power to make new items available, and yet also perhaps withholding them. The missionaries had many discussions amongst themselves as to whether they should acquiesce to the Xiliana's requests. A consideration was that the people making these requests were not children of 12 or 17 years of age, but mature adults. The missionaries at the Mucajai station have not sold items they consider to be non-utilitarian items or products of conspicuous consumption, or extravagant goods such as radios and outboard motors. After returning from the forced FUNAI evacuation in the late 1980s, they kept trade items in their store to a minimum.

Missionaries and the Dynamics of Change

The Xilixana initiated their contact with the outside world. They did not know that this meeting would explode and ricochet the Yanomami into a whole new world, politically, economically, and ideologically. We have no way of evaluating the status of these villages if the missionaries had not established residency in 1958. We know that contact between aboriginals and Westerners would have continued, but probably under a different guise. These Western residents served as shock absorbers, as a cushion to the unknown world. Before the 1970s discussions between the Xilixana and missionaries of events downriver were frequent, and the missionaries often identified areas of exploitation. We know that the behavior of some Brazilians regarding the Xilixana was restrained because they feared that the missionaries upstream would eventually hear news of whatever happened.

The missionaries have not unduly forced on Yanomami culture what they consider the necessary practices of Christianity. They recognize, for instance, that in rituals such as the cremation of the body and keeping the ash close to the hearth for a period of time, the Yanomami are showing respect for the deceased. The missionaries prefer to allow Yanomami to make their own decisions, follow their own practices, on these matters.

The propagating of Christian thought became more covert than overt since the missionaries return after evacuation, with the missionaries now believing that aggressive propagating of the gospel is not appropriate. Missionaries now make less effort to bring Yanomami together for formal Sunday services. They are less likely to broach the subject of spirituality among individuals who have shown no interest for years. Some missionaries feel the Mucajai Yanomami

Christmas Play Day

know about "the Jesus Way," and the decision is theirs. At the same time missionaries do take opportunities to converse with individuals, and sometimes conversations are initiated by the aborigines.

The Xilixana look forward to the annual Christmas festivity at the mission post. The event, an all-day affair initiated as a celebration in which everyone could participate and be happy, has since become institutionalized as a Christmas event. The celebration incorporates a variety of festivities: tests of marksmanship, involving shooting at images of animals; women thread beads; the Xilixana race in cohorts of age and sex; volleyball games. The most prized event is climbing the greased pole. The winners of events get small fish hooks. The missionaries maintain a small field of bananas that are specifically designated for this event, and they dispense candies. The Xilixana participate by bringing food. In 1996 the Xilixana organized and ran the entire Christmas activity.

The missionaries, in recent years, have also wanted to keep an acceptable but uncompromising relationship with FUNAI. They know their presence in Yanomami land is only accepted because of their medical services. Missionaries have and are addressing the medical needs of the Xilixana, expending what knowledge, skills, and resources they have, to alleviate their suffering and their diseases (see chapter 13). Some missionaries have retrained themselves to better address Yanomami medical needs.

The Xilixana have also expanded their knowledge of other people and culture through dialogue with missionaries. During the contact period they were intrigued that there were indigenous peoples in many other parts of the world. Viewing *National Geographic* pictures became a favorite pastime of villagers. They appreciated seeing pictures of animals, fish, and birds from around the world—some of the species extremely foreign to them. They asked me what game and fish I hunted in my land, and made clear that they thought meat from domesticated cattle, swine, and fowl were a poor substitute for the game found in the rainforest. They inquired about Western family obligations and expectations. They were surprised to learn that our daughters would freely accept or decline an offer of marriage. I showed them a picture of Canada's prime minister, and apart from his being partially bald, they found it incomprehensible that he was my headman, because I had never seen or spoken with him. They learned that people lived in urban centers with stores filled with countless goods, that they made transactions with paper (money). Later they heard of satellites, the moon landing, and war. In 1995 one man queried me about the Iran war. They were surprised to know that aboriginals in my land wore clothes, were literate, and drove automobiles. They soon discovered the existence of distinct varieties of Western peoples: Brazilian, American, Canadian, German, and so on. They increasingly came to recognize the construct of Brazil as a land mass and people with a central government. Their worldview has expanded. They are moving in the direction of becoming "Brazilianized."

Missionary presence among aborigines has always aroused a variety of responses. For several decades now, academia and the media have not presented a positive picture, and, indeed, in many cases a bleak portrayal was warranted.

There have been cases of cultural insensitivity, ideological imperialism, and a form of missionary colonialism. But missionaries, of course, are not that different from other humans. We all encounter good and bad relatives, generous and stingy neighbors, reasonable and unreasonable teachers, intolerable and pleasant roommates. So it is too with missionaries.

In the association of so-called "advanced" nations and indigenous peoples, the issues are all the more sensitive because of the power differential. Westerners generally have and wield the balance of power, and this power is often misused. The misuse and abuse of power extends to the entrepreneur, or corporations, government agencies, anthropologists, nongovernmental organizations, and missionaries. We would do well to recognize that each of these entities has a bias, and each, especially in the initial contact with indigenes, tends not to know or understand the meanings of language and behavior, or the internal politics, within the culture. Each person reflects, decides, and behaves within a context of her or his own socialization and experience. Some of that reflection is rational, and some is passion, impulse, or irrational.

Religious people are not the only ones who may be prone to act indiscreetly. The key issue is not whether the person making the intervention is atheist, agnostic, or religious. Westerners among aborigines show indiscretion in a myriad of ways. Anthropologists use video cameras and record the voices of informants, and government personnel might smoke and give cigarettes. NGO staff people might support shamanism because it is native, even though it may perpetuate false hopes or expectations, especially around illness. Indian agencies use their presence for financial gain or status mobility. In most cases the stay of these other agents among aborigines is short-term only.

Today agencies and persons in significant change roles are expected to act more judicially and sensitively than personnel a generation ago. Aboriginals will no longer as easily tolerate violations of human rights. As Westerners we would do well to apply the brush of criticism to all agents, and lend our support to those aborigines who are making strides to achieve their own identity and position in the larger political context of the postmodern world

Thirteen
Health as an Agent of Change

Almost all indigenous people who make contact with Western societies face fatal diseases for which they have little or no immunity. Epidemics of colds, small pox, measles, and whooping cough have ravaged indigenous North and South American populations. As writer Ronald Wright (1992: 14) notes, "Even today, isolated tribes can be decimated by something as 'minor' as the common cold on first contact with missionaries or prospectors. In just two years—1988 to 1990—the Yanomami of Brazil lost 15 per cent of their people, mainly to malaria and influenza."

After the first three Xilixana contacts on the lower Mucajai River in 1957-58, several Xilixana died. Still, the Xilixana continued to build ties with Brazilians, and they allowed outsiders to take up residency in their area in November 1958. Two years later five of them died from colds brought on by contact with a distant Yanomami village. In this new period of their history, medical aid became essential.

There were several marked critical periods of influenza and disease in the Mucajai postcontact period. The first came with the initial contact with Brazilians in early 1957 and continued for another four-year period due to the repeated visits to inhabitants on the lower Mucajai. Colds and pneumonia were the primary concern. Another critical period was between 1985 and 1995, a time when the Xilixana had continual exposure to and contact with other Yanomami, miners, and Brazilians. During FUNAI's presence between 1987 and 1990 the agency recorded 13 deaths in the four Mucajai mission villages.

There were two epidemics of whooping cough, one of measles, and three of chicken pox between 1987 and mid-1991 (Anderson 1991). By the end of 1991, almost one-third of the population was down with malaria. While malaria and TB were the most serious threat after 1986, outbreaks of influenza, kala-azar, Hepatitis B, and venereal disease also occurred.

It is extremely fortunate that the Mucajai communities had capable health care since 1958 or the population statistics would be quite different from what they are today. Dr. Timothy Faul (1997), who spent several years in the state, affirms the positive effects of medical work by both Protestant and Catholic groups amongst Yanomami in Roraima.

The most critical diseases that require continuous care are colds and complications, malaria, influenza, and TB. Colds spread through the villages rapidly, often leading to pneumonia and further complications. Infants and the elderly are particularly vulnerable to this chest infection, which sometimes culminates in death.

Xilixana Modes of Treating Illness

Mark J. Plotkin (1993), who has studied the use of indigenous medicine throughout the Amazon, contends that the Yanomami have not extensively developed the art of indigenous medicine because of the prominence of shamanic powers.

In the contact period several people had three-centimeter-long scars on their foreheads. The cutting was done by stone to release the "thick" blood of the sick person. This practice has been discontinued. Some had leishmaniasis, the disease spread by the sand fly, which they believed they contracted by violating the taboo of not viewing or conversing with a young woman during her puberty rite. They used a knife to cut the flesh in the area of the sore. I have seen scars of at least eight centimeters square on the back, leg, and arm.

They swallowed the inner bark of the quinine tree in liquid form, using this remedy for severe stomach aches. That medication is still used to cleanse the stomach after committing a murder, which suggests its psychosomatic significance. They used a specific leaf for snake bites and another for healing wounds caused by sharp objects (Camargo 1996). In the event of dizziness, which is said to occur from eating raw meat, an Xilixana drops juice from a green tobacco leaf into the eyes. They frequently swish a broad leaf with numerous sharp pricks upon any area of their body that has pain.

The Yanomami perception of health is closely linked to the supernatural world. "Health is harmony, a coherent state of equilibrium between physical and spiritual components of the individual. Sickness is disruption, imbalance and the manifestation of malevolent forces in (the) flesh" (Davis 1996, 280).

Missionaries and Health Care

For at least the first decade after contact, missionaries took full responsibility for Xilixana health care, treating both the trivial and the potentially fatal. They administered Band-aids, iodine, and aspirin. They extracted teeth, taped up cuts, and gave medicine for worms and diarrhoea. They treated scabies, which began to be a problem after contact. Small mites burrow under the skin and lay eggs, usually on the hands, wrists, armpits, or buttocks, or in the genital area. Given unhygienic conditions the mites spread rapidly. Ticks, lice, and chiggers are common. When the missionaries found the local resources inadequate, they had patients flown at their organization's expense to Boa Vista or cities in the south, where professional care could be administered.

Missionaries often make trips by canoe or foot to distant villages to treat Xilixana. Some of the indigenous people come to the mission station to

receive daily care over a longer period of time. The sick are accompanied by at least one other member of the family. Some families do well in supplying food for the sick, others avoid this responsibility. Missionaries meet the patients' need for food from their own tables or from available supplies.

Perhaps most importantly, in the early 1970s the missionaries trained a young man from each village to care for common health needs. These

Leaving the mission for the village after receiving an item from the "store" and medicine from the clinic.

"field nurses" have a kit with bandages, iodine, gauze, aspirin, and medicine to counter toothaches, diarrhoea, and vomiting, and two or three ampules of penicillin. They have medicine for malaria. They give injections after consulting with the missionary. They became effective in treating infections, bronchitis, and pneumonia, but less able to provide adequate care for infants or adults who need constant attention over extended periods. One particularly gifted field nurse sends a patient with a more severe illness to the missionaries with a note indicating exactly the medication he has administered. Even with their limited skills, these field nurses have unquestionably saved lives.

BIRTH OF A DEFORMED BABY

When TI, a woman in her late teens, informed me that she was in labor with her second baby, I invited her to call me when she was about to give birth. She said she would.

The next morning, TI's mother YO ran up our steps, breathless. "Come quickly," she said, "the baby's been born." I raced down the path to TI's house, about five minutes' walk away. Outside the house, on a log, sat TI, her head down, looking dejected. "Where's the baby?" I asked in alarm, for TI was not holding a baby. "Over there," YO said, pointing to a spot in the grass a short distance away. Hidden in the grass lay a tiny baby boy, whimpering, with the umbilical cord tightly wound twice around his neck. Without further thought, I picked him up, unwound the cord, and he howled lustily. I breathed a sigh of relief. As I looked at the baby more closely, I was dismayed to see a large, soft, egg-shaped protrusion, a meningocele, between the baby's eyes. I gave TI her little son to hold, and reluctantly she took him. "We don't want a baby with a bump between his eyes; you find somebody to cut the bump away," YO said to me.

Later I learned that after the baby was born, YO had laid him in the grass, placed a stick across his neck, stepped on each end of it, hoping to snuff out the little boy's life. Deformed babies are considered a blight to the parents and extended family.

We eventually sent the baby to Rio de Janeiro, where doctors performed surgery on him. He barely survived. He still had a small "bump" when he returned, but his parents did receive him back, though reluctantly.

One day, when he was about 12 years old, one of his buddies accidentally hit him with a pointed stick between his eyes while they were playing in the jungle some distance from the mission station. His family quickly brought him to the station, but by the time they arrived, the boy was lifeless. He had probably haemorrhaged to death. It was a sad day for all.

LORRAINE PETERS

Health Treatment Facilities and Organizations

The Fundacão Nacionál do Índio (FUNAI) constructed the Casa do Índio in Boa Vista in the 1970s. By the mid-1980s, along with the Department of Health, the facility was moved to a much more extensive complex about 12 kilometers outside the town. All indigenous peoples in the state receive initial examinations there, and most go there for any necessary treatment. Some are sent to the hospital in the city, or for longer treatment to the Casa da Hekula (House of Spirit Cures) in Boa Vista. A few are sent to other centers such as Brasilia, Belém, or Manaus. Patients stay for a week or even up to six months and are often accompanied by a family member.

In 1989 the Casa do Índio had no isolation ward and an unacceptably low level of hygiene. The risk of contagion from infectious diseases was high. At times the facility did not have adequate food for patients. Two doctors were attempting to meet the needs of 35,000 Indians (Roraima, Brazil: A Death Warning 1989: 13(4) 61).

In the late 1980s the Fundacão Nacionál de Saude (FNS) gained greater authority to meet the sometimes desperate health needs of indigenous peoples in Roraima, and the institution has definitely worked to do this. It became responsible for all treatment at the Casa do Índio, and eventually for any matters of health related to the Yanomami. Its role as regards the Yanomami increased, much to the chagrin of FUNAI personnel. Through the services of FNS, the Xilixana have been immunized against TB, DPT, polio, measles, and, recently, hepatitis B.

The FNS has leased an airplane that flies to any of the several airstrips in which there are FUNAI personnel. They pick up and deliver patients who need care in Boa Vista. From the airport in Boa Vista they are delivered to the Casa do Índio. More serious cases are transferred to the city hospital, a place where Yanomami feel very lonely, because they know no one and no one speaks their language. FUNAI personnel are more likely to transport Yanomami to Boa Vista than are the missionaries, largely because FUNAI workers have less training and experience in health care. Missionaries sense the presence of critical scrutiny of their efforts on the part of FUNAI officials, who seem to believe that the missionaries' efforts in health care are not adequate, despite the diligent endeavors.

In more recent years a few Xilixana have been reluctant to go to the Casa do Índio. They attribute most of their people's deaths to the black magic of other indigenous peoples at the Casa do Índio, rather than to sickness itself.

The other care facility in Boa Vista for indigenes, the Casa da Hekula (sometimes called Casa da Cura, the House of Healing), was constructed in the 1980s by the Consolada (Roman Catholic) missionaries, with equipment supplied by Global Links of Pittsburgh. It has accommodation in hammocks or beds for up to 50 patients, and a staff of 20. The expectation is that the FNS will finance it totally, though this goal had still not been realized by the late

1990s. It is the place for long-term care—for instance, for patients of TB or kala-azar, a severe infectious disease occurring mainly in tropical areas and transmitted by the bite of sand flies.

This facility is now the permanent home of a two-year-old Xilixana girl abandoned at birth by her parents when they realized she was seriously deformed. In 1997, when a child was born with brain damage, she was sent to Brasilia with her parents, and it seemed possible that the parents might eventually return to Mucajai without her and the Casa da Hekula would become her home.

Along with the Casa da Hekula and the Protestant and Catholic missionaries, three other NGO health agents have been active. The Commission for the Creation of the Yanomami Park (CCPY) has two clinics and two doctors among the Yanomami in the state of Amazonas and initiated a pilot program on river blindness. Doctors Without Borders, based in the Netherlands, began work on microscopic diagnosis in the 1990s and hopes to train Yanomami to do that work. Doctors of the World, from France, has a very dedicated doctor who works at Paapiau at the headwaters of the Mucajai. A goal of that organization is to train Yanomami in medical treatment. FUNAI is hoping this group will expand to about a dozen other Yanomami villages.

The Treatment of Diseases

MALARIA

Malaria is transmitted by mosquitos. The parasite is released into the blood stream and can cause harm to the liver. Some 8 to 30 days after being bitten, the individual experiences a full day of headache, weariness, and nausea, followed by 12 to 24 hours of chill and fever, ending with sweating. There are two types of malaria in Brazil, and the worst of those strains (*plasmodium falciparim*) can be fatal in a few days when not treated. All malaria medicine is controlled and provided by the government.

In the early 1970s the missionaries were asked to send a sample of blood of those suspected of having malaria to the Department of Health in Boa Vista. The department asked that the missionaries delay treatment until after the blood samples were tested. This procedure created problems: plasmodia is not always readily detected even under the microscope, and, furthermore, it was sometimes weeks before the department sent its report to Mucajai: the examination could be delayed in Boa Vista, or perhaps the airplane with the information did not return until 20 days later. This created a dilemma for both the missionaries and the indigenes, because meanwhile the patient was suffering from every symptom of malaria.

With the entry of miners into Yanomami territory in 1985 came a new strain of malaria, resistant to medicine. Most Yanomami villages throughout Brazil and on the Venezuela border suffered deaths during this period, a few losing up to 90 per cent of the local population. The Mucajai population was seriously affected in 1987, at which time the government was called in to help, and malaria has continued to be a constant problem since 1990. An epidemic hit in late December 1990 and continued through to March the next year, with six deaths. Another epidemic, which hit in 1994 with even greater severity, lasted for over a year and resulted in several deaths. Missionaries treating patients at Mucajai were exhausted in this epidemic, and at least two of them themselves became critically infected. In 1997 a government health team again assisted with an epidemic of malaria.

The mission of the Brazilian government's Superintendência de Combate a Malária (SUCAM) mission is to control malaria. In the interior of the state of Roraima throughout the 1960s, in an effort to reduce mosquitos, SUCAM sought to spray dwellings with DDT, a chemical outlawed in many Western countries. The spraying included the Yanomami dwellings at the Mucajai station. They supplied the pump and DDT and missionaries did the spraying, generally about twice a year. The Yanomami appreciated this service, not only for the reduction in mosquitos and malaria, but also because it rid their dwellings of hundreds of cockroaches.

At the time no one challenged this wholesale system of DDT use. The effect of the chemical, imported from Indonesia, on children and adults in their habitat is unknown. In the 1980s SUCAM introduced a safer method, spraying only the environs outside the house and sending in its own personnel and using a more acceptable chemical to kill mosquitoes carrying malaria. By 1997 the agency had altered its mode of operation to emphasis diagnostic techniques and treatment rather than preventative measures.

TUBERCULOSIS

TB, another serious ailment among the Xilixana, usually progresses slowly. It commonly shows itself with a reduction in the ability to breathe, a slight fever, night sweats, weight loss, and a dry cough that eventually produces blood and puss-filled phlegm (Kunz & Finkel 1987: 574-75). A person is considered having active TB when there is heavy coughing and frequent sputum. Infection is highly likely. The disease spreads quickly where there is malnutrition, overcrowding, poor housing, and exposure to the elements. The Yanomami living conditions, with 35 to 80 inhabitants in daily close proximity, as well as the custom of drinking liquids masticated by humans, provides a fertile environment for the spread of TB.

In 1966 the missionaries housed possibly the first Yanomami patient of TB in Boa Vista for a six-month period. He then returned to Mucajai for six more months of treatment. He had become infected while employed by Brazilian farmers downstream. He is still alive and has proven a significant informant for data in the precontact period. A Brazilian doctor from the Department of Health immunized the Mucajai population against TB in 1966. Between 1975 and 1977 there were 22 proven cases of TB. This time the source of the

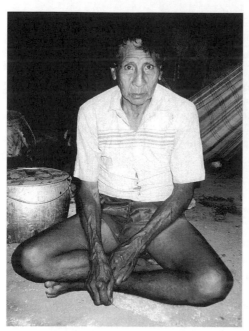

The first Xilixana and possibly Yanomami treated for TB, 1966. Picture taken in 1996.

infection was the Palimi theli and the Aica communities (Anderson 1992). Under K. Taylor and FUNAI, the entire population was vaccinated in November 1975. A doctor from the National Division of Tuberculosis investigated the situation at Mucajai and other Yanomami villages in 1979. A survey in 1992 showed that 27 people had TB. There is TB in every village, and virtually all families have a member with this disease.

Ultimately the government makes the diagnosis of TB and supplies the necessary medicine, but the results of tests are, again, tardy, necessitating frequent trips to town for patients. TB patients are treated at Boa Vista's Casa da Cura. The Yanomami hygiene conditions and living conditions make it exceedingly difficult to treat adequately, let alone eradicate. Communal drinking and eating habits, and the impossibility of meeting the high standards of health care necessary for those fighting TB, militate against control of the ailment. Currently only one of the many who have TB follow the necessary practice of spitting into a hole in the earth in the yãno and covering up the sputum. Dr. Timothy Faul (1997) recognizes that those with TB need vigorous prolonged treatment.

To minimize the spread of TB and colds, the Yanomami would have to alter their festive drinking habits, which involve food being masticated to induce fermentation and then being served in a common gourd. To eradicate TB, authorities would have to initiate the near-impossible task of checking for the disease all the other Yanomami who visit the Mucajai region.

KALA-AZAR

In December 1993 and January 1994, after 200 blood tests, and later some bone marrow tests, the situation was considered an emergency. The government, doing the testing and supplying the medication, treated 22 cases of kala-azar. The treatment consisted of 20 consecutive days of IV injections for each person, representing a considerable commitment for both "nurse" and Yanomami patient. In the more cautious treatment of Kala-azar at Casa da Hekula, patients receive an initial 45 days of intravenous treatment and, after a break of 20 days, another 45 days of treatment. This serious disease, which causes high fever and enlarges the spleen, is passed on by sand flies, and in these cases by infected dogs. The Xilixana reluctantly permitted their infected dogs to be killed, with one exception.

OTHER DISEASES

Venereal disease was first found among the Xilixana at Mucajai in the late 1960s. Several adult Aica women and their children had immigrated from the Apiau River area, where Brazilians had been extracting rubber and sawn lumber for more than a decade. These women were treated by missionary personnel. Venereal disease became more pervasive in the 1980s, when the Xilixana had more contact with Brazilians, particularly in Boa Vista. While making purchases in Boa Vista with money earned working for the miners, a number of men frequented brothels. Missionaries grew accustomed to the prospect of treating Xilixana men soon after they arrived back from the city. With embarrassment, a male would eventually ask for treatment, and soon from two to ten others would begrudgingly seek treatment. Normal treatment is two injections of antibiotics in the hip area, a somewhat painful medication. If husbands had intercourse with their wives after the Boa Vista encounters, the women were also likely to be infected—though this type of VD is difficult to detect in women. Therefore the women also receive full treatments.

Several cases of Brazilians in Boa Vista have tested HIV-positive. Boa Vista is said to have one of the highest rates of HIV infection in Brazil. It would be extremely serious if HIV penetrated Yanomami society.

Immunization against TB, diphtheria, polio, measles, yellow fever, and more recently Hepatitis B are now done on a regular basis. Records are kept at the mission post.

River blindness or onchocerciasis has been found among the Yanomami. It has its origin in Africa and came to Brazil via the slave trade. It is caused by thread-like nematods (round worms) that live in the subcutaneous tissues. The juvenile form, the micro filaria, arrive in the cornea of the eye, which can produce blindness. To date there is no incident of onchocerciasis at Mucajai, though the Yanomami village Paapiu just 100 kilometers to the west has a 90 per cent incidence rate ("Roraima, Brazil: A Death Warning," 1989). The Xilixana have frequent contact with the Palimi theli villages, where 28 per cent of the population have the disease. The occupants of one village of Brazilian Yanomami have been immunized. Two Yanomami in another village recently each lost an eye because of this disease. These were the first cases of blindness caused by this disease in Brazil.

Money is available from international sources to treat all Yanomami in both Venezuela and Brazil against onchocerciasis. A drug company has donated the medicine, and an agency is prepared to give the treatment, which requires pills once every six to twelve months. At a meeting in Boa Vista, FUNAI and FNS withheld their support from such a program because they believed there was inadequate funding for their own specific organizations. There appears to be, on the part of these organizations, an intent to work this treatment process to political and economic gain. But in all likelihood the benefits of consistent treatment should far outweigh the social costs. If we followed the logic of the FUNAI and FNS position, we would have to conclude that all medication, and especially the medication administered in Boa Vista, should have been withheld through the past two to three decades—at an immense cost to Yanomami life and well-being.

INDIVIDUAL MEDICAL NEEDS

From time to time individual medical needs need special attention. In 1966 the missionaries sent a boy of five with his mother to a medical doctor in Guyana for treatment. They returned to the village, and after a number of months and much suffering, he died of Hodgkin's disease. About 1969 a woman in her mid-forties was flown to the city of Belém, at the mouth of the Amazon River, for months of cervical cancer treatment. In 1998 she was the oldest living woman at Mucajai. In the mid-1980s a young man climbed a tree to retrieve his arrows, fell, and broke both wrists and his femur. He was transported to Boa Vista and cared for at missionary expense. In 1993, after years of problems, a woman was finally diagnosed with cirrhosis (commonly due to alcohol) and sent for treatment to the Casa do Índio in Boa Vista before going to a care center for Indians in Manaus. When she returned to the village she went onto a costly drug prescription. In another case in the 1990s a widow in her fifties was given a prescription and placed on a special diet to counter and control the pain of arthritis. The cost of the drugs for these two women, about $70 U.S. per month, was again borne by the missionaries. The patient with arthritis was flown twice to Boa Vista, accompanied by a missionary, in hopes of getting a more specific diagnosis. In the initial stages of her treatment she ventured off with her family to visit a distant village, which meant her first three months of medication were of no value. For the medicine to be effective she required a minimum of six months of consistent treatment. The discipline of persistent regular treatment is a problem medical practitioners consistently encounter among most Yanomami.

In 1982 an epidemic of the shigella (bacillary dysentery) broke out, with four deaths. Shigella comes from contaminated food or water, and an early symptom is diarrhea. The bacteria spread from person to person on fingers, or via contaminated eating utensils, and children are the most vulnerable to the disease.

About 1992 a young man spent considerable time in Boa Vista, during which time he learned some Portuguese. One day, while inebriated, he stepped out of a moving car and a second automobile drove over his foot. He was eventually treated in Brasilia at government expense. He returned to his village disabled and unable to hunt, a critical handicap for a male in Yanomami culture. He eventually acquired a wife and supplies game by fishing. In 1992 a man of almost 70 years of age was flown to Brasilia to be treated for his eyes.

In 1987 twins were born, and with missionaries present both children were kept alive. Since that date two more sets of twins have been kept alive. It is impossible to know how many infants and children have been kept alive because of the care they have received from missionaries or from health care in Boa Vista.

An increasing number of Xilixana require medical treatment because of brawls. In early 1995 all the houses in village D burned due to the negligence of children in one of the peripheral families. A fight erupted and a middle-aged man was flown to Boa Vista and from there to Manaus to receive treatment for serious head gashes. After a drunken brawl in village E in October 1995, the most seriously injured man was given antibiotics intravenously at the mission under advisement by radio from a veteran missionary nurse in Boa Vista. A few weeks later, with no vision in his left eye, he was flown to Boa Vista. According to Carol James (1995), a missionary at Mucajai, he was "bent on revenge," and the village remained in a state of potential explosion for months. In July 1996 another fight erupted during a drinking binge, and nine men and women were pierced with bamboo arrow points. One of these cuts proved fatal.

Infants are particularly vulnerable to infectious diseases. A Xilixana mother whose previous two infants had died was extremely concerned when her infant son showed symptoms of both malaria and whooping cough. Dawn Anderson, who was in charge of medical treatment, reported, "He stopped breathing for several minutes … here at the clinic," although he was soon revived. He may have aspirated a bit of phlegm after he was given aralen, a malaria medicine. According to Anderson (1991): "His cry became weak almost immediately and the mother started the trek home with him saying he was dying. I ran after her and brought her back and no sooner got him inside [the clinic] when the breathing stopped altogether. I tried mouth-to-mouth resuscitation and when [another Xiliana] saw what I was doing she took over. So I grabbed some fenergan, which was the closest to an emergency drug I could find, and gave it to him, then continued with the heart massage and abdominal pressure resuscitation until he gave a little gasp and finally started breathing again." That boy survived, but Anderson reported on the case of another infant that was not so successful. She "was exposed to whooping cough at one week, caught the disease by four weeks, and died a week later."

On my 1995 field trip I witnessed the case of a hunter who had climbed a tree to retrieve his arrow. He slipped, and caught the joint nearest to the tip of his small finger in the slit of a branch. His body momentarily hung from the tree. He became dizzy and fell a few meters to the ground, leaving part of his finger behind. His companions soon joined him, and, fearing the worst, the women began to wail. He regained consciousness. One man scaled the tree to retrieve the finger segment. Hurriedly they paddled downstream to the village.

The Yanomami field nurse was somewhat bewildered, wondering whether to leave the finger detached or attempt to sew it on. The respect for all human body parts in the Yanomami culture motivated him to sew on the detached finger. He then wrote a note of explanation to the missionary and sent the patient to the mission station.

The missionary examined the finger and considered the field nurse's work to have been quite appropriate, but when she consulted a physician by radio she was informed that the finger would not become attached properly and that a bone protruding from the finger had to be covered by skin. This meant cutting a piece of the bone (which I did, with a sterilized wire cutter) and sewing the skin together over the bone. Bravely, she and a second missionary trained in suture procedures methodically did the work while the patient was locally anaesthetized. Within a few days it was evident the finger would not heal. He was flown to Boa Vista for hospital treatment.

The Struggle for Yanomami Health Control: Remaining Questions

In 1995 FUNAI and FNS decided that medicines should only be dispensed at specific centers, and not by the field nurses trained by missionaries—a decision the missionaries perceived as retrogressive, because the trained Yanomami provide an admirable service. Since 1991 the mission society known as Missão Evangélica da Amazonia (MEVA) has required that all missionaries working in the rainforest take a concentrated minimum of one week's training in Boa Vista.

It is clear that the missionaries have had and continue to have an impact upon the health of the Yanomami. Many would have died or be more seriously restricted in body were it not for the missionaries' presence. One might readily conclude that given this medical contribution alone, there could be absolutely no reason for their expulsion from Yanomami land. Missionaries arrived when there was no global concern for the rights of indigenous peoples. They showed interest in the Brazilian Yanomami, and gave of their means and talent, not for a year or two of research, then to retreat, but in many cases a lifelong commitment. They gave unstintingly.

Some questions still linger in terms of Yanomami health care. Who is ultimately responsible for the health of aboriginal peoples? In what way can the Yanomami people or individuals take responsibility? Is it at all possible for at least some of the Yanomami to participate in partial payment in order for the people as a whole to take ownership over their own well-being? How is health care to be exercised? What measure of preventative care might we expect the Yanomami to adopt?

Much remains to be done in preventative health care. Some basic measures such as washing before eating, washing after defecating, cleaning fingernails, washing utensils, spitting outside the house, scraping the earth in the house where people vomit and defecate, and wearing dry clothing would address questions of basic hygiene. If these elementary forms of behavior were adopted, attention to other matters—such as washing skin sores with warm water, wearing clean clothing, and curtailing the mastication of sweet cassava and sugar cane to make drink—could follow. It is a question of how to teach matters of hygiene, and what measures to use to make sure a significant change will take place. Such measures are a radical alteration of existing norms and cultural practices. Missionaries have been minimally effective in their efforts.

The Xilixana now have expectations about receiving treatment from missionaries, health-care workers in Boa Vista, and the government. In their recent politicization they voice human rights demands that air transportation for the ill not be tardy. Some young men are now embarrassed with the loss of their upper front teeth. They ask for a partial denture from the missionary. Two men have gone to Boa Vista to have their front teeth filled, and in one case the teeth were beyond repair. In each case, the treatment was at considerable expense to the Xilixana. On two of my more recent research trips I delivered eye glasses to several older Xilixana males. They appreciated the glasses, but they were not attuned to properly looking after them. The glasses were soon broken, probably by little children, who have ample freedom to meddle with any objects they find interesting. At least one Xilixana now has prescribed glasses.

The mode of health care provided by FUNAI and missionary personnel in the jungle is different. The center for modest and serious health care for FUNAI personnel in the jungle is in Boa Vista. Patients are readily transported by air or canoe and vehicle to Boa Vista. FUNAI personnel are more likely to converse in Portuguese, while Mucajai missionaries go to great lengths to study and use the Ninam language. The term of service for FUNAI personnel in one location among the Yanomami is briefer than that of mission personnel. It is also likely that missionaries have a more thorough understanding of tropical diseases, and use library resources. They often consult with medical professionals by radio. At Mucajai missionaries make frequent visits to the hammocks of the sick and frequently stay at a patient's side for hours through critical periods.

Through their introduction to medicine and basic hygiene the Xilixana quickly recognized the reality of bacteria and germs, as well as some preventative measures for good health. They soon found that some critical cases could be remedied by experts of medicine in larger city centers. But, certainly, if these people are to achieve even a minimal standard of basic general health, including certain standards of hygiene, they will have to adopt radical cultural changes.

Fourteen
Broader Considerations in the Study of Social Change

To the casual observer, it may well appear that inanimate objects have little or nothing to do with social or cultural change. But the effects of the automobile, credit card, television, and computer are all dramatic evidence of objects that have made a solid impact upon Western culture. In the 1940s, and again in about 1953, when the Xilixana returned to the Mucajai river region, the use of canoes altered their transportation patterns. Later on, the introduction of small items—flashlights, fish hooks, or matches, for instance—had a significant impact on the social fiber of their community.

By the end of the initial contact period the Xilixana had replaced several indigenous artifacts with Western goods. Traditionally, women had kept live coals in their hearths, ready to start a fire. In emergencies they would obtain fire from a neighbor's hearth. When they were travelling short distances they carried a piece of wood on fire; for going longer distances they used dry "fire sticks." Within three years of contact they were using matches, which they understandingly saw as being very valuable. They were light, portable, and efficient, but became moist in the humid environment. Fire sticks are now made only for the benefit of tourists.

The Xilixana also replaced the dibble stick with a metal digging tool. (Interestingly, they did not adopt the use of shovels and heavy hoes even though those tools were available.) Soon thereafter enamel pots replaced their heavy earthen pots, and metal griddles replaced the small clay griddles used for cooking. Women lost the art of making clay pots, which involved finding and retrieving the clay, rolling the clay, shaping the pot, smoothing the surface, and finally firing it. The new products were less likely to break. The pots were lighter and therefore readily transportable.

Within a year after the missionaries' arrival every household had access to an axe or knife, whereas prior to 1957 they had only four metal tools, which they shared. They quickly adopted axes, knives, and, later, cutlasses. By the end of the contact period a number of men had several cutlasses, and many women owned their own knives. The use of animal bones or teeth to cut and carve bows and arrow tips, became an extinct art. They could now open fields and trails, make canoes, and cut firewood more efficiently. Domestic work such as cutting meat and peeling manioc became less onerous.

The Xilixana soon considered salt essential in cooking; it remains the only non-garden Western food adopted by them—they now find food tasteless without it. Interestingly, in 1976 William Smole reported that Yanomami rejected salt. Missionaries and Brazilians have shared their food, and most Xilixana are now familiar with coffee, tea, sugar, candies, oatmeal, biscuits, bread, soup, butter, cooking oil, and sardines. They use Portuguese words to identify these foods. The contact with the missionaries provided other garden products, such as pineapple, papaya, and eventually lemons. The Xilixana readily accepted fish lines and hooks and stopped shooting fish with bows and arrows from a scaffold at the edge of the river. In the linking period women began to fish, whereas earlier only the men did. Two or three Xilixana use nets to catch small fish. One man has a long line with about 20 hooks that he extends across the river.

The Xilixana still use the bow and arrow, but carry fewer arrows on a hunt, and have adopted the Palami theli practice of using a quiver. They quickly insert points into the arrow, depending upon the target game. They have reduced the length of their bow and arrow by 30 to 50 centimeters. Many now make bows from the softer, more pliable wood of the black palm tree.

The Xilixana also put considerable pressure upon the missionaries to supply guns, which they quickly found to be more accurate than arrows. At first, the missionaries, myself included, would not do this, but after several years (about 1962 or 1963) we relented, limiting ammunition to those who had the required money. It seemed to us that guns were essential to their livelihood, that they would make their hunting easier and more efficient, and that we had no right to deny them access to this technology. Hunting was not a mere sport. But limiting the ammunition, we believed, would mean that they would continue, to a large extent, using their bows and arrows. The Xilixana promised they would not use the weapons in warfare—an agreement they kept for three or four years. For the Xilixana, guns and ammunition (powder, pellets, caps, and metal shells) also proved to be a significant trade item. When FUNAI and the government banned the sale of guns because of their use in warfare, the missionaries readily supported this position. Currently, FUNAI and missionaries occasionally loan ammunition to the Xilixana to use for a day's hunt.

The Xilixana paid for the purchases of guns with a good jaguar skin or canoe. In 1970 jaguar skins were placed on the world endangered species list, and the Xilixana were no longer able to sell the skins from which they gained valuable trade items. This is a case, again, of a different cultural perspective: the West has enforced a law to prevent the extinction of the jaguar; the Xilixana kill jaguar because the animal kills chickens, dogs, and humans.

The Xilixana first acquired clothing from Brazilians on the lower Mucajai River. The clothes were often torn and patched, unwashed, and sometimes carried diseases. At the time of missionary contact and airstrip construction, one man worked day after day wearing a white, dirty, full-length woman's slip. Several others wore poorly fitting clothing. The Xilixana quickly purchased red loin cloths brought in by missionaries, and missionaries soon began to sell short trousers for the men and cloth for skirts and blouses for the women. By the end of the 1970s the Xilixana were obtaining more clothing directly from Brazilians, including T-shirts, underpants, and brassieres. The Brazilian missionaries who occupied the Mucajai station in 1980 felt modesty should include the wearing of underpants for adults and brassieres for women. Several Xilixana acquired sun glasses and caps—a few men have baseball caps. One man wears prescription glasses. A few wear shoes. When they are around the yãno, the Xilixana now like to wear thongs—a sponge-rubber footwear common in tropical Brazil. On long walks through the jungle they continue to go barefoot.

Clothing has had a strong bearing upon the social life of the community. While it serves as an item of warmth and protection against insects, it has other implications. For instance, at the time of contact the Xilixana covered only their genitalia, using homespun loin cloths and aprons for men and women respectively. In modesty women now cover their breasts, especially in the presence of Westerners. In the environs of the yãno and the mission station they wear a skirt and bra without a blouse. Men now wear shorts and a shirt or T-shirt. Some women have dresses, but never trousers, even though they have long seen missionary women wearing pants or culottes. The Xilixana do not want to be gawked at because of their clothes, or lack of them, by outsiders who visit the mission post. Nor do they wish to be made a spectacle when they visit Brazilians on the lower Mucajai or in Boa Vista. FUNAI has indicated that it wants the Xilixana to again wear the traditional loin cloth and apron, but a *bata* (or senior Xilixana) has told me clearly that this will never happen. The Xilixana now burst into guffaws of laughter when they see pictures of their kin in native dress from the late 1950s. Clothes are now a part of the culture, and in a sense, necessary.

Western clothing has long been a prestige item, and has accordingly become a common item used in bride payment. The Xilixana carefully protect new items of clothing. To some, a bright color is more important than fit or design. Some Xilixana have an ample supply of three or four changes of clothing, while others have only the clothes they are wearing. Three villages now have sewing machines; one has a special house constructed for the machine. Several women and at least one man are adept at sewing. Every woman has needle, thread, and scissors, and they are able to buy cloth.

Young people particularly like Brazilian hammocks which are larger and more colorful than the indigenous hammocks. These hammocks cannot be placed near the fire for warmth because their spread is greater and they become discolored. Their owners use a blanket for warmth. When these imported hammocks become worn, the people will recycle the good thread together with their indigenous cotton thread to weave a new hammock. Now they need to wash their clothes and hammocks, which means they also need to buy laundry soap. Women wash these goods at the river's edge in the same manner as Brazilian peasants. Interestingly, it has become the lot of women to do the work of this new cultural feature—the washing of clothing.

The Xilixana were pleased to purchase small quantities of durable white, blue, red, and eventually other colored beads from the missionaries. They wore bands of beads around the arms, neck, and legs. They traded beads extensively to friends in other Yanomami villages. The women wove beads into symmetrically designed aprons—an amazing feat for a people who do not count beyond two. They sold some of this bead work to the missionaries who in turn exported it to tourists in Boa Vista and Manaus. By the 1970s beads were no longer readily available, and in the 1990s beads are only rarely seen.

The Xilixana, especially the women, appreciate mirrors. They use them to see if their hair is properly groomed, the face correctly painted. Most young people have a toothbrush, and many have toothpaste. Most have hand soap, and particularly appreciate shampoo. They use scissors to cut hair, and almost all men now sport a Western-style haircut rather than the bowl-shaped, blunt cut worn universally at the time of contact. In the 1990s women began to cut their hair short, though a few have opted to leave the hair long, below the neck in what is known as the "Macuxi" cut. Women no longer have tattoo markings on their faces. Old women have allowed the holes at the edges and below the lower lip to fill in. They have abandoned the use of ornaments (short sticks) in these perforations. However, several men and women have tattooed themselves on the upper arm: their names, and in one case the star of David.

The Xilixana have now adopted Western ways of light. They use the cheap and common kerosene lamp used by interior Brazilians for light in the evening within the house. In recent years, during the yãimo events, Xilixana have installed small platforms on posts within the house, upon which they place the lamps. Flashlights are a fairly common item, especially prized for the beam of light they throw upon wild game. They have transformed hunting—functioning well for momentary light in the dark of the yãno, at the river's edge in the evening, or in an emergency to walk the jungle path in the dark. Batteries are always in demand.

Social life has been altered with the purchase of portable stereos. At times the Xilixana will listen to Western music on the radio or on tapes, but more frequently they record and prefer to listen to the festive songs of other Yanomami they encounter. Their use of tape recorders represents a quantum leap from the initial years after contact, when missionaries first began to use a tape recorder for language and linguistic work. At that time some older Yanomami thought the recorders gave the missionaries life and death control over the speaker, so that the missionary might perform black magic at his whim. Currently, it is common to hear sounds from a tape deck or radio coming from a Xilixana house at any time of day.

Most portable stereos are the proud possessions of young men. They were more numerous during the gold boom of the late 1980s than in more recent years, as they tend to become dysfunctional because of improper care, high humidity, infestation by cockroaches, or the lack of batteries. They have become an item that children are not to touch.

The use of these goods brings on other, more indirect changes. The Western goods are imported and must be paid for. The present economy is not adequate to supply the needs of salt, fish hooks, knives, clothing, and soap, let alone radios and outboard motors—three or four men acquired outboard motors which lasted a year or two, then fell to disrepair. As a result, the Xilixana men sometimes have to find paid work; and when one or two individuals leave the village for months to gain employment among Brazilians downriver, their absence alters the cycle of village life, in that they are not present to provide fish and game and do not work the fields. Family and relatives always become anxious about the absentee's well-being. Other men are likely to seduce his wife in his absence.

Women no longer have to make clay pots or griddles. They need not keep busy spinning cotton or weaving aprons, loin cloths, and men's cotton waist wraps. They are not obliged to carve out large gourds in which they once carried water from its source. With pots and large plastic containers they have a larger supply of water in the house. With matches they can be more lax about always keeping hot coals in the hearth.

At the same time the Xilixana find themselves engaged in new and different activities. The women have to wash hammocks and clothing, for which they need soap. Men grind old knife blades to form metal arrow points. They use tin, nails (purchased at the mission store), and cloth to repair or plug cracks in their canoes. They can borrow a hammer or saw from the station. Picture books in the homes of the missionaries are the source of much laughter and comment. Chalk is available, as are paper and pencil. They enjoy doing simple puzzles. Sometimes they send letters to kin at another location. The missionaries' visitors' room is now a place of social exchange, a place to pass the time.

Men spend hours carving miniature canoes and paddles, letter openers, armadillos, and cassava sieves for tourism. Women thread necklaces from a variety of seeds they find in the rainforest. They receive Brazilian currency for these artifacts, which is an aberration from their standard system of exchange. They are forced to distinguish levels of value between notes. They guard this money lest it be lost or stolen.

The Xilixana have modified their houses somewhat to accommodate Western goods. They put up shelves to hold some items. Almost every household has clothing hanging on a rope. Some Western commodities require special care and attention, unlike most indigenous crafts; the Xilixana residences with dirt floors, smoke, dust, cockroaches, and undisciplined children are not conducive to the protection of these items. Guns must be cleaned and oiled. Radios function best without cockroaches and humidity, as do sewing machines. Eye glasses are readily broken by the play of small children.

Clothing must be placed out of the smoke. In the event that a family leaves the permanent dwelling for a day or several weeks, they want to make sure their coveted objects are not accessible to others, so wooden boxes or suitcases with locks have become part of the house furniture. The wooden door of the large house is locked when inhabitants leave the village for a few days. One household built a small mud-walled dwelling in which to store their goods while they are absent from the village.

The pursuit of Western goods has altered dependency relations. They have become the primary items used in bride payment. Usually women depend on their husbands to acquire domestic items such as pots, grater boards, and salt, just as they depended on them to clear fields and bring in fish or game in the past. Families often share their cash to satisfy an individual's request for some desired item—soap, salt, fish hooks—from the mission store. At the same time travel and absences from the village have given individuals greater autonomy. Young people are less constrained to follow the wishes of their parents. Young men are less likely to work in the fields. For the past decade both young men and women have been less likely to enter into or maintain arranged marriages.

The Dynamics of Yanomami Social Change

Still, simply documenting the changes in the use of material goods does not give us the full picture of social change. Other factors are also at play. Some changes may be identified with specific agents, such as the government or missionaries. In other cases change is a result of a much more complex mix of many factors happening over time. The immediate impact within a month or two is not evident, but in four or five years the change does surface; often these changes are irreversible.

Xilixana out-migration has been negligible, while in-migration has been significant. Fertility has increased noticeably. Alliances and visits between several groups have altered the more insular lifestyle of the 1940s and 1950s. With the continual access to Western goods, neighboring villages seek the goods the Xilixana now have, and a supply of Western trade goods has moved into surrounding communities. In the process the Xilixana social status within the larger Yanomami community has been raised, and they have gained the economic advantage in bargaining, which includes negotiating for wives. If missionaries had not been present, providing a ready access to axes and knives, the character of the Xilixana community might be quite different today. Contact with people on the lower Mucajai would probably have been more frequent, with unpredictable consequences. One possibility is that the Xilixana may have become much more fragmented, with some young people relocating to be nearer to Brazilians. Another scenario might also have been greater misunderstandings, clashes, and killings between Brazilian and Xilixana, with resultant police intervention.

For almost 40 years the Xilixana have had good access to health care, which has relieved their suffering and death toll. Thousands of pills, immediate care, effort towards cleanliness, simple hygiene, and diet have had their impact. The provision of care at infancy and early childhood has been of particular importance. The Xilixana are now three times the population they were 40 years ago. In 1996 they were located in six villages, rather than two yãnos in two locations as in 1958. The character of housing has altered. New bonds of cohesion and strains of tension have emerged, both within and outside kin relationships.

The expanded population has altered family patterns. Whereas betrothals used to be made when girls were quite young, they now tend to be made at a later age. The result has been a shorter premarital period of payment and less of a social tie between the son-in-law and his bride's family before the marriage. The taboo of mother-in-law avoidance is now rarely observed.

The contact with other Yanomami has had social implications. The Xilixana have participated in the lives of other Yanomami people—they have hunted and fished with them, heard local gossip, become aware of the activities of neighbors, accompanied them on a few raids, and participated in their yãimos. In some ways their Yanomami identity has been reinforced. Through the discussion of myths, the stories have been modified or expanded. Significant objects of black magic have been adopted, with a few of them planted in their gardens.

The contact with the Palami theli has exposed them to caxiri and brawls that have sometimes proved fatal—a social problem that shows no sign of waning. The cost in physical and mental health is enormous. In my field work in 1995, I heard for the first time a Xilixana discussion about eliminating the fighting at feasts, but when I went back 18 months later there was no evidence of change, although the talk of change continued.

The engagement with Westerners has exposed them to cultures markedly different from their own. Common courtesies are observed: greetings, smiles, a hand shake, and sometimes a Brazilian embrace, or the invitation to sit down. Among Brazilians coffee is served. Objects are paid for with money. Toilets are used. In Brazilian homes food is eaten with the use of silver (or aluminum) ware. Transportation is by automobile, truck, bus, or airplane. Objects can be counted. Westerners engage in social activities, such as seeing a video or movie or watching soccer or basketball games. There are special celebration events such as Christmas and Brazil's national day. Children attend school to learn to read and write. There are micro-organisms in the air as well as in insects and humans, and these micro-organisms spread diseases. Customers enter stores in trust that they will not shoplift. Violations are prosecuted. The services of a prostitute come with payment in money, and prostitutes in the city may pass on diseases. Experience has shown that miners tend not to have the good of the Yanomami at heart.

The world of the *naba* is extensive, comprising many people who are not just Brazilian (and Portuguese-speaking), but possibly German, English, or

American. Some of these people are followers of "the Jesus way," and others are not. The *naba* are sometimes at war with one another. Some of these countries produce specific items such as oil, beads, and adzes. They trade among themselves to gain ownership of these goods. Some of these *naba* have done unusual things, such as travel to the moon and launch satellites into the sky. This means that the land of the sky is intact, even beyond the rainbow.

There is another significant aspect of social change apart from that which is stimulated by artifacts. Ideological change affects the culture in terms of meaning, life and goals—the very foundation of a culture. Yanomami no longer manufacture a large proportion of the artifacts they require. In this sense they are totally dependent upon non-Yanomami. Steel goods come from the *naba*. During illness they know they must use the *naba*'s medicine. As a result, many Yanomami have become less mobile in order to remain close to the foreign resources. And there is a new concern. The once unlimited resources of their land have become limited. The forest and waterways no longer produce the fish and game which only two generations earlier were adequate. The river has been polluted by the mercury used in the mines. Pollution has become such a threat that the Yanomami have been forced to become aware of conservation. In writing about Amazon's indigenous people, Davis (1996: 294) states, "They don't know what it means to destroy.... In a world of such abundance, the meaning of scarcity has no meaning." Although Yanomami do not comprehend this phenomenon, they daily experience this new reality.

Change Agents, and Direct Effects

The Xilixana have resisted some Western interventions—we have seen religious practice as one major example. They did not want to use hoes or shovels, at least until the miners appeared. To till their fields they preferred using their traditional four-centimeter broad chisel-like blade, much like their dibble stick.

FUNAI, the FNS, and missionaries have provided health care of various sorts and with varying degrees of success in the habitat of the Xilixana. Missionaries tend to be better trained, and they have the advantage of communicating in the Ninam language. FNS provides care for more serious and long-term illnesses in an urban setting. In the difficult times of drought, both FUNAI and the missionaries have provided rice and cassava as food.

Undoubtedly the agents of change also want to preserve the traditional practices of care and support shown between members of a defined kin group. This network supplies food, shelter, and emotional support during stable and adverse times. It extends beyond the immediate family, and thus helps to watch over the needs of the orphan, the fatherless child, the widow, and to some degree the elderly. The structure of housing might have an indirect bearing on this network of care. In nuclear family dwellings, contact with extended family members becomes more limited. Now, two of the Mucajai villages are a complex of both yãno and rectangular dwellings. The rectangular houses are home to a mix of immediate and extended families. One Xilixana village consists exclusively of a single yãno. Both the Xilixana villages situated at FUNAI posts have more than one dwelling. The decision to have multiple dwellings in a village is a choice made by the Yanomami quite independently of any external agents of change.

Both FUNAI and missionaries make Western artifacts available to the Xilixana: salt, fish hooks and line, pots. FUNAI has given at least one ghetto blaster to the Xilixana at the mission post, and provides light to village D from a generator at Comara. Western artifacts among Xilixana can no longer be controlled, because with money they can purchase whatever they want: radios, tapes, a bicycle, 10-gallon pots to make drink, outboard motors. In some cases they have stolen or retrieved items from abandoned mining camps: guns, pots, rope, clothing, tarpaulin, and metal or plastic barrels—once, even a foam rubber mattress. Missionaries have tried to establish a broader economic base by encouraging Xilixana to produce tourist items: miniature arrows, bows, paddles and spears, necklaces made of jungle seeds, letter openers, and miniature canoes made of hardwood.

Missionaries, FUNAI, and FNS do not endorse the Xilixana's excessive use of caxiri. These drinking bouts unleash guarded and constrained antagonism and resentment between Yanomami (Camargo 1996). The end result is brutal physical beatings often yielding serious bodily harm, and in some cases, homicide. Resentment and bitterness lingers. The missionaries' position is that the presence of God's spirit within the chest of the Xilixana will eradicate this social problem.

Missionaries endorse the preservation of the Ninam language. They communicate in Ninam and teach it in school sessions. They have printed numerous Yanomami stories so that persons who are literate might read them. FUNAI personnel communicate in Portuguese.

It is possible that the state will soon install a television, as government officers have done among the WaiWai to the southeast. Their aim is to Brazilianize or "civilize" the indigenous people with the Portuguese language, the exposure to Western forms of etiquette and behavior, and patriotism. These goals too, no matter how successful, will have significant social implications.

Both CCYP and FUNAI are not clear in their views on the values and the future for the Yanomami. They want the Yanomami to retain traditional practices, even to the point of returning to the wearing of the loin cloth for the men and the small apron for the women, but the Xilixana will never return to the form of clothing used before contact. Nor will they return to a lifestyle that excludes fish hooks and fish line, salt, aluminum pots, and for that matter, the flashlight and portable stereo with tape recorder. The Xilixana live in a society that now includes Western goods and Western politics. They crave Western possessions, both because it makes their lives easier and because it gives them status in their own communities. They will not return to a mode of life that excludes medical assistance. They will not even return to the Yanomami traditions of the early 1960s.

FUNAI and the FNS clash with the missionaries in spiritual matters. FUNAI encourages the practice of shamanism and sorcery. FUNAI personnel will readily help transport a shaman from one village to another by canoe to assist in the cure of someone who is ill. The approach of both FUNAI and CCYP is to encourage shamanism and not curb sorcery.[1] The missionaries, for their part, see the Yanomami world of spirits as integral to the peoples' lives, but they believe in another viable option as well. They believe that most Yanomami spiritual forces enslave the people, bringing fear and retaliation, and that God's power liberates. At least a few Xilixana have shown their belief that they have experienced this liberation.

FUNAI's approach to the role of shaman and sorcery may rest in a fundamentally different ethos regarding the spiritual world. It is possible that the FUNAI workers have not seen, at close hand, and thus not appreciated, the pervasive place that spirituality has in Yanomami culture. They have not witnessed the practice of these human beings consenting to death because they feel cursed through sorcery or shamanic powers. The Yanomami have a constant preoccupation with the effects of sorcery, and avenge all such acts with murder or with another act of sorcery. This deeply embedded cultural practice establishes a cycle without end, with harsh and negative consequences. FUNAI's approach is to ignore this practice, except in its opposition to warfare.

The FUNAI staff also do not want Christian teaching to permeate or persist among the Yanomami, and they seek whatever means possible to prevent missionaries from teaching Christian beliefs in the rainforest. Missionaries are now forbidden to use anything from the Bible in teaching literacy. In 1995 and 1996 FUNAI and David Kopenawa were successful in expelling four Brazilian missionaries from another mission agency working on the Demini River. FUNAI has refused to give new foreign missionaries permission to work among Yanomami.

With the acceptance of Western medicine, the practice of shamanism may have declined to some extent, but the belief in sorcery and its practice appears to be stronger despite the presence of the Westerners' ideology of rationality and Christianity.

Exchange and Reciprocity

While every society has patterns of exchange, the system of exchange varies. Exchange may be primarily that of object and currency, a system common in Western society, or, where currency has not been adopted, it may be item for item. A more significant aspect of exchange is the degree or quality of social

---

1 Another stance is found in the secular video, *Warriors of the Amazon*: "They believe all diseases are caused by spirits."

involvement. What is the relation or association of the object to the giver, and what is the relationship of giver and receiver? Is the first exchange the end of the encounter between the two actors, or is this the beginning of a life-long special bond?

Ferdinand G. Toennies ([1887] 1963) identifies exchange as being either in the nature of *Gesellschaft* (association) or *Gemeinschaft* (community). *Gesellschaft* (involving an impersonal and goal-specific exchange) is typical of what we think of as "modern," Western society. I pay $25 and receive a book. All matters related to the exchange are terminated; there is no social engagement, except for the sole purpose of receiving the desired object or currency. *Gemeinschaft* recognizes the social component: the means of the exchange as well as its goal (receiving the object) are both significant. Ritual may be involved. The exchange may be one in a series, the fruit of a special bond. The people involved take a human interest in one another: needs, family, health, hospitality, festivity. *Gemeinschaft* best describes the Yanomami exchange practice whereas Western *Gesellschaft* clashes with it.

Reciprocity exchange goes beyond material goods. It engages social principles and moral norms. In most preliterate societies kin are central to reciprocity, but exchange can also engage friends and neighbors (Sahlins 1968: 82). Reciprocity patterns are generally complex and extremely important to social organization. Elman Service (1971) recognized three types of reciprocity: generalized, balanced, and negative.

Virtually all societies have *generalized* reciprocity. Transactions, whether involving objects or service, tend to be altruistic, in a sense approximating the "pure gift." In Western society parents give children gifts and expect none in return. This is also the case among the Yanomami. A donor gives what he or she can give. Personal resources vary. The donor gives, possibly out of his/her or the recipient's need. Even if the item is not reciprocated, the donor may give again. There is a clear sense of mutual aid and generosity, a true sense of sharing: you give because someone else has a need, and because you have the resources that enable you to give. Yanomami giving goes beyond the kin network, extending to visitors. They share their food generously, even though they realize the food supply might be depleted by the next morning. A good Yanomami is a hospitable and generous person.

Balanced reciprocity is generally direct and straightforward, and less personal than generalized reciprocity. It may be bow for bow or large ball of cotton for axe. With the Xilixana, this type of exchange has expanded since the time of contact. Western goods have moved from the Xilixana to Yanomami communities to the south and west. Reciprocity may transpire at one moment in time. Often there is a dramatic staging of the acute need for the item by the hopeful visitor. Of major importance is betrothal, in which a male receives a wife and reciprocates indefinite payment to his in-laws. Sometimes an item from a visitor's distant village may not come into the hands of the recipient until six months after the agreement.

Negative reciprocity, a term coined by Alvin W. Gouldner (1960), indicates "an attempt to get something for nothing" and "ranges through various degrees of cunning, guile, stealth, and violence." The Yanomami use this means of exchange in raids to acquire women and steel goods. At Mucajai they steal from members of a neighboring village. Items include Western goods as well as money. Since the mid-contact period, with the acquisition of Western goods, they place a lock on their boxes of possession, and often on the doors of their houses. Periodically they steal from the missionaries and Brazilians. One Xilixana proudly showed missionaries how he shoplifted countless goods from retail stores in Boa Vista.[2] Negative reciprocity uses pressure or guile to enhance one's own interests.

Western goods in the culture of the Yanomami alter the original exchange system. The Xilixana's desire for Western goods has created another form of dependency. Western goods are only acquired by exchange—labor, product, or money—which entails cultural adaptation and modification. Labor is not likely to take place in the Xilixana habitat except when they work for missionaries. Therefore men intermittently leave the Yanomami community for extended periods of time to work among Brazilians. During this time they do not function as meat providers in their role as husbands and fathers.

A number of men and women produce native artifacts which they market to Westerners: bead aprons, bead necklaces, miniature bows and arrows, paddles. These artifacts require skill and attention to detail, and not all Xilixana want to subject themselves to such precision, such scrutiny. Some are more adept at crafting these artifacts than others. Therefore some use this activity for gain, and others do not. The result is specialization and an altered division of labor, a new dimension in the manufacture of their own artifacts.

The Xilixana appear not to take personally an inability to do this more exact crafting. One is simply *utmuti* (unknowing), as one would be of speaking Portuguese or driving an outboard motor. One similarly has *utmuti* fingers to produce artifacts that Westerners request. However, the Xilixana accuse the missionary of showing favoritism in accepting another's items over their own, perhaps inferior, product. Some Xilixana seek to circumvent the specialized work in "tourist" craft production by using soft wood, and they are embarrassed when they are "found out," or delighted if they succeed in deceiving the purchaser.

Whether they are employed by the missionary to cut grass, retrieve posts from the forest for a new building, or serve as informant, the Xilixana do this activity for another person with the sole goal of gaining money. This same principle applies for labor among Brazilians in cutting fields, planting rice, or assisting miners in transportation and mining. The Yanomami have recognized that employment with Euro-Westerners is generally focused, and is measured by hour or day. Constant vigorous work receives greater monetary reward. The idea of work (for gain) is quite different from the conception of their own labors, their own activities, in and for their community. Yanomami "work" is

2　Most Xilixana dislike him for this behavior, yet he proudly persists in his thievery.

more social, and more directly geared to everyday survival needs. One soon distinguishes work from leisure (Moore 1963: 104). This shift represents a new distinction in their understanding, and usage, of time.

When labor is removed from their habitat for extended periods of time, Yanomami social organization is affected: informal social controls are weakened; the boundaries of kin ties and obligations deteriorate; and bride service and bride payment—central elements in the Yanomami social structure—are redefined and create a new dimension of social tension. The groom pays bride service with Western goods; steel tools and clothing are now required payment among the Xilixana. People become more individualistic. Kin cohesion and obligation are redefined, with greater liberty for the individual. This social process requires a degree of adaptation and accommodation.

The introduction of Western goods has brought about a significant change in the patterns of reciprocity. At the time of contact, the Xilixana were able to produce almost everything they needed by themselves, or trade for what they did not have. Exchanges were frequent and sometimes ritualized. While some items of trade such as tobacco and sugar cane might sometimes be in short supply, they exchanged goods for the sake of person A having B's product. These transactions initiated and maintained unique bonding between specific individuals.

The Yanomami do not find it offensive to ask someone else to give them something they need or want. Westerners are more likely to see such behavior as begging. The Xilixana practise a degree of feigning and drama in asking for a commodity, particularly when visitors are involved. They dramatize their desperate need. Bystanders are often entertained by the deception. If someone does not give (share), that person is seen as stingy, which is a serious cultural offense. Transactions do not have to be completed at one time and place. The exchange may be made in trust, with repayment finalized months later, again often in a ritualized form.

The kin structure contains a second tier of reciprocity. One is generous with one's family, which includes one's parallel-cousins, who are recognized as brothers and sisters. Beyond this inner circle a male is always under obligation to his wife's immediate family. Parents and one's wife's brothers may ask for service and the payment of costly Western artifacts at any time, possibly for a 30-year period. A son-in-law is generally younger than his parents-in-law, which socially binds two generations together.

These reciprocity patterns serve to equalize the items that the Xilixana claim as their possessions. They function to prevent status differences based on material goods. One is obligated to give when one owns more than is fundamentally necessary. At the time of contact a Xilixana with a second knife, axe, or metal pot was obligated to give it to someone else, but with time this norm has taken on greater elasticity. They can accumulate several knives, shirts, and pots—goods beyond the limits of need. In part the original practice might have come about through steel tool deprivation during the years prior to contact. The net effect has been an alteration in the cultural definition of the number of goods a person owns.

The Xilixana have found it difficult to comprehend and integrate fully the mode of reciprocity found among Europeans. On one of their first contacts with Brazilians on the lower Mucajai, they interpreted the Brazilians' reluctance to give steel tools as stinginess, and they considered the option of murder. They left a number of canoes for the Brazilians, expecting repayment on a subsequent visit. As time went on they painfully discovered that promises of payment were not always upheld. They came to understand that they could not apply the Yanomami system of exchange in their new social encounters.

During the early 1960s, when younger men were for the first time going to visit the ranchers and peasants of the lower Mucajai to assist them in some form of field work, I asked them from my Western perspective (in which "work equals money") what they had got for their labor. They told me they had received nothing. I was irritated that they had been exploited, but they didn't see this as a problem. They were satisfied with the unique experience of having lived together with the *naba*. From the 1970s on, their expectations changed. In recent times the Xilixana do voice their discontent with any Western exploitation.

The Xilixana see the Western style of reciprocity as cold and impersonal. The Western exchange medium of money has various strata in value: 10, 20, 50. The Xilixana understood these gradations of money as *usi* (weak) and *lothotho* (strong). Yanomami exchange has "personality ... moral and emotional connotations" (Dalton 1965: 371). One exchange is likely to be the first of many more items that will be traded between the two persons. Western reciprocity is not based upon friendship, commodity exchange, or need. It works independently of bonds of kinship or cultivated friendship. It is void of ritual. In the Western world, trade seldom discriminates by age, sex, religion, race, or social class. If you have sufficient currency (or credit) you receive the commodity. If you do not, you do not receive. The person who gives the item is only significant for the brief time the transaction is made. He/she is not the manufacturer of the commodity, but one whose occupation is to transfer the item to the consumer, a retailer. In contrast Yanomami exchange and reciprocity operate on the basis of kinship rights and obligation (see Dalton 1961).

Social and organizational changes due to technology require further discussion. G. Lenski, P. Nolan, and J. Lenski (1991) posit that social change has its roots in technological change. Modes of productivity, relationships, hierarchical order, and social organization alter because of changing forms of technology. Items such as clothing and steel tools have been integrated into the Yanomami bride payment system. The wearing of appropriate and clean clothing enhances status. Western artifacts can be readily stolen, resulting in feuds and fisticuff duels. Money is now used in exchange between Yanomami, a further significant alteration in the reciprocity process. A shaman may be paid in currency for his service. Family and friends might supplement a buyer's own money at the mission store so that she or he can purchase an item. If a Xilixana purchases 50 small fish hooks, he will likely only have five or six of them left within a few days. He will have yielded to the requests of family and friends and will soon be at the trade store looking to get more. After the accumulation of hard-earned cash from work or from gold in the late 1990s, the Xilixana men made sizeable purchases from stores in Boa Vista. Practising a kind of impulse buying in those expeditions, they often forgot to purchase the smaller items that their wives or offspring had requested. When they returned to their communities, their kin were disappointed, though they would soon forget.

George Dalton reminds us that "primitive" economies differ markedly from Western economies. People in premarket economies exchange on the basis of kinship right and obligation, and kinship ties provide security (Dalton 1961). They give values as well as social advantages. In reading ethnographies of precapitalist marriage systems, we often equate bride price and bride service systems with marital practices in our own economic system, which is inappropriate. They are not synonymous. Most marriage systems among indigenous peoples are a social and political exchange (Dalton 1966). Kinship impedes individual mobility. In the precapitalist economy, labor and land are not items in a commodity market. Among the Yanomami, exchanges are almost always highly personalized, while in our society they are more often impersonal, almost anonymous.

The new Xilixana knowledge of other Yanomami has had an exponential expansion. The contacts with FUNAI and CCYP personnel have helped them recognize that they are a people with rights to land and government services. The Xilixana know that bureaucrats in distant places, unknown to them, make decisions that influence, and even dramatically change, their lives. Government officials carry out the decisions of people in Brasilia and Boa Vista. Exploiters seek to make their own financial gain as well. The Xilixana know that the Yanomami in general inhabit land in both the countries of Brazil and Venezuela. Some are aware that their status is unique: they are Brazilians with special land claims. They recognize an affinity to other aborigines to the east—the Macuxi, Wapishana, and WaiWai. They are encouraged by some agencies to put on a united front before the government. The Xilixana know that the local missionaries will not participate in these political pursuits.

The Xilixana now see themselves as part of a much larger social group, the Yanomami. They realize that exploitation can come in a variety of ways: through outsiders taking natural resources from their lands; unfair wages; inadequate payment for trade items; inadequate compensation by journalists, photographers, researchers, and translators; and substandard health treatment. They have become politicized and recognize that all Brazilian Yanomami have civil rights to land and health care. Their goals will only be achieved if they act in unison against the people in power, such as the government, miners, and entrepreneurs.

Fifteen
Reflections on Social Change Among the Yanomami

On my 1996 visit I was struck by the clutter of possessions now found within the Xilixana's dwelling: gourds, baskets, cloth or plastic bags, or sacks of various sizes, suitcases, wooden or cardboard boxes, and cans containing a variety of objects—clothing, gunshot, cotton, radios, beads, salt, or items for purposes of sorcery. They are placed on shelves against the yãno wall, or hung from a strong wood beam, or to the end of a hammock. Other items such as an old knife blade, can, or gourd are strewn anywhere in the house. Rope dangles from the yãno roof. Pieces of black, blue, or yellow tarp are scattered around, and larger pieces of tarp placed on the yãno itself serve as a shield against wind and rain.

The geographical or social environment has changed. The Mucajai Xilixana are now in eight villages, most of them with multiple dwellings. They do not live in as widely dispersed an area as they did in the 20 years prior to contact. The mission post remains central to most of them, who make almost weekly visits to get medicine or trade goods. A few attend the weekly Sunday religious service. They visit and reciprocate visits to other Yanomami communities, having formed alliances that are significant to their social and political lives.

Attitudes towards Europeans have altered dramatically. The Xilixana no longer view foreigners as spirit or ghost or with fear. Foreigners are now an integral part of Xilixana culture. They no longer covertly see the Brazilian smoker as one who expels black magic when he exhales. Occasionally, when given the opportunity, a few Xilixana smoke, in part to show that they have become "civilized." In the contact period, when government and other people who smoked visited the station the Xilixana showed their disgust in no uncertain terms. They expressed their disapproval with a high pitched "hm!" and tried to move the smoke away with the motion of their hands. To most Xilixana smoke was a means of sorcery.

They have also come to associate with Brazilians in feuds, in drinking or obtaining hard liquor, and in prostitution. They depend upon outsiders for tools, medicine and health care, information, and some entertainment. In turn, though, they have little that the foreigner wants: cultural data, perhaps, a few food items, and some periodical labor. As a result, the process of exchange tends to favor the foreigners, who may grasp opportunities to exploit. Still, the Xilixana also seek to exploit outsiders, particularly in obtaining material goods. In recent years a few Xilixana have learned some fundamentals of politics, such as citizen rights and participation in political decision-making.

While a few Xilixana have become literate, all of them now realize that paper is a significant communicator. Literacy involves a whole new sphere of activity: schooling, exchanging information with other people by picture and written story, the Bible, transmitting messages to Yanomami friends in other villages. At the same time their language has been modified. A few terms, such as *kainai*, the indigenous name of the Mucajai river, have become extinct. They now use Mucajai, the name given the river by the Portuguese colonists.

They have adopted numerous Portuguese words and terms. Initially these words included such items as axe, knife, gun, shirt, and blouse. In the linking period the vocabulary expanded to medical terms such as malaria, colds, and aspirin. Portuguese words for game and field products were increasingly being used: bananas, cassava bread, jaguar, monkey, tapir. In the past decade they have embraced terms of food: tea, coffee, rice, biscuits, sardines. Recently Xilixana leaders have used political terms such as president, governor, chief, and the press. Listeners have noted that their understanding of the word "president" is distinctly different from its Western usage, and our use of "chief" is quite different from theirs.

The Xilixana had a quite different way, embedded in their culture, of naming themselves by description, sometimes publicly acceptable, sometimes not (see chapter 2). Dennison Berwick (1992) contends that the Yanomami's quick adoption of Western names to be used publicly was because those new names were essentially non-names. They did not carry the cultural significance of indigenous names. (In general, Xilixana do not want to name an infant until the child is about six months old.) The use of Portuguese names may alter the fiber of the social network in at least two ways. The use avoids the taboos of name usage found in the precontact period; and the public use of Portuguese names decreases the use of family terms such as son, daughter, and brother, which may well represent a slight shift from the former centrality of the family in their worldview. This could ultimately influence matters of status, prestige, and respect.

Most Xilixana now recognize that Westerners carefully follow an annual cycle of time. A few can identify the 12 months of the year, and most know of the weekly cycle of Sunday through Saturday. They know, for instance, that a service is held at the mission station on Sundays, that the small store is open on Tuesdays and Fridays. They know of Christmas as a time of celebration and a time when the annual day of games and events occurs. They recognize that Westerners annually celebrate birthdays, and they now show interest in their own ages. In 1995 I witnessed my first Yanomami birthday celebration, for a three-year-old boy. Significantly, the young boy had three older sisters, but the father had never prepared a celebration for them—an indication, however minor, of the continuing dominance of the patriarchal system.

Culture and Social Change

Culture is not static, but dynamic, and social change will alter culture. This is clearly the case for the culture of preliterate peoples when meeting Western peoples. Westerners sometimes refer to a "traditional culture" as a "lost culture," but that designation is a misnomer. While some cultures of the past have been truly "lost," and will never again be seen, most traditional cultures are still alive, although reformed and re-created to become the cultures of the present. Jean E. Jackson (1994: 385) helps us understand the vibrant, almost unprogrammed, and unpredictable quality of culture by comparing it to a jazz musician's repertoire. "The pieces the musician plays come out of a tradition, but improvisation also occurs, and the choices made by the musician about the performance take into consideration the acoustical properties of the hall, the property of the instrument played, and the inferred inclinations of fellow musicians and the audience." Culture is not simply revealed in a snapshot, exposing one particular point in time. The clay of culture is always moist, waiting to be shaped.

The Xilixana culture was at the beginning stages of significant change in the early to mid-1950s, when steel axes were few, and those they had were old and worn. Then 11 Kasilapai men went downriver, and the culture of those people on the Mucajai River was forever changed. The contact formed a new thread of the cultural mosaic whose strands soon became thicker and stronger. The new cultural bindings became difficult to remove or replace within a few years, and virtually impossible to remove in a decade. Some threads of the earlier culture became worn and torn and were eventually replaced: pottery, fire sticks, polyandry, perceptions of the cosmos. Some threads were expanded or reinforced: spirit beliefs, the Yanomami as a living, political entity.

In discussing culture among the Tukano in Colombia, Jean E. Jackson (1994: 384) prefers to use the concept of a people acquiring culture—Indian culture—rather than of a people having or comprising a culture. She uses "becoming Indian" to describe not only the dramatic change, but also the nature of the ever-emerging culture after indigenous peoples encounter Western culture.

Yanomami culture now took on the shapings of a different context. In the mid-1950s the Mucajai people necessarily saw themselves in terms of their small villages, their needs as an isolated people in a rainforest habitat, places far removed from an outside world. Their artifacts were mostly self-constructed. Their pool of marriage partners and sexual unions was located within their limited community (which itself created a strain). After contact their culture came quickly to include such items as radios, clothing, flashlights, Brazilian politics, Casa do Índio in Boa Vista, Portuguese language, and money; and people such as the Malaxi theli. An individual's self-perception would now include that person's own perception of what others think of him/her: members in the local village, other Ninam, other Yanomami, and possibly his/her perceived status among non-Yanomami.

But the cultural snapshot of the Yanomami as taken in, say, 1998 will again be altered by the year 2000. The Mucajai people will never return to the pre-contact time. The "lost culture," though not thoroughly lost, is no longer viable. Still, although influenced by NGOs, government, and missionaries, the Yanomami will interpret their position, their being, and their advantages from the vantage point of their own varying perspectives. Yanomami individuals, families, villages, and bata will mold the ever-changing culture through social energies of push, pull, shove, retreat, explosion, passivity, disgust, happiness, and confirmation.

Outsiders, including other Yanomami as well as missionaries, Brazilians, and even North Americans, will have an impact upon these synergistic forces. The Yanomami will be developed in part as the "Indian" (Jackson's term) that "civilized people" want. For the Euro-Westerner, this "Indian" will be measured in terms of stereotypes, clothing worn, means of livelihood, residence, Portuguese-language ability, trade ability, and education.

Social Change: Problems, Bias, and Ethics

Western perspectives regarding social change emerging out of Western and preliterate peoples' contacts require critical evaluation. In this discourse history shows that ideology has altered over time: we have gone through periods of colonialism, cultural purity, cultural personality, cultural relativism, and acculturation. Even as Westerners we do well to recognize that we interpret the impact of European societies upon preliterate peoples with our own biases. Materialists and entrepreneurs see the territories of indigenous peoples as belonging to the ambitious, or to those with the political savvy to make proper use of the land and resources, which really means Euro-Westerners, and they show minimal respect for indigenous cultures. Government personnel have their own political agendas, which are often short-term and based on the goals of capitalist "progress."

Missionaries focus upon the souls of the people, believing that Christianity will bring freedom and peace in the place of gossip, fights, killings, and fear of spirits (Headland & Pike, 1997). They expect ultimately to see a more content people. In some instances, certainly, missionaries have not been sensitive to the fabric of culture. The intentions and behavior of missionaries have not always been pure; at times missionaries become absorbed in myths of their own making. At the same time the public has not recognized the missionaries' contributions of health care, literacy, and ethnographic work; and it is not generally known that missionary work, like much else in society, has altered considerably in the last generation. The missionary program and activity have become more and more scrutinized by governments and an increasingly critical (and skeptical) public, and mission work has responded to this scrutiny. Still, in our secular society, missionaries have readily become the scapegoat for many problems that exist between indigenous and First World peoples.

There has been a cost in the missionary endeavor. One female was threatened by a raging Yanomami with drawn bow. At least one family's child has been sexually abused. All missionaries have suffered one or several tropical diseases. Two missionary couples have had to leave Mucajai station for medical reasons. MEVA Brazilians with children generally leave the jungle locations during the schooling of their children. All missionaries have had to discipline themselves to learn the language and adapt to rainforest life. Most enjoy the rigors of jungle life and the association with the Yanomami.

Social scientists, and anthropologists in particular, carry their own bias. They justify their presence and research into various collective or vulnerable peoples as a matter of the advancement of science. They are reluctant to own up to their participation in social change: the questions they ask, at times subtle and disrespectful; informant payment; using bribery to achieve their "scientific" goals; their material baggage of cameras, tape recorders, Western food, and modes of transportation. (Anthropologists have found mistresses among the people they research. One researcher took a Yanomami as wife.) They, too, compromise their rhetoric of respecting the culture. Anthropologists, perhaps, could be accused of intellectual colonialism (Christie 1996). In many ways they are not much different than missionaries, except their sojourn with indigenous people is usually short-term. They are not present for the long-term dialogue and dialectic between the two cultures. All the while, the public tends to view most of what they write as truth, as authority.

The public has a growing awareness that "disadvantaged" indigenous peoples are being culturally and materially exploited. In some cases a new political energy around this issue has helped to give indigenous peoples a voice in the political process; and in some cases manipulation and exploitation have been stalled or stopped altogether. But the areas of public concern for the well-being of indigenous people may also be somewhat selective, and therefore biased. We target specific areas of culture and are blind or neglectful of others. Westerners who are immersed in the literature often show concern for the life and health of indigenous peoples. They assess resource exploitation, but from a Western model, rather than, in this case, a frontier Brazilian model that has a Southern European and new world mix. Westerners may stress the preservation of culture, but the culture in question is already in flux, and indigenous peoples can't help but welcome some areas of change.

Furthermore, Westerners fall prey to affirming all indigenous cultural practices, even the ones that are exploitive, manipulative, and violate human rights within the local social structure. Most concerned Westerners endorse the Yanomami practice of shamanism and the belief in sorcery. In the name of cultural relativism, many would not interfere with the practice of infanticide. And what is our response to the subjugated status of women? These embedded customs are central both to Yanomami thought and social organization. Some of these prevailing practices bring fear, feuds, and death.[1]

Yanomami culture, as we have seen, includes a trait of deception. The Yanomami bend and embellish truth for the purposes of humor, spite, revenge, and the pursuit of personal goals. Mere rumors readily produce hatred and retaliation, to the point of death. The net effect of such behavior is mistrust and suspicion. A Xilixana cannot be assured of even a brother's or friend's confidence and trust. This makes the Yanomami social fabric volatile. Revenge, feuds, and warfare are central to Yanomami life. Each Yanomami village displays episodes of bigotry and ethnocentrism. Every individual and family seeks its own interest with little tolerance for others, except where personal gain is involved. This intolerance can lead to homicide, with little if any resulting sense of guilt. Their only fear is revenge. This is a picture that fits the Western stereotype of "the law of the jungle."

The Yanomami have little regard for life when it is perceived as an obstacle to routine. They kill infants at birth with no regard for the mother's feelings. In this deeply patriarchal society, they practise female infanticide. Babies born with a physical defect or the weaker of twins are killed, or cared for marginally so that death becomes inevitable. Those with a prolonged illness are sometimes buried alive. In the eyes of the Westerner, Yanomami life is cheap. Males are supreme. Wives are beaten when they inconvenience their husbands. Captured women are often victims to gang rape.

Western silence to these human atrocities speaks volumes. We are selective in our concerns. We address these matters from a distance. We are swayed by media reports. At times we are arrogant about our proposals, our solutions. Our efforts are often patchy rather than holistic. Our commitment is often short-term or sporadic. We tend to condemn all missionary efforts of any kind, making judgments based on stereotypes formulated a half-century ago. In our "objectivity" we do not allow for possible changes in missionary rules and practices. Our "scientific" cultural blinders fail to recognize that the Mucajai missionaries, among others, have tried to address concerns of warfare, infanticide, human dignity, exploitation, revenge, feuds, fear of spirits, and the subordination of women. Missionaries have worked to draw the Yanomami's attention to what they see as an internal violation of human life and dignity.

The past decade has seen increased international intervention in countries dominated by dictatorship or in which human rights are perceived to be violated: South Africa, Cuba, Grenada, Bosnia-Herzgovina, China, Iran. Sanctions have been used to interrupt trade and prevent financial loans. Sometimes a Western peacekeeping force is launched and penetrates the target nation. Governments and international agencies meddle in the internal operations of Western societies or peoples in Third World countries. If people are willing to take these interventionist approaches in nation-states—though they

---

1 Ritchie (1996) portrays a Yanomami shaman's own story of drama and fraud.

are not without their controversies—it would seem logical, and consistent, to apply the same standard to precapitalist peoples when it is clear that human rights are also being grossly violated. If we don't adopt such a position, it would again seem that Western ideals are at best partial and biased. Surely we cannot exempt indigenous peoples from basic standards of human rights simply because we see them are preliterate, or because they provide such a sharp contrast to the realities of Western culture. I do not raise the point to suggest that we place sanctions on Yanomami-like peoples, but to illustrate a possible fault or discrepancy in our international concern and action. Euro-Westerners would do well to critique their motivation and involvement as "advantaged" societies among "simple" and non-capitalistic peoples.

A Response to Change among the Yanomami

Change occurs in all societies, and the degree and rate of social change depend on numerous factors within and contiguous to the specific society. Some changes occur quickly, others more slowly. Some aspects of change are more transparent than other. Change may be manifest, or latent, revealing itself in unanticipated ways.

With increasing sophistication anthropologists have discussed social process, strain, and acculturation patterns involving contact between Western (colonizing) and preliterate peoples for more than a century. This discussion has not abated with the past generation of scholars. Rather, their voices are now being heard by the general public. Magazines such as *Cultural Survival* and *The New Internationalist* speak with clarity and authority about injustice, subjugation, and dominance. At the same time indigenous and minority groups are confronting the government and peoples who resist their claims. In Canada this is evidenced by the Oka incident and the resistance of the Labrador peoples against low-flying military aircraft over indigenous hunting lands. In Brazil a national and international front was established to push for a Yanomami Park.

The Yanomami have been confronting the state as a growing collective and soliciting the media to voice their cause since 1994. While they are still a people whom we would classify as officially nonliterate, they are claiming their right as Brazilian citizens. In a small way they are participating in the "democratic" process. They want to influence existing powers for what they perceive to be their best interests. They face the formidable fortress of capitalism, entrepreneurship, prejudice, and intolerance. This almost impenetrable wall is found at the local, state, and federal levels.

The Yanomami face their foes from a disadvantaged position. Only two generations of Xilixana have had contact with Western society, and until recently this contact has been extremely limited. As a people they have not had enough time to come to a complete or full understanding of Western ways. Then again, the only Westerners who want to understand their culture seem to be scholars and missionaries, and perhaps a few activists. These groups have minimal political clout. No politician has as yet shown that he or (less likely) she is taking on the interests of the Yanomami as a central issue. Politicians tend to respond to issues only because of pressure from lobbying groups, or because other power institutions such as the National Security or the Brazilian Air Force want to penetrate Yanomami land, and thus impinge on Yanomami culture. The ultimate goal of many politicians at the state and federal level in Brazil is the acculturation of the Yanomami—an approach that leaves little room for their Yanomami uniqueness and identity.

Magic and shamanism are but fragile protection against the steel force of Western culture. The evidence of history, according to Wilber Moore (1963: 78), "is fairly overwhelming that as a rule superior technology wins out." The odds are not in the favor of the aborigines (Lenski, Nolan & Lenski 1991). The "rationality" of the Western world would appear to be overpowering. Despite numerous compromises on the part of indigenous peoples, few groups are able to keep their cultures entirely intact, although I would not agree with Lucien Bodard's conclusion in his book *Green Hell* (1973: 291), in which he posits that among Brazil's indigenous peoples, "There is no solution. There never will be. It is civilization that kills them."

Their dependence on that outside "civilization" has its materialistic component: three Western commodities have become accepted and uncompromising Xilixana cultural artifacts—tools, salt, and clothing. These basic items have expanded to other commodities as well: beads, guns, flashlights, watches, sunglasses, outboard motors, ghetto blasters with tape decks. The list will only expand in the coming years. It is important to recognize that the Xilixana made the choice to adopt Western goods. Despite several deaths after their initial contacts, even before the missionaries arrived they were resolved to keep avenues open for steel tools. Since that time their appetite has not abated but, rather, has been augmented. The Xilixana must take responsibility for this change. The Xilixana have a lever of control on the change process.

The general population of Brazil wants to see the indigenous peoples within their boundaries "civilized." While the term "civilized" can mean many things, as a society the Mucajai Yanomami have met several of the criteria. They are no longer "fierce killers" (despite a few recent incidents involving miners). Many of them fit the Western criterion of being relatively clean and clothed, most are courteous and congenial, some understand Portuguese, and a few speak it. Most are employable for domestic, field, or day labor. Brazilians would be even more satisfied if these fellow occupants of their country could read, write, and speak Portuguese, but those conditions would still not give the Yanomami carte blanche entry to Brazilian society. Their third-class status in Brazilian society is likely to remain fixed for at least another three generations—basically because of the Westerner's reluctance to accept them; as well as because the common criteria for being "Brazilian" (or "Canadian" or "American") do not include their sort of lifestyle and history.

Social change among the Xilixana has not been exclusively a matter of Euro-Western influence. It has also involved exchange with other Yanomami.

Excessive drinking and its effects, especially in the joint festivities, the resulting violence, and the undue loss of their food resource overnight are symptomatic of cultural problems that the Xilixana themselves will have to deal with. Only they can stop the wave of destruction that begins with the structure of the yãimo festival.

The cultural trait of violence continues to be a controversial, and important subject. Chagnon's (1977) description of a "fierce people" is accurate for the 1900-80 period, and in Western eyes it is a characterization that will be difficult to live down. It is difficult to argue that the Yanomami peoples have indeed not been "fierce" when they strangle infants at birth, stab someone within their own family, or bash a fellow tribesman on the basis of rumor or personal mood. The cultural practice creates a cycle of violence that continues—and will continue on, perhaps, until a Yanomami leader dares to take a stand, most likely at great personal cost, to turn the tide (Early 1996). This particular cultural transformation is an achievable dream, and when it becomes reality the results will be a significant force in Yanomami society.

The Clash of Values Revisited

The European value of rationalism conflicts with the Yanomami world of magic and spirit. The relations between these two societies challenge germane Yanomami values and social structures. Outside social forces compete around the issue of keeping or altering the traditional structure. The rational model of the European, in its ideal form, does not make distinction by kin, tribe, status, or gender. The nation-state cannot tolerate different regulations for each community or village. Euro-Westerners operate on the basis of codified rules known as law. This kind of uniform standard is foreign to the Yanomami. The principle of "might is right" is changing for the Yanomami. Until the awareness period their sense of respect for others did not include all peoples. The concern of an institution such as the United Nations for global human rights is incomprehensible to the Yanomami. The Xilixana have historically, and skilfully, bluffed, deceived, stolen, and if necessary killed to achieve their ends. The raids on the Xili theli (1960), Hewakema (1968), and miners (1987-97) are examples of the Yanomami sense of justice.

Given the disparate views of justice, how do Westerners respect the "law of the jungle" among the Yanomami? Brazilians now appear to endorse two judicial systems in matters relating to homicide: Western laws for Brazilians in general; and the rule of the Yanomami in the frontier rainforest terrain. A consistent practice of Brazilian law has yet to be tested when warriors raid and kill more than a few Yanomami. For their part, the Yanomami are aware that they need to keep such incidences secret. Any testimony by a Yanomami in a Brazilian court is not likely to be based upon what Westerners would consider to be "fact" but rather upon a cultural base of self-interest.

If the Yanomami go before the courts as a result of breaches of the state law, and are found guilty, a further moral dilemma would arise around the question of punishment. The Yanomami think of Brazilian jails as places to be dreaded because of the imposed isolation, food, and smell. How long does one wait to enforce Brazilian law in the jungle? Should the state discriminate between communities near a mission or FUNAI post and the other Yanomami who live in somewhat more isolated areas?

The issues of indigenous rights, government and NGO responsibility, and the accountability and participation of the Xilixana in major decisions that have an impact on their lives pull many of us in various directions. The government did not act responsibly in allowing the deluge of miners into Yanomami lands, but at the same time dependence on an outside group of people—in determining what happens on their land or in their villages, or in reliance on Western health care, for instance—can result in a loss of dignity and self-respect for the peoples involved.

The Yanomami have adopted Western goods because they are more efficient than their own created artifacts. (The constant search for greater efficiency appears to stimulate change in almost all societies.) Other cultural changes have emerged, some readily recognizable, others more covertly. Missions use the radio to monitor flights, obtain information for medical treatment, and on occasion to exchange news. The Xilixana insist that the missions relay news regarding impending visits between Yanomami villages, as well as information to relatives in treatment in Boa Vista. They want any serious illness or death to be communicated to others. This places missionaries in a position of some power, able to comply with or restrict communicable radio messages (see Ramos 1995: 253).

Missionaries, tourists, and researchers have not been hesitant to photograph Yanomami. Chagnon used pictures of the Yanomami extensively to do genealogical research. Foreigners have often shown little discretion in their photography practices. Camera crews sanctioned by anthropologists did extensive filming of several Yanomami villages in Venezuela as early as 1970, and most recently in 1995, when the Yanomami headman cooperated with the six-week presence of the crew making the film Contact because he would be materially rewarded. By the 1980s the Xilixana had adapted to the world of the photograph and film. The Xilixana requested pictures of themselves or of their families. Frequently they pose for someone to get a personal photo. In the mid-1990s several begged me for copies of the snapshots of people, now deceased, which I had taken in the contact period. They wanted a tangible memory of their relatives—in marked contrast to the prohibition of even using the names of the deceased in the contact period.

Conclusion

Wilber Moore (1963: 85) argues that our studies of acculturation have been too simplistic. Change occurs at various rates, affecting specific phenomenon at different times, and in general change accelerates with time. It is feared that what sociologists define as the acculturation process will soon bring "primitive" cultures to a close (Murphy 1989: 234). A component of change is that work becomes more clearly distinguished from leisure (Moore 1963: 104), and as well, according to Murphy (1989: 24), the trade commodity also changes: "The utilitarian law of the steel axe in a past period is matched by the charms of transistor radios today."

To add to this mix, Robert Murphy (1989: 24) states that missionaries and government have served "boundary roles" or as "culture brokers," although adding, "the strongest ties are through trade and labor," which is true, not only in the Amazon but in other areas of the world as well. We would do well to allow for some type of syncretism, possibly a fusion of the old and the new, and we must recognize that change should occur at a pace that is acceptable to indigenous people (Murphy 1989: 85).

Drawing on Murphy's (1989: 163-84) research, it is possible to identify specific areas of change in the order and authority of Yanomami society. Individuals in every society engage in a search for prestige and respect. Rank differs by sex and age, as well as position in the community. In many aboriginal tribes social standards are enforced through witchcraft, which is a powerful ideology controlled by shaman. When illness reaches epidemic proportions, as it did in early 1960 among the Kasilapai, a witch hunt targeted the Malaxi theli as the cause, then the Xili theli.

In aboriginal societies, for the most part people gain legal status from kin-group membership. They do not gain it as individuals, as is frequently the case in modern society, as a Member of Parliament perhaps, or a lawyer, journalist, or market analyst. Modern society expands the roles existing within a community and therefore multiplies the relations between its members. Similarly, to some degree the Yanomami now have individuals who are spokespersons for the government. They have traders, river guides, paramedics, crafters of tourist items, and domestics. All of these roles carry prestige to a greater or lesser degree. They can be a source of money. They represent links to the outside world. The roles are new: they have altered the role of the recognized leaders of the precontact period: headman, shaman, older males. Western peoples have had difficulty understanding the nature of the status of a headman among the Yanomami. The Xilixana, for their part, have difficulty understanding how there could be one supreme leader of a people, while amongst them a number of men always have degrees of power. The usual concept of chief as applied by Westerners does not adequately explain the power situation. In any case, with the contact with Europeans and the frequent travel of youth, the *bata* power in the context of the family has diminished.

In the aboriginal community a person's relationships are informal, face to face, *Gemeinschaft*. In capitalist, industrial societies these relations are formal, contractual, *Gesellschaft*. Within the village, societies are homogeneous and personal. In capitalist society the role of the state adds a completely different dimension. The state depersonalizes relations, operating on universal criteria. The Yanomami themselves will most likely enter this new reality, first in terms of recognizing, and working along the lines of, a universal Yanomami people, then by forming an association with other aboriginals in Brazil, and finally, perhaps, as Brazilians. It is quite another question as to whether Brazilians will accept the Yanomami as full, bona fide, equal citizens.

Among the Yanomami the dependency upon medicine, Western tools, and extra survival items is evident. But this new ongoing syncretism requires a process in which the people working their way through it can maintain their dignity. The procedure has all too often been one of deculturalization and detribalization and not acculturation (see, for instance, von Graeve on the Pacaa Nova in Brazil, 1989).

Central to the preservation of any aboriginal's dignity is land. Julio Carduño, a Mexican Indian leader, declared at the First Congress of South American Indian Movements in 1980: "Perhaps what most unites us is the defense of our land. The land has never been merchandise for us, as it is with capitalism, but it is the support of our cultural universe" (quoted in Bodley 1990, 167). While indigenous peoples have different systems of regulating individual access to land, one constant is that their land cannot be sold. They view their land system as equitable, and industrial nations have no similar treatment of land. According to John Bodley (1990: 154), "They consider themselves more sensitive to the need to protect their land from environmental deterioration than are those who would take the land from them."

The Yanomami are now in a precarious situation. Tribal systems develop more slowly than industrial states and are less destructive environmentally, in part because of their smaller populations. The new Western presence among the Yanomami is the last thrust of the industrial revolution upon a precapitalist people. It is the inevitable product of a culture of consumption. A consumption-oriented society carries no constraint upon expansion (Bodley 1990: 6). The culture of consumption recognizes no boundaries. Unfortunately, the "quality of life often suffers as economic development accelerates" (Bodley 1990: 139). The quest to extract the mineral resources found in Yanomami lands in the last decade has sped up the process of Western domination and exploitation, as has the nation-state's need to secure its territory and boundaries, to build a unified state infrastructure. Missionary work and anthropological research have contributed to the establishment, and spread, of unbreakable ties.

The Yanomami encounter with miners beginning in 1985 is a reminder of the colonization of the industrial nations of Africa and the Pacific islands and North America by the "civilized" Europeans in the centuries since 1492. It seems paradoxical that we have not learned from the atrocities of the French, English, Portuguese, and Spaniards in the Americas. Our research, history-telling, and filmmaking have not stemmed the flow of the capitalistic greed for possessions and power. They have not taught us respect for people and culture. Westerners, rather, have tended towards a ruthless sense of justification for their behavior, based on thought patterns that have historically categorized indigenous people as subhumans and our culture as superior. We have felt and still feel (erroneously) that our culture and the Western way of life are superior to that of preindustrialized or partially industrialized peoples. We glorify our industrialized, mechanized, computerized, and scientific cultures—our society that is the end product of materialism, nationalism, and entrepreneurship.

It may well be time to take account of our sins, our greed, our pride, even at some sacrifice. Christians, anthropologists, governments, the military, multinational corporations, and entrepreneurs would do well to evaluate and alter the shortsighted, insensitive, exploitative, and selfish behavior that has resulted not only in the loss of the identity of many peoples around the world, but also, at times has led to the destruction of whole peoples and cultures.

Again, not all those cultural practices that are intact are healthy and need to prevail. Among the Yanomami, for the sake of human safety, human rights, and human dignity, the degree of violence and the prevalence of sorcery must be curbed. Since the Yanomami themselves are not addressing this destructive and dysfunctional practice, it would seem that other peoples and/or institutions should attempt to do so. We might also ask whether we would find national or international support for some agent or agencies to work long-term among the Yanomami, to work against the ethos of murder, brutality, and deceit, and the subjugation of females. The road to Yanomami human dignity, while making social, economic, and political adjustment in the frontier regions of civilization, will be a long and arduous task.

It is possible that the Xilixana and all Yanomami can weather the tornado force of Western influence in a project of participation alongside the external agents. To do this, however, the external agents will have to steer a course radically different from the "civilized" world's history of involvement with indigenous peoples over the past 450 years. They must bravely move in a direction that opposes, or at least tempers, the tide of consumption and capitalism. Although contrary to the practice of capitalism, "Technical experts can and should evaluate the practices of other people and decide which ones should be modified" (Bodley 1990: 102). Together with the Yanomami they must bravely confront the existing institutions and practices of government, economies, modernization, and Western religion. Along with the external agents, the Yanomami must carve out their new identity and be tenacious and *waithili* (fierce). They will have to be steadfast, persistent, at times crafty, and always resistant to the historical patterns of the West's subtle and overt domination of a vulnerable people.

Appendix
Language-Learning

In English we have phonemes of *a*, *o*, *c*, *t*, and so on. The Ninam dialect of Yanomami has vowels similar to those of the English language—*a, e, i, o, u*—but Ninam also has a sixth vowel, a sound somewhere between an *a* and an *e*. Linguists have used the *è* to distinguish this sound. In our study of Ninam we soon recognized that all vowels could be nasalized. For example, Yanomami have an ordinary *a* and a very strongly nasalized *a*. In the orthography, the nasalized vowel was identified with *ã* as in yãno and yãimo. Linguists determine whether to mark the presence of vowel nasalization in the orthography by analysing the sound environment of words. In Ninam language *la* has a different meaning than *lã*. Thus the need for nasalization in the orthography.

Consonants present a problem all their own. The phones *b*, *d*, *g*, *h*, *j*, *k*, *l*, *m*, *n*, *r*, *sh*, *t*, *v*, and *w*, as pronounced in English, are all found in speech. Note that in English we have virtually the same sound for *c*, *k*, and *qu*. Were linguists to rewrite the English orthography today, they would likely eliminate two of these three consonants with no change in our manner of speech and understanding. In many languages, a sound often influences its sound environment. In Ninam this was true of the *b* and *p*, *k* and *g*, and *t* and *d* sounds. In this case the *p*, *k*, and *t* were adopted into the alphabet. Similarly, the phoneme environment predicts the use of *r* or *l*, so eventually only the *l* was adopted. In the international phonemic code the *sh* sound is identified *x*, so the letter or orthographic symbol of *x* was adopted. (Note Shirishana becomes Xilixana.) The final decision regarding the use of phonetics was discussed with other Yanomami linguists in both Venezuela and Brazil. Ninam ended up with the orthographic symbols of consonants *h*, *k*, *l*, *m*, *n*, *p* (usually pronounced like the English *b*), *s*, *t*, *w*, *x* (pronounced *sh*), and *y* (pronounced like the English *j* or *y* depending if it was followed by a nasalized vowel). That makes a total of eleven consonants and six vowels (each vowel also is nasalized). (Other Yanomami dialects have twelve consonants and seven vowels [Swain 1996].)

A morpheme is the smallest unit of grammar. In English, cat, by, the, and run are morphemes. Let us examine some specific Xilixana morphemes. *Ta* means to see and *tha* means to do. The difference between the two words is a gentle *t* compared to an explosive *t* as found in "take" (English). The explosive Yanomami *t* phone (sound) is orthographically written as *th* to distinguish it from the softer *t* phoneme.

We were puzzled in our early language learning to find that the Xilixana lengthened some vowels. For example, the word for fish is *paa* and not *pa*. The distinction is not always evident when words or sentences are spoken quickly. The word meaning "see" is sometimes *ta* and sometimes *taa*. Some words were heard with either a single or a lengthened vowel. Another puzzle was an apparent precise break (glottal stop) between a vowel. The word for bush turkey is *pa?ali*. (The *?* marks an abrupt stop.)

In English, *s* is a bound (fixed to a word) morpheme denoting plurality; cow versus cows and dog versus dogs. Other bound morphemes in the English language are *ed*, which denotes past tense (walked), and the prefix *sub*, which means lower in status or position (subordinate, submarine). In Ninam we found that bound morphemes had meanings very foreign to our accustomed way of thinking. For example, *lã* is a negative bound morpheme. The negative of "I do" is really "I do it not." Another bound morpheme, *ha* before the verb, indicates that the speaker has heard of the incident, rather than actually witnessing it.

All these bound morphemes are found with verbs. It is rather easy to write about them now, more than three decades after the struggle to comprehend the language and culture began, but it seemed next to impossible to grasp what was being said then, in the contact period.

References

Albert, Bruce, & Gale Goodwin Gomez. 1997. *Saúde Yanomami*. Belem, Brasil: Museu Paraense Emilio Goeldi.

Albright, Sue. 1965. "Aikamateli Higher-level Phonology." *Anthropological Linguistics* 7.

Albright, Sue. 1970. "Kind of Knowledge, Information Source, Location and Time in Shirishana Predicates." Department of Linguistics, Seminar Papers, series no. 1. California State College, Fullerton.

Aldous, Joan. 1978. *Careers*. New York: John Wiley.

Anderson, Dawn, & Steve Anderson. Correspondence and interviews, 1990-1997.

Berwick, Dennison. 1992. *Savages: The Life and Killing of the Yanomami*. London: Hutchison.

Bodard, Lucien. 1973. *Green Hell: Massacre of the Brazilian Indians*. New York: Ballantine Books.

Bodley, John N. 1990. *Victims of Progress,* 3rd ed. Menlo Park, Cal: Benjamin/Cummings.

Bodley, John N. 1997. *Cultural Anthropology: Tribes, States, and the Global System.* 2nd ed. Mountain View, Cal.: Mayfield Publishing.

Borgman, D.M., & S.L. Cue. 1964. "Sentence and Clause Types in Central Waica (Shiriana)." *International Journal of American Linguistics* 31 (3).

Borgman, D.M., S.L. Cue, S. Albright, M. Seeley, & J. Grimes. 1965. "The Waican Languages." *Anthropological Linguistics* 7 (7).

"Brazilian Government Reduces Yanomami Territory by 70 Percent." 1989. *Cultural Survival Quarterly*. 13-1: 47.

Brooks, E., R. Fuerst, J. Hemming, and F. Huxley. 1973. *Tribes of the Amazon Basin in Brazil 1972*. London: Charles Knight.

Carduño, Julio. 1990. Quoted in John H. Bodley, *Victims of Progress*, 3rd ed. 167.

Carmargo, Milton. Correspondence and interviews, 1994-1996..

Chagnon, Napoleon A. 1972. "Tribal Social Organization and Genetic Micro-differentiation." *The Structure of Human Population*. Ed. L.A. Harrison & H.J. Boyce. London: Oxford.

Chagnon, Napoleon A. 1992. *Yanomamo*. 4th ed. Toronto: Holt, Rinehart and Winston.

Chagnon, Napoleon A. 1997. *Yanomamo*. 5th ed. Toronto: Holt, Rinehart and Winston.

Chagnon, Napoleon A., and Raymond Hames. 1979. "Protein Deficiency and Tribal Warfare in Amazonia: New Data." *Science* 203: 910-13.

Chagnon, N., J. Neel, L. Weitkamp, H. Gershowitz, & M. Ayres. 1970. "The Influence of Cultural Factors on the Demography and Pattern of Gene Flow from the Makiritare to the Yanomama Indians." *American Journal of Physical Anthropology* 32: 339-49.

Christie, Laird. 1996. Conversation.

Colchester, Marcus. 1985. Introduction. *The Health and Survival of the Venezuelan Yanomama.* Ed. M. Colchester. Copenhagen: Anthropology Resource Center/International Work Group for Indigenous Affairs, no. 53, 1-11.

Contact: The Yanomami Indians of Brazil, 1990. Video. Geoffrey O'Conner, producer. Realis Pictures.

Correio da Manha. 1959. Rio de Janeiro. Sept. 17.

Dalton, George. 1967. "Biographical Essay." *Tribal and Peasant Economies: Readings in Economic Anthropology.* Ed. G. Dalton. New York: Natural History Press.

Dalton, George. 1967. *Tribal and Peasant Economics.* Garden City, New York: Natural History Press.

Davis, Wade. 1996. *One River.* New York: Simon and Schuster.

de Alguier, Bras Dias. 1944. "Geografia Amazonica: Nas Fronteiras de Norte." *Revista Brasileira de Geografia.* July-September: 19-40.

Dowdy, Homer. 1964. *Christ's Witch Doctor.* New York: Harper.

Dowdy, Homer. 1995. *Christ's Jungle.* Gresham, Or.: Vision House.

Dufour, Darna. 1995. "A Closer Look at the Nutritional Implications of Bitter Cassava Use." *Indigenous Peoples and the Future of the Amazonas.* Ed. L. Sponsel. Tucson: University of Arizona Press: 149-65.

Durkheim, Emile. 1933 (1893). *The Division of Labor in Society.* Trans. George Simpson. Glencoe, Ill.: The Free Press.

Duvall, Evelyn M. 1971. *Family Development.* 4th ed. New York: Lippincott.

Early, John D. 1988-1997. Discussions.

Early, John D. & John F. Peters. 1990. *The Population Dynamics of the Mucajai Yanomami.* New York: Academic Press.

Early, John D. & John F. Peters. 2000. "Eight Yanomami Villages: Population Dynamics." *The Xilixana Yanomami in the Amazonian Rain Forest: History, Social Structure, and Population Dynamics.* Gainsville, FL: University Press of Florida.

Faul, Timothy. 1996, 1997. Conversations.

Ferguson, Brian. 1995. *Yanomami Warfare.* Sante Fe, NM: School of America Research Press.

Good, Kenneth. 1991. *Into the Heart.* New York: HarperCollins.

Gomez, Gale Goodwin. 1997. "The Impact of Gold Mining in Yanomami Health." Presentation, American Anthropological Association meetings, Washington, November.

Gouldner, Alvin W. 1960. "The Norm of Reciprocity." *American Sociological Review.* 25: 161-78.

Guemple, Lee. 1979. *Inuit Adoption.* National Museum of Man, Mercury Series, Ottawa.

Harris, Marvin. 1984. "A Cultural Materialist Theory of Band Village Warfare: The Yanomamo Test." *Warfare, Culture and Environment.* Ed., R.B. Ferguson. Orlando: Academic Press: 111-40.

Hawkins, Neill. 1963. Correspondence.

Headland, Thomas. 1996. "Missionaries and Social Justice: Are They Part of the Problem or Part of the Solution?" *Missiology* 24 (2) (April): 167-78.

Headland, Thomas N., & Kenneth L. Pike. 1997. "SIL and Genocide: Well-Oiled Connections?" *Anthropology Newsletter.* 38.2: 4-5.

Hill, Reuben, & Roy H. Rodger. 1964. "The Developmental Approach." *Handbook of Marriage and the Family.* Ed. Harold T. Christensen. Chicago: Rand McNally.

James, Carol. 1988-1996. Correspondence and conversations.

Jackson, Jean, 1994. "Becoming Indians: Politics of Tukanoan Ethnicity." *Amazonian Indians from Prehistory to the Present: Anthropological Perspectives.* Ed. A. Roosevelt. Tucson: University of Arizona Press: 383-406.

Kopenawa, David. 1989. "Letter to All the Peoples of the Earth." *Cultural Survival Quarterly.* 13(4): 68-69.

Kunz J., & A. Finkel, eds. 1987. *Family Medical Guide.* New York: Random House.

Lee, Richard. 1984. *The Dobe !Kung.* New York: Holt, Rinehart, Winston.

Lenski, Gerhard, Patrick Nolan, & Jean Lenski, 1995. *Human Societies: An Introduction to Macrosociology.* 7th ed. New York: McGraw Hill.

Lévi-Strauss, Claude. 1969 [1949]. *The Elementary Structures of Kinship.* Boston: Beacon Press.

Lizot, Jacques. 1976. *The Yanomami in the Face of Ethnocide.* Copenhagen: IWGIA Documents.

Lizot, Jacques. 1985. *Tales of the Yanomami.* New York: Cambridge University Press.

Maybury-Lewis. 1989. "Indians in Brazil: The Struggle Intensifies." *Cultural Survival Quarterly:* 13(1):2-5.

Migliazza, Ernest E. 1972. "Yanomama Grammar and Imitation." Diss. Indiana University.

Migliazza, Ernest. 1996, 1997. Conversations.

Moore, Wilbert. 1963. *Social Change.* Englewood Cliffs, NJ: Prentice Hall.

Murphy, Robert. 1989. *Culture and Social Anthropology.* 3rd. ed. Englewood Cliffs, NJ: Prentice-Hall.

The New Internationalist. Toronto, Canada.

Peters, John F. 1973. "Demography of the Shirishana." *Social Biology* 21 (1): 58-69.

Peters, John F. 1980. "The Shirishana of the Yanomama: A Demographic Study." *Social Biology* 27 (1): 272-85.

Peters, John F. 1982. "Polyandry Among the Yanomama-Shirishana Revisited." *Journal of Comparative Family Studies* 13 (1): 89-95.

Peters, John F. 1984. "Role Socialization Through the Life Cycle of the Yanomami: The Developmental Approach to the Study of Family in a Preliterate Society." *Journal of Comparative Family Studies* 15 (2): 151-74.

Peters, John F., & Chester L. Hunt. 1975. "Polyandry Among the Yanomama Shirishana." *Journal of Comparative Family Studies* 6 (2) (Autumn): 197-207.

Plotkin, Mark J. 1993. "The Semen of the Sun." *Tales of a Shaman's Apprentice.* Ed. Mark J. Plotkin. New York: Viking Press: 239-71

Rabben, Linda. 1993. "Demarcation—And Then What?" *Cultural Survival Quarterly:* 17(2): 12-14.

Ramos, Alcida Rita. 1995. *Sanuma Memories.* Madison: University of Wisconsin Press.

Ramos, Alcida Rita. 1997. "Indigenous Organizations in Brazil." Paper delivered at American Anthropological Association meetings, Washington, November.

Reis, Artur Cesar Ferreira. 1944. "As Cabeceiras do Orenoco e a Fronteira Brasileiro-Venezuelana." *Revista Brasilera de Geografia,* April-June: 93-105.

Rice, A. Hamilton. 1921. "The Rio Negro, The Casiquiare Canal, and the Upper Orinoco, September 1919-April 1920." *The Geographical Journal* 58: 321-43.

Rice, A. Hamilton. 1928. "The Rio Bronco, Uraricuera and Parima." *The Geographical Journal* 71: 113-43, 209-23, 345-57.

Richardson, Don. 1974. *Peace Child.* Glendale, Cal.: Regal Books.

Ritchie, Mark. 1996. *Spirit of the Rainforest.* Chicago: Island Lake Press.

Rodger, Roy, H. 1975. *Family Interaction and Transaction: The Development Approach.* Englewood Cliffs, NJ: Prentice Hall.

"Roraima, Brazil: A Death Warning." 1989. *Cultural Survival Quarterly.* 13(4): 59-67.

Ross, E.B. 1976. *The Achuara Jivaro: Cultural Adaptation in the Upper Amazon.* Diss. Columbia University, New York.

Sahlins, M. 1968. *Tribesmen*. Englewood Cliffs, NJ: Prentice Hall.

Saffirio, Giovanni. 1985. "Ideal and Actual Kinship Terminology among the Yanomami Indians of the Catrimani River Basin (Brazil)." Diss. University of Pittsburgh.

Saffirio, G., & R. Hames. 1983. *The Forest and the Highway, In The Impact of Contact: Two Yanomami Case Studies*. Working papers on South American Indians, no.6 / Cultural Survival Occasional Papers no.11.

Salzano, Francisco M. and Didia M. Callegari-Jacques. 1988. *South American Indians: A Case Study in Evolution*. Oxford: Clarendon Press.

Service, Elman Roger. 1971. *Primitive Social Organization: An Evolutionary Perspective*. 2nd ed. New York: Random House.

Shapiro, Judith. 1980. *Sex Roles and Social Structure Among the Yanoama Indians of Northern Brazil*. Ann Arbor: University of Michigan.

Smole, William J. 1976. *The Yanomami Indians: A Cultural Geography*. Austin: University of Texas.

Sponsel, Leslie E. 1986. "Amazon Ecology and Adaptation." *Annual Review of Anthropology*. 15: 67-97.

Sponsel, Leslie E. 1995. "Relationships Among the World System, Indigenous Peoples and Ecological Anthropology." *Indigenous Peoples and the Future of Amazonia*. Tucson: University of Arizona Press: 263-93.

Steward, Julian H., ed. 1963. *Handbook of South American Indians*. Vol. 3. New York: Cooper Square Publishers.

Swain, Carole. 1993-96. Correspondence and conversations.

Taylor, Kenneth I. 1974. *Sanuma Fauna, Prohibitions and Classifications*. Monograph 18, Caracas, Fundacion La Salle de Ciencias Naturales.

"The Threatened Yanomami." 1989. *Cultural Survival Quarterly*. 13(1): 45-46.

Toennies, Ferdinand. 1963 [1887]. *Community and Society*. New York: Harper & Row.

Tierney, Pat. 1997. *The Last Tribes of Dorado*. New York: Viking.

von Graeve, Bernard. 1989. *The Pacaa Nova: Clash of Cultures on the Brazilian Frontier*. Peterborough, Ont.: Broadview Press.

Warriors of the Amazon. 1996. Video. Corporation for Public Broadcasting, Nova.

Wilbert, Johannes, and Karen Simonean. 1990. *Folk Literature of the Yanomami Indians*. Los Angeles: University of California.

World Council of Churches. 1972. "Declaration of Barbados for the Liberation of the Indians." *The Situation of the Indian in South America*. Geneva. Chap. 19. Includes a declaration for Indians, anthropologists and for missionaries.

Wright, Ronald. 1992. *Stolen Continents: The "New World" through Indian Eyes*. Toronto: Penguin Books.

Index